YOUR Health

CONSULTING AUTHORS

Charlie Gibbons, Ed.D.
Associate Professor
Auburn University at Montgomery
Foundation, Secondary, and
    Physical Education Department
Montgomery, Alabama

Kathleen Middleton, MS, CHES
Administrator for Health and
    Prevention Program
Monterey County Office of Education
Monterey, California

Jan Marie Ozias, Ph.D., R.N.
Consultant, School Health Programs
Austin, Texas

Carl Anthony Stockton, Ph.D.
Professor and Department Chair
Department of Physical and
    Health Education
Radford University
Radford, Virginia

Harcourt Brace & Company

Orlando • Atlanta • Austin • Boston • San Francisco • Chicago • Dallas • New York • Toronto • London

http://www.hbschool.com

SENIOR EDITORIAL ADVISOR

Larry K. Olsen, Dr. P.H., CHES
Professor and Chair, Department of Health Science
Towson University
Towson, Maryland

REVIEWERS AND FIELD TEST TEACHERS

Linda Ashby
A.D. Harvey Elementary
Kingsville, Texas

Sandra J. Belle
John H. Vohr Elementary
Gary, Indiana

Kristen Bullis
Centennial Elementary
Fargo, North Dakota

Gary Callahan
Goodland Elementary
Racine, Wisconsin

Ada Cuadrado
PS 112 Elementary
New York, New York

Cynthia Gadson
CC Spaulding Elementary
Durham, North Carolina

Kimberly Gay
Mango Elementary
Seffner, Florida

Kenya Griffin
Sanders Elementary
Louisville, Kentucky

Sarah Grycowski
Goodland Elementary
Racine, Wisconsin

Sharon S. Henry
Chancellor Elementary
Houston, Texas

Mary Jane Hollcraft
Washington Irving, School #14
Indianapolis, Indiana

Carolyn R. Jones
Johnston Elementary
Asheville, North Carolina

Rhonda Kelley
Middletown Elementary
Louisville, Kentucky

Susan Lomanto
Valley View Elementary
Longview, Texas

Jane Milner
Estes Elementary
Asheville, North Carolina

Beverly Sanney
Lakewood Elementary
St. Albans, West Virginia

John Torres
PS 41 Elementary
Staten Island, New York

Sandra Wade
Sylvan Hills Elementary
Sherwood, Arkansas

CONSULTING HEALTH SPECIALISTS

Harriet Hylton Barr, B.A., M.P.H., CHES
Clinical Associate Professor Emeritus
Department of Health Behavior
    and Health Education
School of Public Health
University of North Carolina
    at Chapel Hill
Durham, North Carolina

David A. Birch, Ph.D., CHES
Associate Professor
Department of Applied
    Health Science
Indiana University
Bloomington, Indiana

Glen Ceresa, D.D.S.
Clinical Instructor
Las Vegas Institute for Advanced
    Dental Studies
Las Vegas, Nevada

Michael J. Cleary, Ed.D., CHES
Professor
Department of Allied Health
Slippery Rock University
Slippery Rock, Pennsylvania

Lisa C. Cohn, M.M.Sc., M.Ed., R.D.
Nutrition Educator and
    Research Consultant
New York, New York

Mary Steckiewicz Garzino, M.Ed.
Director, Nutrition Education
National Dairy Council
Chicago, Illinois

Mark L. Giese, Ed.D., FACSM
Professor
Northeastern Oklahoma
    State University
Tahlequah, Oklahoma

Michael J. Hammes, Ph.D.
Associate Professor
University of New Mexico
Albuquerque, New Mexico

Betty M. Hubbard, Ed.D., CHES
Professor of Health Education
Department of Health Sciences
University of Central Arkansas
Conway, Arkansas

Rama K. Khalsa, Ph.D.
Director of Mental Health
Santa Cruz County
Soquel, California

Darrel Lang, Ed.D.
Health and Physical
    Education Consultant
Kansas State Department
    of Education
Emporia, Kansas

Gerald J. Maburn
National Vice President for Planning
    and Evaluation
American Cancer Society
Atlanta, Georgia

Cheryl Miller-Haymowicz, B.S., CHES
Health Educator
Salem-Keizer Public Schools
Salem, Oregon

John A. Morris, M.S.W.
Professor of Neuropsychiatry
    and Behavioral Science
University of South Carolina
    School of Medicine
Director of Interdisciplinary Affairs
South Carolina Department
    of Mental Health
Columbia, South Carolina

Patricia Poindexter, M.P.H., CHES
Health Education Specialist
Tucker, Georgia

Janine Robinette
Health Program Administrator
Monterey, California

Spencer Sartorius, M.S.
Administrator
Health Enhancement and
    Safety Division
Montana Office of
    Public Instruction
Helena, Montana

Jeanne Marie Scott, M.D.
Staff Physician
San Jose State University
San Jose, California

David A. Sleet, Ph.D.
Centers for Disease Control
    and Prevention
Atlanta, Georgia

Becky J. Smith, Ph.D., CHES
Reston, Virginia

Howard Taras, M.D.
Associate Professor
(Specialist in Medical Consultation
    to Schools)
University of California at
    San Diego
San Diego, California

Pamela M. Tollefsen, R.N., M.Ed.
Program Supervisor,
    Health Education
Office of Superintendent of
    Public Instruction
State of Washington
Olympia, Washington

Mae Waters, Ph.D., CHES
Executive Director of Comprehensive
    Health Training
Florida State University
Tallahassee, Florida

Contents

The Amazing Human Body **1**

Sense Organs **2**

Skeletal System **4**

Muscular System **6**

Digestive System **8**

Circulatory System **10**

Respiratory System **12**

Nervous System **14**

Chapter 1

Emotional, Intellectual, and Social Health

About Myself and Others **16**

1 Feeling Good About Myself **18**

2 Understanding My Feelings **20**

3 Dealing with Fear, Stress, Anger, and Grief . . **24**

Life Skills Manage Stress at School **28**

4 Relationships with Family and Friends **30**

5 Communicating Well with Others **34**

Life Skills Resolve Conflicts with Friends **36**

Chapter Review **38**

Activities **40**

Chapter Test **41**

Chapter 2

Family Life, Growth, and Development

Me and My Family **42**

1 What Is a Family? **44**

2 Changes in Families **48**

Life Skills Communicate with Family Members **52**

3 Everyone Grows and Changes **54**

4 People Grow at Different Rates **58**

5 Taking Care of My Body **62**

Chapter Review **64**

Activities **66**

Chapter Test **67**

Chapter 3

Personal Health and Physical Fitness

Keeping My Body Fit **68**

1 Caring for My Skin **70**

2 Caring for My Teeth and Gums **74**

3 Caring for My Ears and Nose **78**

4 Exercise and Rest for Fun and Health **82**

Life Skills Set Goals for Learning **86**

5 Staying Safe While Exercising **88**

Chapter Review **92**

Activities **94**

Chapter Test **95**

Chapter 4

Nutrition

Food for a Healthy Body **96**

1 Why My Body Needs Food **98**

2 The Food Guide Pyramid and
Healthful Meals **102**

3 Healthful Snack Choices **106**

Life Skills Make Decisions About Snacks . . . **108**

4 Being a Wise Food Shopper **110**

5 Handling Food Safely **114**

Chapter Review **116**

Activities **118**

Chapter Test **119**

Chapter 5   Preventing Disease 120

Disease Prevention and Control

1 What Is Disease? 122

2 Some Diseases and Their Causes 124

3 Fighting Disease 128

4 Diseases You Can't Catch 132

5 Fighting Disease with a
Healthful Lifestyle 136

Life Skills Manage Stress to
Control Disease 140

Chapter Review 142

Activities 144

Chapter Test 145

Chapter 6   Medicines and Other Drugs 146

Drug Use Prevention

1 Learning About Drugs 148

2 Medicines and Their Uses 150

3 How Can Medicines Be Used Safely? 154

4 What Is Caffeine? 156

5 Inhalants and Other Drugs 158

6 How Can I Say No to Drugs? 162

Life Skills Refuse Inhalants 164

Chapter Review 166

Activities 168

Chapter Test 169

Chapter 7

Avoiding Alcohol and Tobacco . . . 170

Drug Use Prevention

1 Learning About Tobacco and Alcohol **172**

2 How Tobacco Affects the Body **174**

3 How Alcohol Affects the Body **178**

4 Refusing to Use Alcohol and Tobacco **182**

Life Skills Refuse Alcohol and Tobacco **186**

Chapter Review **188**

Activities **190**

Chapter Test **191**

Chapter 8

Keeping Safe **192**

Injury Prevention

1 Being Responsible for Your Safety **194**

2 Safety Around Strangers and Bullies **198**

Life Skills Resolve Conflicts Using Negotiation **202**

3 Safety at Home—Fire, Electricity, and Poisons **204**

4 Safety for Sports and Bicycling **208**

Life Skills Make Decisions with Safety in Mind **212**

5 Getting Help and Giving First Aid **214**

Chapter Review **216**

Activities **218**

Chapter Test **219**

Chapter 9 Health in the Community 220

Community and Environmental Health

1 Health Departments, Hospitals, and Clinics **222**

2 Keeping the Environment Healthful **226**

3 Controlling Water Pollution **230**

Life Skills Set Goals to Improve Community and Environment **234**

4 Reduce, Reuse, and Recycle **236**

Chapter Review **240**

Activities **242**

Chapter Test **243**

Health Handbook 244

Life Skills **246**

Good Nutrition **248**

Preparing Foods Safely **250**

Being Physically Active **252**

Using a Computer Safely **260**

Being Safe at Home **262**

Bicycle Safety **264**

Safety in Emergencies **266**

First Aid **268**

Glossary **272**

Index **283**

The Amazing Human Body

Sense Organs 2
Your sense organs let you see, hear, smell, taste, and
touch everything around you.

Skeletal System 4
Your skeletal system holds your body up and allows
you to move in many directions.

Muscular System 6
Your muscular system works with your skeletal system
to allow your body to move and function.

Digestive System 8
Your digestive system turns the food you eat into the
energy your body needs to work and grow.

Circulatory System 10
Your circulatory system delivers helpful materials all over
your body and carries away waste products.

Respiratory System 12
Your respiratory system takes in the oxygen you need to
survive and releases carbon dioxide.

Nervous System 14
Your nervous system is the control center of your body.
It is responsible for everything your body does or feels.

*Getting enough rest,
staying active, and
eating right are important
steps to a healthful life.*

1

Sense Organs

Eye

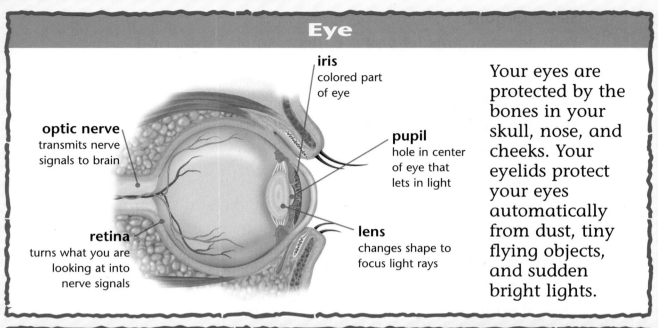

iris
colored part of eye

optic nerve
transmits nerve signals to brain

pupil
hole in center of eye that lets in light

retina
turns what you are looking at into nerve signals

lens
changes shape to focus light rays

Your eyes are protected by the bones in your skull, nose, and cheeks. Your eyelids protect your eyes automatically from dust, tiny flying objects, and sudden bright lights.

Ear

Earwax is made inside your ears to help keep them clean. Dust, dirt, and germs stick to the earwax instead of going farther into your ear. When you move your mouth by chewing and talking, old wax works its way to your outer ear.

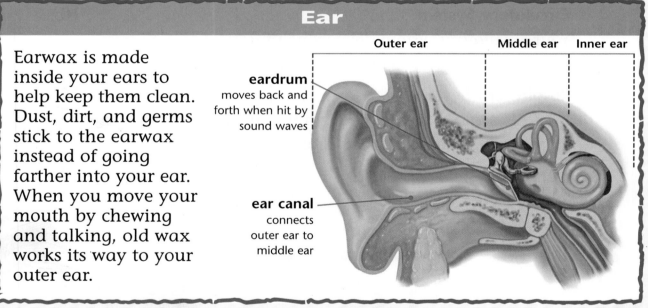

Outer ear Middle ear Inner ear

eardrum
moves back and forth when hit by sound waves

ear canal
connects outer ear to middle ear

Caring for Your Eyes and Ears

- Have your eyesight (vision) checked every year.

- Wear safety glasses when participating in activities that can be dangerous to the eyes, such as sports and mowing grass.

- Wash in, around, and behind your outer ear. Do not try to clean your ear canal with cotton-tip sticks or other objects.

Nose

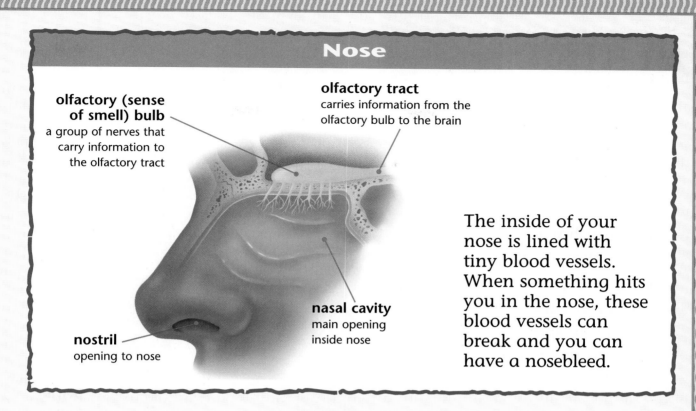

olfactory (sense of smell) bulb
a group of nerves that carry information to the olfactory tract

olfactory tract
carries information from the olfactory bulb to the brain

nostril
opening to nose

nasal cavity
main opening inside nose

The inside of your nose is lined with tiny blood vessels. When something hits you in the nose, these blood vessels can break and you can have a nosebleed.

Caring for Your Nose, Tongue, and Skin

- If you get a nosebleed, sit, lean forward slightly, and pinch just below the bridge of your nose for ten minutes. Breathe through your mouth.

- When you brush your teeth, brush your tongue too.

- Always wear sunscreen when you are in the sun.

Tongue

Germs live on your tongue and in other parts of your mouth. Germs can harm your teeth and give you bad breath.

taste buds

Skin

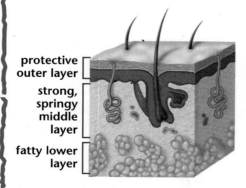

protective outer layer

strong, springy middle layer

fatty lower layer

Your skin protects your insides from the outside world. It keeps fluids you need inside your body and fluids you don't need, such as swimming pool water, outside your body.

Skeletal System

Each of your bones has a particular shape and size that allow it to do a certain job. You have bones that are tiny, long, wide, flat, and even curved. The job of some bones is to protect your body parts.

skull

clavicle
(collar bone)

rib cage

humerus

spine

ulna

pelvis

radius

femur

tibia

fibula

Bones that Protect

Rib Cage Your rib bones form a cage that protects your heart and lungs from all sides. Your ribs are springy. When something strikes you in the chest, your ribs push the object away instead of letting it hit your heart and lungs.

Your ribs are connected to your breastbone (sternum) by springy material called cartilage. The springy connection lets your ribs move up and down. This happens when your rib cage gets bigger and smaller as you breathe in and out.

Skull The bones in your head are called your skull. Some of the bones in your skull protect your brain. The bones in your face are part of your skull too.

cartilage

rib

sternum

jaw

Caring for Your Skeletal System

- Calcium helps bones grow and makes them strong. Dairy products like milk, cheese, and yogurt contain calcium. Have 2–3 servings of dairy products every day.

- Exercise also makes your bones strong. When bones aren't used, they can become brittle and may break.

Activities

1. Look at the picture of the skeleton. Name a long bone. Name a short bone. Name a curved bone.

2. Put a tomato inside a wire cage. Gently throw a wad of paper at the cage. What happens? The cage protects the tomato in the same way your ribs protect your heart.

3. Measure around your rib cage with a string. How big is it when you breathe in? How big is it when you breathe out? Which measurement is greater?

Muscular System

Like your bones, each muscle in your body does a certain job. Muscles in your thumb help you hold things. Muscles in your neck help you turn your head. Muscles in your arms help you pull or lift objects.

deltoid

biceps

triceps

flexors

abdominal muscles

quadriceps

flexors

Muscle Pairs Your arm can reach forward and pull back. Your hand can open and close. Muscles can only pull. Moving part of your body in more than one direction takes more than one muscle. It takes a pair of muscles for your arm to bend and straighten.

triceps contracts when you straighten your arm

biceps contracts when you bend your arm

tendon

tendon

Tendons Tendons are strong strips of tough cord-like material. They connect your muscles to your bones. Your Achilles tendon is just above your heel. It connects your calf muscle to your heel bone. Your calf muscles and Achilles tendon allow you to stand on tiptoe.

Caring for Your Muscular System

- Exercise makes your muscles stronger.

- Stretching before you exercise makes muscles and tendons more flexible and less likely to get hurt.

Activities

1. **Tie your shoe without using your thumb. What happens?**

2. **Pull up on a desk with one hand. With your other hand, feel which arm muscle is working. Now push on the desk. Which arm muscle is working?**

3. **Ask a friend to push down on your arms for one minute while you push up as hard as you can. When your friend lets go, what happens?**

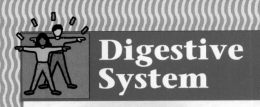

Food is broken down and pushed through your body by your digestive system. Your digestive system is a series of connected parts that starts with your mouth and ends with your large intestine.

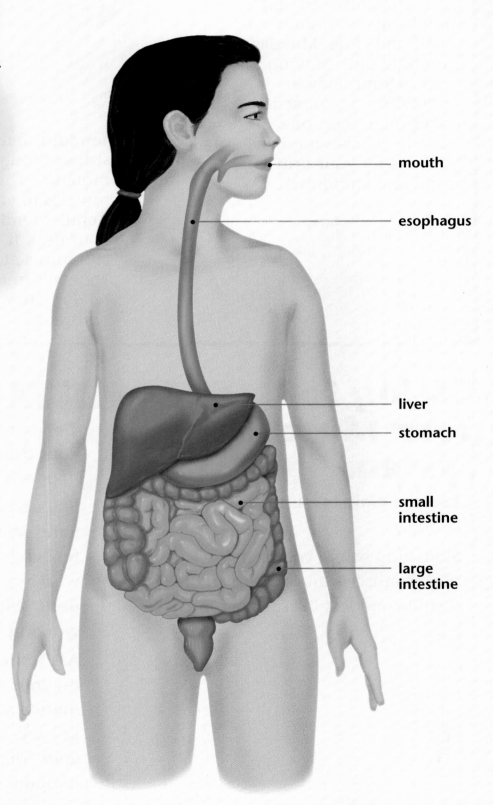

mouth

esophagus

liver

stomach

small intestine

large intestine

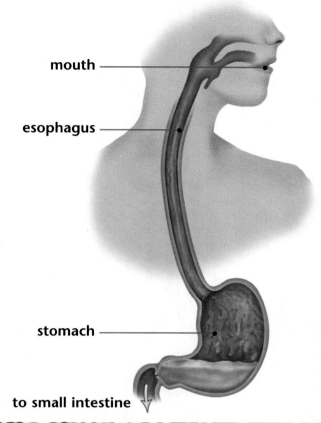

mouth

esophagus

stomach

to small intestine

Esophagus Your esophagus, or food tube, is a tube that connects your mouth to your stomach. After you swallow a bite of food, muscles in your esophagus push the food into your stomach.

Stomach Your stomach is filled with acid that helps dissolve food. The stomach walls are strong muscles that mix food with the acid. The stomach walls are protected from the acid by a thick layer of mucus. From your stomach, food moves to the small intestine and then to the large intestine.

Caring for Your Digestive System

- Chew everything you eat carefully. Well-chewed food is easier to digest.
- Do not overeat. Overeating can cause a stomachache.

 Activities

1. Measure 25 feet (about 8 m) on the floor. This is how long your digestive system is.

2. Cut a narrow balloon so that it is open on both ends. Put a wad of paper in one end. Squeeze the outside of the balloon to push the paper through and out the other end. This is similar to how your esophagus pushes food to your stomach.

Food and oxygen travel through your circulatory system to every cell in your body. Blood moves nutrients throughout your body, fights infection, and helps control your body temperature. Your blood is made up mostly of a watery liquid called plasma.

arteries

blood vessels

veins

heart

Blood Vessels

Arteries Arteries carry blood away from the heart. Blood in arteries is brighter red because it has come from the lungs and has lots of oxygen. Arteries bring oxygen and nutrients to all parts of the body.

Veins Veins carry blood to the heart. Veins have one-way valves that allow blood to move only toward the heart.

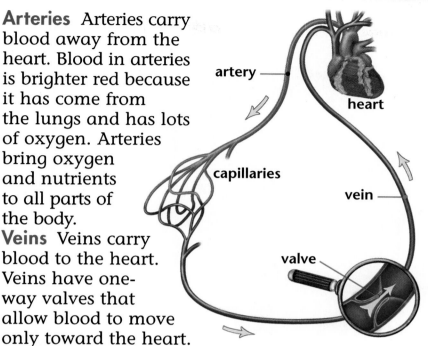

artery

heart

capillaries

vein

valve

Capillaries Capillaries are very small pathways for blood. When blood flows through capillaries, it gives oxygen and nutrients to the cells in your body. Blood also picks up carbon dioxide and other waste.

Caring for Your Circulatory System

- Never touch another person's blood.

- Eat a healthy, balanced diet throughout your life to keep excess fat from blocking the blood flowing through your arteries.

- Get regular exercise to keep your heart strong.

Activities

1. **Take the bottom out of a paper cup. Bend the top together like a clamshell. Hold the cup and drop a marble through from the bottom. Now try to drop one into the top. The clamshell-shaped cup is like the one-way valve in a vein.**

2. **Find the blue lines under the skin on your wrist. These are veins. Press gently and stroke along the lines toward your elbow. Now stroke toward your hand. What do you see?**

Respiratory System

Your body uses its respiratory system to get oxygen from the air and get rid of excess carbon dioxide. Your respiratory system is made up of your nose and mouth, your trachea (windpipe), your two lungs, and your diaphragm—a dome-shaped muscle under your lungs.

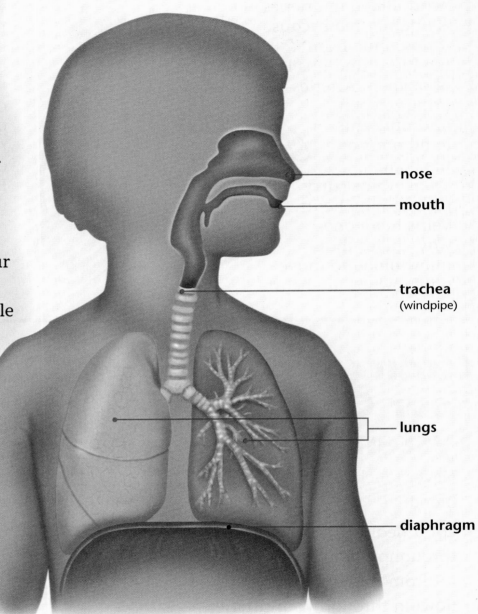

nose

mouth

trachea
(windpipe)

lungs

diaphragm

Breathing

When you inhale, or breathe in, air enters your mouth and nose and goes into your trachea. Your trachea connects your nose and mouth to your lungs. Your trachea divides into two smaller tubes that go to your lungs. Your lungs fill with air. When you exhale, or breathe out, your diaphragm pushes upward. Air is forced up your trachea and out your mouth and nose.

INHALING

air goes into mouth and nose

lungs fill with air

diaphragm moves down

EXHALING

air comes out of mouth and nose

air leaves lungs

diaphragm moves up

Caring for Your Respiratory System

- Exercise. When you exercise your body, you exercise your respiratory system too. Your muscles use more oxygen, so you breathe faster and deeper.

- Get enough sleep to help your resistance to colds.

Activities

1. Sit in a chair and count how many breaths you take in 30 seconds. Then exercise for two minutes. When you stop, count how many breaths you take in 30 seconds. Do you breathe more while sitting or after exercise?

2. Put your hand on your bellybutton and take a deep breath in and out. How does your hand move?

Nervous System

Your nerves send information to your brain from various parts of your body and from the outside world. Your brain decides what to do with the information and sends instructions through your nerves back to your body parts.

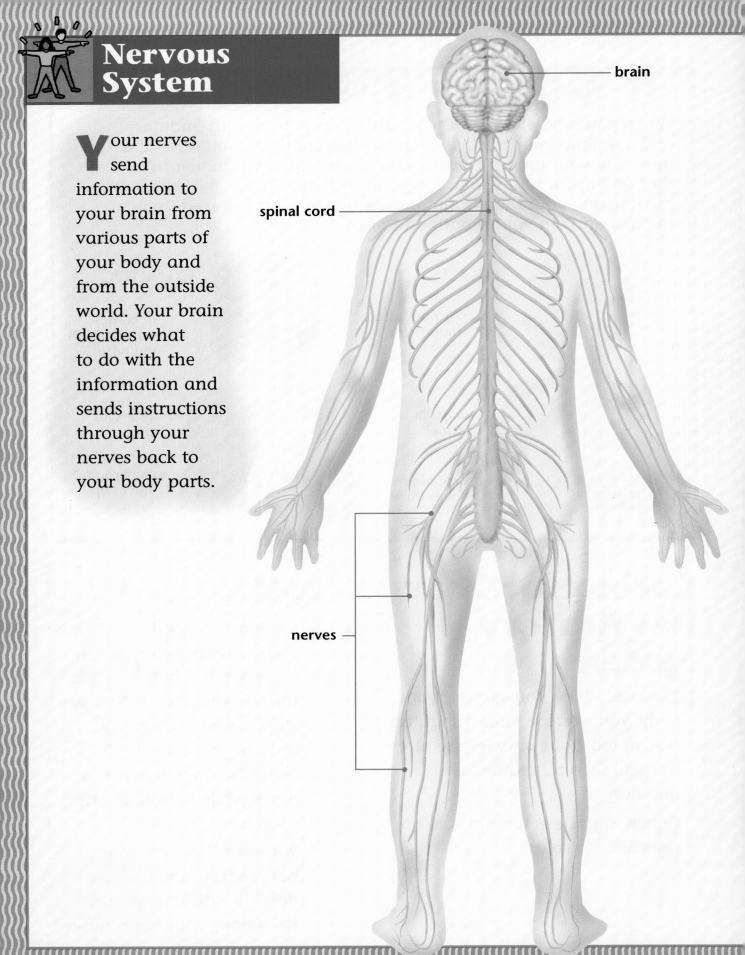

brain

spinal cord

nerves

Your Brain

Your brain is about two pounds of wrinkled, pinkish-gray material. It's protected by your skull and cushioned by a thin layer of liquid. The brain's main connection to the body is the spinal cord.

Different parts of the brain send signals to different parts of your body. For example, the part right behind your forehead tells your body how to move. The area near the base of your neck controls your breathing and heartbeat. If you are left-handed, the right half of your brain controls your handwriting.

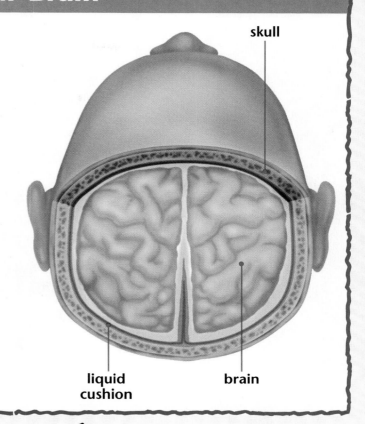

skull

liquid cushion

brain

Caring for Your Nervous System

- Many injuries to the brain are caused by car crashes. Wear your safety belt and sit in the backseat when you are in the car.

- Always wear a helmet when you ride your bike, skate, or use a skateboard.

Activities

1. Make a list of signals your nerves are sending to your brain right now. Also list instructions your brain is sending to your nerves.

2. Read a paragraph out of a book while the television is on. Do you know what the paragraph was about? Do you know what happened on television?

3. Write your name with your opposite hand ten times. Does your writing improve?

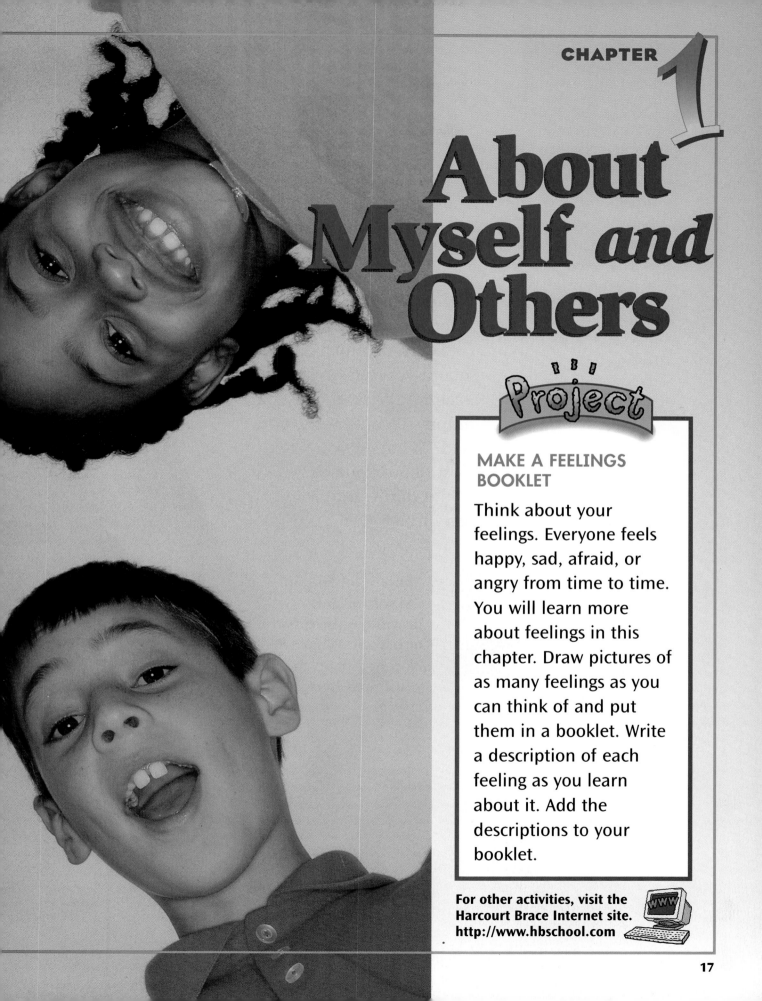

CHAPTER 1

About Myself and Others

Project

MAKE A FEELINGS BOOKLET

Think about your feelings. Everyone feels happy, sad, afraid, or angry from time to time. You will learn more about feelings in this chapter. Draw pictures of as many feelings as you can think of and put them in a booklet. Write a description of each feeling as you learn about it. Add the descriptions to your booklet.

**For other activities, visit the Harcourt Brace Internet site.
http://www.hbschool.com**

MAIN IDEA
Treating yourself like a good friend is a way to respect yourself.

WHY LEARN THIS? When you feel good about who you are, it is easier to be happy and get along better.

VOCABULARY
• feelings
• respect
• responsible
• honest

Feeling Good About Myself

Look in the mirror. Whose face do you see? A very special person is looking back at you. In the whole world there is no one else just like you.

Your feelings make you special. **Feelings** are the way you react to people and events.

Learn as much as you can about yourself and your feelings. What makes you happy? What makes you sad? What do you like best about yourself? What don't you like very much?

► Maria is looking in the mirror and drawing a picture of herself. What kind of person do you think she sees?

It is important to treat yourself like the special person you are. Treat yourself the same way you would treat a good friend. This means you feel proud of yourself when you do something well.

Being a friend to yourself also means you respect yourself. If you **respect** (rih•SPEKT) yourself, you believe in yourself. You stand up for yourself. You listen to your feelings and take good care of yourself.

Taking care of yourself shows you are learning to be responsible. Being **responsible** (rih•SPAHNT•suh•buhl) means that other people can count on you. It also means that you are **honest**—you tell the truth. Being responsible is a sign of growing up.

LESSON CHECKUP

Check Your Facts

❶ What are feelings?

❷ What can you do to be a good friend to yourself?

❸ CRITICAL THINKING Give an example of something you could do that shows you respect yourself.

Set Health Goals

❹ Name one way you have been responsible at school today. Name another way you can be responsible today.

MAIN IDEA
You can choose how to show your feelings. You can also decide how to express what you are feeling.

WHY LEARN THIS? Knowing as much as you can about your feelings is an important part of growing up.

VOCABULARY
• body language
• emotions
• self-control

Understanding My Feelings

Your feelings are a part of what makes you a special person. You choose when and how to express your feelings. Learning to name your feelings and express them in a safe way shows that you are growing up.

Where do my feelings come from?

Sometimes feelings come from an event. You are happy working on a project with friends. Feelings also come from thinking about an event in the past. You feel sad thinking back to the day you moved. You also have feelings about events to come. You are excited for winter vacation to arrive.

▼ Working in a group can be a lot of fun. How do you think these children feel as they practice their math skills together?

All right!

How do I show feelings?

You show your feelings in different ways. One way is through your words. Actions are another way to show feelings. When you cry, you may be saying you are sad, hurt, or angry. When you pet your dog, you are showing how much you care. Writing a thank-you note expresses your feelings in actions *and* in words!

Did you know that your body helps you show your feelings? Your face often tells others how you are feeling. A big smile lets people know that you are happy. Other parts of your body express your feelings, too. Your **body language** is how your body shows your feelings.

When your face gets red, your body is saying you are embarrassed or shy. If you say you aren't afraid, but your hands are shaking, your body is telling the truth for you.

When you know and can name a feeling, it is easier to choose how to express it. When feelings take you by surprise, they can explode out of you in words or actions. They can make you feel uncomfortable or not in control. This can be scary.

JOURNAL

In your Health Journal describe a time when you felt happy. How did you express it in words, in your actions, and in body language?

MAIN IDEA
You can learn how to deal with unpleasant feelings such as fear, stress, anger, and grief.

WHY LEARN THIS? When you know about unpleasant feelings, you can make wise choices about how to deal with them.

VOCABULARY
• fear
• stress
• anger
• grief

I'm afraid!

Dealing with Fear, Stress, Anger, and Grief

It is important to learn as much as you can about unpleasant feelings. Understanding them will make it easier to help yourself or a friend deal with one of these feelings.

How can I deal with fear?

There are many reasons you might feel **fear**, or be scared.

• You are in a new school or class.

• You are alone in your house.

• Some older children bully you.

When you feel afraid, your heart beats faster. You are nervous and upset. It is important to trust how you feel and to do something about it. It is part of being a good friend to yourself.

You can deal with some fears by yourself. If you are afraid of missing the school bus, you can set your alarm so you get up earlier. Other fears may be much more serious. Sometimes you need to talk to a trusted adult right away.

WHEN TO ASK FOR HELP
• Something makes you feel uncomfortable or scared.
• You are afraid to go to school.
• You have trouble sleeping.
• Someone touches you in a way you don't like.

I'm stressed!

How can I deal with stress?

When you feel **stress**, you may have butterflies in your stomach. Your hands may sweat. Your heart may even beat fast.

It is important to know why you are feeling stress. Are you worried about a test? Is there not enough time to finish your homework? If you have felt stress for a long time, you should talk to a parent or a trusted adult. He or she may have ideas to help you.

There are many ways to deal with stress. One way is to manage your time. First, make a list of what you have to do. Then, write down how long each task will take. Other ways to deal with stress are listed in the table.

DEAL WITH STRESS

- Talk to a family member or an adult.
- Plan your time wisely.
- Set goals you can reach.
- Get some exercise and take time to have fun.

How can I deal with angry, hurt, or sad feelings?

When you feel **anger**, you are very mad. It is all right to be angry. Everyone gets angry sometimes. You may get angry if you don't get your way or if someone teases you. Hurt and sadness are other common feelings. You may feel hurt if you are blamed for something you didn't do. You may feel sad if your best friend moves away.

You can learn to manage your anger in ways that keep you safe and in control. You can learn to make wise choices about how you show your anger. Then you can decide what you want to do.

Communicate

Murray feels angry because his brother left the tops off his colored markers. He feels like telling his brother, "You are so stupid." Suggest a better way for Murray to tell his brother how he feels. Use the steps for communicating shown on pages 246 and 247. What if he began by saying "I feel . . ."?

MANAGE ANGER

1. Stop what you are doing.
2. Count to ten to cool down or take three long, slow breaths.
3. Think about what is happening.
4. Take action. Either walk away or tell the person what you are feeling.
5. Use messages that tell how you feel. Begin with "I feel . . ."

I'm angry!

I'm hurt!

I'm sad

How can I deal with grief?

When you feel **grief**, you feel a deep sadness. This sadness may last for a while.

You may feel grief when a person or a pet dies. You may feel like being alone, or you may feel like crying. It is important to find a way to express your feelings.

Talking about how you feel is another way to express your grief. Family members, a teacher, and a member of the clergy are people who will listen to you. You can also take care of yourself by exercising, eating well, and getting enough sleep.

You can write a poem in your journal or draw a picture that expresses your sadness. Did you know that many famous artists express their feelings of grief and sadness in their artwork?

► Visual artists express their feelings through art.

Career

Visual Artist

What They Do

Visual artists include painters, illustrators, photographers, and sculptors. Visual artists express many different ideas and feelings in their artwork. A painter may express grief by doing a painting in memory of a person who died.

Education and Training

Some visual artists go to art school. Others learn and practice on their own. Some visual artists teach art classes for children or adults.

LESSON CHECKUP

Check Your Facts

1. When should you ask for help if you are scared?
2. CRITICAL THINKING How can planning ahead help you feel less stress?
3. How can you express your anger but stay in control?
4. Who can help you deal with grief?

Use Life Skills

5. COMMUNICATE Pretend that you are angry with a friend who broke your favorite toy. How could you manage your anger in a way that keeps you in control?

27

MANAGE STRESS
at School

Everyone faces stress from time to time. Learning the following steps will help you handle your stress in a healthful way.

Learn This Skill

Tran's class is having a spelling bee next week. He is worried that he will be one of the first students to miss a word. How can Tran handle the stress he feels?

1. Know what stress feels like and what causes it.

Tran cannot fall asleep. He can feel his heart pounding and his muscles tightening. He is worried about the spelling bee.

2. When you feel stress, think about ways to handle it.

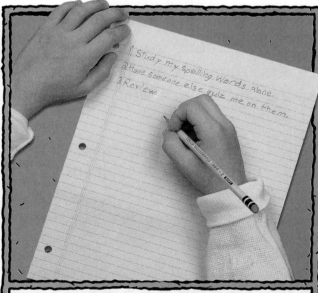

"My dad says I should make a list of what I need to do to get ready for the spelling bee."

3. Focus on one step at a time.

"Dad and I made a list of the words I still need to work on."

4. Learn to relax.

Tran takes a deep breath. "I am prepared, and I know that I will do my best!" he tells himself.

Practice This Skill

Use this summary to help you solve the problems below.

Steps for Managing Stress

1. Know what stress feels like and what causes it.

2. When you feel stress, think about ways to handle it.

3. Focus on one step at a time.

4. Learn to relax.

A. Sara is joining a Little League team. She has heard people say mean things to players who make mistakes. What can Sara do to deal with her fear about making a mistake?

B. Luis didn't do his homework because he left his math book at school. He is worried that his teacher will call on him. What should Luis do?

Relationships with Family and Friends

MAIN IDEA
Having good relationships with family and friends helps you have healthy relationships with other people.

WHY LEARN THIS? Getting along with family members and friends makes you feel good about yourself.

VOCABULARY
• relationship
• peers
• peer pressure

A **relationship** (rih•LAY•shuhn•ship) is the way you get along with someone. You spend a lot of time with your family and friends. It is important to get along well. When you have good relationships with your family and friends, it makes you feel good about yourself.

What makes good relationships with family?

Each person in a family has a special role. It is important to respect everyone in your family—from the youngest to the oldest. Talking and listening to all family members are ways of showing respect.

▼ How would you describe the relationships of the family members in these four photos?

Families work together better when family members respect and trust each other. When you tell the truth, you let your family members know they can trust you.

Being a responsible family member makes you feel good about yourself. It also lets your family know that they can depend on you to do your part. It means you are growing up. Some people your age do the dishes, set the table, take out the trash, or care for a pet. What chores do you do at home?

Families need time to play together, too. When you and your family have a good time together, it reminds you of how special it is to be a family. Some families like to ride bikes, make pizza, play games, or plan surprises together.

All families have problems at times. That's when family members need to work together and support each other. Taking time to talk together about what each family member can do helps families feel close. It's another way for family members to show they care about each other.

What do you like to do with your family?

What makes good relationships with friends?

Roller skating, birthday parties, school projects, and playing sports are fun ways to be with friends. Even doing a chore such as raking leaves is more fun with a friend!

Do you like to swim or build models? It's fun to find friends who like the same things you do. School clubs, neighborhood centers, and church groups can be good places to see old friends and make new friends.

Sometimes, however, even best friends disagree. When you and a friend don't agree, try to listen and talk things over. Say you're sorry if you do something that hurts a friend. Be ready to forgive your friend if he or she hurts you. Sometimes others do not know that their actions affect you.

► How are these children enjoying their friendship?

◄ Friends can have differences and still have many things in common.

It's important to have **peers**—friends your age— who share your interests. However, if some of your friends want you to do something just because "everyone is doing it," they are using **peer pressure**. If it doesn't feel right to you, or it is against your family rules, stand up for yourself and make another choice. When you do that, you can be proud of yourself. It's a sign that you respect yourself and your family. You are also setting a good example for your peers.

LESSON CHECKUP

Check Your Facts

① How can you show respect for each member of your family? How can family members show respect for you?

② What jobs can children your age do to be responsible family members?

③ What are some ways to meet new friends?

④ CRITICAL THINKING Why is it important to be able to talk over problems with your friends?

Set Health Goals

⑤ Give an example of peer pressure. Describe what you could do to stand up for yourself.

MAIN IDEA
Speaking and listening respectfully to others helps you understand yourself and others better.

WHY LEARN THIS? You can use what you learn to improve your listening and communication skills.

VOCABULARY
• communicate
• compassion
• apologize

Communicating Well with Others

To **communicate** (kuh•MYOO•nuh•kayt) means to share information. You can learn to communicate in a way that helps you understand yourself and others better.

Using I-messages helps communicate your feelings. "I feel bad when you don't keep a promise" is an I-message. It helps others understand your feelings. It gives them a chance to respond.

It is important to take turns listening and speaking. When others are speaking, listen carefully so you can understand them. Listening carefully, even when you disagree, is a way to respect other people.

If you have **compassion** (kuhm•PA•shuhn), you can feel what others feel. You treat people in a kind and caring way. You don't use put-downs or act like a bully, because you want to show respect and communicate well.

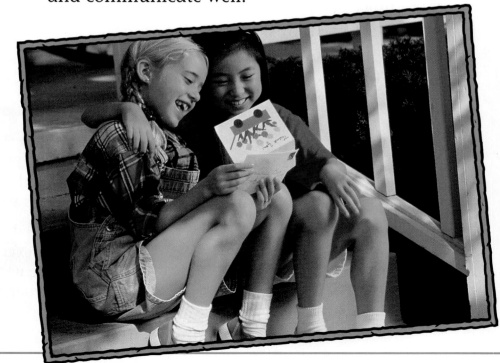

▶ There are many ways for friends to communicate.

▲ These brothers are communicating with a friend who lives far away. How else could they communicate with him?

When you are wrong, you should **apologize** (uh•PAH•luh•jyz)—say you are sorry. You are asking the other person to forgive you. When people tell you they are sorry, you can forgive them.

Using words to communicate your feelings and listening respectfully to other people are signs that you are becoming more responsible.

Activity **Use Communication Skills** Choose one of the pictures on these pages. Write a paragraph about the picture. Include how these friends are using good communication skills.

LESSON CHECKUP

Check Your Facts

❶ Name four helpful communication skills.

❷ CRITICAL THINKING Why might you apologize to a friend?

Set Health Goals

❸ Which communication skill is easiest for you? Which communication skill is the hardest for you? Describe a time when communication skills might come in handy.

RESOLVE CONFLICTS
with Friends

Ignoring how other people feel can lead to conflicts. Learning how to resolve conflicts will help you have more healthful relationships.

Learn This Skill

Some of the students are making fun of Martha, the new girl, because she wears glasses. When Dennis arrives, they expect him to join in. Dennis wants to go along with his friends, but he knows that teasing is wrong. What should Dennis do?

1. Use I-messages to tell how you feel.

"I feel sad when Martha is teased," says Dennis.

2. Listen to each other.

"You may think what you are saying is funny, but it isn't funny if it makes someone sad." "We weren't trying to be mean," the group replies.

3. Think of the other person's point of view.

"Look—Martha's new. That's hard enough. Let's include her in our group."

4. Decide what to do.

"Dennis is right—let's all try to get to know each other."

Practice This Skill

Use this summary to help you solve the problems below.

Steps for Resolving Conflicts

1. Use I-messages to tell how you feel.

2. Listen to each other.

3. Think of the other person's point of view.

4. Decide what to do.

A. Your friend's parents say it's OK to walk to the store. You want to go, but you know your parents wouldn't want you to. Explain how you feel and why you can't go.

B. You are the youngest one on a family vacation. Your parents want you to go to bed earlier than everyone else. Write down why your parents might think you need to go to bed early.

USE VOCABULARY

anger (p. 26)	**emotions** (p. 22)	**peer pressure** (p. 33)	**self-control** (p. 22)
apologize (p. 35)	**fear** (p. 24)	**peers** (p. 33)	**stress** (p. 25)
body language (p. 21)	**feelings** (p. 18)	**relationship** (p. 30)	
communicate (p. 34)	**grief** (p. 27)	**respect** (p. 19)	
compassion (p. 34)	**honest** (p. 19)	**responsible** (p. 19)	

Use the terms above to complete the sentences. Page numbers in ( ) tell you where to look in the chapter if you need help.

1. Friends your own age are ____.

2. To ____ means to share information.

3. ____ are strong feelings.

4. If you feel ____, you are very mad.

5. When you say you are sorry, you ____.

6. Being ____ means that other people can count on you.

7. When you feel ____, you may have butterflies in your stomach.

8. If you have ____, you can feel what others feel.

9. ____ are the way you react to people and events.

10. When you are ____, you tell the truth.

11. ____ is a deep sadness.

12. A ____ is the way you get along with someone.

13. If you ____ yourself, you believe in yourself.

14. Your ____ is how your body shows your feelings.

15. ____ may cause you to do something because "everyone is doing it."

16. If you have power over your emotions, you have ____.

17. If you feel ____, you are afraid.

CHECK YOUR FACTS

Page numbers in ( ) tell you where to look in the chapter if you need help.

18. What is an I-message? (p. 34)

19. What are three ways to let go of emotions? (p. 23)

20. Name two things you can do to be a good friend to yourself. (p. 19)

21. What are two things you can do when you and a friend disagree? (p. 32)

22. Name four things you can do to deal with stress. (p. 25)

23. Describe three things you do that make you a responsible member of your family.

24. Pretend that you are sad because your best friend is moving away. How would you express your sadness in your words, actions, and body language?

APPLY LIFE SKILLS

25. **Manage Stress** Suppose you are worried about a math test you will have tomorrow. Write the steps for managing stress and tell how you can deal with the stress you feel.

26. **Resolve Conflicts** Suppose you and a friend have a disagreement because he wants you to play baseball instead of finishing your homework. Write the steps for resolving conflicts and tell how you can work out your disagreement.

Promote Health **Home and Community**

1. Talk with family members about things all of you do to get along with each other.
2. Make a poster that shows at least four important communication skills. Display it at your school or at home.

Activities

Mirror, Mirror, on the Wall

On Your Own • Look in the mirror and study your face. Imagine that you are angry. How does your face look? Now imagine that you are about to go to the beach with your family. How does your face look now? Draw pictures of yourself showing each of these emotions.

Getting to Know You

With a Team • On poster board write down five things you could do to get to know a new student. Draw pictures to go with your words.

Communicating Your Feelings

With a Partner • Imagine that you and a friend have a disagreement over which game to play. Write down at least four I-messages you could use to help you communicate your feelings. Take turns reading your I-messages.

Managing Your Time

At Home • Imagine that you never have time to finish all your chores. Make a time management chart to help you.

Multiple Choice

Choose the letter of the correct answer.

1. You can show your feelings through _____ .
   a. actions
   b. words
   c. body language
   d. all of the above

2. You're feeling _____ when you have butterflies in your stomach and your hands are sweaty.
   a. stress
   b. grief
   c. anger
   d. sadness

3. It's important to have good _____ with family members and friends.
   a. responsibility
   b. emotion
   c. relationships
   d. feeling

4. Using I-messages helps you _____ your feelings.
   a. respect
   b. communicate
   c. forgive
   d. apologize

Modified True or False

Write *true* or *false*. If a sentence is false, replace the underlined term to make the sentence true.

5. Taking care of yourself shows that you are learning to be <u>responsible</u>.

6. Having <u>self-control</u> over your emotions can help you deal with unpleasant feelings.

7. Families work together better when family members <u>respect</u> each other.

8. It is <u>not all right</u> to feel angry.

9. Your <u>feelings</u> are the way you respond to people and events.

10. Using <u>you-messages</u> is a good way to communicate your feelings.

11. Talking and listening to others is a way of showing <u>respect</u>.

Short Answer

Write a sentence to answer each item.

12. What are two things families might do when they have problems?

13. Name two things you do for yourself when you respect yourself.

14. Give an example of something you could do to show compassion.

15. Name three types of visual artists.

16. What are three things you can do to improve your communication?

Essay

Write a paragraph to answer each item.

17. Luis feels lonely. What are three things he could do to let go of that feeling?

18. Roberta is feeling stress because she doesn't think she can finish her social studies project on time. How could she deal with her stress?

Me and My Family

MAKE A FAMILY BOOK

Make a book titled "Things Families Do Together." Include fun things as well as jobs families might work on together, such as making meals.

For other activities, visit the Harcourt Brace Internet site. http://www.hbschool.com

MAIN IDEA
Families enjoy working and playing together.

WHY LEARN THIS? When family members play and work well together, they learn to respect each other.

VOCABULARY
• family
• values

What Is a Family?

Your **family** is the group of people you live with. There are many kinds of families. Some families have children and two parents. Other families have one parent, a grandparent, or another adult. A stepparent or stepchildren may be part of a family. Who is in your family?

Your family makes sure your basic needs are met. They give you food, a place to sleep, and clothes to wear. They love you, help you when you are ill or scared, and make rules to keep you safe.

Families also teach values. **Values** (VAL•yooz) are strong beliefs, such as honesty and caring about others. Children first learn about right and wrong in their families.

Most parents love their children. They try hard to give their children what they need to grow up strong and healthy.

▼ There are many kinds of families.

How does a family play together?

Family members can play together in many ways. Some families like to play sports or go hiking. Other families choose books to read out loud. Some work on jigsaw puzzles. Others play games or watch videos. How do the people in your family play together?

Playing together can make everyone in a family feel good. You laugh together as you plan a special surprise. You talk as you put together a puzzle. You have a chance to relax together as you ride bikes or walk the dog.

Playing together gives family members a chance to talk and listen to each other. You get to know each other better. You talk about what you are feeling. You learn to respect each other.

When members of a family have fun together, it makes everyone happy. It makes everyone glad to be part of the family.

LANGUAGE ARTS CONNECTION

"I'll Never Forget the Time . . ."

On Your Own Write a story about a funny or exciting time with your family that you will never forget. Tell what you liked best about the event.

○ ○ ○

45

How does a family work together?

It's important for family members to work together. When people in a family work together, it makes everyone in the family feel proud.

In some families the children are responsible for certain jobs. One child may always set the table, carry in firewood, or take care of a pet. In other families parents and children take turns doing some jobs, such as washing the dishes or taking out the trash.

You may have different jobs depending on where your family lives. If you live in a city apartment, you will have different jobs from someone who lives on a farm.

Taking Care of Maggie

1. Feed her. ✓
2. Give her clean water. ✓
3. Pet her. ✓
4. Brush her for 10 minutes. ○
5. Keep her litter box clean. ✓

◀ **Taking care of a pet is a good way to show responsibility.**

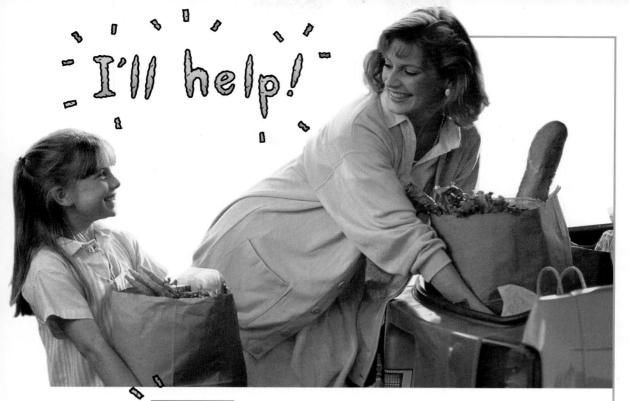

I'll help!

Activity **Think of New Jobs** List the ways you help your family. What three new ways could you add to your list?

It feels good to be a responsible member of your family. You are being responsible when you do a job without waiting to be asked. For example you can keep your room clean or offer to help with big jobs.

When everyone in a family works together, no one person has to do all the work. Jobs get done more quickly. And that leaves more time for play!

LESSON CHECKUP

Check Your Facts

1. How does your family meet your basic needs?

2. Name three reasons it's important for family members to play together.

3. CRITICAL THINKING What jobs could people in your family take turns doing?

Set Health Goals

4. Think of three things you would like to do with your family. Give other family members a chance to add to the list. With your family, choose an activity from the list, and make a plan for doing it.

MAIN IDEA
All families go through changes. Some changes are harder than others.

WHY LEARN THIS? It helps to know ways that family members can help each other during good times and bad times.

VOCABULARY
• divorce
• sibling

Changes in Families

Have you ever seen a snow globe—a glass ball that "snows" when you turn it upside down? When big changes happen in a family, you may feel as if you're inside a snow globe. Everything may suddenly seem to be turning upside down.

What happens when families change?

Changes happen all the time. Many changes are fun, but some are hard. Moving, divorce or remarriage, a new baby, and the death of a pet are all big changes. Everyone in the family will need time to get used to changes like these.

Moving to a new place can feel confusing. If you move, you may feel sad about leaving your old friends and your old home. But you may also feel excited about going to a new school.

Moving day can bring mixed feelings.

Activity **Write About Change** These snow globes show big changes that can turn a family upside down for a time. Choose one, or think of another big change. Write about all the feelings you might have as you get used to the change.

When parents **divorce** (duh•VORS), it means they are no longer married to each other. If parents divorce or remarry, it is normal to feel sad, scared, and confused for a while.

When a pet dies, you may feel sad a long time. Even if you get another pet, you will always remember the pet that died.

When a new baby joins your family, you have a new brother or sister, or **sibling**. You may feel excited but also jealous of the time your parents spend with the baby. It may take some time for you to get to know your new brother or sister.

If a big change happens in your family, it's all right to feel whatever you are feeling. Be patient with yourself and with other family members.

How can family members help each other?

When you were little, your parents did everything for you. Now that you are older, you can begin to help them. When family members help each other, they feel as if they're part of the same team.

It's easier for a family to be a good team when family members share the same values. If all the people in your family speak politely to each other and tell the truth, it helps your family stay strong.

Family rules also help family members work as a team. When all the people in your family respect the rules, family members argue less often and have more fun together.

Team members help each other. You may help by reading stories to a younger sibling. Sometimes the whole family might pitch in for a big project such as painting the house. By helping, you are being a responsible member of your family.

◀ Reading a book out loud is a good way to spend time with a younger sibling.

▲ Mealtime is a good time for family members to listen to each other's ideas and feelings.

LIFE SKILLS FOCUS

Resolve Conflicts

Your younger brother and sister always interrupt when you are talking. This makes you angry. How can you help them learn to listen politely and wait their turn to speak? Use the steps for resolving conflicts shown on pages 246 and 247.

For a family to be a good team, family members need to communicate. It takes practice to learn to talk and listen respectfully to each family member. Some families spend time talking while eating meals, riding in the car, or making breakfast.

When family members can talk to each other, work together, and have fun together, they feel like a team. They feel close to each other. Feeling close makes it easier for family members to help each other when big changes happen.

LESSON CHECKUP

Check Your Facts

1. Name some times when all the members of a family can talk together.
2. What kinds of feelings might you have when a new sibling is born?
3. CRITICAL THINKING How are family team rules like a sports team's rules?
4. Why are family rules important?

Set Health Goals

5. Write one goal you would like your family to work toward. What could each family member do to help?

COMMUNICATE
with Family Members

Even when planning fun activities, family members need to communicate with each other. This skill will help you do just that.

Learn This Skill

Jenny's family is planning which restaurant to go to on Friday night. Each family member gets to present an idea.

1. Understand your audience.

Jenny knows each family member has certain likes and dislikes. They will have to work together to choose a restaurant all will accept.

2. Give a clear message.

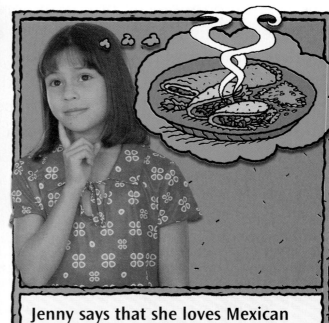

Jenny says that she loves Mexican food and that she'd like to go to the Mexican Fiesta.

3. Listen.

Jenny listens to the rest of the family. Her brother says they eat Mexican food too often. He wants to go to the Little Italy restaurant.

4. Gather feedback.

Everyone talks and listens. They decide to go Italian this Friday and Mexican next Friday.

Practice This Skill

Use the steps to help you solve the problems.

Communicating with Family Members

1. Understand your audience.
2. Give a clear message.
3. Listen.
4. Gather feedback.

A. Kathy gets angry when her brother borrows her bike without asking. How can Kathy communicate her feelings to her brother?

B. Larry is upset. His sister promised to help him clean the kitchen, and then she forgot. How can Larry communicate how he feels?

Everyone Grows and Changes

The Human Life Cycle

birth to two

two to ten

ten to adult

adult to senior

▲ Birth to two

What is the human life cycle?

The next time you're at the mall, look around. You will see babies, children, teenagers, and adults. Each group is in a different stage of the life cycle. The human **life cycle** includes four stages of growth that people go through.

Birth to Two During the first stage of growth in the human life cycle, you were a tiny, helpless baby. You were not able to care for yourself. To stay alive, you had to be cared for by your parents or other adults.

During this first stage of your life, you grew at an amazing rate. From before you were born until about age two, you grew faster than you ever will again. You changed from a baby into an active, more independent two-year-old.

Two to Ten Between the ages of two and ten, you grow more slowly. You grow only about 2 or 3 inches a year.

Your language skills develop quickly during this stage. Now you can read and write. You can use your thinking skills to solve problems.

You can run faster and throw a ball farther than ever before. You can put your physical and mental skills together to learn a complex task, such as riding a bicycle.

▼ Two to ten

Career
Pediatrician

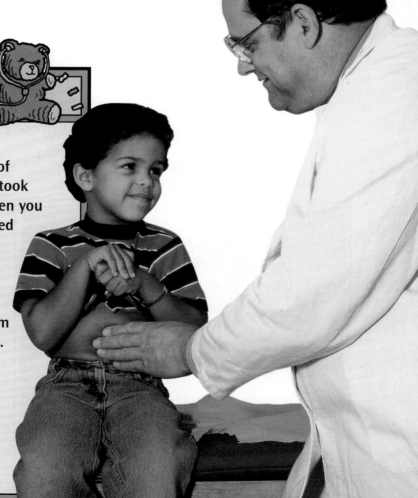

What They Do

Pediatricians are doctors who take care of babies and children. Your parents probably took you to a pediatrician for many checkups when you were a baby. You were measured and weighed to make sure you were healthy and growing normally. Pediatricians make sure children have their vaccinations. They also help children get better when they are ill. Pediatricians may see the same children from the time they are babies until they are adults.

Education and Training

Pediatricians go to college for four years and medical school for four more years. After they go through training in pediatrics for three more years, they can practice medicine.

LIFE SKILLS FOCUS

Communicate

Peggy's teenage sister gets a bigger allowance and can stay up later than Peggy does. Peggy thinks this is unfair. Write a script for a conversation in which Peggy talks to her parents about her feelings. Use the steps for communicating shown on pages 246 and 247.

▶ **Ten to adult**

Ten to Adult

At about age ten or twelve, you will enter the next stage of growth. You will begin to change from a child into an adult. As a teenager you will again grow very fast. Your body will become taller and heavier.

This growth stage usually happens sooner for girls than for boys, but boys catch up and often grow faster at about age fourteen or fifteen. Your body will grow and change when it is the right time for you.

Adult to Senior When you are an adult, you will stop growing taller. As an adult you will decide what kind of job you want to have, whether or not you will get married, and whether or not you will have children. As an older adult, or senior, you will have more free time to learn new things and to enjoy your family and friends.

◀ **Adult to senior**

younger

older

younger

older

JOURNAL

Ask family members to tell you their favorite stories about things you did when you were a baby. Choose your favorite story, and write it in your Health Journal.

Activity **See How You've Changed** What can the older children in these photos do that they needed help with when they were younger? Make a list of things you needed help with when you were younger.

Remember when you were a baby?

You probably don't remember yourself as a tiny baby, but this is what you were like. You had a large head and wobbly legs. You could grasp a finger and suck to get milk, but adults had to take care of you.

Your fastest growth period began before you were born and lasted until you were two. Your body and brain grew quickly. By the age of two, you could sit up, walk, and talk. Look at pictures of yourself as a baby. Think of all the ways you have changed since then!

LESSON CHECKUP

Check Your Facts

❶ During which two stages of the human life cycle do you grow most quickly?

❷ CRITICAL THINKING What kinds of decisions will you make when you are an adult? What do you think you'll decide to do?

❸ What skills do you learn during your second stage of growth?

Set Health Goals

❹ List three things you can do now that you couldn't do three years ago. Now list three things you hope to do three years from now.

People Grow at Different Rates

How do people grow?

Everything from your nose to your toes grows because of the tiny cells inside you. A **cell** is the smallest working part of your body. Your growth began with one cell. Now you have many cells. During periods of rapid growth, the cells inside your body multiply quickly.

Your bones, skin, blood, and muscles are all made up of cells. Cells contain information your body needs to be able to eat, breathe, and think. By taking good care of your body, you help your cells do their important work.

Activity **List Differences** Each person starts out as one cell, yet no two people are alike. List ten ways you are different from the people in the photo and from anyone else you know.

nerve cells

bone cells

skin cells

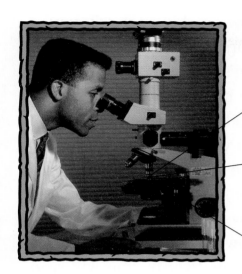

▲ You need a microscope to see most cells. Each cell's shape helps it do its job.

What do cells do?

Cells come in different shapes and sizes that help them do special jobs. Nerve cells are long and thin. They carry signals through your body. Bone cells surround themselves with a hard material. They help hold your body up. Skin cells are flat. They form layers to protect and cover your body.

Cells that work together to get a job done are called **tissues** (TIH•shooz). Muscle tissue is one kind of tissue in your body. Groups of tissues join together to form **organs**. Your heart is one of your organs. It is made up of different tissues that work together to pump blood through your whole body. Many organs work together in an **organ system**. Your blood, heart, and all your blood vessels together make up your circulatory system.

HUMAN BODY CONNECTION

Examine Organ Systems

Look through the organ systems, also called body systems, on pages 1–15. Pick one organ in each system, and tell what it does.

● ● ●

"We all grow at our own rate."

What is the special way you grow?

Your **growth rate** is how quickly or slowly you grow. Everyone goes through the same basic periods of growth, but each person's growth rate is different.

From before birth to age two, you grew very quickly. Your family can tell you how much you changed in a short amount of time when you were a baby. As a teenager you will again grow quickly. In between, your growth rate will be very slow. By the time you are an adult of about age twenty, you will stop growing taller.

Sometimes you may compare yourself to your friends and wonder if you are normal. You may worry that you are growing too much or not enough. Remember, no two people are alike. And there is no one way to grow. You grow in your own time and at your own speed to the height that is right for you.

▲ Have fun and don't worry! Your body is growing just the way it should.

birth | twelve months | eighteen months

▲ Growth happens all through your body. When you were born, you had no wrist bones. But they developed by the time you were eighteen months (one and a half years) old.

| six months | one year | three years | five years | seven years | ten years |

▲ A newborn baby's head is very large. As a person grows, the body gets bigger, but the head size remains about the same.

You grow because the cells inside you divide to make many new cells. You add inches to your height as your bones get longer. You grow stronger as your muscles stretch to cover your growing bones. You also add weight to your body.

Your physical growth is easy to see, but you are growing in other ways, too. As your brain cells grow larger and make new connections, you learn new things. You can think about and solve harder problems. You can begin to be more responsible for yourself. People can count on you in new ways.

LESSON CHECKUP

Check Your Facts

1 What happens when cells multiply and make many new cells?

2 Why are cells different shapes?

3 CRITICAL THINKING Do you ever stop growing?

4 Tell how cells, tissues, organs, and organ systems are related.

Set Health Goals

5 Name two ways your growth can let you be a more responsible family member.

Taking Care of My Body

The best way to grow healthy and strong is to take good care of your body. When you feel well, your body is telling you that you are doing a good job of taking care of it. When you feel tired or weak, or if you are often ill, your body may be telling you to make some changes.

Getting regular exercise and eating a balanced diet are important. Your body also needs to rest. With enough sleep you will be ready for the day ahead. Keeping your body, hair, nails, and teeth clean is important, too. You will learn more about exercise and diet in Chapters 3 and 4 of this book.

Support good health habits!

Eat healthful foods!

Get regular checkups!

Get plenty of rest!

Be vaccinated against disease!

Keep your body clean!

Exercise!

You may have a box of special treasures that you keep **private**, which means they belong only to you. Each family member has a right to private things. You need to respect the privacy of others. Knock before entering a room. Ask before using things that belong to someone else.

Your body is special. There are parts of your body you have a right to keep private. It feels good to get a hug from someone you trust. A pat on the back for a job well done makes you feel great. But there are some touches that don't feel good. It is not proper for someone to touch you on a private part of your body or in a way that makes you feel uncomfortable. Talk to a trusted adult if this happens.

When You Need Help, Talk to a Trusted Adult
- Parent
- Teacher
- Doctor
- Religious leader
- Counselor or nurse
- Police officer

▶ **A kind touch on the shoulder can make someone feel better.**

LESSON CHECKUP

Check Your Facts
❶ Why is it important to take good care of your body?

❷ Tell where to get help with a problem.

Use Life Skills
❸ MAKE DECISIONS Imagine that your friend invites you over to have ice cream. You want to go, but you haven't eaten dinner yet. Use your decision-making skills to make a healthful choice.

USE VOCABULARY

cell (p. 58)

divorce (p. 49)

family (p. 44)

growth rate (p. 60)

life cycle (p. 54)

organ system (p. 59)

organs (p. 59)

private (p. 63)

sibling (p. 49)

tissues (p. 59)

values (p. 44)

Use the terms above to complete the sentences. Page numbers in ( ) tell you where to look in the chapter if you need help.

1. Your brother or sister is called your ____.

2. Tissues work together to form ____.

3. Your ____ is very fast between birth and two years of age.

4. Your growth began with one ____.

5. Birth to age two is one stage in the human ____.

6. When you keep something ____, it belongs only to you.

7. When parents ____, they are no longer married to each other.

8. Cells that work together are called ____.

9. Strong beliefs taught in families are called ____.

10. Your ____ is the group of people you live with.

11. Many organs work together to form a(n) ____.

CHECK YOUR FACTS

Page numbers in ( ) tell you where to look in the chapter if you need help.

12. Name three jobs you can do to help as a member of your family. (p. 46)

13. Name four big changes that can happen in families. (pp. 48–49)

14. List the four stages of growth in the human life cycle. (pp. 54–56)

15. Name the types of cells in the pictures shown here. (p. 59)

16. Name three good ways to take care of your body. (p. 62)

17. How can you respect each family member's right to privacy? How can family members respect yours?

18. Study the photo below. Why is it important to understand that all people grow at their own rates and in their own time?

19. **Resolve Conflicts** Suppose a friend invites you over on the night your family has planned to do something together. What will you say to your friend, and why?

20. **Communicate** Suppose someone touches you in a way that does not feel comfortable to you. What would you say or do, and why?

Promote Health - Home and Community -

1. In your school, take a survey of the chores children do around the house. Sort the chores by grade level. Design and make a poster to show your results.

2. Make a growth chart, and ask your family members to record their heights on the chart each month for a year. Be sure to record your height, too. As each month passes, notice how much some family members are growing taller. At the end of the year, add up the number of inches each person grew. Use the numbers to show which stage of the life cycle each person is in.

Activities

At Home • Interview older family members, and list the jobs they did when they were your age. Which jobs are the same as the ones you do? Which are different?

Circles of Life

With a Team • Find out about the life cycles of other living things. How are their stages of growth the same as the stages in the human life cycle? How are they different?

Picture Perfect

With a Partner • Make a poster of the human life cycle. Draw a big circle, and divide it into four parts to represent each stage. Then cut out pictures, and paste them in each section. Be sure your chart shows how humans may look and what they may do at each stage of life.

Movin' On

On Your Own • Imagine that you have moved several times and you have been asked to help other children your age who are moving. Make a booklet suggesting ways to help them deal with the move.

Multiple Choice

Choose the letter of the correct answer.

1. Basic needs are met in your ____.
   a. club   b. family
   c. cells   d. life cycle

2. Your whole body is made up of ____.
   a. growth   b. cells
   c. organs   d. water

3. Cleaning your room shows you are ____.
   a. responsible   b. healthy
   c. honest   d. happy

4. When tired, your body needs ____.
   a. food   b. exercise
   c. rest   d. water

5. Your first stage of growth ended at ____.
   a. two   b. adulthood
   c. twelve   d. sixteen

Modified True or False

Write *true* or *false*. If a sentence is false, replace the underlined term to make the sentence true.

6. Listening respectfully is a good way to <u>communicate</u>.

7. A new <u>doctor</u> causes family changes.

8. Tissues that work together form <u>organs</u>.

9. During the <u>third</u> stage of growth, you are becoming a senior.

10. A pediatrician is a doctor who specializes in the care of <u>adults</u>.

11. Families teach <u>jobs</u>, like honesty.

12. It is important to respect other people's <u>privacy</u>.

13. Teenagers grow at <u>the same</u> rates.

14. As an <u>adult</u> you make lots of decisions.

15. Once you are about <u>twelve</u> years old, you will not grow any taller.

Short Answer

Write a complete sentence to answer each question.

16. What important jobs do cells do?

17. Who can you talk to if someone touches you in a way that makes you uncomfortable?

18. How can families help each other?

19. List two skills that develop between the ages of two and ten.

20. If a younger sibling is having a hard day, how can you show you care?

Essay

Write paragraphs to answer each item.

21. Describe what it feels like when big changes happen in families.

22. During the two-to-ten stage, many children learn to ride a bicycle. List some skills needed to ride a bike.

CHAPTER 3

Keeping My Body Fit

Project

PLAN A FITNESS GAME

Running, swimming, riding a bike, jumping rope, and even walking are different kinds of exercise. As you read through this chapter, you will learn that exercise is an important part of taking care of your body. Plan a fitness game for your class to play. Be sure your game includes several kinds of exercise that will help your body in different ways.

For other activities, visit the Harcourt Brace Internet site. http://www.hbschool.com

Caring for My Skin

MAIN IDEA
Caring for your skin helps you stay healthy.

WHY LEARN THIS? You can use what you learn to practice good skin care.

VOCABULARY
• pores
• bacteria
• sunscreen

Have you ever had an itchy rash? If so, you know skin problems can be annoying. You can't stop all skin problems. But you can stop many of them. Caring for your skin helps you stay healthy and look good too.

How can I keep my skin clean?

Do you know your skin has holes in it? These tiny holes are called **pores** (POHRZ). Sweat comes up through your pores. Sweat helps cool your body. Oil comes up to the surface of the skin along hairs. Oil helps keep your skin soft.

Oil, sweat, and dirt collect on your skin. Bacteria grow on your skin too. **Bacteria** (bak•TIR•ee•uh) are living things that are so tiny you cannot see them. Some bacteria cause illness. Washing with soap and warm water is the best way to get rid of oil, sweat, dirt, and bacteria on your skin.

HUMAN BODY CONNECTION

Under Your Skin

Your skin is more than a simple covering for your body. Turn to page 3 of The Amazing Human Body to find out what lies beneath the surface of your skin.

• • •

▶ It's a good idea to wash your hands several times a day.

Washing your hands is very important. When your hands are clean, you are less likely to catch or spread illnesses such as colds. Always wash your hands before you eat. Wash your hands after using the bathroom. Wash your hands right away if you sneeze or cough into them. If you touch an animal, wash your hands soon afterward.

To clean your whole body, take a bath or shower. Bathe whenever you are dirty or sweaty. Some people need to bathe every day. Others can skip a day if they don't get too dirty or sweaty.

▼ Bath time can be relaxing and fun. A back brush helps you wash hard-to-reach spots.

71

How can I protect my skin from the sun?

The sun gives off harmful rays. You cannot see the rays, but they can burn you. This kind of burn is called a sunburn. A sunburn goes away in a few days. The real harm from too much sun shows up years later. Skin may get tough. It may get very wrinkled. Skin cancer, a disease that can be deadly, may occur.

Skin damage can happen even if you never get a sunburn. It can happen if you get a tan. Everyone needs protection from the sun.

Everyone needs to use sunscreen!

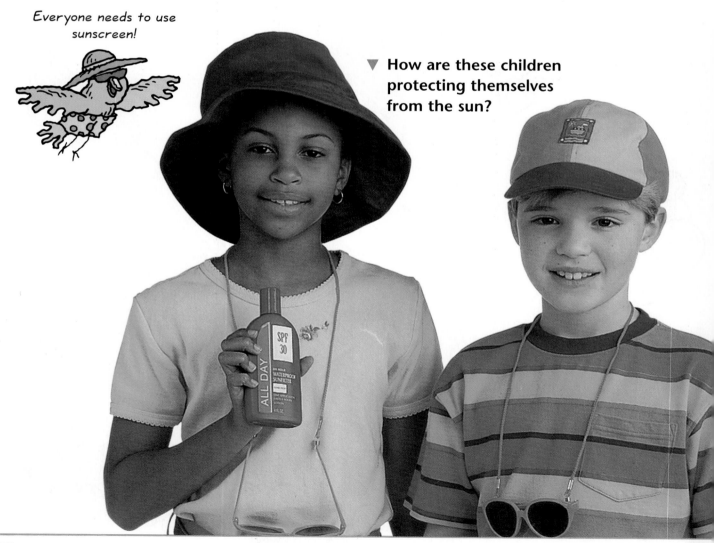

▼ **How are these children protecting themselves from the sun?**

The sun is strongest in the middle of the day. So try to limit your time outdoors to early morning, late afternoon, or evening. If you do go out in the middle of the day, cover up. Your clothes will help protect you from the sun. Wear long sleeves and long pants. If it is hot, wear loose clothes that are light in weight and light colored. They will help you stay cool. Wear a hat to shade your face.

Rub sunscreen on any uncovered skin. **Sunscreen** is a lotion or cream that can protect you from the sun's harmful rays. Some sunscreens block almost all harmful rays. Other sunscreens give you just a little protection. Before you go outside, ask an adult in your family which sunscreen is best for you.

Your eyes also need protection from the sun. Over time the sun's rays can harm your eyes. Wearing sunglasses is the best way to protect them. Never look right at the sun, even if you're wearing sunglasses. With sunglasses, sunscreen, and the right clothing, you can have fun in the sun and still be safe.

ART CONNECTION

Draw Your Day in the Sun

On Your Own
Make a picture of yourself having fun at the beach. Show how you would protect yourself from the sun. Write labels on your picture.

LESSON CHECKUP

Check Your Facts

1. Why is it important to wash your hands often?

2. CRITICAL THINKING Think about what oil does for your skin. What do you think might happen if you used harsh soap or bathed too often?

3. List three ways to protect your skin from the sun.

Set Health Goals

4. Think back over the past two days. How many times did you go outside, and how long did you stay out each time? Write down the different ways you protected yourself from the sun. Then think of ways you could do even better next time. Write these ideas down too.

MAIN IDEA You can take good care of your teeth and gums by learning how to floss and brush and how to protect your teeth from injury.

WHY LEARN THIS? Caring for your teeth and gums helps you stay healthy.

VOCABULARY
• plaque
• cavity
• dental floss
• fluoride

Caring for My Teeth and Gums

Some of your adult teeth may grow in this year. You will need them for biting, chewing, and even talking. These teeth will last for the rest of your life if you take good care of them.

What can cause problems with teeth and gums?

Plaque (PLAK) is a sticky coating that is always forming on teeth. Plaque has bacteria that break down bits of food and give off acids. These acids can make a hole called a **cavity** (KA•vuh•tee) in a tooth.

Look at the diagram below. A cavity can grow through the enamel, into the dentin, and even into the pulp. A deep cavity can even kill the tooth.

When plaque stays on a tooth and hardens, it can make the gum weak. If the gum gets very weak, teeth may fall out.

▼ You can protect your teeth by flossing and brushing away plaque. Chewing a *disclosing tablet* makes areas with plaque dark red.

The Parts of a Tooth

enamel

dentin

crown

gum

pulp

root

74

How can I floss my teeth?

Plaque can build up on all the surfaces of your teeth. It can also build up between your teeth. To remove plaque from between your teeth, you need a special thread called **dental floss**. Using this thread is called flossing.

▲ Plan to floss once a day. It's a good idea to floss just before you brush your teeth.

Look at the pictures to see how to floss. Break off about 18 inches of dental floss. Wrap one end of it around the middle finger of one hand. Guide the floss with your thumbs and index fingers. Push the floss gently between two teeth. Rub gently back and forth as you move the floss toward the gum. Also rub near the gum line of one tooth and then the other. Remove the floss. Unwind it a bit to reach a clean part. Repeat for each tooth.

How can I brush my teeth?

Brushing gets rid of plaque on the front, back, and top of each tooth. Use a toothbrush with soft bristles. Soft bristles will clean your teeth without hurting your gums. Use a toothpaste that has **fluoride** (FLAWR•yd). Fluoride is a chemical that makes teeth stronger and harder. Strong, hard teeth are less likely to get cavities.

Look at the pictures to see how to brush. Brush with short, tooth-wide back and forth movements on all your teeth. Brush along the gum line too. Spend extra time on your back teeth. They have deep pits where plaque can collect. Turn your toothbrush to reach the inner sides of your front teeth. When you finish brushing, spit out the toothpaste. Rinse your mouth with water.

JOURNAL

Keep a record of how you care for your teeth and gums every day for a week. Then look over your journal to make sure you're taking good care of your teeth and gums.

Activity **Practice Flossing and Brushing** Look carefully at the pictures on pages 75 and 76. With a partner, take turns acting out how to floss and brush your teeth. Explain each step as you act it out.

▶ Brush your teeth at least twice a day, once in the morning and again at night.

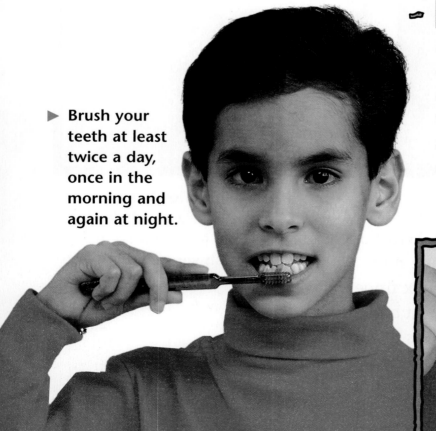

How can I protect my teeth from injury?

Your teeth are very strong and hard. But if you use them for cutting or tearing things other than food, you can harm the tooth enamel. For example, you should never open food packages with your teeth.

If you play sports, wear a mouth guard to protect your teeth from being hit or injured in a fall. A mouth guard is made of plastic. You can buy one at a store, or a dentist can make one for you.

If a tooth gets knocked out, lightly rinse it in running water. Then put it back in place. Hold it, and go right to the dentist. The dentist may be able to save the tooth.

LIFE SKILLS FOCUS

Make Decisions

Alan plays roller hockey. His coach recommends that all players wear mouth guards, but his friends say they aren't going to wear them. Use the decision-making steps shown on pages 246 and 247 to help Alan decide what to do.

◄ **Dentists recommend mouth guards for football, baseball, basketball, hockey, and soccer players.**

LESSON CHECKUP

Check Your Facts

❶ CRITICAL THINKING **How do you help your gums when you remove plaque from your teeth?**

❷ **When should you floss your teeth? When should you brush?**

❸ **What kind of toothbrush and toothpaste should you use? Why?**

Use Life Skills

❹ MAKE DECISIONS **Make a list of your favorite activities. Circle the activities you need a mouth guard for. Make up your own list of rules to help you decide when to use your mouth guard.**

MAIN IDEA
Caring for your ears and nose helps you stay healthy.

WHY LEARN THIS? Learning about your ears and nose will help you take good care of them.

VOCABULARY
• ear canal
• eardrum

Caring for My Ears and Nose

You go for a walk after it rains. You hear splashes as you walk through a puddle. Everything smells clean and damp. Your ears and nose help you enjoy the things around you, so take good care of them.

What can cause problems with hearing?

Your ear has three main parts—the outer ear, the middle ear, and the inner ear. The diagram below shows the three parts. Sound enters your ear through your **ear canal**. This is part of your outer ear. The opening you can see in your ear is the beginning of your ear canal.

▶ The part of the ear you can see collects sound waves and channels them into your ear canal.

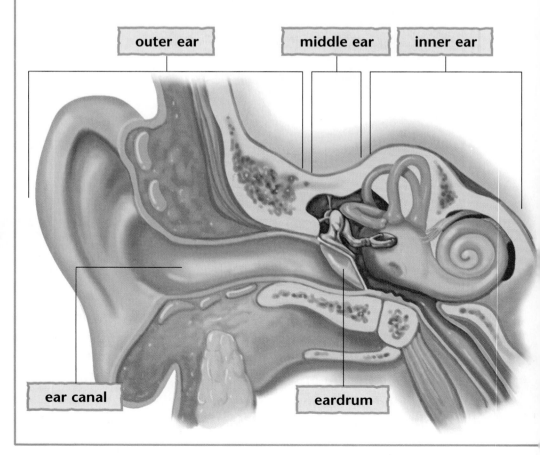

outer ear   middle ear   inner ear

ear canal   eardrum

Noise can hurt!

Your **eardrum** is at the other end of your ear canal. Sound waves make the eardrum move back and forth. This movement sends the waves on to the inner ear. The inner ear turns the waves into nerve signals. These signals travel to your brain, and you hear a sound.

Some things can harm your ears. Bacteria in your ear can give you an ear infection. An ear infection can make your ear hurt. You may also have trouble hearing. If this happens, tell an adult. The adult may take you to a doctor. The doctor may give you medicine to help your ear heal.

Loud sounds also can harm your ears. Over time such sounds can cause you to have trouble hearing. Loud music, loud machines, and loud traffic all can cause hearing problems. You may not notice these problems for many years. By then it will be too late to correct the harm to your ears.

▲ Noise from these things can cause hearing problems over time. What are some other sounds that might harm your hearing?

How can I take care of my ears?

You cannot stop all the things that might hurt your hearing, but you can avoid most of them. Stay away from noisy places. Turn the sound down when you listen to the TV, radio, or CD player. Also keep the sound low when you play video games. When you use headphones, you should still be able to hear sounds around you. If you can't, you may be hurting your ears.

Getting hit on your ears also can hurt your hearing. Wear a helmet when you play rough sports. This will help protect your ears.

You can wash the outsides of your ears with a washcloth. But do not stick anything into the ear canal. Doing this can poke a hole in the eardrum and damage hearing.

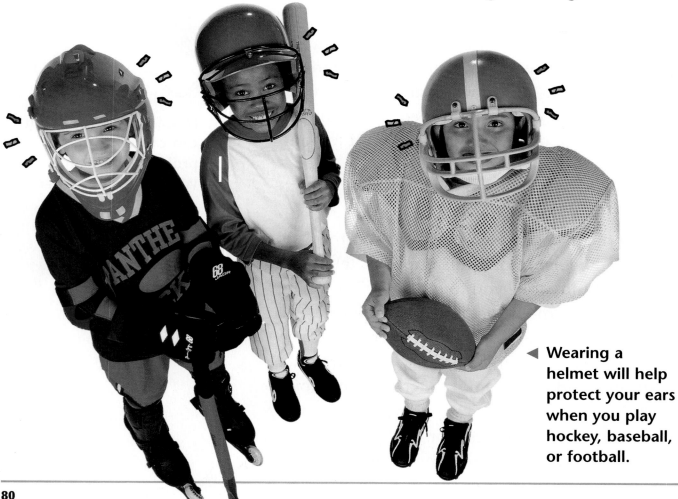

◀ Wearing a helmet will help protect your ears when you play hockey, baseball, or football.

How can I protect my nose?

Have you ever had a hard bump to your nose? If you have, you know how much it can hurt. Injuries to the nose usually heal quickly. Still, you need to take care of your nose to feel your best.

Taking care of your nose is especially important when you have a cold. Always blow your nose gently. Keep both nostrils and your mouth open. If you blow your nose too hard, you can send bacteria from your throat through a tiny tube into your middle ear. This can give you an earache.

Blowing your nose too hard also can break blood vessels. When that happens, your nose may bleed. If you get a nosebleed, stand or sit up and lean forward. Gently pinch your nose. Breathe through your mouth. The bleeding should stop soon.

▶ **If bleeding from your nose doesn't stop after a short time, visit your doctor for help.**

HUMAN BODY CONNECTION

The Sense Organs

When your nose feels stuffed up, what happens to your senses of smell and taste? Turn to pages 2 and 3 of The Amazing Human Body to learn more about the nose and your senses.

LESSON CHECKUP

Check Your Facts

❶ Explain how your eardrum helps you hear.

❷ What can happen if you listen to loud sounds over a period of years?

❸ CRITICAL THINKING Why might spicy foods taste good to you when you have a cold?

❹ What should you do if you get a nosebleed?

Set Health Goals

❺ Make a list of common noises that could hurt your hearing over time. Next to each noise, write one or more ways you could protect your ears from that noise. Share your list with your family. Make plans to put your ideas into action.

MAIN IDEA
You need a balance
of exercise, rest,
and sleep to be
physically fit.

**WHY LEARN
THIS?** Learning
about exercise, rest,
and sleep can help
you plan ways to
feel and look fit.

VOCABULARY
• exercise
• aerobic exercises

Exercise and Rest for Fun and Health

You come in from playing outside. You are laughing and have lots of energy. In fact, you feel great. That's because you have good physical fitness.

How can I exercise for fitness?

Exercise helps you become and stay physically fit. **Exercise** (EK•ser•syz) is any activity that makes your body work hard. Running games and sports are exercise. Swimming is exercise. Jumping rope is exercise. Riding a bike is exercise. Even walking is exercise.

Different kinds of exercise help your body in different ways. Some exercises make your muscles strong. For example, bicycling uphill strengthens your leg muscles. Some exercises stretch your muscles. Doing gymnastics stretches your arm, leg, and back muscles.

Aerobic exercises (air•OH•bik EK•ser•sy•zuhs) strengthen your heart and lungs by making them work harder.

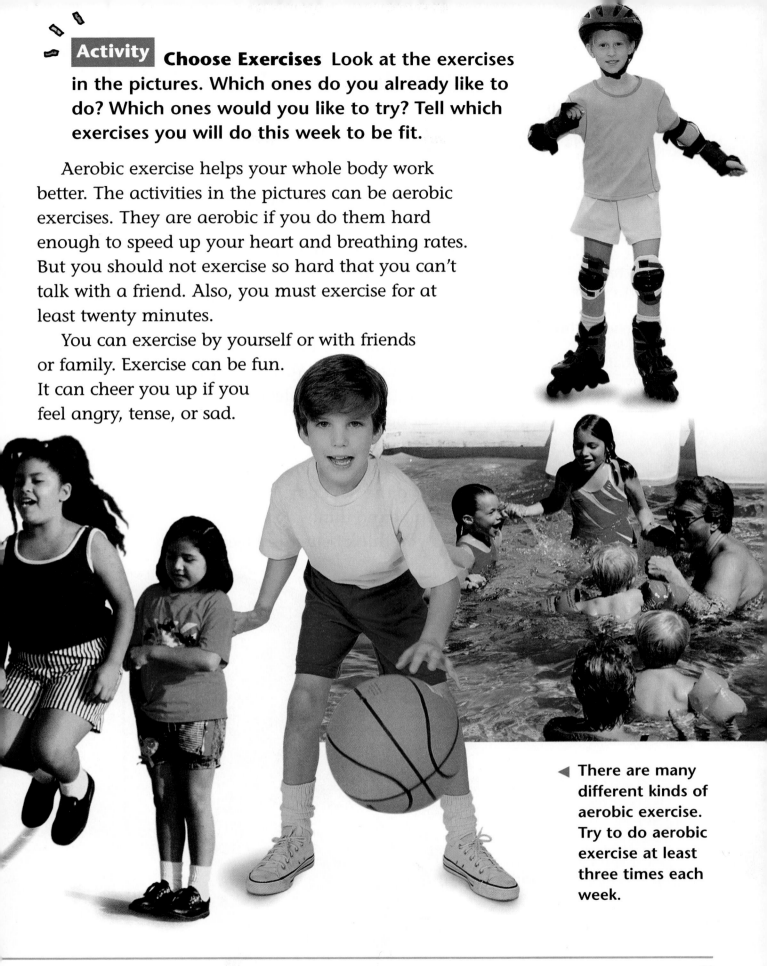

Activity **Choose Exercises** Look at the exercises in the pictures. Which ones do you already like to do? Which ones would you like to try? Tell which exercises you will do this week to be fit.

Aerobic exercise helps your whole body work better. The activities in the pictures can be aerobic exercises. They are aerobic if you do them hard enough to speed up your heart and breathing rates. But you should not exercise so hard that you can't talk with a friend. Also, you must exercise for at least twenty minutes.

You can exercise by yourself or with friends or family. Exercise can be fun. It can cheer you up if you feel angry, tense, or sad.

◀ There are many different kinds of aerobic exercise. Try to do aerobic exercise at least three times each week.

Did you know?

You dream for several hours every night. When you dream, your eyes dart back and forth. Your eyelids may flutter. But your arms and legs probably don't move much at all.

How do rest and sleep help me stay fit?

Exercise is good for your body. Rest is also good for you. After exercise your body needs to rest. When you rest, you breathe more slowly. Your heart beats more slowly too. Your muscles have a chance to relax. After resting, you may have more energy. You may want to do something active again.

Sleep is an important way to rest. When you sleep, your whole body slows down. Your senses become dull. You breathe slowly and deeply. Your heart beats slowly. Your muscles relax. Your body repairs itself during sleep. It makes new blood cells and bone cells.

Sleep gives your brain a chance to rest too. If you do not sleep much one night, you may have trouble thinking the next day. You may have a hard time remembering things. Extra sleep the next night will help you think better and feel better.

▶ Sleep is your body's deepest form of rest. People naturally sleep at night. But many animals, including cats, spend all or part of the night awake.

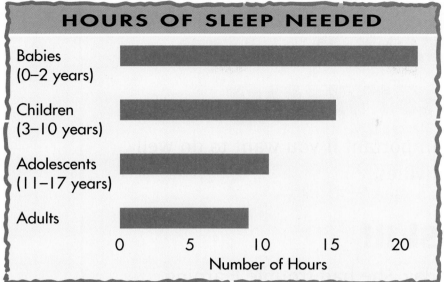

HOURS OF SLEEP NEEDED

Babies (0–2 years)	
Children (3–10 years)	
Adolescents (11–17 years)	
Adults	

Number of Hours
0   5   10   15   20

▲ At different ages, people need different amounts of sleep. How much sleep do you need to feel your best?

LIFE SKILLS FOCUS

Make Decisions

Amber's friends want to play computer games on Saturday. Amber likes to be with her friends, but she also wants to get some exercise. Use the decision-making steps shown on pages 246 and 247 to help Amber satisfy both needs.

As you grow, the amount of sleep you need changes. Right now you need ten to fourteen hours of sleep every night to stay healthy. Babies need more sleep than you do. Most adults need less.

LESSON CHECKUP

Check Your Facts

1. What are two ways exercise can help your body?

2. CRITICAL THINKING Of the exercises you do, which are aerobic exercises?

3. CRITICAL THINKING Why do you think babies need so much more sleep than adults do?

4. Why is sleep important?

Use Life Skills

5. REFUSE Imagine that you are spending the night at a friend's home. Your friend wants you to stay up late and play games. You know you need your sleep. Write down three ways you could politely say *no* to your friend.

SET GOALS
for Learning

Getting enough rest is important if you want to do well in school and other activities.

Learn This Skill

Lisa was very sleepy today. She had trouble learning. She could not pay attention and had trouble sitting still and listening.

1. Set a goal.

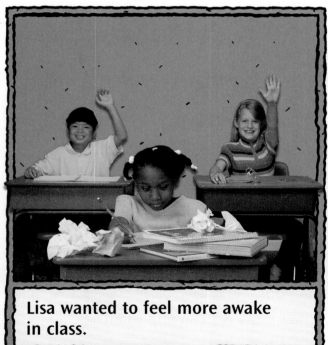

Lisa wanted to feel more awake in class.

2. Plan steps to help you meet the goal.

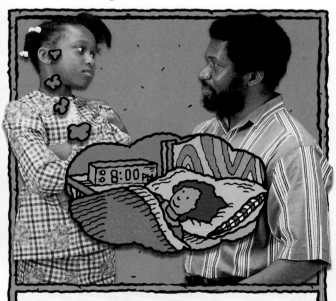

Lisa's dad suggested she go to bed earlier so she could get the rest she needed.

3. Monitor progress toward the goal.

4. Evaluate the goal.

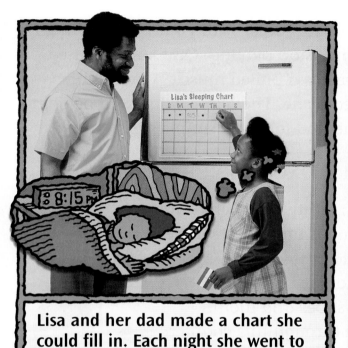

Lisa and her dad made a chart she could fill in. Each night she went to bed on time, she gave herself a star.

When Lisa got the sleep she needed, she felt better at school. She could pay attention in class.

Practice This Skill

Use the steps to help you solve the problems.

Steps for Setting Goals

1. Set a goal.
2. Plan steps to help you meet the goal.
3. Monitor progress toward the goal.
4. Evaluate the goal.

A. Gene wants to spend more time reading. Use the goal-setting steps to help Gene find time to read.

B. Carrie wants to exercise at least three times each week. Use the goal-setting steps to help her.

► Doing a warm-up before hard exercise and a cool-down afterward can help keep you from getting hurt. Both your warm-up and your cool-down should include stretching activities.

Staying Safe While Exercising

You are playing soccer with your friends. One by one your friends stop playing. One has a bruised shin. Another has a pulled muscle. One is thirsty and has a headache. The game would still be going on if everyone had followed simple safety rules.

How can I exercise safely?

Putting on safety gear before you start exercising is important. Soccer players should protect their legs with shin guards. They also need special shoes and mouth guards. Look through this chapter for pictures of different kinds of safety gear.

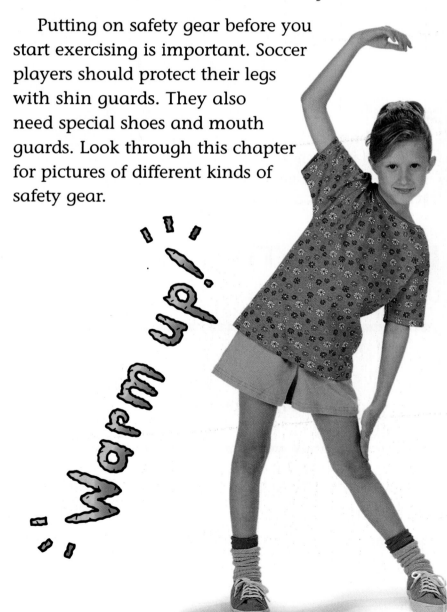

warm up!

Warming up your muscles gets them ready for hard exercise. During your **warm-up**, stretch and do slow exercises for about five minutes. This helps prevent pulled muscles. After hard exercise, do slow exercise and stretching again. This is called a **cool-down**. A five minute cool-down helps prevent muscle soreness later.

Your body loses a lot of water during exercise. You see this when you sweat. Drinking water before, during, and after exercise can help prevent discomfort and illness.

▲ **During exercise you can take small sips of water. This will cool you and replace some of the water you lose.**

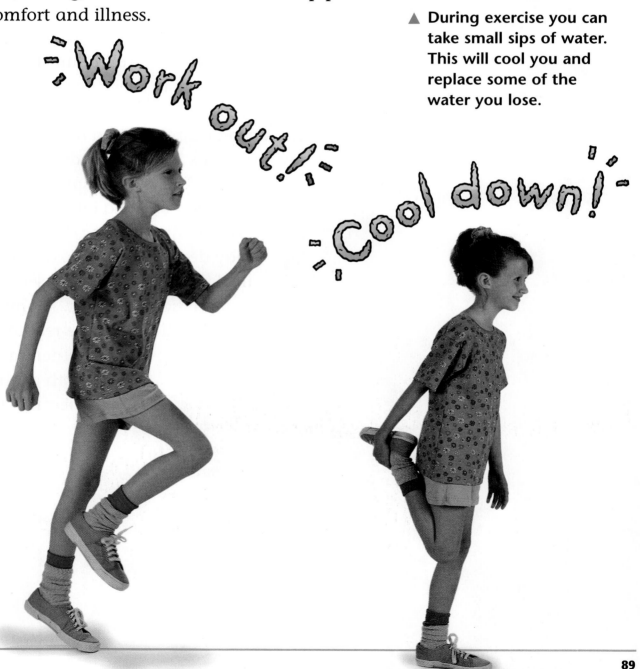

Work out!

Cool down!

What should I do if I get injured while exercising?

A little muscle soreness is normal after certain exercises. However, if you feel more than a mild soreness when you exercise, tell an adult. The adult will probably tell you to stop exercising for a while. You can see how you feel the next day. If you still feel sore, you can try a different exercise. Or you can do light exercise to give your muscles a chance to recover.

If you feel pain while exercising, you may have an injury. Stop right away. Tell an adult. The adult may give you an ice pack to keep the injury from swelling. Hold the ice on the injured spot for about fifteen minutes two or three times a day.

If you have a serious injury, the adult may take you to the doctor. The doctor may give you medicine or put a bandage or cast on the injured area. The doctor may decide you need extra help to heal. If so, he or she will send you to a physical therapist. A physical therapist helps people regain movement and strength so they can become active again soon.

▼ **If you put ice on an injury, wrap the ice in a towel or other cloth so it will not freeze your skin. The picture shows a reusable frozen gel pack.**

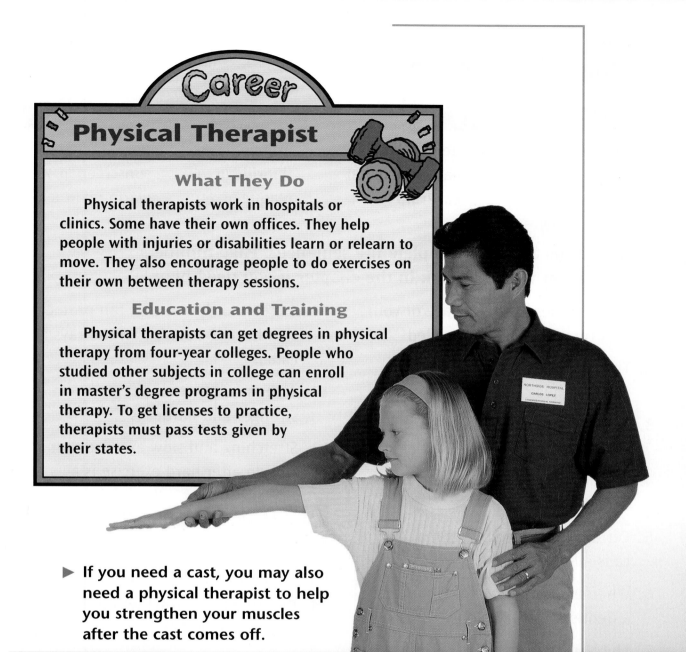

Career

Physical Therapist

What They Do

Physical therapists work in hospitals or clinics. Some have their own offices. They help people with injuries or disabilities learn or relearn to move. They also encourage people to do exercises on their own between therapy sessions.

Education and Training

Physical therapists can get degrees in physical therapy from four-year colleges. People who studied other subjects in college can enroll in master's degree programs in physical therapy. To get licenses to practice, therapists must pass tests given by their states.

▶ If you need a cast, you may also need a physical therapist to help you strengthen your muscles after the cast comes off.

LESSON CHECKUP

Check Your Facts

❶ CRITICAL THINKING List the safety gear for your favorite sport. Tell how each item helps keep players safe.

❷ Why is it important to do a warm-up and a cool-down when exercising?

❸ Why is it important to drink water before, during, and after exercising?

❹ CRITICAL THINKING You fall while jumping rope. Your ankle hurts. What should you do?

Set Health Goals

❺ Plan a weekly exercise program. Write which activity or activities you will do for aerobic exercise. Describe the warm-up and cool-down you will do during each exercise session. Try your plan for a week. Then write how you could make it better.

USE VOCABULARY

aerobic exercises (p. 82)   **dental floss** (p. 75)   **exercise** (p. 82)   **pores** (p. 70)

bacteria (p. 70)   **ear canal** (p. 78)   **fluoride** (p. 76)   **sunscreen** (p. 73)

cavity (p. 74)   **eardrum** (p. 79)   **plaque** (p. 74)   **warm-up** (p. 89)

cool-down (p. 89)

Use the terms above to complete the sentences. Page numbers in ( ) tell you where to look in the chapter if you need help.

1. Sweat comes to the surface of your skin through tiny holes called _____.

2. The sticky coating that forms on your teeth is called _____.

3. The opening that you can see in your ear is the beginning of your _____.

4. Any activity that makes your body work hard is _____.

5. Certain tiny living things that may cause illness are called _____.

6. When acids make a hole in a tooth, a dentist must fill the _____.

7. The part that moves back and forth at the end of the ear canal is the _____.

8. Exercises that strengthen your heart and lungs by making them work harder are called _____.

9. The special thread you use to remove plaque between teeth is _____.

10. Stretching and slow exercise that you do before hard exercise is a _____.

11. A cream or lotion that can protect skin from the sun's harmful rays is called _____.

12. A chemical that makes teeth stronger and harder is _____.

13. Stretching and slow exercise that you do after hard exercise is a _____.

CHECK YOUR FACTS

Page numbers in ( ) tell you where to look if you need help.

14. Describe the correct way to brush your teeth. (p. 76)

15. Tell two things you can do to exercise safely. (pp. 88–89)

16. List three ways to take good care of your ears and prevent hearing problems. (p. 80)

17. Explain why you need to protect your skin from the sun. (p. 72)

18. Use the bar graph to tell the greatest number of hours of sleep needed by people in each age group. (p. 85)

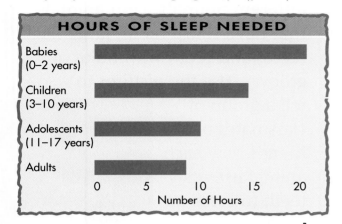

HOURS OF SLEEP NEEDED

Babies (0–2 years)

Children (3–10 years)

Adolescents (11–17 years)

Adults

Number of Hours
0   5   10   15   20

THINK CRITICALLY

19. Why might someone who seldom washes his or her hands be likely to get or spread a cold?

20. Would it be a good idea to clean the inside of your ears with cotton swabs? Explain.

APPLY LIFE SKILLS

21. **Manage Stress** Imagine that you are feeling tense or angry about something that happened at school. What could you do for half an hour when you get home that would help you feel happier and build your fitness? Give details.

22. **Make Decisions** Imagine that you are spending the night at a friend's house. When you unload your backpack, you realize that you forgot your toothbrush. Decide what you would do. Tell how you made your decision.

Promote Health **Home and Community**

1. Talk to family members about what you have learned in this chapter. Together, make a plan for taking care of yourselves. For example, you might go to the store together to choose a good sunscreen or toothpaste. Or you might come up with a family exercise program that everyone can enjoy.

2. Make posters about exercise safety. Get permission to display them at places in your community where people play sports or do other kinds of exercise.

Activities

Warm-up and Cool-down Collage

With a Team • Brainstorm good ways to warm up before and cool down after different kinds of hard exercise. A warm-up and a cool-down should use the same muscles that the hard exercise does. Make a collage using pictures of the exercises you brainstormed.

Teeth of Different Sorts

With a Partner • Look for pictures that show the teeth of different animals. Find animals that have sharp teeth, large flat teeth, and teeth with holes or grooves. Use the pictures to tell a group of classmates or friends how each animal uses its teeth to catch or eat its food.

Sleepy Time

On Your Own • Keep track of your sleep for a week. Write down the time you go to sleep each night and the time you wake up each morning. Make a bar graph that shows how long you slept each night.

The Nose Knows

At Home • Ask an adult to help you gather some "mystery foods" for family members to sample. Have those family members put on blindfolds, hold their noses, and try to identify the foods by taste. Then have them try to identify the foods without holding their noses. Talk about how the nose affects taste as well as smell.

Multiple Choice

Choose the letter of the correct answer.

1. What should you do before you eat?
   a. apply sunscreen   b. bathe
   c. wash hands   d. floss

2. Brushing gets rid of _____.
   a. minerals   b. plaque
   c. cavities   d. fluoride

3. Avoiding loud sounds is one way to protect your sense of _____.
   a. hearing   b. smell
   c. sight   d. taste

4. Bicycling uphill _____ leg muscles.
   a. speeds up   b. stretches
   c. strengthens   d. slows down

5. If you get hurt while exercising, _____ is the best thing to help stop the swelling.
   a. hot water   b. bandages
   c. cold water   d. ice

Modified True or False

Write *true* or *false*. If a sentence is false, replace the underlined term to make the sentence true.

6. Washing with soap is <u>a poor way</u> to get rid of bacteria on your hands.

7. One way to protect uncovered skin from the sun is to put <u>sunscreen</u> on.

8. Remove plaque from between teeth by <u>rinsing your mouth</u>.

9. Baseball players should wear <u>mouth guards</u> to protect their ears.

10. Blowing your nose too hard can give you an <u>earache</u>.

11. You should do aerobic exercise for <u>at least twenty minutes</u> at a time.

12. People your age need <u>seven to nine hours</u> of sleep each night to stay healthy.

13. Drinking <u>water</u> before, during, and after exercising can help prevent discomfort and illness.

Short Answer

Write a complete sentence to answer each question.

14. How can the sun harm you?

15. Tell what to do if a tooth is knocked out.

16. How can you protect your hearing when listening to music at home?

17. Tell what to do to stop a nosebleed.

18. When you exercise, how should you warm up and cool down?

Essay

Write paragraphs to answer each item.

19. Describe a perfect "healthful habits day."

20. Someone doesn't want to exercise because it's "boring." Tell how you would change his or her mind.

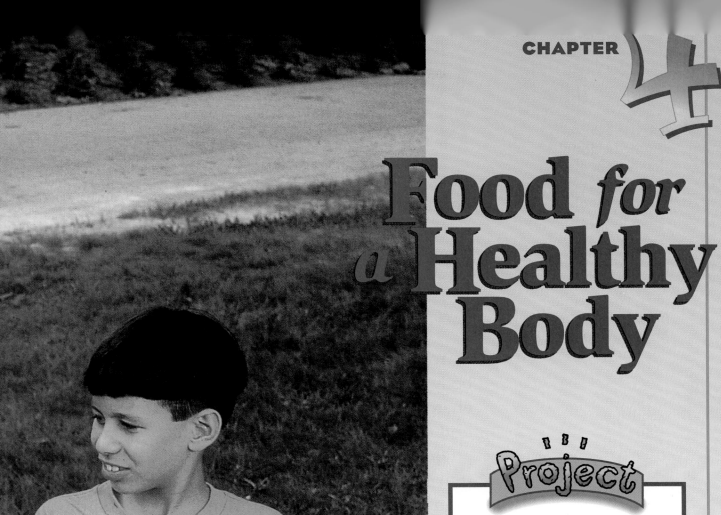

CHAPTER 4

Food *for a* Healthy Body

Project

MAKE A FOOD DISPLAY

As you work through this chapter, think about which foods you need to eat to stay healthy. Cut out pictures from magazines and food labels, and arrange them on paper plates. Include information about each food, and explain why it is healthful. Put your food display in the school cafeteria.

For other activities, visit the Harcourt Brace Internet site.
http://www.hbschool.com

MAIN IDEA
Eating healthful foods from plants and animals is important to good health.

WHY LEARN THIS? In order to eat a healthful diet, you need to understand which foods are good for you.

VOCABULARY
• nutrients
• nutrition
• diet
• fiber

Why My Body Needs Food

When you eat, does it matter whether you eat bananas or potato chips? Yogurt or french fries? Carrots or cookies? You bet it does! Some foods are more healthful than others. Eating healthful foods is important in keeping your body healthy.

Why is food important?

You cannot live without food. Food gives your body energy. You need energy to grow. You need energy to be active. You need energy to read, write, and think. You even need energy to sleep!

Nutrients (NOO•tree•uhnts) are the parts of food that help your body grow and get energy. There are many different kinds of nutrients. You get all the nutrients you need by eating different kinds of foods.

Nutrition (nu•TRIH•shuhn) is the study of food and how it affects the body. Knowing about nutrition can help you stay healthy.

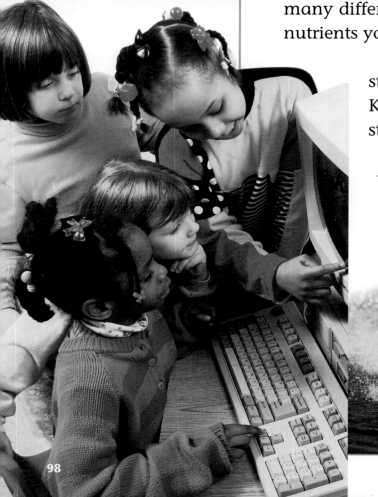

◀ What are some ways people use energy? ▼

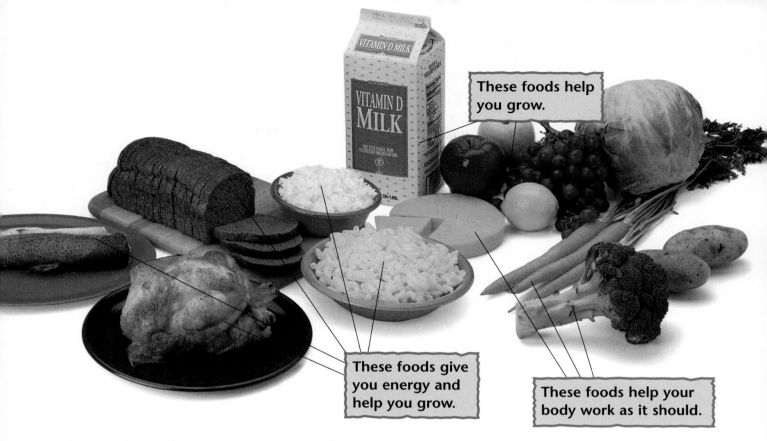

These foods help you grow.

These foods give you energy and help you grow.

These foods help your body work as it should.

Why should you eat different kinds of foods?

Loni eats leftover pizza for breakfast. Ali snacks on popcorn and pretzels. Cathy often has rice and vegetables for dinner. The foods a person usually eats and drinks make up his or her **diet** (DY•uht). What foods are a part of your diet?

Some diets are more healthful than others. For you to stay healthy, your diet must give your body all the nutrients it needs. Your diet also must include **fiber**, the woody part of plants. Fiber helps keep you healthy. Many fruits and vegetables contain fiber. Grains, such as brown rice, and foods made from grains, such as oatmeal and bread, also contain fiber.

Variety is important in a diet. Some foods give your body energy. Some foods help you grow. Other foods help parts of your body work well. The photograph shows some healthful foods that do these jobs. Which of these foods do you eat?

The Intestines

Fiber helps keep food moving through your small and large intestines. Look at the digestive system on page 8 at the front of the book. Trace the intestines from one end to the other.

• • •

▲ Wheat is needed to make bread. Wheat is a grain that is harvested in the late summer.

▲ The wheat is taken to a factory to be ground into a fine powder called flour.

Where does food come from?

Many of the foods we eat come from plants. Fruits and vegetables come from plants. So do beans, nuts, and seeds. Grains used to make cereals and breads also come from plants. Some common grains are corn, wheat, oats, and rice. Look at the pictures to see how bread is made.

When plant crops are ripe, they are harvested. Some plant foods are sold fresh. Others are sent to factories where they are canned, packaged, or frozen.

Career

Farm Operator

What They Do

Farm operators raise grains, fruits, vegetables, livestock, and dairy cows. They plan, plant, and care for crops. They care for animals. They harvest crops and send foods to market.

Education and Training

Many farm operators grow up on farms. Farm operators need strong science and math skills. Some may use computers. People without farming experience can go to college to learn how to grow crops or raise animals.

▲ At large bakeries wheat flour is made into loaves of bread. The loaves are packaged in plastic bags.

▲ Trucks bring loaves of fresh bread to grocery stores every day.

Most of the other foods people eat come from animals. We eat meat from cows, sheep, pigs, chicken, and fish. Most of the eggs we eat come from chickens. Most of the milk we drink comes from cows. After the cows are milked, the milk is heated to make it safe to drink. Then it is put into containers. Some milk is made into cheeses, butter, ice cream, or yogurt.

All kinds of plant and animal foods come from farms across the United States. Some foods even come from other countries. When ready for sale, fresh and prepared foods are sent to markets. They may be sent by truck or train. In a market food is placed on shelves or in cold storage. Finally, it ends up on your table.

LESSON CHECKUP

Check Your Facts

1. Why are nutrients important to good health?
2. What is nutrition?
3. Where does food come from?
4. Describe how wheat becomes the bread you eat.

Set Health Goals

5. What kinds of foods make up your diet? List the foods you eat often. Tell which are plant foods and which are animal foods. What can you do to make your diet more healthful?

MAIN IDEA
The Food Guide Pyramid shows how many servings from each food group you need to eat each day to have a healthful diet.

WHY LEARN THIS? You can use what you learn to make sure you eat a balanced diet.

VOCABULARY
• Food Guide Pyramid
• serving
• fluoride
• balanced diet

LIFE SKILLS
FOCUS

Make Decisions
Make a list of all the foods you eat in one day. Sort each food into its food group. Use the steps for making decisions to change your diet so that you get the right number of servings of each group. Use the steps for making decisions shown on pages 246 and 247.

• • •

The Food Guide Pyramid and Healthful Meals

The Cortéz family wants to be healthy. Every Sunday they sit down and plan their meals for the week. They plan for three meals and two snacks each day. The family chooses a variety of foods. They want to make sure everyone gets all the nutrients he or she needs.

What makes a meal healthful?

By itself a potato is not a healthful meal. But if you eat it with salad, chicken, and a glass of milk, you will have a healthful meal. A healthful meal includes a variety of foods. Eating a variety of foods gives your body the nutrients it needs.

The **Food Guide Pyramid** (FOOD GYD PIR•uh•mid) is a tool to help you choose foods for a healthful diet. It has six groups. The Food Guide Pyramid tells how many servings you should eat from each group each day. A **serving** is the amount of food you would probably eat during a meal or as a snack.

The bread group is the largest group in the Food Guide Pyramid. It includes bread, pasta, rice, and cereal. The smallest section of the pyramid is the fats, oils, and sweets group. You don't need to eat many of these foods.

Fruits are one group. Vegetables are another. Milk products make up a group. Meat, fish, poultry, eggs, nuts, and dried beans make up another group.

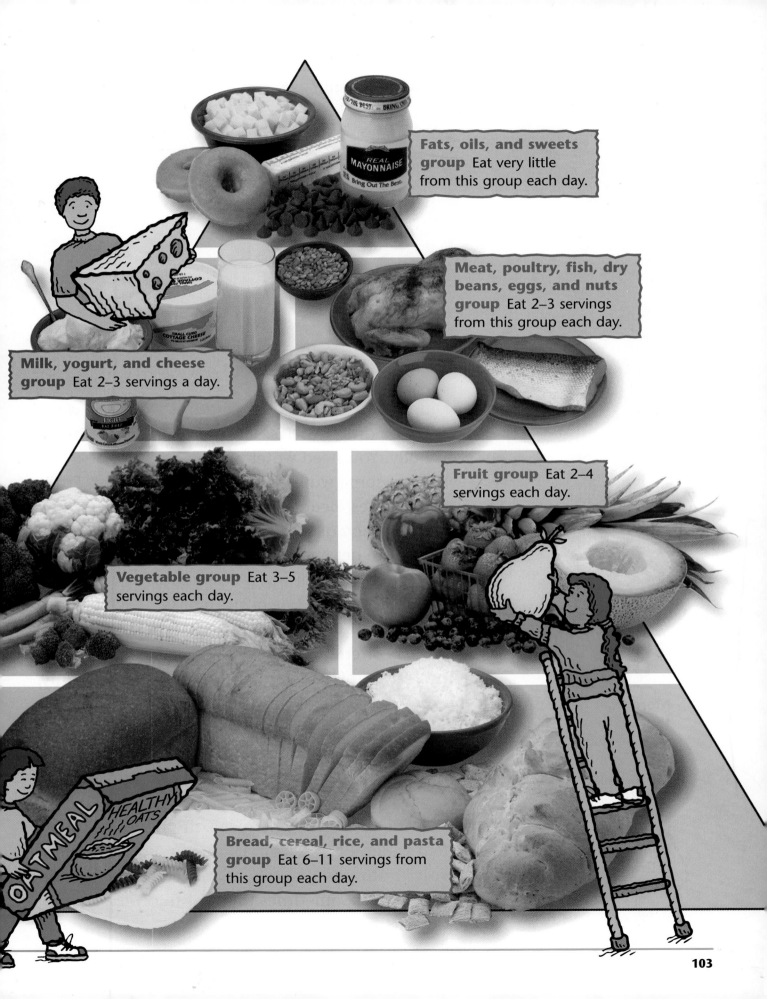

Fats, oils, and sweets group Eat very little from this group each day.

Meat, poultry, fish, dry beans, eggs, and nuts group Eat 2–3 servings from this group each day.

Milk, yogurt, and cheese group Eat 2–3 servings a day.

Fruit group Eat 2–4 servings each day.

Vegetable group Eat 3–5 servings each day.

Bread, cereal, rice, and pasta group Eat 6–11 servings from this group each day.

▼ All these foods contain water. Which foods do you eat? What other foods might have water in them?

Where do you get your water?

Did you know your skin contains water? So do your bones and muscles. Water is everywhere in your body. You need water to stay healthy.

You get some water from the foods you eat. Fruits such as apples, peaches, and melons contain water. Vegetables such as lettuce and carrots also have water. But to get enough water, you need to drink six to eight glasses of water each day.

Fluoride (FLAWR•yd) is a nutrient your body needs in small amounts. It helps keep your teeth healthy. Fluoride is often added to the water that is piped to homes. If you get your water from a water company, you may get some of this fluoride each time you drink water from your faucet.

Some people don't drink water that is piped to their homes. They buy bottled water to drink or get their water from a well.

Fluoride and other chemicals are removed from bottled water. People who drink only bottled water or water from private wells may need to get fluoride in other ways. Sometimes they get fluoride treatments from a dentist.

Did you know?

More than half the weight of your body is made up of water. There is water everywhere in your body. Even your bones are one-fifth water!

• • • • • • •

Why eat three meals a day?

Everything you do uses energy. Even when you are not doing anything, your body is using energy. Your body needs energy all day.

Different activities use different amounts of energy. When you ride your bike, your body uses a lot of energy. When you sit and read, it uses less.

All the energy your body uses comes from the food you eat. Your body uses energy throughout the day. The Food Guide Pyramid can help you eat foods to provide your energy needs. If you use the guide to eat foods from each food group each day, you will have a **balanced diet** (BA•luhnst DY•uht).

Suppose you ate all the foods you need each day at one meal. Your body could not use all that food at once. It's important to eat meals throughout the day. Spacing meals gives your body the energy and nutrients it needs all day.

LIFE SKILLS
FOCUS

Make Decisions
Kim is always late. She often skips breakfast so she won't miss the bus. This makes Kim tired and cranky. Use the steps for making decisions on pages 246 and 247 to help Kim get the energy she needs and still catch the bus.

▶ **What provided these boys with the energy they need to play their favorite sport?**

LESSON CHECKUP

Check Your Facts

❶ What is the Food Guide Pyramid?

❷ What are the food groups in the Food Guide Pyramid?

❸ How can you make sure you get enough water?

❹ CRITICAL THINKING How can you eat a balanced diet?

Set Health Goals

❺ Think back over what you've eaten for lunch the last three days. Did you eat foods from every food group in the Food Guide Pyramid? How many things did you eat from each group? How can you make your lunches more healthful?

MAIN IDEA
Snacks are an important part of a healthful diet.

WHY LEARN THIS? You can use what you learn to help you choose healthful snacks.

VOCABULARY
• snacks

Healthful Snack Choices

Seth gets home from school every day at three o'clock. He heads straight for the refrigerator. He's starving! Milk, cheese, grapes, apples, carrots, celery. What will Seth choose today?

Like most children, Seth eats a few **snacks**—food between meals—every day. Snacks are a part of a healthful diet. They keep you from getting too hungry. They also give you the energy and nutrients you need. Snacks are especially important if you are active.

People eat snacks for many reasons. You might be hungry. You may eat snacks when you are with friends. You may want a snack when you are tired. You may have a snack to celebrate a happy time, such as a birthday.

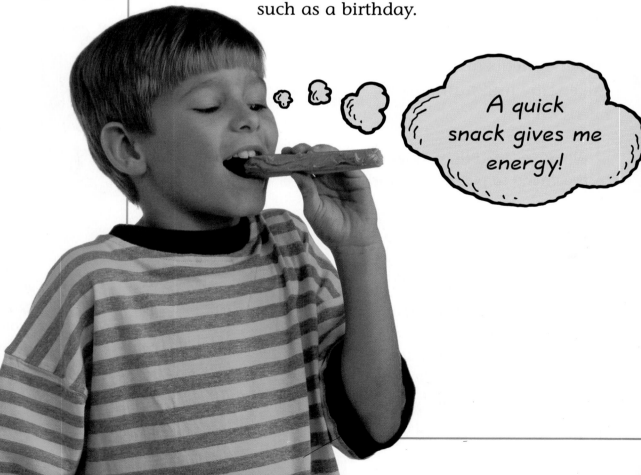

A quick snack gives me energy!

What makes a snack healthful?

As you use the Food Guide Pyramid, remember to include snacks in your diet. Snacks help you get nutrients you may not get during meals. A plum or pear as a snack gives you a fruit serving. A granola bar or half a bagel gives you a serving from the bread, cereal, rice, and pasta group.

This snack counts as a serving of fruit.

Some snacks are not healthful. They don't give you the nutrients you need most. Potato chips and chocolate bars are mostly fats and sweets. You should eat these foods only in small amounts.

Healthful snacks don't contain a lot of fats, oils, or sweets. Some healthful snacks are listed below.

- fresh fruit
- raw vegetables
- whole grain cereal
- orange juice
- milk
- raisins
- lowfat yogurt
- unbuttered popcorn
- whole wheat crackers
- cheese
- peanut butter sandwich

Which foods in the healthful snacks list do you like? Remember these foods the next time you race for the kitchen. Find yourself a healthful snack!

LESSON CHECKUP

Check Your Facts

1. What is a snack?
2. CRITICAL THINKING What are two reasons snacks are important?
3. What are two unhealthful snacks?
4. Give four examples of healthful snacks.

Use Life Skills

5. COMMUNICATE Write a letter to an adult family member. Explain why you like to eat healthful snacks. Include suggestions for five healthful snacks that you would eat. Ask if you might help shop for these foods.

MAKE DECISIONS
About Snacks

Choosing snacks is something most people do every day. This skill will help you make healthful choices.

Learn This Skill

Belinda has a skating lesson in thirty minutes. Her friends are ready to go, but she wants to eat a healthful snack that will give her energy during her lesson.

1. Find out about the choices you could make.

Belinda opens the refrigerator to check out her choices. What will she choose?

2. Imagine the possible result of each choice.

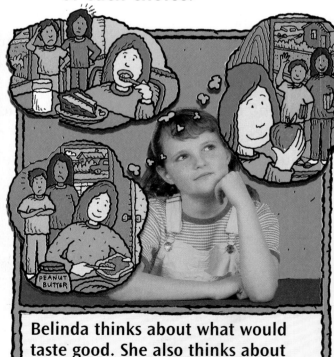

Belinda thinks about what would taste good. She also thinks about how long each snack will take to fix and eat.

3. Make what seems to be the best choice.

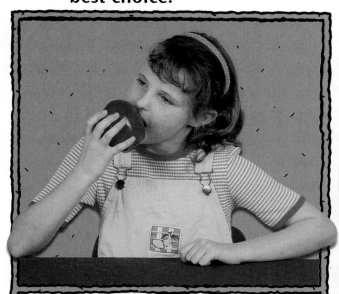

Belinda chooses an apple because it's her favorite fruit. It's also ready to eat!

4. Think about the result of your choice.

Belinda got a healthful snack and didn't keep her friends waiting.

Practice This Skill

Use this summary as you solve the problems below.

Steps for Making Decisions

1. Find out about the choices you could make.

2. Imagine the possible result of each choice.

3. Make what seems to be the best choice.

4. Think about the result of your choice.

A. Howard is bringing drinks for the baseball team. He may bring cola, fruit juice, or water. Use the steps to help Howard make his choice.

B. Ann is planning a snack for a hike. She needs a healthful snack she can carry easily. What are some possible choices? What is the best choice? Why?

Being a Wise Food Shopper

Sabrena and her father go shopping together every week. By shopping together, they each get a variety of foods they like. As they shop, Sabrena and her father carefully look at all the labels. They want to be sure the foods they buy are healthful.

How can you choose among food products?

Many foods are packaged. Packaged foods include cake mixes, canned fruits, and bread. These foods are made of more than one thing. The things that go into a food are its **ingredients** (in•GREE•dee•uhnts).

► Look at all the different cereals! What do you think helped Sabrena and her father make their choice?

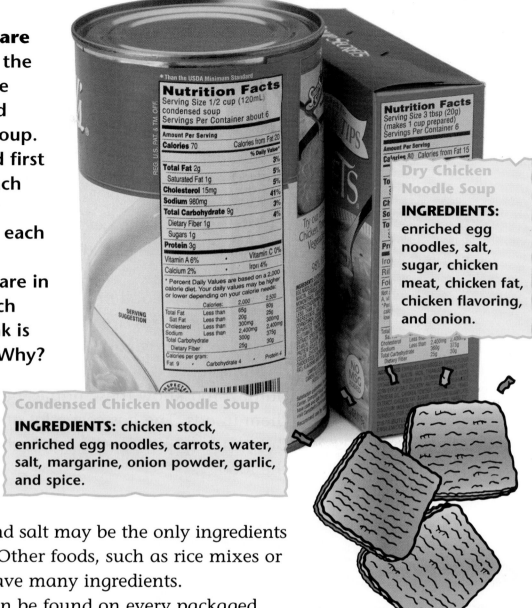

Activity **Compare Soups** Compare the ingredients in the canned and dried chicken noodle soup. See what is listed first and second in each food. How many ingredients does each have? Look for ingredients that are in both soups. Which soup do you think is more healthful? Why?

Condensed Chicken Noodle Soup

INGREDIENTS: chicken stock, enriched egg noodles, carrots, water, salt, margarine, onion powder, garlic, and spice.

Dry Chicken Noodle Soup

INGREDIENTS: enriched egg noodles, salt, sugar, chicken meat, chicken fat, chicken flavoring, and onion.

Corn, water, and salt may be the only ingredients in a can of corn. Other foods, such as rice mixes or frozen dinners, have many ingredients.

A **food label** can be found on every packaged food. It gives information about how nutritious a food is. The information is called Nutrition Facts.

A food label also lists the ingredients in a food. You can use food labels to compare the ingredients in different foods. The ingredients are listed in order of amount. The first ingredient is the one used most in the food. The last ingredient is the one used least.

Food labels also show the amounts of different nutrients. Similar foods may have different nutrients. They may also have different amounts of each nutrient.

Nutrition Facts
Serving Size 16 Crackers
Servings per Container About 4

Amount per Serving	
Calories 140	Calories from Fat 50
	% Daily Value
Total Fat 6g	9%
Saturated Fat 1g	5%
Polyunsaturated Fat 0g	
Monounsaturated Fat 2g	
Cholesterol 0mg	0%
Sodium 180mg	8%
Total Carbohydrate 19g	6%
Dietary Fiber 2g	
Sugars 2g	
Protein 2g	
Vitamin A 0% • Vitamin C 0%	
Calcium 2% • Iron 4%	

Why the price difference?

Kito and his brother need to buy orange juice. They can buy fresh juice, canned juice, or frozen juice. They can buy a big package or a small package. They can buy juice in cartons, cans, bottles, or boxes.

The boys want to get the best deal. But each package of juice has a different price. They are so confused!

One kind of food may have many different prices. Fresh foods are often most expensive. Frozen foods may cost more than canned foods.

Some foods cost more because they carry brand names. You know these names because you see them in ads. The ads cost a lot of money to make. But you help pay for the ads each time you buy the food.

▼ **Orange juice comes in many different packages.**

A large supermarket may have its own store brand. You do not see many ads for these foods. So store brand foods are usually cheaper than brand-name foods.

Foods are sold in different amounts. A small can of juice costs less than a large can. But be careful. The juice in the small can may really be more expensive! You must compare the cost by weight or unit. The cost per ounce of the small can is probably higher than that of the large can. You can often find the unit cost on tags near the food on the store shelf.

Sometimes foods are packaged together. You can buy packages of boxed juice. Each box is a single serving. This type of package is expensive. You can save money by buying the juice in larger packages and using a clean, tightly closed jar to carry it in your lunch.

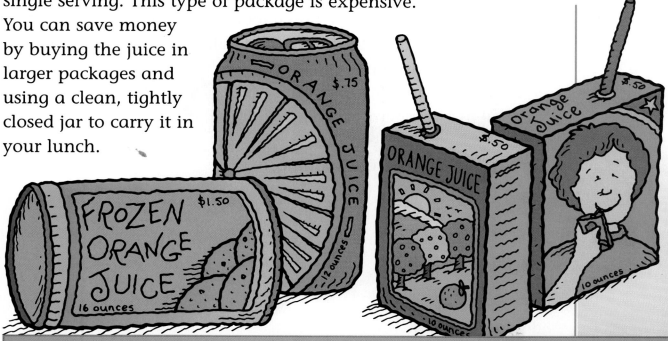

LESSON CHECKUP

Check Your Facts

❶ What are ingredients?

❷ How are food labels useful?

❸ What are three things that can affect the cost of food?

❹ CRITICAL THINKING Why do you have to be careful when comparing the prices of small and large packages?

Use Life Skills

❺ RESOLVE CONFLICTS Tess wants the small boxes of orange juice. Her sister wants to buy the frozen juice. Why might Tess want the small boxes? Why do you think her sister wants the frozen juice? How might they resolve their conflict?

Handling Food Safely

Jen is helping unload groceries. First, she quickly places the frozen foods in the freezer. Next, she puts the meat, chicken, and eggs in the refrigerator. She puts some of the fruits and vegetables in the refrigerator, too. Finally, Jen stacks the canned and dry foods in the cupboard.

Which foods need refrigerating?

Some foods spoil. A **spoiled** food is one that is unsafe to eat. Some foods spoil quickly. These foods usually need to be kept cold or frozen. You should store meat, milk, eggs, and leftovers in the refrigerator. This helps keep these foods from spoiling.

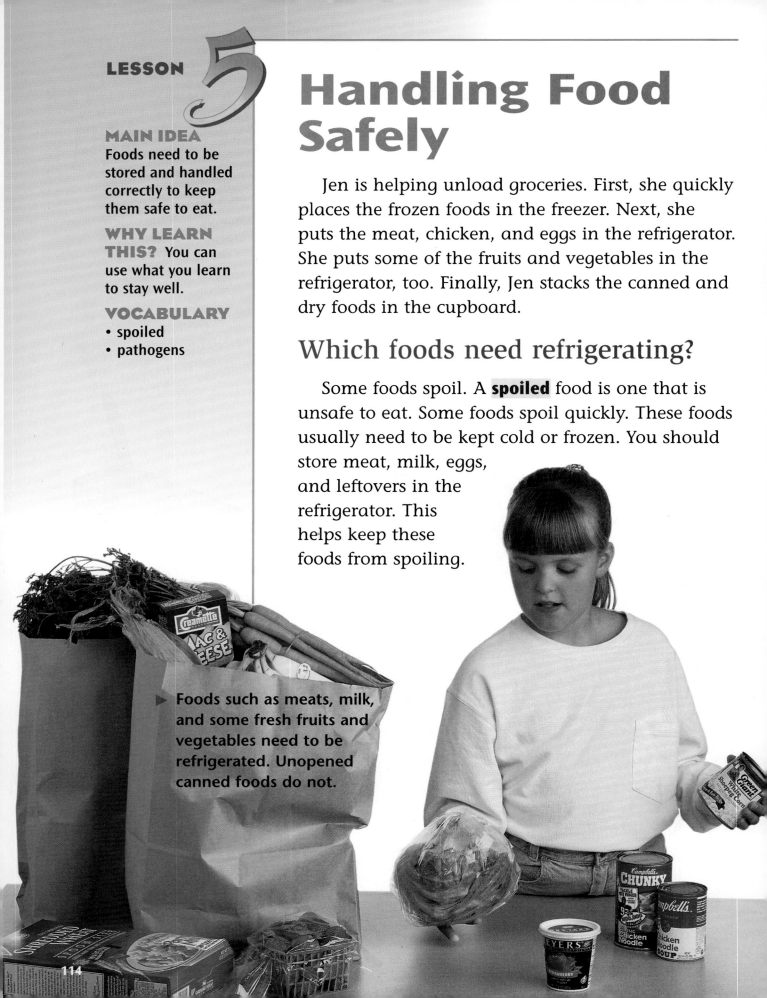

▶ Foods such as meats, milk, and some fresh fruits and vegetables need to be refrigerated. Unopened canned foods do not.

Some foods need to go into the freezer. Already frozen foods, such as frozen vegetables, must stay frozen to be safe. Foods that are not frozen, such as meats, can be kept longer in the freezer.

What are some safety tips for preparing a meal?

Pathogens (PA•thuh•juhnz), or germs, in food can cause illness. If a food with pathogens touches another food, the pathogens can spread.

You can help keep pathogens from spreading. Before and after working with food, wash your hands with soap and warm water. Also wash and keep your work areas clean.

Meat and poultry can carry pathogens. You should not cut other foods on a surface that meat and poultry have touched. Cutting boards must be washed with soap and hot water.

Wrapping foods keeps out air and pathogens. It helps keep food safe. Always wrap foods before putting them away.

▶ **Wrapping your food helps keep it fresh.**

JOURNAL

Write in your Health Journal the things you do to help keep food in your home safe. What can you do to help keep food even safer? Share your ideas with your family.

LESSON CHECKUP

Check Your Facts

❶ Why shouldn't you eat spoiled food?

❷ Name four foods that must be kept in the refrigerator.

❸ CRITICAL THINKING Why might you want to store meat in the freezer instead of the refrigerator?

Set Health Goals

❹ When should you wash your hands throughout the day? When **do** you wash your hands? Set goals for keeping your hands cleaner. Try to meet your goals.

USE VOCABULARY

balanced diet (p. 105)	**fluoride** (p. 104)	**ingredients** (p. 110)	**serving** (p. 102)
diet (p. 99)	**Food Guide Pyramid** (p. 102)	**nutrients** (p. 98)	**snacks** (p. 106)
fiber (p. 99)	**food label** (p. 111)	**nutrition** (p. 98)	**spoiled** (p. 114)
		pathogens (p. 115)	

Use the terms above to complete the sentences. Page numbers in ( ) tell you where to look in the chapter if you need help.

1. The woody part of plants is _____.

2. Foods you eat between meals are _____.

3. The _____ is a tool to help you choose foods for a healthful diet.

4. A _____ gives you information about a food.

5. Parts of a food that help your body grow, get energy, and work well are _____.

6. When you have a _____, you eat foods from each food group every day.

7. The foods you usually eat or drink make up your _____.

8. A food that is unsafe to eat has _____.

9. _____ are the things that go into a food.

10. The study of food and how it affects the body is _____.

11. A _____ is the amount of food you would probably eat during a meal or as a snack.

12. Germs in food that can cause illness are _____.

13. _____ is a nutrient that helps keep your teeth healthy.

CHECK YOUR FACTS

Page numbers in ( ) tell you where to look in the chapter if you need help.

14. What are some jobs of a farm operator? (p. 100)

15. How many glasses of water do you need each day? (p. 104)

16. How do snacks help you get the nutrients you need? (p. 107)

17. What does listing an ingredient first on a food label tell you about the ingredient? (p. 111)

18. Why is it important to wash your hands before eating? (p. 115)

THINK CRITICALLY

19. Name four plant foods and four animal foods.

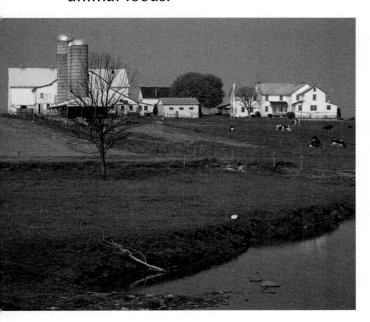

20. What are three things you can do at home to help keep foods safe?

21. **Make Decisions** Imagine you are going to the movies with friends. They want to share hot buttered popcorn. You are trying to eat healthful snacks. Use the steps for making decisions to choose a more healthful snack you could have with your friends.

22. **Make Decisions** You go shopping with your parents. They want to buy the same kind of macaroni and cheese they usually get but they think the store brand, which comes in a larger box, is cheaper. How can you use the steps for making decisions to help your parents decide which product is a better buy?

Promote Health **Home and Community**

1. Sit down with your family to discuss what healthful snacks the whole family can enjoy. Make a shopping list that includes the snacks you agree on.
2. Talk with a farmer or a gardener who grows plants for food. Find out what kinds of things plants need to grow well. Share what you learn with your class.

Activities

Make Your Own Food Guide Pyramid

With a Team • Use boxes to make a model of a Food Guide Pyramid. Use pictures cut from food labels or magazines to show which foods belong in each part of the pyramid. Add labels to the pyramid that name each food group and tell how many servings a person should eat from the group each day.

Choosing Healthful Foods

On Your Own • On a sheet of paper, make a list of 20 foods you really like. Next to each food, write the name of its food group. Use your list and the Food Guide Pyramid on page 103 to plan two days' worth of healthful meals.

cereal
pizza
popcorn
cheese
apple
animal crackers
corn

Local Foods

With a Partner • Find out what kinds of plant and animal foods are raised in your state. Draw a map of your state, and include pictures of the different types of foods.

Select Your Snacks

At Home • Look through your kitchen to see what kinds of snack foods are there. Make a list of the foods you find. Place a check beside each food you think makes a healthful snack.

Multiple Choice

Choose the letter of the correct answer.

1. ____ helps keep food moving through the digestive system.
   a. Nutrition   b. Fiber
   c. Fat   d. Cheese

2. Fluoride is a nutrient you may get from ____.
   a. juice   b. water
   c. fiber   d. vegetables

3. Snacks help you get the ____ you may not get during meals.
   a. nutrients   b. oils
   c. fats   d. nutrition

4. Your ____ is what you eat each day.
   a. serving   b. snack
   c. nutrition   d. diet

5. Foods such as ____ need to be refrigerated.
   a. canned fruit b. chips
   c. meats   d. bread

Modified True or False

Write *true* or *false*. If a sentence is false, replace the underlined term to make the sentence true.

6. Nutrition is the study of <u>fiber</u> and how it affects the body.

7. Fruits and vegetables come from <u>animals</u>.

8. The <u>fruit</u> group is the largest group in the Food Guide Pyramid.

9. You need to drink extra <u>water</u> when you exercise.

10. You should eat fats and sweets in <u>large</u> amounts.

11. Fresh foods are usually <u>less</u> expensive than canned foods.

12. The first ingredient on a food label is the one used <u>least</u> in the food.

13. Some foods cost more because they carry <u>brand</u> names.

14. A spoiled food is <u>safe</u> to eat.

15. Wrapping foods helps keep <u>pathogens</u> from spreading.

Short Answer

Write a complete sentence to answer each question.

16. Why should you wash your hands before and after working with food?

17. How can you compare the costs of foods sold in different amounts?

18. Name two things on a food label.

19. Name three healthful snacks.

20. Name three foods that contain water.

21. Name a food that comes from animals.

22. List three common grains.

Essay

Write paragraphs to answer each item.

23. Why should you eat a variety of foods?

24. Explain some safety tips for preparing a meal.

CHAPTER 5

Preventing Disease

Project

MAKE A GERM-FIGHTER BULLETIN BOARD Make a bulletin board with pictures that show things you can do to avoid spreading germs. Make your own drawings, and cut out or copy pictures from magazines and newspapers. For each picture, include a short sentence telling how the activity shown prevents the spread of germs.

For other activities, visit the Harcourt Brace Internet site. http://www.hbschool.com

What Is Disease?

MAIN IDEA
Diseases keep the body from working normally.

WHY LEARN THIS? What you learn can help you understand what is happening when you feel ill.

VOCABULARY
• symptom
• disease

Patty was not eating her favorite meal. "Don't you feel well?" her father asked. Patty said her head and throat hurt. Her father knew she was ill because of her symptoms. A **symptom** (SIMP•tuhm) is a sign that something is wrong in the body. A headache and sore throat are common symptoms of a cold or flu.

How do you feel when you are ill? Like Patty, you probably don't feel very well. An illness is a disease. A **disease** (dih•ZEEZ) is something that causes the body not to work normally.

There are many kinds of diseases. Some diseases spread from one person to another. Sneezing without covering your mouth is one way to spread diseases such as a cold or the flu. Some other diseases can't be spread to other people.

JOURNAL

In your Health Journal, describe how you felt the last time you had a cold or the flu. What were your symptoms? How long did you feel ill? Remember that your journal is private.

▼ **You know you are ill if you have symptoms. Some common symptoms are fever, scratchy throat, coughing, headache, and body aches.**

▶ People with disabilities might not be able to do some things. But there are many other things they *can* do.

How should you act toward people who are ill?

When friends have diseases that can spread, you should know how you can keep the disease from spreading to you. Different diseases spread in different ways.

Sometimes people have diseases or health problems that you cannot catch. Stacy has an illness that keeps her from walking. She uses a wheelchair to get around. Stacy's illness can't be spread to others, but it has caused her to have a disability. A disability is a physical or mental problem. You can't catch a disability.

People with illnesses and disabilities may feel bad because their bodies aren't working normally. You should treat people with diseases and disabilities the same way you treat your other friends. Imagine how you would feel if you were that person. Think about how an illness or a disability would affect you and how you would want to be treated.

LESSON CHECKUP

Check Your Facts

1 What is a disease?
2 How do you know if you have a disease?
3 CRITICAL THINKING Suppose a student in your class is home with a cold. Should you visit him? If not, what could you do instead?

Set Health Goals

4 Think about a time when you were ill. How did you feel? What made you feel better? List some ways to help a person with an illness feel better.

MAIN IDEA
Bacteria and viruses are two kinds of pathogens that cause disease.

WHY LEARN THIS? You can use what you learn to keep from getting a disease.

VOCABULARY
• infectious disease
• pathogens
• bacteria
• virus
• fever

Some Diseases and Their Causes

A friend at school gets a cold. She sniffles and sneezes all day Monday. By Friday several people in your class are ill. A cold is an infectious disease. An **infectious disease** (in•FEK•shuhs dih•ZEEZ) is a disease that can spread from one person to another. Infectious diseases are caused by pathogens. **Pathogens** (PA•thuh•juhnz) are germs that cause disease. When your friend sneezed, she spread the pathogens that caused her disease to others.

What are some kinds of pathogens?

Two main kinds of pathogens cause infectious diseases. One kind is bacteria. **Bacteria** (bak•TIR•ee•uh) are very simple living things. They are each made of just one cell. They are so small that you can see them only with a microscope.

Activity **Find the Ways Pathogens Spread** How are these students spreading pathogens? List other ways that pathogens can be spread.

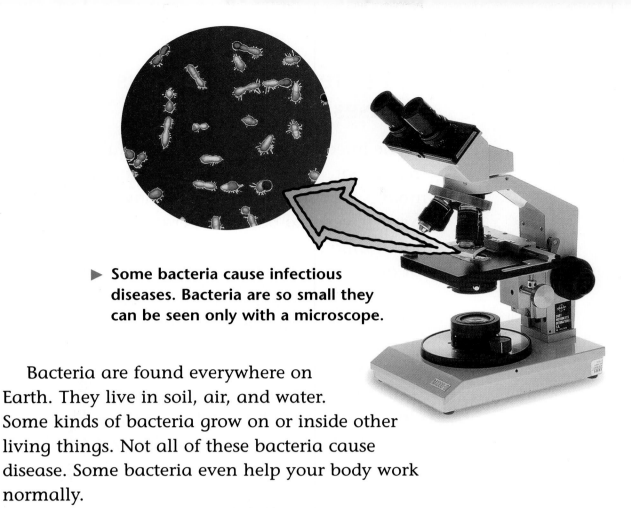

▶ Some bacteria cause infectious diseases. Bacteria are so small they can be seen only with a microscope.

Bacteria are found everywhere on Earth. They live in soil, air, and water. Some kinds of bacteria grow on or inside other living things. Not all of these bacteria cause disease. Some bacteria even help your body work normally.

However, a few kinds of bacteria *do* cause disease. When they get into your body, they can begin to multiply. They can grow into such large groups that your body cannot work normally. Then you become ill.

Another kind of pathogen is a virus. A **virus** (VY•ruhs) is one of the tiniest pathogens that cause disease. Viruses are even smaller than bacteria. Viruses must use cells in other living things to make more viruses. Viruses cause disease by destroying the cells they use.

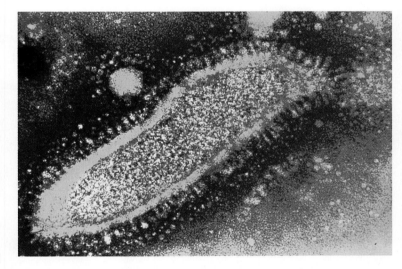

▲ Viruses also cause some infectious diseases. Viruses are even smaller than bacteria. Special microscopes must be used to see them. This virus has been magnified many hundreds of times.

What are some infectious diseases?

One infectious disease that bacteria cause is strep throat. When you have strep throat, your throat is very sore and you may have a fever. A **fever** (FEE•ver) is a body temperature that is higher than normal.

Colds and flu are two kinds of infectious diseases viruses cause. When you have a cold, you may have a stuffy nose, a scratchy throat, and a cough. You may even have a fever. Colds usually last about a week.

The flu has many of the same symptoms as a cold. You also may have chills, fever, and body aches. The flu can make you feel very tired. The flu usually lasts one day to a week.

▼ If you have a very sore throat, your doctor may take a swab of your throat. The doctor will try to grow what's on the swab. If bacteria grow, you may have strep throat.

▲ When you have a cold or the flu, you need plenty of rest.

▲ Head lice are tiny insects. To get rid of them, you must use a special shampoo that kills them and their eggs.

What are other health problems that can spread?

Another common problem that can spread is head lice. People who have head lice can spread the lice by being near other people or by sharing things like combs, brushes, and hats.

Head lice are very small insects that crawl on skin and hair and feed on blood. As the lice feed, the head becomes very itchy. Other symptoms of head lice are tiny red bumps near the root of the hair on the head.

People who have head lice must use a special shampoo that kills the insects. Louse eggs in the hair must be removed with a fine comb or tweezers. All combs, brushes, clothing, and bed linens must be washed in very hot water to kill the lice and their eggs.

LIFE SKILLS FOCUS

COMMUNICATE
Joyce is making a picture book to help a kindergarten class learn how infectious diseases spread. What should Joyce think about while she's planning her book? How can she communicate her message clearly? Use the steps for communicating shown on pages 246 and 247.

LESSON CHECKUP

Check Your Facts
1. What are pathogens?
2. How do pathogens cause infectious diseases?
3. CRITICAL THINKING Is it a good idea to share a cup with a friend who doesn't seem ill? Why or why not?

Set Health Goals
4. Think of a time when you caught an infectious disease from a friend or relative. How do you think you got the disease? Write down some things you might have done to keep from getting the disease.

Fighting Disease

MAIN IDEA
Most diseases can be prevented and treated.

WHY LEARN THIS? You can use what you learn to help keep yourself and others healthy.

VOCABULARY
• immune
• vaccine
• medicine

Pathogens are all around us. Sometimes pathogens get into your body and cause disease. Luckily, there are ways to treat most diseases. Often your body can fight the disease on its own. Sometimes you need a doctor's help.

How can you prevent disease?

Reggie wants Juan to come outside and play. Juan's mom says that Juan has the flu. He can't play with other children until he is well. She tells Reggie that she doesn't want him to catch the flu from Juan.

Staying away from people who are ill is only one way to prevent disease. A very important way to prevent disease is by washing your hands with soap and water. Many objects that people touch a lot, such as doorknobs and handrails, have pathogens on them. Washing with soap and water helps get rid of the pathogens on your hands. Keeping your hands clean helps prevent disease.

▶ Reggie can't play with Juan because Juan is ill. Learning how diseases are spread helps you know how to stay healthy.

128

◀ An oral vaccine is taken by mouth and swallowed. It will prevent a certain disease.

You can also prevent diseases by becoming immune to them. A person is **immune** (ih•MYOON) when a pathogen that causes a disease cannot make that person ill. People often become immune to a disease after they have had that disease. They also become immune when they get a vaccine for that disease. A **vaccine** (vak•SEEN) is a substance given to keep you from getting a certain kind of disease.

When you get a vaccine, a pathogen for a disease is put into your body. The pathogen has been weakened or killed so it can't make you ill. But it does cause your body to make a substance to fight the pathogen. If that pathogen gets in your body again, this substance will destroy it right away. You won't become ill.

When you are ill, you must also keep from spreading the disease to others. There are several easy things you can do. Wash your hands often. Cover your mouth and nose with a tissue when you cough or sneeze. Don't share anything that you have put in your mouth or near your nose. Doing these things will help keep others from catching your disease.

Some Diseases for Which There Are Vaccines

- **Chicken pox**
- **Diphtheria**
- **Haemophilus Type B (Meningitis)**
- **Hepatitis B**
- **Measles**
- **Mumps**
- **Pertussis (Whooping Cough)**
- **Polio**
- **Rubella (3-Day Measles)**
- **Tetanus**

Body Temperature

On Your Own How do you know when you have a fever? Find out what normal body temperature is. Then find out how high a body temperature must be to be a fever.

○ ○ ○

How are diseases treated?

Before a disease can be treated, you must know what the symptoms are. Always tell a parent, teacher, or caregiver when you feel ill. Then you will get the care you need.

Diseases are treated in different ways. Many diseases, such as colds and flu, are treated by resting in bed and drinking liquids. Sometimes diseases are treated with medicines. A **medicine** (MEH•duh•suhn) is a liquid, powder, cream, spray, or pill used to treat illness.

Not all medicines work alike. Some medicines kill the pathogen causing the disease. Medicines for strep throat and ear infections work like this. Other medicines treat the symptoms of a disease to make the person feel better. Cold medicines work like this. These medicines can help clear a stuffy nose and soothe a sore throat. But they cannot cure a cold.

▼ **Tell an adult when you are feeling ill so that you can be cared for right away.**

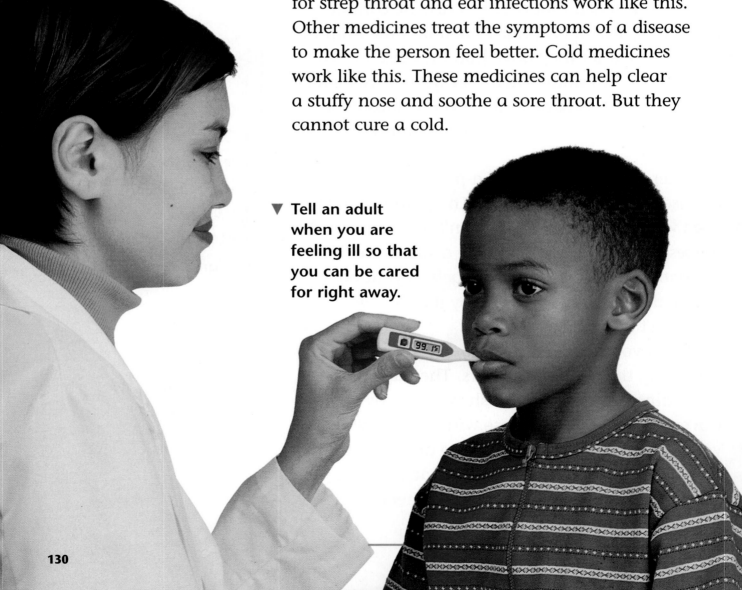

Fever is a symptom of many diseases. To bring your temperature back to normal, an adult can give you a fever medicine. Some fever medicines are very safe for children to take. However, one kind—aspirin—is not safe for children. It can cause a serious illness in children. For this reason, take medicine only when a trusted adult gives it to you. The adult should read the labels or consult a doctor to decide which medicine to use, how much to give you, and how often you need it.

Take medicine only from a parent or other trusted adult.

▶ **This child is getting fever medicine. Fever medicines help the body temperature return to normal.**

LESSON CHECKUP

Check Your Facts

1. What are two ways to prevent disease?
2. What does it mean to be immune to a disease?
3. CRITICAL THINKING If you feel ill, should you take medicine that another student gives to you? Why or why not?

Use Life Skills

4. COMMUNICATE List three ways to keep from spreading or getting disease. Post your list where family members can see it.

Diseases You Can't Catch

You have been learning about infectious diseases. Infectious diseases are spread from one person to another by pathogens. Other diseases are not spread by pathogens. **Noninfectious diseases** cannot be caught from or spread to other persons. Some examples of noninfectious diseases are allergies, asthma, and diabetes.

What is an allergy?

One common noninfectious disease is an allergy. An **allergy** (A•ler•jee) is the body's reaction to some substance. People with allergies are not all allergic to the same things. Some people are allergic to just one thing. Other people are allergic to many things.

◀ People can have allergies to things that are harmless to most people.

Animals, plants, medicines, dust, bee stings, and foods can all cause allergies. Some foods that can cause allergies include eggs, peanuts, strawberries, wheat, and milk.

Not all people have allergies. Those who do have allergies have symptoms like sneezing, itchy and watery eyes, a runny nose, or an itchy skin rash. Some people have only mild symptoms. Others react strongly and may need to see a doctor right away. A very serious allergic reaction can cause death.

Doctors can help people with allergies. If you have an allergy to something, your doctor may tell you to stay away from it. Doctors can give medicine to help symptoms go away. They use skin tests to find out what things cause allergies. Sometimes people get allergy shots to reduce their symptoms.

Myth: Hay fever is a hay allergy.

Fact: Hay fever is an allergic reaction to tiny bits of plants or animal skin, feathers, and molds carried in the air.

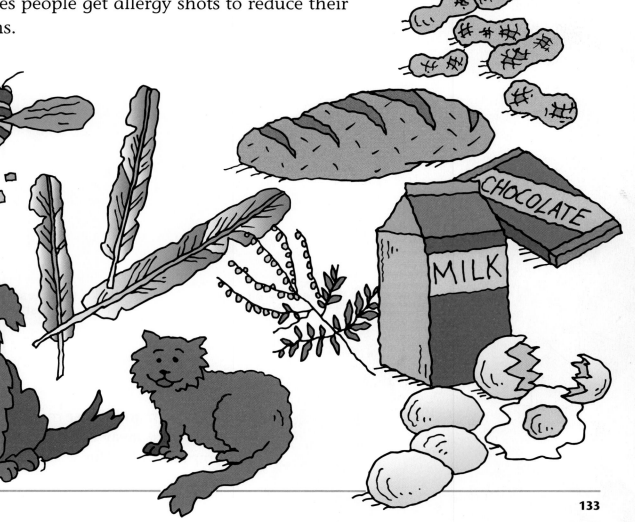

What is asthma?

Another noninfectious disease is asthma. **Asthma** (AZ•muh) causes people to have difficulty breathing. During an asthma attack, airways in the lungs become very narrow. This makes it hard for air to move in and out of the lungs. Compare the pictures below of the healthy airways and airways with asthma.

People who have asthma do not feel ill all the time. Their attacks are usually set off by allergies, exercise, or diseases that affect the lungs. Symptoms include tightness in the chest, difficulty breathing, and coughing and wheezing. Wheezing can be very loud and sometimes sounds squeaky.

Doctors can give medicine to help the symptoms of asthma go away. If you have asthma, your doctor may tell you to avoid the things that cause your asthma attacks.

HUMAN BODY CONNECTION

The Respiratory System

Study the respiratory system found on pages 12 and 13 of The Amazing Human Body. Find the lungs in the picture. How does asthma affect these organs?

Healthy airways

Airways during an asthma attack

◄ Medicine from an inhaler reaches the lungs right away to help ease the symptoms of asthma.

What is diabetes?

Your digestive system changes some of the food you eat to a kind of sugar. The blood carries this sugar to the body cells. The cells use the sugar to make energy. **Diabetes** (dy•uh•BEE•teez) is a noninfectious disease that prevents the body from using sugar properly. The sugar doesn't go into the cells. Instead, it stays in the blood. Too much sugar in the blood can make people ill. They may feel very thirsty and tired and lose weight.

A doctor uses a blood test to find out if someone has diabetes. People with diabetes must eat a special diet. Often they must also take medicine. The medicine helps the body use the sugar from food.

Jill has just learned that she has diabetes. A home health nurse has come to help Jill and her mother. He shows them how to check the amount of sugar in Jill's blood. He talks to them about Jill's diet. He also shows Jill's mother how to give Jill medicine for her diabetes.

Career

Home Health Nurse

What They Do

Home health nurses go to patients' homes to observe their health, give medicines, give baths, and prepare meals. They may tell patients how to take medicine. They also may tell or show a patient's family how to take care of the patient.

Education and Training

Home health nurses must have some college education and training in nursing. Many states also require them to pass a special test. Home health nurses must have good communication skills, a desire to help others, and good judgment.

LESSON CHECKUP

Check Your Facts

1. What is an allergy?
2. What are some symptoms of asthma?
3. CRITICAL THINKING Why would someone with diabetes feel tired?

Use Life Skills

4. COMMUNICATE Choose one of the diseases described in the lesson. Imagine that you have this disease. Tell how it might affect your life.

MAIN IDEA
Having a healthful lifestyle can help you fight disease.

WHY LEARN THIS? You can use what you learn to keep your body well.

VOCABULARY
• abstinence

Fighting Disease with a Healthful Lifestyle

You can do many things every day to keep your body healthy. Your lifestyle can make a difference in your health. *Lifestyle* refers to the choices a person makes about how to live his or her life. If you make healthful choices, then you have a healthful lifestyle. A healthful lifestyle helps your body fight disease.

How does the food you eat help you stay healthy?

Every morning for breakfast, Paul has orange juice and oatmeal with milk. Paul never feels tired during the school day. Lucas likes to have doughnuts and a soft drink for breakfast. Lucas is often sleepy at school.

 Activity **Identify Healthful Foods** Compare these lunches. Which lunch is more healthful? Make a list of other healthful lunches.

Which is healthful?

Always read labels.

◄ Check the amounts of fat, sugar, and salt in foods. Eating less of these can help reduce your risk for some noninfectious diseases.

The foods you choose to eat are important to your health. Food gives your body energy. Food also gives your body the things it needs to grow and fight disease.

Every day you should eat a variety of healthful foods. Use what you know about the Food Guide Pyramid to make smart choices about the foods you eat. When you make smart choices, your body gets the right amounts of nutrients and fiber.

If you choose foods that are not healthful, your body doesn't get the things it needs. You may have less energy, gain extra weight, and catch infectious diseases easily. If you eat a lot of foods low in fiber and high in fats, sugar, and salt, you may increase your risk of developing some noninfectious diseases, too.

At the grocery store you may have noticed foods labeled "fat-free," "sugar-free," or "low in salt." Are these foods really more healthful? The only way to know for sure is to read the labels on the food packages. Each food package is labeled with the amounts of fat, sugar, and salt in that food. By reading and comparing labels, you can find out which foods are more healthful.

How does exercise help you stay healthy?

Jane's gym teacher always has the class begin with a jog around the playground. At first Jane couldn't make it all the way around. Now she can always finish. And she seems to have more energy.

Exercise is important to good health. It makes your muscles, heart, and lungs stronger. It helps your body use food and keeps you at a healthful weight. Exercise also helps your body fight disease.

Exercise helps you manage stress, too. You may be stressed when something makes you worried, nervous, angry, sad, or tired. You may also be stressed when things around you change or when you begin something new. Symptoms of stress include headache, stomachache, and trouble sleeping. Stress also can make your heart pound and your muscles feel tight. Too much stress can make you ill.

Exercise can help you feel calmer. It can help make the symptoms of stress go away. If you exercise regularly, your body will also handle stress better.

JOURNAL

In your Health Journal, describe your favorite kinds of exercise. Tell when, where, and how often you do them. How do you feel after exercising? Remember that your journal is private.

How does tobacco use affect a person's health?

Using tobacco is not a healthful lifestyle choice. When people smoke, they breathe tobacco smoke into their mouths, noses, throats, and lungs. Tobacco smoke has many harmful substances.

Smoking weakens the body. People who smoke are more likely to catch diseases such as colds and flu than those who don't smoke. People who use chewing tobacco usually have problems with their teeth and gums. Over time any kind of tobacco use may cause cancer, lung disease, and heart disease.

To have a healthful lifestyle, you must practice abstinence from tobacco. **Abstinence** (AB•stuh•nuhnts) means avoiding a behavior that will harm your health. Choosing not to use tobacco is one of the best things you can do for your health.

LIFE SKILLS
FOCUS

Refuse

Deborah's mom has asthma. A neighbor who is visiting asks Deborah's mom if she can smoke in the house. Use the steps for refusals shown on pages 246 and 247 to help Deborah's mom respond.

◄ **When you breathe in other people's smoke, you get the same harmful substances that smokers breathe in. Many public places have made special areas for smokers. This helps keep the smoke away from nonsmokers.**

LESSON CHECKUP

Check Your Facts

❶ List two healthful lifestyle choices.

❷ Why is it important to eat healthful foods?

❸ CRITICAL THINKING If you feel worried about a test that's coming up, what might make you feel better?

❹ CRITICAL THINKING Some of your friends think that smoking is cool. What should you tell them?

Set Health Goals

❺ Joe gets exercise one day a week. How can he change his lifestyle to make it more healthful?

MANAGE STRESS
to Control Disease

We all feel stress sometimes. Learning to manage stress will help keep you healthy.

Learn This Skill

Marcy has to give an oral report tomorrow, and she is feeling a lot of stress. She is sitting quietly, but her muscles feel tight, her heart is pounding, and her head hurts. Here are four things Marcy can do to manage her stress.

Exercise.

"Maybe I'll feel less tense if I go for a walk."

Imagine yourself doing well in the situation.

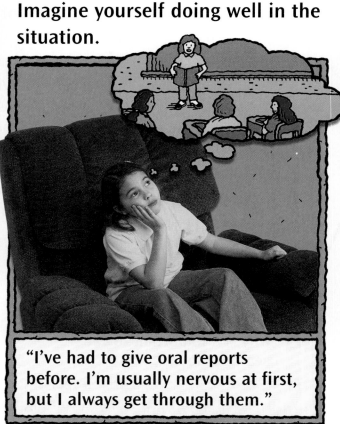

"I've had to give oral reports before. I'm usually nervous at first, but I always get through them."

Find a way to relax.

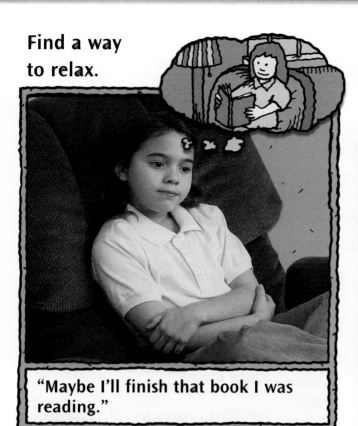

"Maybe I'll finish that book I was reading."

Talk to someone about how you're feeling.

"Maybe I'll call Maria. She always knows just what to say to make me feel better."

Practice This Skill

Here are some ways to help you solve the problems.

Ways to Manage Stress

- Exercise.
- Imagine yourself doing well in the situation.
- Find a way to relax.
- Talk to someone about how you're feeling.

A. Ann is worried about her first visit to the hospital to see her grandfather. She can feel her heart pounding. Use what you know about managing stress to help Ann.

B. Clay has a big math test tomorrow, and he can't get to sleep. Use what you know about managing stress to help Clay.

USE VOCABULARY

abstinence (p. 139)   diabetes (p. 135)   infectious disease (p. 124)   pathogens (p. 124)

allergy (p. 132)   disease (p. 122)   medicine (p. 130)   symptom (p. 122)

asthma (p. 134)   fever (p. 126)   noninfectious diseases   vaccine (p. 129)

bacteria (p. 124)   immune (p. 129)   (p. 132)   virus (p. 125)

Use the terms above to complete the sentences. Page numbers in ( ) tell you where to look in the chapter if you need help.

1. When a pathogen cannot make a person ill, that person is ____.

2. A body temperature that is higher than normal is called a ____.

3. The body's bad reaction to some substance is an ____.

4. One of the tiniest pathogens that cause diseases such as colds is a ____.

5. Something that causes the body not to work normally is a ____.

6. A liquid, powder, cream, spray, or pill used to treat illness is called ____.

7. ____ are simple living things made of just one cell.

8. A disease that prevents the body from using sugar properly is ____.

9. Germs that cause disease are called ____.

10. A sign such as a headache that something is wrong in the body is a ____.

11. Diseases, such as diabetes or asthma, that cannot be caught are ____.

12. A disease that causes people to have difficulty breathing sometimes is ____.

13. A substance given to keep you from getting a certain kind of disease is a ____.

14. A disease that can spread from one person to another is an ____.

15. You practice ____ when you avoid a behavior that will harm your health.

CHECK YOUR FACTS

Page numbers in ( ) tell you where to look in the chapter if you need help.

16. Tell what disease is. How do you know if you have a disease? (p. 122)

17. Name the two kinds of pathogens in the photos below, and tell how they cause infectious diseases. (p. 125)

18. List three diseases that you can't catch. What are their symptoms? (pp. 132–135)

19. List two things that are part of a healthful lifestyle. Tell how they help you stay healthy. (pp. 136–138)

20. Name three ways you can prevent a disease from spreading. (pp. 128–129)

THINK CRITICALLY

21. Mike has the chicken pox. A virus causes chicken pox. Could Mike spread chicken pox to others? Explain.

22. Jenny eats many high-fat foods and rarely exercises. Explain how and why Jenny should change her lifestyle.

APPLY LIFE SKILLS

23. **Manage Stress** Suppose you will be playing soccer on a new team this year. How can you manage your stress to help you feel comfortable about playing on the new team?

24. **Communicate** Suppose your friend begins to feel ill at school. She wants to stay because there is a special program today. What would you tell her? How could you help her get care for her illness?

Promote Health — Home and Community

1. Explain to your family what you have learned about how important exercise is for good health. Think of some ways family members can exercise together.
2. Make an advertisement that describes the importance of getting vaccines. Display the ad someplace in your school.

Activities

Health Collage

With a Partner • Look through old magazines to find pictures that show healthful lifestyle choices. Cut out these pictures. Use them to make a collage about healthful lifestyles. Be sure to give your collage a title.

Gathering Cheer

With a Team • Make a list of things other than medicine that would help an ill person feel better. If possible, gather these items together to make a "cheer-up kit." Send your kit to someone who is in the hospital or at home with an illness.

Disease Search

On Your Own • Find out more about smallpox. It is a dangerous infectious disease that many people died from until about 200 years ago. Write a paragraph about smallpox. Tell what causes it, what its symptoms are, and how it has been stopped.

Germ Stoppers

At Home • Ask a family member to help you find items in the house that are used to kill pathogens. Find out how they are used to keep pathogens from spreading.

144

Multiple Choice

Choose the letter of the correct answer.

1. To treat a disease, your doctor might give you ____.
   - a. diabetes
   - b. viruses
   - c. medicine
   - d. pathogens

2. A fever is a ____, or a sign that something is wrong in the body.
   - a. disease
   - b. pathogen
   - c. lifestyle
   - d. symptom

3. Which health problem can be spread from one person to another?
   - a. allergies
   - b. head lice
   - c. asthma
   - d. diabetes

4. Choosing not to ____ is an example of abstinence.
   - a. exercise
   - b. smoke
   - c. diet
   - d. study

5. A disease that causes people to have difficulty breathing is ____.
   - a. strep throat
   - b. diabetes
   - c. asthma
   - d. cancer

Modified True or False

Write *true* or *false*. If a sentence is false, replace the underlined term to make the sentence true.

6. You are immune to a disease when its pathogen <u>cannot</u> make you ill.

7. <u>Food</u> gives your body things it needs to grow and fight disease.

8. <u>Asthma</u> is a disease that prevents the body from using sugar properly.

9. A <u>disease</u> is something that causes the body not to work normally.

10. Using tobacco is a <u>healthful</u> lifestyle choice.

11. A <u>pathogen</u> is given to keep you from getting a certain kind of disease.

12. An <u>allergy</u> is the body's reaction to some substance.

13. An infectious disease <u>can</u> be spread from one person to another.

Short Answer

Write a complete sentence to answer each question.

14. Name two ways to prevent disease.

15. What are some ways that infectious diseases are spread?

16. What does exercise do for the body?

17. Describe how smoking affects the body.

18. Why should you tell an adult when you are feeling ill?

Essay

Write paragraphs to answer each item.

19. Samantha is going to perform in her first play. Describe how she can manage her stress and relax.

20. Explain why living a healthful lifestyle helps prevent disease.

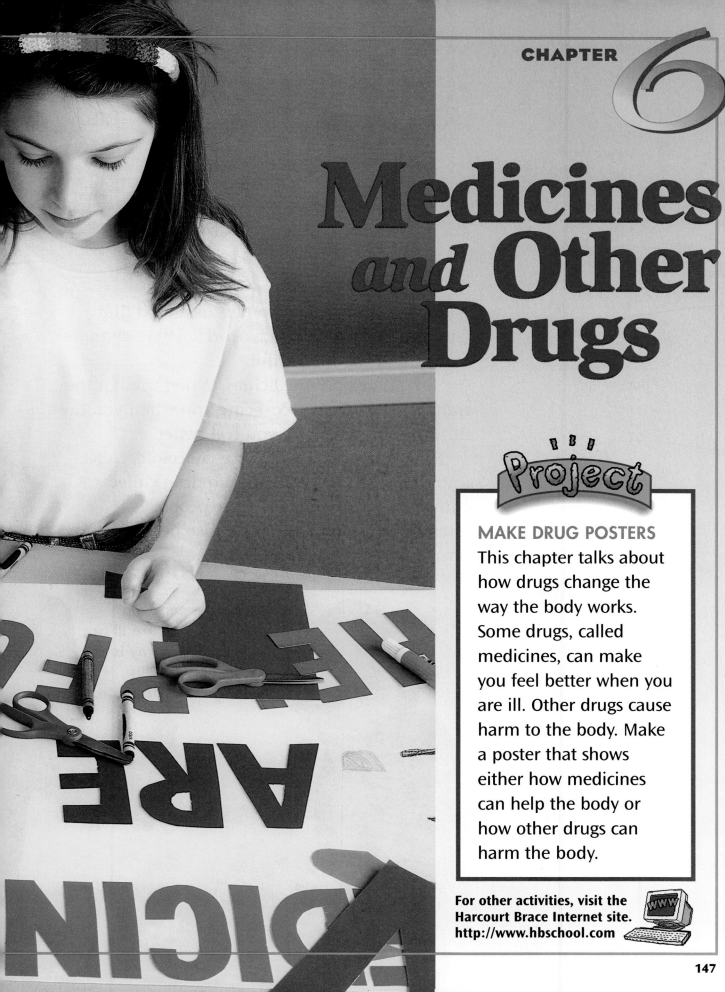

Medicines and Other Drugs

Project

MAKE DRUG POSTERS

This chapter talks about how drugs change the way the body works. Some drugs, called medicines, can make you feel better when you are ill. Other drugs cause harm to the body. Make a poster that shows either how medicines can help the body or how other drugs can harm the body.

For other activities, visit the Harcourt Brace Internet site. http://www.hbschool.com

Learning About Drugs

MAIN IDEA
Drugs change the way the body works. They can help you or harm you.

WHY LEARN THIS? Knowing the difference between helpful and harmful drugs will help keep you healthy.

VOCABULARY
• drug

Some drugs can help you when you are ill. Other drugs can make you ill. Do you know which drugs are helpful and which are harmful?

What are drugs?

A **drug** is something other than food that changes the way the body works. These changes can be helpful or harmful.

Some drugs are medicines. When used in the right way, medicines can cure you when you are ill. They can also help you feel better.

Some foods and drinks, like chocolate, coffee, and some soft drinks contain a drug called caffeine. Caffeine makes some people feel more awake. But caffeine can also be harmful if you have too much.

SOCIAL STUDIES
CONNECTION

Ancient Medicines

On Your Own Long ago Native Americans found that drinking tea made from the bark of a willow tree took away pain. The bark contains the same chemical that is in aspirin. Find out about other ancient medicines.

▼ Medicines can help you when you are ill or in pain. This spray is a medicine that kills pathogens on the skin.

◀ Many products around the home contain dangerous substances. The warning labels on these products warn the products should only be used as directed. They can hurt the body when used incorrectly.

Some drugs, like marijuana and cocaine, are harmful. They change the way people think, feel, and act. They can also make people very ill. Because they are so harmful, marijuana and cocaine are illegal. It is against the law for anyone to buy, sell, have, or use them.

Many household products give off dangerous fumes. Some people use the fumes as a drug. They sniff the fumes to get high. A "high" is a common way of describing how people feel when they use drugs. But the fumes are poisons that can cause illness, brain damage, or even death.

LESSON CHECKUP

Check Your Facts

1 What do drugs do to the body?

2 CRITICAL THINKING All medicines are drugs. But are all drugs medicines? Explain your answer.

3 How can household products be dangerous?

Set Health Goals

4 With your teacher, read the labels on some products in your classroom that contain dangerous substances. What kinds of warnings do they give to keep people safe? Are you and your classmates using the products safely?

MAIN IDEA
Medicines can help you get well when you use them correctly.

WHY LEARN THIS? You can find out how different medicines can help you.

VOCABULARY
• over-the-counter medicine
• prescription medicine

Medicines and Their Uses

When you get ill, an adult may give you medicine to help you get better. How do grown-ups know what kind of medicine you need? Where does it come from?

What are the different kinds of medicine?

There are two kinds of medicines. An **over-the-counter medicine** (OTC medicine) is a medicine that an adult can buy without a doctor's order. Drugstores and grocery stores sell OTC medicines. OTC medicines are for minor health problems, such as sore throats, colds, and headaches. Cough syrups, pain relievers, and first-aid sprays are all OTC medicines. The label on an

▼ There are thousands of over-the-counter medicines. An adult can buy these medicines without a doctor's order.

150

Career

Pharmacist

What They Do

Pharmacists fill orders for prescription medicines. They can explain how to use medicines safely. Pharmacists work in places such as drugstores, hospitals, care centers, grocery stores, and drug companies.

Education and Training

Pharmacists must graduate from college with a degree in pharmacy. While in college they usually work part-time with a pharmacist to get practice. After graduating, they must pass a state exam to be licensed.

▲ This pharmacist is filling a prescription.

OTC medicine tells what the medicine treats. It also gives directions for using the medicine. Adults must always follow these directions exactly so the medicine will be used safely.

A **prescription medicine** (prih•SKRIP•shuhn MEH•duh•suhn) is a medicine that must be ordered by a doctor. A doctor writes the order, called a prescription. Then a pharmacist fills the order.

Prescription medicines are strong and must be used correctly. That is why a doctor must order them. A doctor or pharmacist can explain exactly how to use them.

How can medicines help you?

Medicines can help you get well when you are ill. They can also help you feel better while you are ill.

Some medicines kill pathogens that can make you ill. For example, the doctor might give you a medicine called an antibiotic to kill the bacteria that cause an ear infection. An adult might put a first-aid spray on a cut to kill the pathogens on the skin near the cut.

Some medicines don't cure illnesses. But they make you feel better while you are ill. A medicine won't cure a cold or the flu. But a medicine will make a headache feel better or lower a fever caused by the flu. One medicine children your age should *not* take is aspirin. Aspirin is only safe for adults. Aspirin can cause an illness in children that can lead to death.

JOURNAL

Write about a time you took a medicine that helped you get well or feel better. First write down your health problem. Then tell which medicine you took and describe how it helped you.

▼ Antibiotics are prescription medicines that kill bacterial pathogens. This mother is giving her child an antibiotic to help cure an ear infection.

Some OTC medicines can help when you are in pain. There are many different kinds of pain relievers.

Medicines come in many different forms. There are pills, liquids, sprays, and creams. Some pills can be chewed. Other pills are swallowed whole. Some liquid medicines are meant to be swallowed. Other liquids, creams, and sprays are put directly on the area being treated. All medicines should always be given by an adult.

LESSON CHECKUP

Check Your Facts

1. Name the two kinds of medicines.
2. Which kind of medicine can an adult buy without a doctor's prescription?
3. CRITICAL THINKING Why must a pharmacist be able to read a doctor's prescription?
4. CRITICAL THINKING Can a medicine help you even if it does not cure you? Give an example.

Set Health Goals

5. Make a chart with two columns. Label one column OTC Medicines and the other Prescription Medicines. Look through magazines for ads of different kinds of medicines. Write down the name of each medicine in the correct column. Describe how each medicine should be used.

MAIN IDEA
Medicine can harm the body if it is used in the wrong way.

WHY LEARN THIS? Using medicine correctly will help you stay healthy.

VOCABULARY
• side effects

How Can Medicines Be Used Safely?

Medicines can help you when you are ill. But they can also be harmful if used in the wrong way. Always remember to follow the rules when you must use a medicine.

Refuse

Bryan started sneezing while he was playing at Linda's home. Linda offered Bryan some of her prescription allergy medicine. Tell ways that Bryan could refuse this offer. Use the steps for refusing shown on pages 246 and 247.

• • •

OPEN
PUSH DOWN & TURN
CLOSE

Safety Rules for Medicine Use

Be careful! Medicines can be dangerous.

• Only an adult should give you medicine. Never take a medicine on your own.
• Always follow the directions on the medicine label.
• Never take someone else's prescription medicine.
• Don't use old medicines. They can change when they get old and make you ill. Look at the date on the label.
• Leave the labels on all medicines.
• Keep medicines on high shelves in locked cabinets.
• Keep medicines away from small children.

◀ Medicines on store shelves have safety seals. The seals keep the medicines clean. They also stop other people from opening the medicine before someone buys it. Never buy medicine with a broken safety seal.

What should you do when you think you need a medicine? Tell an adult! An adult can help you. Before buying a medicine, an adult should check the safety seal. The seal should not be broken. An adult should give you the correct amount listed on the label, not more and not less. Watch for any side effects. **Side effects** are unwanted changes in the body caused by a medicine. If you feel any side effects, such as dizziness, itching, or a headache, tell an adult.

Activity **Follow Medicine Safety Rules**
Read the safety rules on page 154. Then look at the pictures on pages 152 and 153. How are the people in the pictures following the safety rules? What are some other safety rules you should follow?

LESSON CHECKUP

Check Your Facts

❶ What does the label on a medicine do?

❷ Why should you never use old medicines?

❸ CRITICAL THINKING Why do you need to take medicines carefully?

❹ What are side effects?

Set Health Goals

❺ Make a small poster listing the safety rules for medicine. Put it up at home where medicines are kept. How can the poster help you use medicines safely?

What Is Caffeine?

Do you enjoy iced tea, chocolate, and soft drinks? Many people do. But watch out! Some of these items contain caffeine. **Caffeine** (ka•FEEN) is a drug that speeds up the heart. Some OTC medicines contain caffeine, too.

It is not harmful to take in a small amount of caffeine. Many adults drink coffee in the morning. It helps them feel more awake. But large amounts of caffeine can make adults feel jittery. Smaller amounts of caffeine can keep children from sleeping. Too much caffeine also can strain the heart and upset the stomach.

It is hard for people who take in a lot of caffeine to stop using it. When they don't have caffeine, they can get tired and upset. They might also get headaches.

▼ Caffeine is in many drinks and foods, such as coffee, tea, and chocolate. Colas and fruit-flavored soft drinks often contain caffeine, too.

CHOCOLATE LOWFAT MILK
VITAMIN A AND D • 1/2% MILKFAT

CHOCOLATE
LOWFAT MILK
VITAMIN A AND D
1/2% MILKFAT
SEE SIDE PANEL FOR
NUTRITION INFORMATION
PINT (473 mL)

COLA
WITH NATURAL FLAVOR

◀ Does your favorite drink have caffeine? Look for drinks that are labeled "caffeine-free."

How can you avoid caffeine?

Many people drink a lot of soft drinks filled with caffeine or eat a lot of chocolate. They may not even know that they are taking in caffeine. If you know which foods have caffeine, you can avoid letting caffeine become a habit.

Chocolate, coffee, tea, and soft drinks often have caffeine. If you often eat or drink foods with caffeine, try to find foods without caffeine instead.

LESSON CHECKUP

Check Your Facts

1. List four sources of caffeine.
2. Why should people limit caffeine?
3. CRITICAL THINKING Name four drinks that don't have caffeine.

Set Health Goals

4. Cola drinks and many other soft drinks contain caffeine. Think about the drinks you've had in the last two days. List the ones that contain caffeine. If you drank several drinks with caffeine, think about what you can do to cut back on the amount of caffeine you take in each day.

MAIN IDEA
There are many harmful drugs. Some are household products that can be misused.

WHY LEARN THIS? Knowing the effects of dangerous drugs will help you avoid them.

VOCABULARY
- inhalants
- marijuana
- cocaine

Inhalants and Other Drugs

You probably know about harmful drugs such as marijuana and cocaine. But did you know that some household products are also dangerous drugs?

What are inhalants?

You walk into the bathroom and know right away that it has been cleaned recently. How do you know? You smell the fumes from the cleaning products. You can also smell fumes at a gas station.

Some people breathe in fumes from products such as spray paints, glues, markers, cleaners, and nail polish remover. These people are trying to get high. This can be very dangerous. The fumes are poisons. Substances that give off fumes are **inhalants** (in•HAY•luhnts). Labels on inhalants warn people to avoid breathing them.

▶ You must use some glues only where there is a lot of fresh air. Look at the label for warnings when you use glue.

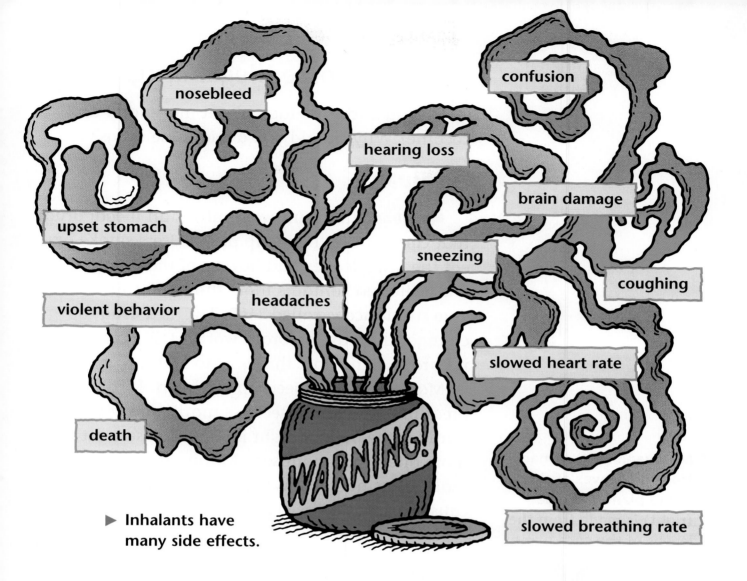

confusion

nosebleed

hearing loss

brain damage

upset stomach

sneezing

coughing

violent behavior

headaches

slowed heart rate

death

WARNING!

slowed breathing rate

▶ Inhalants have many side effects.

Inhalants distort how you see, hear, and feel. Yet many people do not think of inhalants as drugs because they are sold as common household products.

Inhaling the fumes can cause nosebleeds and headaches. Inhalants can cause brain damage. Inhalants can also slow your heart and breathing rates, which can kill you. Many people have died instantly by breathing in too much of the poisonous fumes at one time.

HUMAN BODY CONNECTION

Inhalants

Study the picture showing how inhalants affect the body. List all the organs of the body that inhalants affect. Find these organs in the human body diagrams on pages 1–15 at the front of the book.

• • •

What are some illegal drugs?

Do you know the facts about marijuana and cocaine? Why should you avoid these drugs?

Marijuana

Marijuana (mair•uh•WAH•nuh) is an illegal drug that comes from the hemp plant. Users smoke or eat the dried leaves and flowers of the plant.

Marijuana contains more than 400 substances. One substance is called THC. THC is a drug that changes the way the brain works. THC can make it hard to remember things or to learn.

Marijuana can speed up the heart. It can cause breathing problems. Because marijuana makes it hard for the body to fight infections, users get ill more often than nonusers. Marijuana can also make users nervous. When it is smoked, it can cause cancer, just as cigarettes do.

▼ Marijuana (left) is made from the leaves of the hemp plant. Cocaine (right) is made from the leaves of the coca plant.

▲ It is against the law to have, use, sell, or buy cocaine or marijuana. People who use these drugs can go to jail.

Cocaine

Cocaine (koh•KAYN) is an illegal drug made from the leaves of the coca plant. Most users sniff powdered cocaine. Some users inject it with a needle. Others smoke a strong form of cocaine, called "crack."

Cocaine can make people feel good for five to forty minutes. Then users often feel sad, nervous, confused, angry, or tired. They want to use more and more of the drug to get the same feeling back.

Cocaine users may get dizzy. Cocaine can also cause lung or brain damage. Even one use of cocaine can cause a stroke, heart attack, or death.

LESSON CHECKUP

Check Your Facts

❶ CRITICAL THINKING Why is it a good idea to turn on a fan when using certain types of glue?

❷ List two products that people misuse as inhalants.

❸ What are the harmful effects of marijuana?

❹ What are the harmful effects of cocaine?

Use Life Skills

❺ REFUSE Make a list of the harmful effects of inhalants. Keep this list in mind if anyone asks you to try an inhalant.

How Can I Say *No* to Drugs?

Sometime someone may ask you to try a drug. It is important to decide ahead of time how to refuse. To **refuse** is to say *no*.

You can practice ways to refuse with your family or friends. You might say something like, "I want to have fun, not hurt my body" or "I can have fun without it." Think of something that feels right for you. Then you will be ready if someone asks you to use drugs.

▶ Avoid dangerous drugs. Get involved in an activity you enjoy instead, like sports, music, or art.

▲ **More and more kids are saying *no* to drugs.**

LIFE SKILLS FOCUS

Communicate

Cathy's friend told her that someone on the playground had drugs. Cathy's friend said she might like to try the drugs. What should Cathy say to her friend? Use the steps for communicating shown on pages 246 and 247.

• • •

If you have doubts about saying *no*, remember how harmful drugs can be. A person can go to jail for using drugs. Drugs can change the way the brain works so a person cannot think well. They can cause illness and even death.

Some people use drugs to get high or to escape from their problems. But the high feeling doesn't last long. When that feeling wears off, users feel very low. And their problems are still there.

If someone asks you to use drugs, say *no*. Then talk to a trusted adult about it. That adult can be a family member, teacher, or doctor. You do not have to face the problem alone.

LESSON CHECKUP

Check Your Facts

❶ CRITICAL THINKING Why should you choose friends who don't use drugs?

❷ What should you remember if you have doubts about saying *no* to drugs?

❸ Whom can you talk to for help if someone asks you to try drugs?

Use Life Skills

❹ REFUSE Make a list of three ways you can say *no* to drugs.

REFUSE
Inhalants

There may be a time when someone asks you to use drugs. Know ahead of time how to refuse.

Learn This Skill

Kamil went shopping with his friend Roger. They were looking at art supplies. Roger opened a tube of glue and started sniffing it. He wanted Kamil to try it.

1. Say *no*.

"Try it. It will make you feel really weird," Roger says.
"No," says Kamil.

2. State your reasons for saying *no*.

Warning—Sniffing glue can cause brain damage.

"I don't want to fry my brain!" says Kamil.

3. Suggest something else to do.

"I want to look for some new paintbrushes," Kamil says.

4. Repeat *no*; walk away.

"I don't want to be anywhere near that stuff!" Kamil says as he walks away.

Practice This Skill

Use the steps to help you solve the problems below.

Steps for Refusing

1. Say *no*.

2. State your reasons for saying *no*.

3. Suggest something else to do.

4. Repeat *no*; walk away.

A. Marta is visiting her cousin Jane. Jane has found some pills in her mother's purse. She wants Marta to try them with her. How can Jane refuse?

B. Tara's older brother Mike wants her to try some pills that will give her more energy. How can Tara say *no*?

USE VOCABULARY

caffeine (p. 156)   inhalants (p. 158)   prescription medicine (p. 151)

cocaine (p. 161)   marijuana (p. 160)   refuse (p. 162)

drug (p. 148)   over-the-counter medicine (p. 150)   side effects (p. 155)

Use the terms above to complete the sentences. Page numbers in ( ) tell you where to look in the chapter if you need help.

1. The unwanted changes in the body caused by a medicine are _____.

2. An illegal drug made from the leaves of the coca plant is _____.

3. Something other than food that changes the way your body works is a _____.

4. Coffee and chocolate contain _____, a drug that speeds up the heart.

5. A medicine that an adult can get only with a doctor's order is a _____.

6. To say *no* is to _____.

7. An illegal drug that comes from the hemp plant is _____.

8. _____ are substances that give off dangerous fumes and are sometimes used as drugs.

9. A medicine that an adult can buy without a prescription is an _____.

CHECK YOUR FACTS

Page numbers in ( ) tell you where to look in the chapter if you need help.

10. What are medicines? (p. 148)

11. What does the label on an OTC medicine tell you? (pp. 150–151)

12. What is a prescription medicine? (p. 151)

13. List two possible side effects of medicine. (p. 155)

14. List two foods that contain caffeine. (p. 156)

15. List four side effects people may develop if they misuse the products shown here. (p. 159)

16. Which substance in marijuana changes the way the brain works? (p. 160)

17. Name a fun activity that does not include the use of drugs. (p. 162)

THINK CRITICALLY

18. Why is it important to read the labels on over-the-counter medicines?

19. Illegal drugs, such as marijuana and cocaine, are dangerous. Why do some people use them anyway?

20. Why should you read warning labels on substances such as glue?

APPLY LIFE SKILLS

21. **Refuse** You go to a party at a friend's house. After a while many of the people go into the basement to sniff glue. They tell you to try it. Everyone is looking at you, waiting for your answer. How would you refuse?

22. **Communicate** You can refuse drugs when someone offers them to you. But how can you communicate to others that they should never offer drugs to you?

Promote Health **Home and Community**

1. Look at the place where your family stores medicines. Is it safe, according to the Safety Rules for Medicine Use? If so, why? If not, where can your family store the medicine more safely?
2. Make a poster that tells other kids to stay off drugs. Hang your poster up in the classroom.

Activities

Safety Cartoons

At Home • Look at the Safety Rules for Medicine Use shown here. Pick one. Then draw a cartoon to illustrate the rule. Print the rule at the bottom of the drawing. Display your cartoon with those of your classmates.

Drug Messages

With a Partner • How do ads and TV programs show the use of alcohol and other drugs? Watch several TV programs and ads. Take notes. What messages do these shows and ads send to kids about alcohol and other drugs? Report to your class.

Safety Rules for Medicine Use

- Only an adult should give you medicine. Never take a medicine on your own.
- Always follow the directions on the medicine label.
- Never take someone else's prescription medicine.
- Don't use old medicines. They can change when they get old and make you ill. Look at the date on the label.
- Leave the labels on all medicines.
- Keep medicines on high shelves in locked cabinets.
- Keep medicines away from small children.

Antidrug Party

With a Group • Plan a party or rally at your school to celebrate saying *no* to drugs. Think of fun activities for the celebration. Include music and food. Ask speakers to take part. Make posters and buttons with antidrug messages. Show that you can have lots of fun without drugs—and that most kids don't want to use them.

Talk to Your Pharmacist

On Your Own • Talk with a pharmacist about his or her job. What do pharmacists do each day? Is the work fun? How did he or she become a pharmacist? Write down what the pharmacist says, or record the interview. Share what you find out with your class.

Multiple Choice

Choose the letter of the correct answer.

1. Drugs change the way the body ____.
   a. looks
   b. works
   c. tastes
   d. smells

2. Pharmacists prepare ____ medicines.
   a. no
   b. OTC
   c. prescription
   d. all

3. Caffeine is a drug that ____ the heart.
   a. speeds up
   b. destroys
   c. slows down
   d. copies

4. The fumes that come from inhalants are ____.
   a. poisons
   b. medicines
   c. safe
   d. air

5. It is important to decide ahead of time how to ____ drugs.
   a. accept
   b. buy
   c. try
   d. refuse

Modified True or False

Write *true* or *false*. If a sentence is false, replace the underlined term to make the sentence true.

6. Drugs can change the way people <u>think</u>, feel, and act.

7. A <u>doctor</u> uses a prescription to make your medicine.

8. Some over-the-counter medicines <u>relieve pain</u> or stop coughs.

9. Never take someone else's <u>medicine</u>.

10. Always read the <u>safety seal</u> on a medicine.

11. Caffeine is in coffee and some <u>soft drinks</u>.

12. Marijuana is an illegal drug that comes from the <u>corn</u> plant.

13. Cocaine use can cause <u>brain</u> damage.

Short Answer

Write a complete sentence to answer each question.

14. What kinds of health problems do over-the-counter medicines treat?

15. Why should you always leave the labels on medicines?

16. How can you cut down the amount of caffeine in your diet?

17. List some of the harmful effects that marijuana can have on the body.

18. How can inhalants harm the body?

Essay

Write paragraphs to answer each item.

19. What is the safe way to take medicine?

20. What could happen to someone who uses drugs?

CHAPTER 7

Avoiding Alcohol and Tobacco

Project

MAKE A MODEL With a small group, make a life-size model of the human body on cardboard or drawing paper. On the model, draw the body organs that are affected by alcohol and tobacco.

For other activities, visit the Harcourt Brace Internet site.
http://www.hbschool.com

Learning About Tobacco and Alcohol

You may have seen adults using tobacco (tuh•BA•koh) or alcohol (AL•kuh•hawl) products. You may think these products are safe to use. But did you know that tobacco and alcohol are drugs? Drugs change the way a person's body works. Tobacco and alcohol can harm a person who uses them.

Why are tobacco and alcohol drugs?

The tobacco in cigarettes and cigars comes from the leaves of the tobacco plant. Tobacco that is smoked in pipes is made from the same leaves. Other tobacco products are chewed or sucked. These products look different, but they all contain tobacco.

Types of Tobacco

snuff

smoking tobacco

chewing tobacco

► Smoking tobacco includes cigarettes, cigars, and loose tobacco smoked in pipes. Snuff and chewing tobacco are smokeless tobacco products.

All tobacco products have nicotine. **Nicotine** (NIH•kuh•teen) is the drug in tobacco. People who use tobacco products are putting this drug into their bodies. Like other drugs, nicotine causes changes in the body. Some drugs, such as the medicines a doctor gives, cause good changes. The changes nicotine causes are not good.

Nicotine is a poison. Farmers and gardeners use it to kill insects on plants. Nicotine can kill people, too. A small amount of pure nicotine—about a tablespoonful—can kill an adult. Smaller amounts harm the body. Many tobacco users know that tobacco can make them ill. But the nicotine also makes them keep wanting tobacco.

Alcohol is also a drug. Like nicotine, alcohol causes changes in the user's body. Alcohol is found in drinks such as beer, wine, and mixed drinks. Some adult liquid medicines also have alcohol. Most children's medicines are made so that they have no alcohol.

Drinking alcohol is harmful, especially for children. Using alcohol for many years also causes health problems. Some people who use alcohol can't stop using it.

Types of Alcohol

beer

wine

mixed drinks

LESSON CHECKUP

Check Your Facts

❶ What drug is found in beer, wine, and mixed drinks?

❷ CRITICAL THINKING Most people know that tobacco and alcohol can harm the body. Why do people still use these drugs?

❸ What drug is found in tobacco?

Set Health Goals

❹ List three reasons to avoid using tobacco and alcohol. Then write ways you can keep from using these drugs.

How Tobacco Affects the Body

All kinds of tobacco have nicotine in them. Nicotine can get into the body through smoke or through juice from the tobacco.

Nicotine can cause addiction. **Addiction** (uh•DIK•shuhn) makes people keep using drugs even when they want to stop. Nicotine affects the way the brain works. It also makes the heart beat faster and harder and can cause heart disease. Tobacco users sometimes die from heart disease.

How do people use tobacco?

Most people who use tobacco smoke it. Some smoke it in a pipe or cigar. Most smoke it in cigarettes. To make smoking tobacco, the green leaves of the tobacco plant are dried. Then the dried tobacco leaves are shredded. Pipe tobacco and the tobacco in cigars look similar to the tobacco in cigarettes. The outside of a cigar is made from tobacco leaves that have not been shredded.

Some people chew small wads—or plugs—of moist tobacco. This moist tobacco for chewing is called **chewing tobacco**.

Some people put clumps of powdered or shredded tobacco between their cheeks and gums and suck it. This tobacco is called **smokeless tobacco**, or snuff.

◀ Some people think chewing tobacco is safer than smoking it. It's not! Nicotine in the tobacco still gets into the body.

How does tobacco affect the body?

Tobacco smoke has more than 4,000 different things in it. Many of these things can harm a person's body. You have already learned how harmful nicotine is. Tobacco smoke also contains tar. **Tar** is a dark, sticky substance. It coats the lungs and air passages of people who breathe in tobacco smoke. Tar makes breathing hard. It can also lead to lung diseases and **cancer** (KAN•ser), a disease that makes cells grow wildly. Other problems that tobacco causes are shown in the diagram below.

Your Lungs

Your lungs are part of your respiratory system. To learn more about how your lungs get air in and out of your body, turn to pages 12 and 13. How would tobacco smoke travel through your body?

Mouth Using tobacco causes bad breath. Smokeless tobacco stains the users' teeth. It makes their gums and lips crack and bleed. It can lead to mouth cancer.

Throat Smoking causes coughing. It can cause throat cancer.

Heart Nicotine makes blood vessels shrink. The heart beats faster and harder. This can lead to heart disease.

Lungs Tar coats smokers' lungs. They have trouble getting enough air. Smokers may die from lung cancer or other lung diseases.

▲ This girl isn't smoking. But smoke from the pipe and cigar in the room is affecting her. The ETS harms her eyes, nose, throat, and lungs.

LIFE SKILLS
FOCUS

Communicate
Martha knows that tobacco can harm her body. She wants to write a poem to tell others about the dangers of tobacco. How can Martha use her communication skills to write this poem? Use the steps for communicating shown on pages 246 and 247.

• • •

How is tobacco harmful to people who don't use it?

Have you ever been in a room with someone who was smoking? If so, you could probably see smoke in the air.

The smoke that fills a room when someone is smoking is called **environmental tobacco smoke** (in•vy•ruhn•MEN•tuhl tuh•BA•koh SMOHK), or *ETS*. Some ETS comes directly from burning cigarettes, pipes, or cigars. The rest is smoke that is breathed out by smokers.

ETS carries poisons that can hurt people who breathe it—even if they don't smoke themselves. Some people live or work in places filled with ETS. These people may become ill more often than people who live and work in smoke-free places.

Adults and children who live in homes with ETS may get more colds, coughs, and sore throats than those who do not live with smokers. Nonsmokers who breathe ETS for many years may get the same diseases as smokers. They have a higher risk of getting lung diseases, heart diseases, and cancer than people who live or work in smoke-free places.

One way you can avoid ETS is to sit in the nonsmoking section of a restaurant. You can have an adult politely ask people sitting near you not to smoke. If necessary, leave a room where many people are smoking.

JOURNAL

Have you ever been in a room where ETS bothered you? In your Health Journal, write about ways other people's smoke has affected you. Tell what you might have done to solve the problem.

Cough! Cough! Please don't smoke!

Activity **Avoid ETS** Imagine you are in a place where people are smoking. Suggest ways you could protect your health from ETS. Tell what you might do or say. Be sure your suggestions are polite!

LESSON CHECKUP

Check Your Facts

1 List four products that have tobacco in them.

2 Name two substances in tobacco smoke that can harm you.

3 CRITICAL THINKING How can you be harmed by tobacco even if you don't smoke?

4 How does nicotine affect the heart of a tobacco user?

Set Health Goals

5 List three things you like to do that require a strong heart and lungs. How would smoking affect your ability to do these activities?

MAIN IDEA Any amount of alcohol is dangerous for young people.

WHY LEARN THIS? Knowing how dangerous alcohol is will help you refuse it.

VOCABULARY
• bloodstream
• alcoholism

How Alcohol Affects the Body

Drinking alcohol regularly can be harmful. An adult who drinks too much alcohol can have serious health problems. Alcohol is especially harmful to young people, because they are still growing.

What happens when a person drinks alcohol?

Most food you eat has to be digested. It takes several hours for food to travel through your digestive system. Chemicals there break food into nutrients. Nutrients move from your digestive system to your bloodstream. Your **bloodstream** is the blood flowing through your body. Look on pages 10–11 to see how your bloodstream carries nutrients to all parts of your body.

Alcohol doesn't need to be digested. It begins to enter the bloodstream as soon as it reaches the stomach and small intestine. Just minutes after a person drinks alcohol, the alcohol has traveled to all parts of the body.

Alcohol slows down the brain's ability to collect information. It also slows down the messages the brain sends to other parts of the body. After drinking alcohol, the user might find it hard to walk or speak. He or she cannot see clearly. Making decisions isn't easy. Paying attention or remembering things becomes hard, too.

Alcohol can even change the user's personality. Different people change in different ways. Some people get silly when they drink alcohol. Others feel sad. Still others become loud or angry.

▲ Alcohol enters the bloodstream from the stomach and small intestine. Within a few minutes it reaches the brain and other parts of the body.

Often people who drink too much feel sleepy. They may even fall asleep while driving. People who drink too much may also get dizzy. Sometimes the dizziness is so bad it makes them ill. They may still feel ill the next day. Many people get headaches after they drink. These headaches can last a few hours or a whole day.

Alcohol in the Body

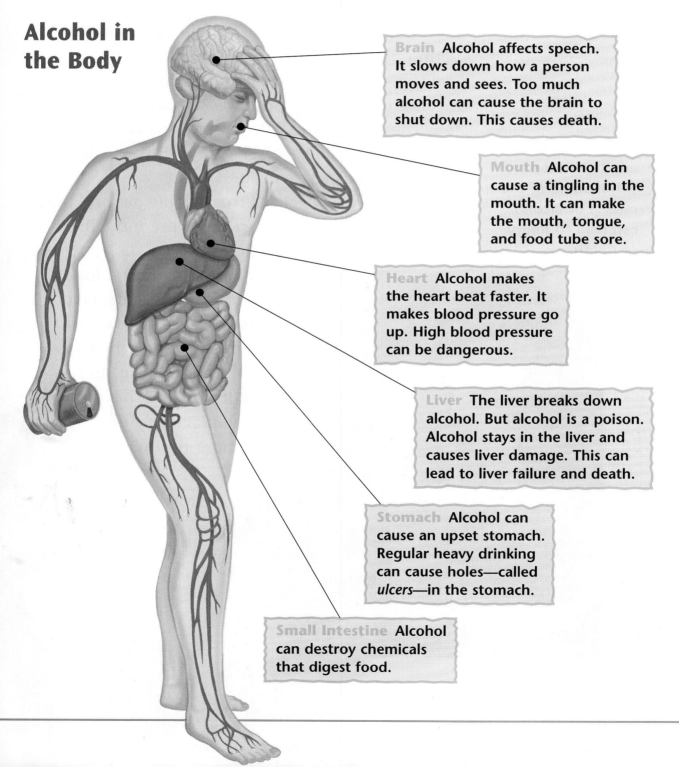

Brain Alcohol affects speech. It slows down how a person moves and sees. Too much alcohol can cause the brain to shut down. This causes death.

Mouth Alcohol can cause a tingling in the mouth. It can make the mouth, tongue, and food tube sore.

Heart Alcohol makes the heart beat faster. It makes blood pressure go up. High blood pressure can be dangerous.

Liver The liver breaks down alcohol. But alcohol is a poison. Alcohol stays in the liver and causes liver damage. This can lead to liver failure and death.

Stomach Alcohol can cause an upset stomach. Regular heavy drinking can cause holes—called *ulcers*—in the stomach.

Small Intestine Alcohol can destroy chemicals that digest food.

How is alcohol harmful?

Even a small amount of alcohol can be harmful—especially for young people. Alcohol prevents normal brain and body growth. That's one reason why it is against the law for young people to buy or drink alcohol. A young person will feel the effects of alcohol more quickly than an adult. No amount of alcohol is safe for a young person to drink.

People who drink even small amounts of alcohol are at risk for injuries. Sometimes they fall. They might run into things. Alcohol users who drive can cause crashes that hurt or kill themselves or people around them.

Alcohol can affect the way people act and treat others. People who drink alcohol are more likely to feel angry and cause fights.

Some people drink a lot of alcohol for many years. Over time heavy drinking can hurt almost every part of the body. Alcohol can kill brain cells, making it hard for the user to think clearly or to remember things.

▼ Alcohol affects adults in different ways. Some of the effects of alcohol can lead to injury or death.

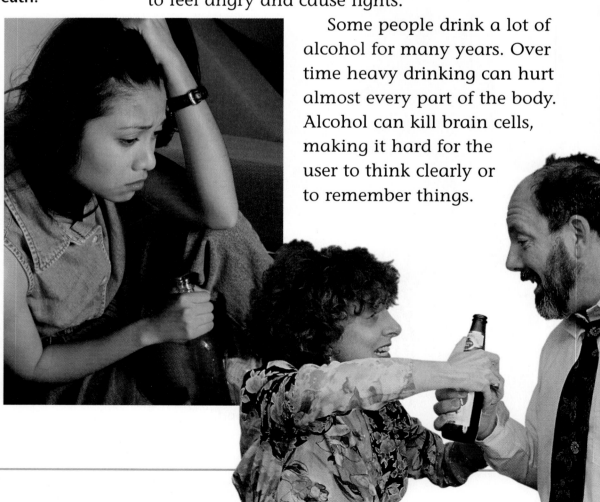

The liver is an organ that is often damaged by alcohol. The liver removes poisons from the blood. It does other jobs as well. Alcohol can scar the liver. Then the liver can't clean the blood. The liver may stop working. This can cause death.

Finally, for some people, drinking alcohol can lead to a disease called **alcoholism** (AL•kuh•haw•lih•zuhm). Alcoholics, or people with alcoholism, can't stop using alcohol. They know alcohol causes problems for them and for people they care about. But they still need to drink it. If they don't, they become nervous and ill.

Myth: Alcoholics wear dirty clothing and drink in alleys.

Fact: Only about 6 out of 100 alcoholics in the United States are like this. Most alcoholics appear to live normal lives.

▼ **People who drink and then drive are responsible for many car crashes.**

LESSON CHECKUP

Check Your Facts

1. Why is alcohol especially dangerous for young people?
2. Why is drinking alcohol a safety risk?
3. CRITICAL THINKING Why might a person who uses alcohol have trouble learning?
4. List three organs that are affected by alcohol use.

Use Life Skills

5. MANAGE STRESS Some adults drink alcohol because they don't know other ways to relax. List three healthful things you do to relax.

Refusing to Use Alcohol and Tobacco

MAIN IDEA
To stay safe from alcohol and tobacco, avoid places where people use these drugs. Plan ahead by thinking of ways to say *no*.

WHY LEARN THIS? Avoiding alcohol and tobacco is an important skill that will protect your health and safety.

You may hear people say "Just say *no* to drugs!" Maybe you think it's not always that easy—especially when friends urge you to smoke or drink. But saying *no* is important. That little word could save your life!

What are some laws about the use of alcohol and tobacco?

It is against the law for young people to buy alcohol and tobacco. You must be at least 21 years old to buy alcohol. In most places you must be 18 years old or older to buy tobacco products. It is against the law for anyone your age to buy alcohol or tobacco.

Laws also protect people from the harmful effects of ETS. Most government buildings are smoke-free. Many other places, such as restaurants, have nonsmoking areas.

The government requires warning labels on alcohol and tobacco packaging that tell about the dangers of using these products. The government hopes warnings will help people avoid the dangers of these products.

◀ **You can choose many healthful drinks.**

How can you stay safe from alcohol and tobacco?

Many adults use more alcohol and tobacco than they really want to. Using these drugs has become a habit they can't quit. Understanding why people use these drugs can help you decide never to start using them.

Many people first try alcohol and tobacco when they are young. They think it will make them look grown up, but many adults don't use these drugs. You may be afraid to say *no* if your friends urge you to try them. To stay safe from alcohol and tobacco, stay away from places where people use them. Find friends who don't want to use these products.

Some people use alcohol and tobacco because ads make using alcohol and tobacco products look fun. The truth is that these products are dangerous.

LIFE SKILLS FOCUS

Refuse Bill and his friend, Lyle, find an open bottle of alcohol at Lyle's house. Lyle tells Bill he has heard it is fun to drink alcohol. Lyle wants to try the alcohol. He wants Bill to try it too. How can Bill use what he knows about alcohol to refuse to try it? Use the steps for refusing shown on pages 246 and 247.

Career

Health Spokesperson

What They Do
Community health spokespersons get information about health-care groups. They tell the public about health information by sending it to newspapers and to TV and radio stations. They also hold events such as health fairs to make people aware of health-care information.

Education and Training
Some community health spokespersons earn college degrees in public relations or health education. Others start as journalists. Some train by getting jobs with public health departments.

How can you say *no* to alcohol and tobacco?

It's important to decide ahead of time that you don't want to use alcohol and tobacco. Then you'll be ready if someone wants you to try them.

skate

read

sing

Think of some ways you can say *no*. Here are ideas you might try.

- Say *no*, and walk away. You don't have to explain why.
- Make a face. Say, "It doesn't taste good."
- Look surprised. Say, "That's against the law."
- Say, "It's against my family's rules."
- Say, "No, thanks." Then change the subject.
- Laugh and say, "I want to have fun, not hurt my body."
- Look at a clock. Say, "I have to get going."
- Say, "I can have fun without it."
- Say, "I need to be at my best for sports"— or for whatever activities you enjoy.

Practice with your family ways to say *no*. Or practice with a friend who has also decided not to use alcohol or tobacco. Try out different ways. Choose the ways you are most comfortable with. When the time comes to say *no*, one of them is sure to feel right. Remember, when you say *no*, you might be saving your health—or your life!

Activity **Say *Yes* to Good Health** When you say *no* to alcohol and tobacco, you can say *yes* to the many activities you enjoy. Without alcohol or nicotine your mind and body work at their best. What activities would you like to say *yes* to? List five things you like to do. Then list ways in which using alcohol or tobacco could affect these activities.

LESSON CHECKUP

Check Your Facts

❶ What are two laws about alcohol and tobacco?

❷ How can you avoid people who want you to use alcohol and tobacco?

❸ CRITICAL THINKING Why is it important to say *no* to alcohol and tobacco?

Use Life Skills

❹ REFUSE Think of a time when you refused to do something a friend wanted you to do. How did you say *no*? What did you think about when you said it? How was that situation like saying *no* to alcohol and tobacco?

REFUSE ALCOHOL and Tobacco

What will you do if someone asks you to use alcohol or tobacco? Practice learning how to say *no*. Then you'll be ready to refuse to use these drugs.

Learn This Skill

Amy is at Pam's house. Pam's big sister smokes cigarettes. Pam thinks it looks cool. She wants Amy to try it with her. How can Amy say *no*?

Say, "It's against the law."

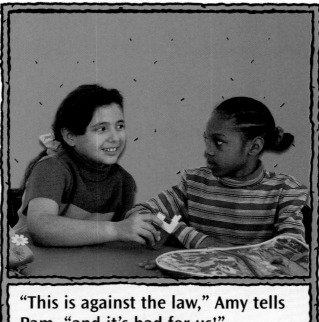

"This is against the law," Amy tells Pam, "and it's bad for us!"

Say, "I don't want to get into trouble or get sick."

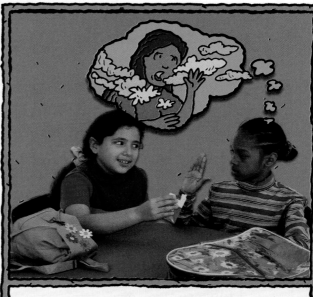

"It won't hurt us," says Pam. "We'll be in big trouble if we get caught," Amy says. "We could get really sick."

Suggest something else to do.

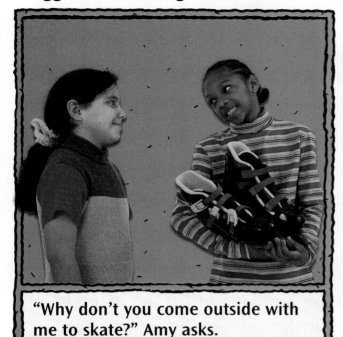

"Why don't you come outside with me to skate?" Amy asks.

Walk away.

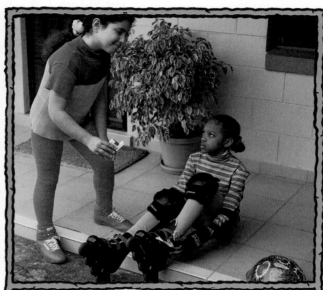

"Just try one," Pam says.
"I am not going to try cigarettes," Amy says. "I'm going skating."

Practice This Skill

Use these ideas to help you solve the problems.

Ways to Refuse

- Say, "It's against the law."
- Say, "I don't want to get into trouble or get sick."
- Suggest something else to do.
- Walk away.

A. Derrel's friends say that the tobacco some baseball players chew doesn't hurt the lungs. Help Derrel use refusal skills to end this discussion.

B. Cheryl's friends want to go to a park to play. Cheryl knows that people who use drugs hang out there. How could Cheryl say she doesn't want to go?

USE VOCABULARY

addiction (p. 174)

alcohol (p. 173)

alcoholism (p. 181)

bloodstream (p. 178)

cancer (p. 175)

chewing tobacco (p. 174)

environmental tobacco
   smoke (p. 176)

nicotine (p. 173)

smokeless tobacco (p. 174)

tar (p. 175)

Use the terms above to complete the sentences. Page numbers in ( ) tell you where to look in the chapter if you need help.

1. It is hard to quit using tobacco because the nicotine in tobacco causes ____.

2. ____ is a disease in which people "need" alcohol.

3. ____ is a poisonous substance found in all tobacco products.

4. The drug ____ is found in beverages such as beer, wine, and whiskey.

5. The smoke in the air that comes from burning cigarettes is ____.

6. ____ is a dark, sticky substance that coats the lungs of smokers.

7. People who put moist tobacco in their mouths are using ____.

8. Alcohol is carried through the ____ to the brain and the heart.

9. ____ is a dry, powdered form of tobacco that is held between the cheek and gum.

10. A disease that makes cells grow wildly is ____.

CHECK YOUR FACTS

Page numbers in ( ) tell you where to look in the chapter if you need help.

11. Using the diagram, choose three organs that are affected by alcohol and describe the effects. (p. 179)

12. How is nicotine harmful to the body? (pp. 173, 175)

13. How does ETS affect nonsmokers? (pp. 176–177)

14. What law about alcohol and tobacco is the most important for young people? (p. 182)

THINK CRITICALLY

15. You hear someone say, "People who don't like alcohol and tobacco shouldn't use them. But they shouldn't try to stop others from using them." Do you agree or not? Explain why.

16. Why do you think advertisers make ads for alcohol and tobacco that show people using these products while having fun?

APPLY LIFE SKILLS

17. **Refuse** A good friend of yours is excited. She has met some older students she really likes. She wants you to go to the mall with her to meet these older students. You go, but as you get near the mall entrance, you see that they are smoking. What would you do?

18. **Communicate** You're at a friend's house after school one day. Your friend's parents aren't home, and your friend says, "Want to try something?" He goes into the refrigerator and takes out a beer. He tells you, "Drink it. It will make you feel great." What would you say?

Promote Health — Home and Community

1. Is there a place your family goes to, such as a favorite restaurant, that has environmental tobacco smoke? Discuss ETS with your family. Think of ways your family can avoid ETS there and at other places.

2. A federal law says alcohol can not be sold to anyone under 21 years old. However, states, towns, and counties can have other laws about selling and using alcohol. Make a poster showing local alcohol laws. Display the poster someplace where people in your community can see it.

Activities

Conduct an Interview

At Home • With your family's permission, talk with some people who use tobacco. Ask them how and when they started using tobacco. Ask whether they would like to change the way they use it. Ask them what advice they would offer to someone your age who wants to try tobacco.

Please Don't Smoke

With a Partner • Think of polite ways to ask people near you not to smoke. Present your ideas in a cartoon booklet.

Have a Heart

On Your Own • Cut a large heart shape from construction paper. Use it to record all the activities you do in a day. At the end of the day, list the ways your heart helped you. Write what you have learned about decisions you can make that will help keep your heart healthy.

Body Parts Skit

With a Team • Put on a body parts skit. Have people in the skit play different body parts. Each character can explain how alcohol and tobacco affect the body part.

Multiple Choice

Choose the letter of the correct answer.

1. Nicotine is found in _____ products.
   a. tar b. alcohol
   c. tobacco d. drug

2. Nonsmokers can get ill by breathing _____.
   a. ETS b. nicotine
   c. alcohol d. oxygen

3. Alcohol makes the brain _____.
   a. more alert b. slow down
   c. speed up d. bigger

4. Alcoholism is _____.
   a. a disease
   b. a drug
   c. fear of drinking
   d. dislike of alcohol

5. If offered tobacco, _____.
   a. pretend to smoke, but don't
   b. give it a try
   c. impress people with how much you can smoke
   d. say *no* and leave

Modified True or False

Write *true* or *false*. If a sentence is false, replace the underlined term to make the sentence true.

6. Nicotine and alcohol are both <u>drugs</u>.

7. Nicotine causes <u>addiction</u>.

8. ETS affects <u>nonsmokers</u>.

9. Alcohol reaches the heart through the <u>bloodstream</u>.

10. A person's ability to speak and walk are affected by <u>tobacco</u> products.

11. The <u>liver</u> can be scarred by alcohol.

12. <u>A small</u> amount of alcohol is safe for adults to drink.

13. It is harder to <u>keep</u> using alcohol and tobacco than it is to never start at all.

Short Answer

Write a complete sentence to answer each question.

14. What are three tobacco products?

15. What are some health risks caused by smokeless and chewing tobacco?

16. How does alcohol affect the actions of people who drink it?

17. Why can even small amounts of alcohol be harmful to young people?

18. Why is it against the law for people to drive after they drink more than a small amount of alcohol?

Essay

Write paragraphs to answer each item.

19. Explain why using tobacco in ANY form is harmful.

20. Explain why young people who refuse to use drugs are more grown up than those who use them.

CHAPTER 8

Keeping Safe

SAFETY COLLAGE As you read through this chapter, you will learn tips to help keep you safe at home, at school, and at play. Make a collage showing ways to stay safe. You can use photos, draw pictures, or cut out pictures from magazines.

For other activities, visit the Harcourt Brace Internet site. http://www.hbschool.com

Being Responsible for Your Safety

Who is responsible for your safety?

Many people help protect you and keep you safe. At home your family watches over you. Family members have a responsibility, or duty, to protect you.

At school the principal and teachers share the duty of keeping the students safe. Others may also help. The bus driver and the crossing guard help you get safely to school. A hall monitor may help keep the school hallways safe and peaceful. All these people help protect you from harm.

You also have a duty. Your important job is to keep yourself safe. The person most responsible for your safety is **YOU**.

Who is most responsible for your safety? You!

family

bus driver

194

What does it mean to be careful?

Being careful means that you know and follow safety rules. **Safety rules** are rules that help protect you from injury. An **injury** (INJ•ree) is harm done to a person's body.

One safety rule is to watch out for hazards wherever you are. A **hazard** (HA•zerd) is a danger, like broken glass on a playground, that could lead to an injury. Another safety rule is to obey the limits set by adults. A **limit** (LIH•muht) is a point at which you must stop. Your family probably sets limits by letting you play only in places that are safe.

▼ The pictures show some of the people who help you stay safe. How does each person help protect you? Who is missing? (**Hint**: Who is most responsible for your safety?)

coach

principal

crossing guard

teacher

How can you stay safe on the way to and from school?

These safety rules can help keep you safe.

When riding the bus,

- do not bother the driver.
- stay in your seat.
- talk quietly—never yell.

When riding in a car,

- always buckle your safety belt.
- sit in the backseat. It is the safest place for passengers. A **passenger** (PA•suhn•jer) is someone riding in a car or bus with a driver.

When walking,

- stay on the sidewalk.
- walk with others, not alone.
- cross streets only at corners or crosswalks. Before crossing, STOP, LOOK, and LISTEN. THINK about what might be a hazard.

▼ The pictures show ways to keep safe on the road and at school. Which safety rules do you follow?

Talk quietly.

Use safety belts.

How can you stay safe at school?

At school everyone must obey the safety rules. Otherwise, both you and others could get injured.

- Never run in the hallways.
- Don't stand on chairs or other furniture.
- Follow game rules on the playground.
- Don't push or shove.

Sometimes the best safety rule is to get help. Here are two times to get adult help.

- If you see a fight, tell an adult.
- If you see a weapon, such as a gun or a knife, get an adult right away.

JOURNAL

In your Health Journal, write about how you go to and from school. What are the hazards along the way? What safety rules can you follow to make your trip safer?

Use sidewalks.

Walk in school.

LESSON CHECKUP

Check Your Facts

1. Who is most responsible for your safety?
2. Why do you need to watch out for hazards?
3. CRITICAL THINKING What are five safety rules that you follow at school? Name at least two that are not mentioned in this lesson.

Use Life Skills

4. MAKE DECISIONS Imagine that you walk to school with two friends who don't follow safety rules. How could you use the decision-making steps to help them make safer choices? Look on pages 246 and 247 if you need help.

Safety Around Strangers and Bullies

MAIN IDEA You can take steps to keep safe around strangers and bullies.

WHY LEARN THIS? What you learn can help protect you from strangers and bullies.

VOCABULARY
• stranger
• trusted adult
• bully

What should you do if you are approached by a stranger?

You need to be very careful around strangers. A **stranger** (STRAYN•jer) is someone you don't know well. You must stay away from people you don't know because some strangers are not safe to be around.

If a stranger approaches, or comes near you, look for a trusted adult to help you. A **trusted adult** is a grown-up you know well or an adult in a responsible position. Usually your family members, teachers, good neighbors, security people, and police officers are adults you can trust.

Strangers in Cars Suppose someone in a car stops next to you and calls to you. What should you do? Follow the rules listed here to be safe.

• Ignore him or her.

• Leave the area. Keep walking, cross the street, or change directions.

• If the stranger gets out of the car or follows you, run away, and yell, "I don't know you!"

Four Safety Rules About Strangers

1. Stay more than an arm's reach away from a stranger.
2. Don't talk to a stranger.
3. Don't take anything from a stranger— not even your own things.
4. Don't go anywhere with a stranger.

 Activity **Review Safety Rules** Read this list of safety rules about strangers. What other rules can you add to the list?

Strangers Asking for Help Adults ask other adults, not children, for help. If someone you don't know well asks you for help, here's what to do.

- Tell him or her NO.
- Leave the area.
- Tell a trusted adult.

The Most Important Rule There is one rule that will help you keep safe from strangers. *Always* tell your family where you are going and whom you are with. Don't go *anywhere* with *anyone* unless your family knows about it.

Career

Security Guard

What They Do

Security guards work in banks, amusement parks, museums, and other places where people shop, visit, or live. They help protect people and property. They watch for troublemakers or criminals. They answer questions and help people who are lost or in trouble. Police officers may act as security guards during crowded events such as parades.

Education and Training

Most security guards are high school graduates. They must have good character and have committed no crimes on record. They usually get special training in giving first aid and handling emergencies. They are also trained to stop or capture people who break laws. Some are trained on the job.

This girl cannot find her parents. Why is she asking a security guard for help?

What can you do if someone tries to bully you?

A **bully** is someone who hurts or frightens others, especially those who are smaller or weaker. Here is a story about a bully from one student's journal.

One day a new boy named Justin came to school. He looked mad and did not smile. He was bigger than all the other boys.

The trouble started after school. Justin started calling me names. He pushed me against the wall. I got away. My friends saw it. We told Ms. Díaz, our teacher.

The next day, our class talked about bullies. We drew pictures of what bullies do. We made "No Bullying" posters from our pictures. We acted out ways to get along with others instead of bullying.

It turns out that Justin and I both like to play baseball. We're not really good friends or anything, but he's teaching me how to slide into home plate.

Communicate
Laura teases Helen because she has freckles and red hair. Helen feels sad when someone teases her. Role-play with a partner to show how Helen could handle how she feels about being teased. Use the steps for communicating shown on pages 246 and 247.

Remember the following safety rules if you have to face a bully.

- Ignore mean remarks. You are not the problem. The bully's problems are causing his or her actions.
- Don't talk back or fight. Walk away.
- Get help if the bully follows you.
- Stay with others. Bullies pick on people who are alone.
- Choose friends who stay away from bullies.

▶ Finding common interests is one way to get along with a bully.

LESSON CHECKUP

Check Your Facts

1. What should you do if a stranger approaches you?

2. CRITICAL THINKING Why should you always tell your family where you are going and whom you are with?

3. What should you do if someone tries to bully you?

4. CRITICAL THINKING Describe a situation in which you should ask a trusted adult for help.

Use Life Skills

5. REFUSE Suppose you see an adult stranger looking for a lost dog. The adult asks you to help find the dog. What should you do?

RESOLVE CONFLICTS
Using Negotiation

Conflicts happen, even among friends. Knowing ways to work things out will help you get along better.

Learn This Skill

Pascal, Susan, and Keith want to play table tennis. There are only two paddles. They argue about who gets to play. How can they negotiate, or work together, to resolve their conflict?

1. Agree that you disagree.

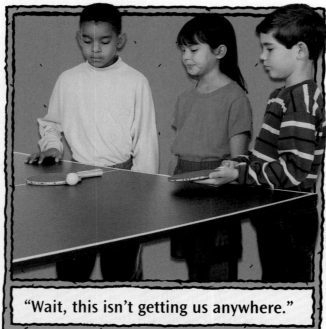

"Wait, this isn't getting us anywhere."

2. Listen to each other.

"Let's face it—we can't all play at once. We need a fair way to decide who gets to play."

3. Negotiate.

"We could flip a coin, and the winner will play first."
"We could draw names from a hat."
"We could go in alphabetical order."

4. Compromise on a solution.

"Let's take three pieces of paper and write our names on them. Keith can mix them up, and Pascal will pick two names to play first."

Practice This Skill

Use this summary to help you solve the problems below.

Resolve Conflicts

1. Agree that you disagree.

2. Listen to each other.

3. Negotiate.

4. Compromise on a solution.

A. You and a friend decide to play a game. You both want to go first. Use what you know about resolving conflicts to solve this problem.

B. Your friend comes home with you after school. You want to play outside, but your friend would rather play computer games. What do you do?

MAIN IDEA You and your family can take steps to protect yourselves from fire, electricity, and poisons.

WHY LEARN THIS? What you learn can help keep you and your family safe at home.

VOCABULARY
• emergency
• poison

Safety at Home—Fire, Electricity, and Poisons

How can you stay safe in a fire?

The smoke alarm beeps. You smell smoke. Someone yells, "Fire!" A house fire is an **emergency** (ih•MER•juhnt•see)—a situation in which help is needed right away. To be prepared, you and your family can work together to make an escape plan and practice fire drills.

Make an Escape Plan Draw a map of your home. Draw arrows to show two ways to escape from each room. Windows or doors may be used. Make sure everyone knows both ways to escape. Choose a place outdoors to meet after you escape. The meeting place could be a tree or a neighbor's house.

Practice Fire Drills Here's how to escape a fire.

- **Crawl out quickly.** If you notice fire or smoke, drop down and stay low. Keep below the smoke so you don't breathe it. As you crawl, hold a damp cloth over your mouth and nose. Breathe through the cloth.

- **Warn others.** Shout or blow a whistle loudly to alert your family.

- **Follow the escape paths.** Crawl along the walls if the smoke is too thick to see through. If you come to a closed door, feel it with your hand. If the door is cool, you may open it.

HUMAN BODY
CONNECTION

Smoke Alarm
Look at the human respiratory system on pages 12 and 13. Find out where smoke goes in your body if you breathe it in during a fire. Make a list of the organs that are affected by smoke.

If it is warm, stop.
Do not open the door. Escape using a different path.

- **Go to the meeting place.** This is very important. If you don't come, your family may think you are trapped inside the house.

- **Call 911 or the fire department.** You need to know your address to tell the 911 operator. The operator may also ask how big the fire is, what is burning, and whether anyone is trapped inside. Don't hang up before the operator does.

- **Stop, drop, and roll.** If your clothing catches fire, stop and drop to the ground. Roll slowly back and forth to smother the fire.

▶ Smoke, heat, and dangerous gases rise and reach the smoke detector. The smoke sets off a loud alarm signal. When you hear the alarm, get low and crawl. Cover your mouth and nose with a damp cloth. The cloth helps keep out the smoke.

DO	DON'T
DO hold the plug.	DON'T hold the cord.
DO use only one plug in each outlet.	DON'T overload extension cords.
DO use wall outlets properly.	DON'T poke things into outlets.

Activity **Identify Safety Rules** The pictures in the chart show some ways to be safe or unsafe with electricity. What other safety rules can you add?

How can you stay safe around electricity?

Lighting rooms. Drying hair. Keeping food cold. Electricity is very useful. But it also can be dangerous. Practice the safety rules shown and listed here when you use electricity.

- Electrical cords are safe to use only when they aren't cracked or frayed. If you can see the wires inside a cord, don't use it.
- Hold the plug, not the cord, when plugging or unplugging things.
- If there are young children in your home, an adult may want to put covers over the outlets that are not in use.
- Use only one plug in each outlet.
- Never run cords under a carpet.
- To prevent a shock, never plug in or turn on electrical things when you have wet hands.
- NEVER touch outdoor power lines, especially fallen power lines.

How can you stay safe around poisons?

A **poison** (POY•zuhn) is a substance that causes illness or death when it gets in the body. Many useful home products become poisons if they are not used in the right way.

Many products must not be breathed, swallowed, or touched. Even medicines become poisons if too much is taken. These rules will help you stay safe.

- Keep household cleaning products locked up where small children cannot reach them.
- Keep all medicines, even vitamins, locked up and out of the reach of small children.

▲ These products can be poisons if not used correctly. Most families keep products like these in their homes. How is each one normally used? Which ones are in your home?

LESSON CHECKUP

Check Your Facts

1 When a fire breaks out, what information does the 911 operator need?

2 CRITICAL THINKING Think about the household products in your home. Name four products other than those pictured on this page that could be poisons if used in the wrong way.

3 List five electricity safety rules.

Set Health Goals

4 Make a map or floor plan of your home. Draw arrows to show the fire escape paths. Make sure each room has two escape paths such as a door and window. Show where your family members can meet after they escape.

Safety for Sports and Bicycling

MAIN IDEA
Wearing the proper safety gear helps prevent injuries.

WHY LEARN THIS? What you learn can help keep you safe when you play a sport, skate, or ride a bicycle.

VOCABULARY
• safety gear
• mouth guard

How can you stay safe when playing on a team?

In many team sports, players must wear safety gear in order to play. **Safety gear** is clothing or equipment worn to protect players from injury.

Football In football all players need to wear helmets with face guards. Pads for legs, knees, and shoulders protect players from falls and hits.

Players also wear shoes that have small pegs called cleats on the bottom. Cleats help keep players from slipping on wet grass.

Football players also wear mouth guards. A **mouth guard** is a protective plastic shield worn in the mouth. Mouth guards help protect the teeth, gums, face bones, and jaw. Doctors and dentists recommend wearing mouth guards for most team sports.

Hockey Hockey players are likely to fall or get hit by the sticks or puck. Players wear padding, helmets, and face guards as safety gear. Players also should wear mouth guards.

Softball Softball safety gear includes cleated shoes and padded gloves. However, players are most likely to get injured when batting or running to a base. Batting helmets with ear guards protect batters and runners. A mouth guard also can protect a player.

helmet

shoulder pads

face guard

mouth guard

padded pants

knee pads

cleated shoes

Always wear your safety gear!

Soccer Soccer players wear shin guards to protect their legs from kicks. Mouth guards and shoes with cleats also protect players from injury.

Following the Rules No matter where you play team games and sports, your teachers and coaches want you to stay safe when you play. They give you instructions so that you will not get hurt. They teach you to obey the rules. Some of the rules are for safety. Other rules tell you how to play and how to win. Always follow the directions given by your teachers and coaches.

mouth guard

shin guard

shoes with cleats

Activity **Compare Safety Gear** Study the safety gear worn by the players on these two pages. How is the safety gear different for the three sports? How does each piece of safety gear protect the players?

helmet with ear guards

padded glove

chest protector

cleated shoes

helmet with face guard

How can you stay safe on wheels?

▼ What safety gear do you need for skating?

helmet

knee pads

elbow pads

wrist guards

People playing sports on wheels have high rates of injuries. Skaters, skateboard riders, and bicyclists risk falling. They need to wear special safety gear.

Skating and Skateboarding The pictures on the left show the safety gear for skating and skateboarding. Wrist injuries are the most common injuries in these sports. Skaters and skateboarders need to wear wrist guards. They also need to wear pads to avoid elbow and knee injuries.

Skaters and skateboarders also need to protect the fronts, sides, and backs of their heads. Skating helmets protect all sides of the head.

Bicycling The most important safety gear for bicycling is a helmet. Head injuries are likely when a rider falls off a bike. In fact, many states and cities have laws that require bicyclists to wear helmets.

Skate and bicycle helmets are made of thick, hard foam. The foam will crush if you fall and hit your head. This spreads out the force of a fall, so your head doesn't receive all of it. The foam is covered by a slick, hard plastic shell. The slick shell slides when it hits the ground. This takes away some of the force of a fall.

SAFETY RULES FOR BICYCLING

- Always wear your helmet.
- Walk your bike across streets. Stop and look in all directions before you cross. Listen for traffic. Obey all traffic lights and stop signs.
- Carry only one person—YOU! It is never safe to give rides to others.
- Be careful around driveways and parked cars. Watch for cars that might be backing out or car doors that might be opening.
- Ride only in daylight. Use reflective clothes if you must ride in cloudy or rainy weather.

What should you look for when buying a helmet?

There are many important things to consider when buying a helmet.

- Look for a hard shell and an approval sticker that shows the helmet meets safety standards.

- Buy a bright color to help others see you.

- Wear the helmet level on your head. Make sure it sits evenly between your ears and low on your forehead.

- Make sure the helmet fits. Take the time to fit all the pads and straps. Adjust them so that the helmet is snug but not too tight. Try hard to pull the helmet off. If it comes off, adjust the straps again. If it still comes off, try another helmet.

After buying a helmet, the most important thing to do is to wear it every time you ride. The best helmet in the world won't help you if it's not on your head while you ride.

approval sticker

quick-release strap

air vent

padding

hard shell

LESSON CHECKUP

Check Your Facts

1. Tell what a mouth guard protects and when you should wear one.

2. CRITICAL THINKING How does following the rules of a game help protect the players?

3. What safety gear should be worn while skating and skateboarding?

4. CRITICAL THINKING Why do you think it is important to fit a bicycle helmet properly before buying it?

Set Health Goals

5. List the sports you like to play. Make a chart or drawing that shows the safety gear you need to wear for each sport.

MAKE DECISIONS
with Safety in Mind

Staying safe and avoiding injuries doesn't just happen. The decisions you make are what keep you safe.

Learn This Skill

Brian met his friends after school to play soccer. When he checked his gear, he saw he had left his shin guards at home. How can the steps for making decisions help Brian make a choice for safety?

1. Find out about the choices you could make.

What are Brian's choices?

2. Imagine the possible result of each choice.

What does Brian think might happen?

3. Make what seems to be the best choice.

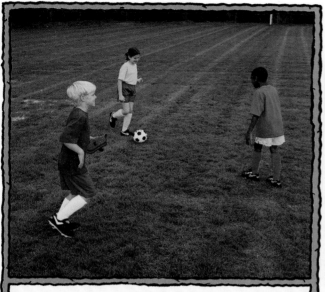

"I live only two blocks away. I'll ask my friends to wait for me."

4. Think about what happened as a result of your choice.

Being safe is being smart.

Practice This Skill

Now it's your turn to use your decision-making skills.

Steps for Making Decisions

1. Find out about the choices you could make.

2. Imagine the possible result of each choice.

3. Make what seems to be the best choice.

4. Think about what happened as a result of your choice.

A. You ride your bike to school. When it is time to go home, you can't find your helmet. Decide what to do.

B. An adult you don't know stops his car and offers you a ride. Decide what to do.

MAIN IDEA You can take steps to help when someone gets injured.

WHY LEARN THIS? What you learn can help you treat small injuries and get help in an emergency.

VOCABULARY
• first aid

Getting Help and Giving First Aid

You see a friend trip and fall on the playground. You find your little brother playing with an open bottle of pain killers. Your parent suddenly becomes very ill. What should you do? Get help! At home, tell your family or the baby-sitter. At school, tell a teacher or another adult.

Calling 911 If you can't find an adult, use a telephone to get help. Dial 911 or the emergency number for your area. Tell the operator

• where you are.

• your name and phone number.

• what happened and who needs help.

Calling the Poison Control Center If someone has been poisoned, call the Poison Control Center. Look for the number on the first page of the telephone book, and keep the number handy. Different poisons need different treatments. The people at the Poison Control Center know what to do for each kind of poison.

First Aid No matter how careful you are, you may get small injuries from time to time. Caring for them is called **first aid**. Here are some first-aid tips. Remember, the first thing you should do is tell an adult about the injury, no matter how small. First aid that is properly given can keep a person's injury from getting worse.

First Aid for Cuts and Scrapes

- Wash your hands. Put on gloves to keep the other person's blood off your skin. Blood can carry pathogens.

- Run water over the injury. Rinse away any dirt. Then wash the injury with soap and water.

- Dry the area and put on a clean bandage. Change the bandage every day and when it gets wet or dirty. Keeping the injury clean will help it heal.

First Aid for Insect Bites or Stings

- Find out what kind of insect made the sting or bite.

- Scrape any stinger out. Don't pull it out because more venom may get squeezed into the skin.

- Wash the injury and put ice or a cold pack on it for a few minutes.

LANGUAGE ARTS CONNECTION

First-Aid Book

With a Team On index cards, write the steps to care for small injuries, such as sunburn, insect bites and stings, blisters, scrapes, cuts, and bruises. Look up any steps you don't know.

◄ **These products are from a first-aid kit. How is each product used?**

gauze

gloves

bandages

soap

antibiotic cream

LESSON CHECKUP

Check Your Facts

1. What should you do if someone is badly injured?

2. CRITICAL THINKING If someone has been poisoned, should you give first aid or call the Poison Control Center first? Why?

3. Why is it important not to touch other people's blood?

Set Health Goals

4. Look up the emergency phone numbers on the first page of your local telephone book. Make a card that lists the numbers, such as 911 and the Poison Control Center.

USE VOCABULARY

bully (p. 200)
emergency (p. 204)
first aid (p. 214)
hazard (p. 195)

injury (p. 195)
limit (p. 195)
mouth guard (p. 208)

passenger (p. 196)
poison (p. 206)
safety gear (p. 208)

safety rules (p. 195)
stranger (p. 198)
trusted adult (p. 198)

Use the terms above to complete the sentences. Page numbers in ( ) tell you where to look in the chapter if you need help.

1. An _____ is harm done to the body.

2. A danger that could lead to an injury is called a _____.

3. Rules to keep you from injury are called _____.

4. A _____ is a point at which you must stop.

5. A person who rides in a car or bus with a driver is a _____.

6. A _____ is someone you don't know well.

7. A _____ is a grown-up you know well or someone who is responsible for you.

8. Someone who hurts or frightens others is called a _____.

9. A substance that causes illness or death can be called a _____.

10. Clothing or equipment that can help protect you from injury is _____.

11. A protective shield you wear in your mouth is called a _____.

12. An _____ is a situation in which help is needed right away.

13. The care given to small injuries is _____.

CHECK YOUR FACTS

Page numbers in ( ) tell you where to look in the chapter if you need help.

14. What are two safety rules to follow when riding in a car? (p. 196)

15. Why should you stay away from strangers? (p. 198)

16. What might a 911 operator need to know about a fire emergency? (p. 205)

17. Why do dentists recommend that people wear mouth guards for most team sports? (p. 208)

18. Name four things you need to have in a first-aid kit, and tell how each is used. (p. 215)

19. You are walking to school when a car stops beside you. The driver asks for directions to school. What should you do?

20. Your mom is driving you to school. You want to be safe in the car. Name two things you should do and two things you shouldn't do.

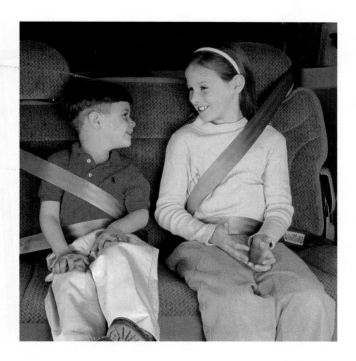

21. Resolve Conflicts Jerome and Carlos are on the playground when a bully starts to bother them. How can they negotiate to solve their problem?

22. Make Decisions Janine is shopping with her family when she becomes lost. What should she do? Use the steps for making decisions in your answer.

Promote Health **Home and Community**

1. With your family, plan an outdoor hazard hunt. Look for places around your home that could be hazardous. Then discuss ways to correct the hazards.
2. On cards, list emergency numbers for your community. Hand the cards out at school or at a community event.

Activities

A Safer Bicycle

On Your Own • Find out what kind of safety gear bicycles need to have. Then make a poster showing safety gear on bicycles.

Best Helmets

With a Partner • Research and compare bicycle and skating helmets. You might want to visit a store to look at different helmets. Make a chart that compares the safety features of each helmet. You might compare prices, too.

First-Aid Kit

With a Team • Visit the school nurse or office to find out which first-aid supplies the school has. List the supplies that a classroom first-aid kit might need. Get together with others, and make a kit for your classroom.

Safety Search

At Home • Look up *safety* and *fire* in an encyclopedia or in library books. Make a list of fire hazards that are common in homes. Talk about them with your family. Help an adult in your family correct the fire hazards that you find.

Multiple Choice

Choose the letter of the correct answer.

1. The person most responsible for your safety is ____.
   a. your mom   b. your brother
   c. you   d. your teacher

2. Cross a street ____.
   a. at a crosswalk   b. on the left
   c. in the middle   d. on the right

3. If a bully follows you, ____.
   a. turn and talk   b. tell a friend
   c. yell   d. get help

4. If you are trying to escape a fire, ____.
   a. run   b. find water
   c. crawl   d. hide

5. A bicycle helmet should ____.
   a. not have straps   b. fit properly
   c. be black   d. be loose

Modified True or False

Write *true* or *false*. If a sentence is false, replace the underlined term to make the sentence true.

6. Before crossing the street, STOP, LOOK, <u>BLINK</u>, and THINK.

7. The safest place for car passengers to sit is in the <u>front</u> seat.

8. Stay a <u>hand's</u> reach from a stranger.

9. When bullied, <u>stay and fight</u>.

10. One piece of safety gear hockey players wear is a <u>mouth guard</u>.

11. A bicycle helmet should fit <u>loosely</u> on your head.

12. In a fire the cleanest air is <u>up high</u>.

13. Hold the <u>cord</u> when you unplug something.

14. A 911 operator <u>should</u> hang up first.

15. You should put <u>ice</u> on an insect bite.

Short Answer

Write a complete sentence to answer each question.

16. Describe a limit set by an adult.

17. How does a safety belt protect you?

18. Why is safety gear important when you play sports?

19. How could medicine be a poison?

20. Tell what you should do after a fire.

21. Why shouldn't you plug in a toaster when you have wet hands?

22. Tell why a helmet is important safety gear.

23. What are two safety rules for crossing the street?

Essay

Write paragraphs to answer each item.

24. Give an example of an emergency. Tell what safety steps should be followed in the emergency.

25. What should you look for when you shop for a bicycle helmet?

Health in the Community

Project

REUSE CLASSROOM ITEMS Develop a plan for reusing items in your classroom. Find out what kinds of things would be useful for art projects or other classroom projects. Decide where those things can be collected. Write a plan to share with other classes.

For other activities, visit the Harcourt Brace Internet site. http://www.hbschool.com

MAIN IDEA
Health departments, hospitals, and clinics treat people who are hurt or ill. They help people stay well, too.

WHY LEARN THIS? You can use what you learn to find places in your community to get health care.

VOCABULARY
• community
• health department
• hospital
• clinic

Health Departments, Hospitals, and Clinics

A **community** (kuh•MYOO•nuh•tee) is a place where people live, work, play, and go to school. Doctors, nurses, and other health care workers help keep the community healthy.

What does a health department do?

A **health department** is a group of health workers that serves a community. Health department workers are also called public health workers. The pictures on pages 222 and 223 show some of the jobs they do.

This public health nurse is giving this girl a shot that will protect her from a disease such as mumps or measles. The health department also gives adults shots that protect them from diseases such as flu.

This public health nurse is visiting an older adult in his home. The nurse checks the man's blood pressure. She asks questions to find out if he is well. She checks to see that he is taking the medicine his doctor ordered.

This public health nurse is visiting a new mother at home. The nurse is teaching the mother to care for her baby. Health department workers began helping before the baby was born. They taught the mother which foods to eat and how to take care of herself so that she and the baby would be healthy.

Public health officers keep records of diseases that can spread. They file reports on diseases carried by unsafe food and water. The health department keeps records of animal bites, too. Animals can spread diseases such as rabies.

223

JOURNAL

In your Health Journal, write about a time that you went to a hospital. Perhaps you were visiting a friend or a new baby. If you've never been to a hospital, describe what you think it would be like. Remember, your journal is private and need not be shared with others.

How do hospitals help the community?

A **hospital** (HAHS•pih•tuhl) is a place where hurt or ill people get medical treatment. Hospitals care for people who are too ill to get well at home.

Doctors take care of people who come to the emergency room. For example, they sew up deep cuts and set broken arms or legs.

Surgeons are doctors who do operations. A surgeon might remove a person's unhealthy appendix. Surgeons also repair organs, such as a person's damaged heart.

Doctors or midwives help women give birth in hospitals. New mothers and their babies get nursing care. Nurses teach mothers how to feed their babies.

How do clinics help the community?

A **clinic** (KLIH•nik) is another place where people go for medical treatment. Sometimes the cost is low or even free. Clinics also teach things such as baby care and car-seat safety.

Doctors and nurses in clinics treat people who are ill or have small injuries. (Very ill or badly hurt people go to the hospital.) Women who are going to have babies often see doctors in clinics.

Clinics offer health screenings—tests to check for diseases. Technicians take blood for tests. Nurses check blood pressure and give eye exams. Nurses also give shots to prevent diseases.

◀ Have you ever had your ears or throat examined? How did the doctor examine your ears or throat?

LESSON CHECKUP

Check Your Facts
1. Describe three things a health department does.
2. Name two places in the community where ill or hurt people can get care.
3. CRITICAL THINKING Why is it important for the health department to keep good records?
4. Name two services offered at clinics.

Use Life Skills
5. MANAGE STRESS Write about a health problem that could cause stress. How could a nurse help with this problem?

225

MAIN IDEA
Clean air and protection from noise are important to your health.

WHY LEARN THIS? You can use what you learn to reduce air pollution and to protect your hearing.

VOCABULARY
- environment
- pollution
- air pollution
- pollution control technician
- noise pollution

Keeping the Environment Healthful

Everything around you is part of the **environment** (in•vy•ruhn•muhnt). The environment includes all nonliving things, such as rocks and air. It also includes living things, such as trees. You are part of the environment, too.

The environment can be made unhealthful by pollution. **Pollution** (puh•LOO•shuhn) is dirt and harmful materials in the air, water, or land.

How do people keep the air safe?

Dirt and harmful materials in the air are **air pollution**. Some things that people use or do cause air pollution. For example, many people drive to get from one place to another. Cars, trucks, and buses give off materials that pollute the air.

▶ The exhaust from cars and trucks has harmful gases and other materials in it. In some areas laws limit the amounts of polluting gases cars and trucks can give off. Drivers in these areas must have their vehicles tested to make sure they meet pollution control laws.

▶ This pollution control technician tests cars and trucks to see if they meet pollution control laws. He will attach a hose to a vehicle's exhaust pipe. Then he will examine the collected exhaust to see how much harmful material it contains.

Many communities have laws to help reduce air pollution. These laws limit the amount of smoke and harmful fumes released into the air. The laws apply to smoke and harmful fumes from factories, cars and trucks, and tobacco products.

Burning trash outside causes air pollution too. Why? Smoke from the trash causes pollution. Also, many things that people throw away give off harmful gases as they burn. Burning things such as batteries or plastic, for example, pollutes the air.

Many cities burn trash inside special buildings to help reduce air pollution. These buildings have pollution control devices. As the trash is burned, gases and solids that can pollute the air are removed.

Some people have jobs working to reduce air pollution. A **pollution control technician** (puh•LOO•shuhn kuhn•TROHL tek•NIH•shuhn) tests water, air, or soil for harmful substances.

How does noise pollution affect people?

Noise can pollute the environment, just as dirt in the air can. Disturbing or harmful sounds made by human activities cause **noise pollution**. Sirens, vacuum cleaners, jackhammers, and loud radios are just a few sources of noise pollution. What other sources can you think of?

Noise pollution makes people tired and angry. It gives people headaches and stomachaches. Worst of all, it hurts people's ears. Noise pollution causes most people in the United States to lose some hearing by the time they are 30 years old. If you need to raise your voice for people to hear you, then you are in a place with enough noise to damage your hearing.

Pollution control experts help reduce noise pollution. They check factories to make sure workers are not being harmed by unsafe noise levels. Cities make noise control laws. People can help reduce noise pollution by turning down the volume of radios, CD players, and televisions. They can also replace noisy machines, such as lawn mowers, with quieter ones.

Protect your ears from loud noises.

▶ **This airport worker spends each day directing airplane traffic. He wears earmuffs to protect his hearing.**

LOUDEST ⟶
jet plane
thunder
train
lawn mower
jackhammer
stereo
traffic
conversation

Activity **Compare Noises** This chart shows several sources of noise pollution. List the sounds from softest to loudest. Put a star next to the sounds that are hard to get away from. Put a check mark next to the sounds that can hurt your hearing if they go on for a long time. How can people control some of these sounds?

LESSON CHECKUP

Check Your Facts

1. Name two kinds of pollution.
2. What does a pollution control technician do?
3. Name two things people can do to help reduce noise pollution.
4. CRITICAL THINKING Name two noises that hurt your ears. How can you protect yourself from those noises?

Set Health Goals

5. Make a list of places you have gone in a car, bus, or truck in the past two days. Make a check mark beside any places you could go safely on foot or on a bike. How does walking or biking when you usually go by car help reduce air pollution?

MAIN IDEA
Water is polluted in many ways. Pollution technicians and other people can help control water pollution.

WHY LEARN THIS? You can use what you learn to help protect our water.

VOCABULARY
• water pollution
• groundwater

Controlling Water Pollution

Harmful material in lakes, oceans, or rivers is called **water pollution**. Harmful things poured on the ground can also pollute the water. Garbage and chemicals in a river are examples of water pollution.

How is water kept clean?

Because there is only a certain amount of water in the world, communities use the same water again and again. The water used to do dishes today will be used for drinking later. Of course, water must be clean when it is used for cooking, cleaning, and drinking. That is why dirty water that washes down the drain or flushes down the toilet flows through underground pipes to a sewage treatment plant.

After it enters the treatment plant, sewage flows through screens. The screens filter out floating objects, such as stones, trash, and rags.

The sewage moves into a settling tank. Solids that are too small to get caught in the screens settle, or drop, to the bottom.

The liquid that is left flows into another tank. Tiny living things called bacteria remove more wastes. Many of these wastes are too small to see.

At the sewage treatment plant, the used water, or *sewage*, is treated to make it clean. The pictures on pages 230 and 231 show the main steps in sewage treatment.

The man on this page is a pollution control technician. He is checking water that has been treated at a sewage treatment plant. He tests it to make sure the water is clean.

Pollution control technicians also check a community's water sources. They take samples from places where communities get their water. They check the samples for pollutants. Some pollutants include used motor oil from cars and trucks and many kinds of chemicals from factories.

If a pollution control technician finds a pollutant, such as oil, in the water, he or she reports it. Then the people or factory that spilled the oil must usually pay to clean it up.

In another tank, chemicals are added. A chemical called chlorine makes the water clear and kills pathogens.

▲ Groundwater fills cracks and spaces in rocks under Earth's surface. Why is it important to keep groundwater clean?

SOCIAL STUDIES CONNECTION

Locate Water Sources

With a Partner On a map of your community, find water sources such as streams and lakes. After you have located these water sources, talk to an adult in your family about where your community's water comes from.

● ● ●

How is groundwater protected?

Many people think we get all our drinking water from lakes and rivers. Yet a lot of drinking water comes from groundwater. **Groundwater** is water that sinks into the soil and fills cracks and spaces in buried rocks. The picture on this page shows an area under Earth's surface where groundwater lies.

Chemicals, such as those used on farms, can travel into the ground and pollute groundwater. Other chemicals, such as those used in factories, pollute groundwater, too. And salt used on icy highways pollutes groundwater. So do many products that people use to grow grass and to kill garden pests.

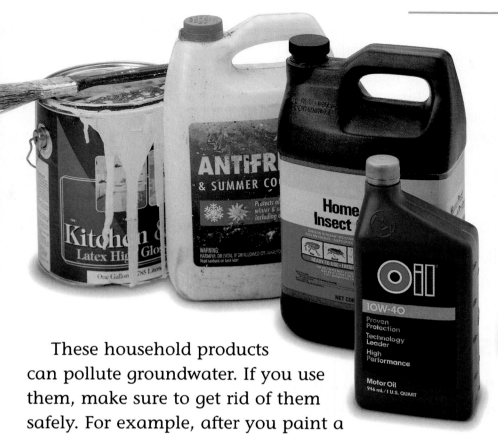

LIFE SKILLS
FOCUS

Communicate

You and a friend have been painting signs at his house. Your friend wants to pour the leftover paint down the drain. He says it's okay because the water will get treated. What would you say to him? Use the steps for communicating shown on pages 246 and 247.

• • •

These household products can pollute groundwater. If you use them, make sure to get rid of them safely. For example, after you paint a picture, store the paint jar with the lid on tight. Never put leftover paint into the trash or down the drain. Set it aside for a special trash pick-up of toxic, or poisonous, wastes.

Clean water is important to everyone's health. You need clean water for drinking, cooking, bathing, and washing. Talk with friends and classmates about things you can do to help protect groundwater.

LESSON CHECKUP

Check Your Facts

❶ What happens to sewage?

❷ Where does most drinking water come from?

❸ CRITICAL THINKING Would it be a good idea to eat a fish that you caught in a lake that is too polluted to swim in? Explain.

❹ CRITICAL THINKING List three ways you can think of to protect rivers where people fish, boat, and swim.

Use Life Skills

❺ COMMUNICATE Draw a picture to show a younger student why it is important to keep groundwater clean.

SET GOALS
to Improve Community and Environment

You can do things to improve your community and your environment. Using the steps for setting and reaching goals can help you make a difference in your surroundings.

Learn This Skill

George's family went to a lake for a picnic. When they arrived, they saw trash all around. Follow George as he uses goal-setting steps to clean up the picnic area.

1. Set a goal.

George wanted to make the lake a cleaner place.

2. List steps to reach that goal.

George mapped out an area that needed to be cleaned and asked his Cub Scout friends to help.

3. Monitor progress toward the goal.

4. Evaluate the goal.

George and the other scouts worked together to clean the area around the lake. When each boy finished, he put an X through his section on the map.

After George and his friends cleaned up the litter, the Cub Scouts enjoyed a picnic at the lake.

Practice This Skill

Use the steps to help you solve the problems below.

Steps for Setting Goals

1. Set a goal.
2. List steps to reach that goal.
3. Monitor progress toward the goal.
4. Evaluate the goal.

A. Ellen's family recycles aluminum cans. She was upset when she saw all the cans thrown away at school. Use what you know about goal setting to help Ellen.

B. Ray found out that some household products can pollute the groundwater. What goal setting steps could Ray take?

Reduce, Reuse, and Recycle

How can you help the trash problem?

The children in the picture are helping protect the land and water. How? By picking up litter.

Littering (LIH•ter•ing) means dropping trash on the ground or in water. Littering makes beaches, parks, and roadsides ugly. It also harms ocean animals. Many sea turtles die because they eat balloons or plastic bags in the water. They mistake them for jellyfish, their favorite food.

▼ The children cleaning up the beach are wearing heavy gloves. They do this to keep from getting cut by glass or other sharp things found on the beach.

You can help the trash problem by never littering. You might encourage your friends and family members not to litter. You might also pick up litter left by others. If you want to pick up litter in your neighborhood, take a trash bag the next time you take a walk. Spend a few minutes picking up litter at the park or at the beach, too.

Follow two safety rules when you pick up litter. Wear heavy gloves to protect your hands, and get an adult to help you.

The picture below shows many, colorful balloons. The balloons are filled with helium gas, which makes them rise. Never let go of helium balloons. The balloons can travel for many miles and litter the land or the ocean.

LIFE SKILLS FOCUS

Make Decisions

You are outdoors at a friend's house for her birthday party. Her grandfather gives everyone helium balloons. What should you do with your balloon? Use the steps for making decisions shown on pages 246 and 247.

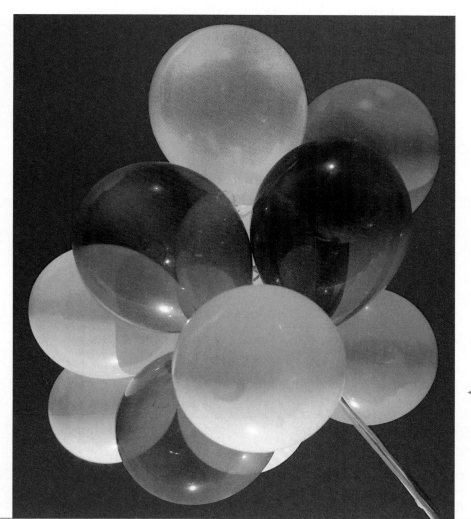

◀ If you get a helium balloon, do not let go of it outside. Keep it indoors.

How can you reduce, reuse, and recycle?

Clean land is important to your health. Litter left in uncovered dumps draws flies, mosquitoes, and rats, which carry disease. We should **reduce**, or make less, trash to stay healthy. For example, you could drink from a glass instead of from a paper cup that would be thrown away.

Another way to reduce trash is to **reuse** something, or use it again. You could reuse outgrown clothes by giving them to someone smaller. You could also reuse books by borrowing them from the library.

Recycling also helps lessen the trash problem. To **recycle** (ree•sy•kuhl) means to collect used things so they can be made into new things.

Some communities recycle newspapers, glass and plastic containers, and cans.

▼ Plastics are stamped with a number code. The numbers 1 through 7 help people at the recycling center sort the plastics. Most (88 percent) of recycled plastics are marked with a 1 or a 2. What products are made from the plastics you recycle?

RECYCLING PLASTICS

Code	Original Objects		New Products
1	Soft-drink bottles, peanut butter jars, frozen-food trays	become...	surfboards, skis, carpets, soft-drink bottles.
2	Detergent bottles, milk and water jugs, toys	become...	flowerpots, trash cans, stadium seats, toys.
3	Shampoo bottles, clear food wrap	become...	floor mats, pipes, hoses, mud flaps on trucks.
4	Grocery bags, bread bags, frozen-food bags	become...	grocery bags, other types of bags.
5	Ketchup bottles, yogurt cups, other food containers	become...	food trays, car battery parts.
6	Videocassette cases, plastic spoons, food trays, foam cups	become...	trash cans, egg cartons, hangers.
7	Packages with many layers of materials	become...	plastic lumber.

Activity **Learn to Reuse** Look at the things on this page. Tell how each thing was used. Think of at least one new way each thing could be reused. (Hints: You could think about making art. You could also think about gardening.) Tell which of the things are easy to reuse and which are hard to reuse.

LESSON CHECKUP

Check Your Facts

❶ Name four ways you can help solve the trash problem.

❷ What two safety rules should you follow when you pick up litter?

❸ CRITICAL THINKING Which helps the trash problem, buying a cone or a cup of frozen yogurt? Explain.

❹ What types of plastic items are commonly recycled? Give at least three examples.

Set Health Goals

❺ Write a plan for how you can help solve the trash problem in your classroom. Include in your plan ways you can reduce, reuse, and recycle.

USE VOCABULARY

air pollution (p. 226)   groundwater (p. 232)   noise pollution   recycle (p. 238)
clinic (p. 225)   health department   (p. 228)   reduce (p. 238)
community (p. 222)   (p. 222)   pollution (p. 226)   reuse (p. 238)
environment (p. 226)   hospital (p. 224)   pollution control   water pollution
                          littering (p. 236)   technician (p. 227)   (p. 230)

Use the terms above to complete the sentences. Page numbers in ( ) tell you where to look in the chapter if you need help.

1. Many Americans get their drinking water from ____.

2. A place where people may be able to get health care at a low cost is a ____.

3. Dirt and harmful materials in the air are called ____.

4. When you give a sweater you have outgrown to a younger child, you ____.

5. A place where people live, work, and play is a ____.

6. People who are badly hurt or very sick can get health care at a ____.

7. When you collect glass jars so they can be made into new jars, you ____.

8. Everything around you is part of the ____.

9. If you throw a banana peel on the ground, you are ____.

10. Home health care workers and public health nurses work for the ____.

11. Disturbing or harmful sounds made by human activities cause ____.

12. When you make less trash, you ____.

13. Dirt or harmful materials in the air, water, or land are called ____.

14. Materials that harm lakes, oceans, or rivers are called ____.

15. A worker who tests air, water, or soil for harmful substances is a ____.

CHECK YOUR FACTS

Page numbers in ( ) tell you where to look in the chapter if you need help.

16. Tell three things a health department does. (pp. 222–223)

17. Name three sources of noise pollution. Tell how noise pollution harms health. (p. 228)

18. Describe what happens at a sewage treatment plant. (pp. 230–231)

19. What are some things that can be made from recycled milk jugs? (p. 238)

THINK CRITICALLY

20. If someone has a broken leg, should he go to the hospital or a clinic? Why?

21. Suppose you buy a loaf of bread at the store. The clerk asks if you want a bag for it. Do you say yes or no? Why?

22. Why do you think it is important for clinics to offer low-cost or free health care?

APPLY LIFE SKILLS

23. **Communicate** Maria's older sister has the radio on very loud. Maria is getting a headache from the loud music. What could Maria say to her sister?

24. **Set Goals** You may have seen your classmates throw away lots of trash every day. Using the goal-setting steps, make a plan to reduce the amount of trash in your classroom.

Promote Health Home and Community

1. Cars, trucks, and buses cause air pollution. Talk to your classmates about ways you can help reduce the air pollution problem. For example, could you walk or bike instead of going by car? Make a poster that shows your ideas.

2. With several classmates, think of some new ways your school could recycle. (For example, teachers and staff could use only recycled paper.)

Activities

In the News

On Your Own • Have an adult help you write a letter to your local newspaper. Give ideas for how your community can reduce noise pollution.

Checking Up

With a Partner • Call or visit the health department to find out what children's services they provide. Make a poster to show what you learned.

Save the Groundwater

At Home • Call your trash collection company to find out how your community handles household hazardous wastes such as batteries, paint, and motor oil. Then make a plan for safely getting rid of these harmful wastes in your home.

Payback Time

With a Team • Many states and communities have laws that charge deposits on soft-drink bottles and cans. Then you can return the empty bottles and cans to the grocery store for money. Find out if your state or community has such a law. If so, ask what the grocery does with the bottles and cans. Tell how this can help protect the environment.

Multiple Choice

Choose the letter of the correct answer.

1. Many people in the United States get their drinking water from ____.
   a. oceans
   b. groundwater
   c. rivers
   d. lakes

2. A place where people live, work, play, and go to school is ____.
   a. a health department
   b. a clinic
   c. a community
   d. a hospital

3. Workers who test water, air, or soil for harmful substances are ____.
   a. pollution control technicians
   b. home health care workers
   c. public health officers
   d. registered nurses

4. A place where a person can get health care is ____.
   a. a hospital
   b. a clinic
   c. a health department
   d. all of these

5. Used water is treated at ____.
   a. a clinic
   b. a hospital
   c. the health department
   d. a sewage treatment plant

Modified True or False

Write *true* or *false*. If a sentence is false, replace the underlined term to make the sentence true.

6. People who are badly hurt can get care at a <u>health department</u>.

7. Harmful materials in the air, water, or land are called <u>pollution</u>.

8. Rocks, air, and trees are all part of the <u>environment</u>.

9. Farm chemicals and salt used on icy roads pollute the <u>air</u>.

10. Giving your clothes to a younger child is an example of <u>reusing</u>.

Short Answer

Write a complete sentence to answer each question.

11. How does burning trash outside harm the environment?

12. Why is it important to keep groundwater clean?

13. What safety rules should you follow when you pick up litter?

Essay

Write paragraphs to answer each item.

14. Tell what happens at a sewage treatment plant.

15. Why do some communities have laws that require car and truck exhaust to be tested for pollutants?

Life Skills
Understanding Life Skills 246

Good Nutrition
The Food Guide Pyramid 248
Estimating Serving Sizes 249

Preparing Foods Safely
Fight Bacteria 250
Food Safety Tips 251

Being Physically Active
Planning Your Weekly Activities 252
Guidelines for a Good Workout 253
Warm-Up and Cool-Down Stretches 254
Building a Strong Heart and Lungs 256
The President's Challenge 258

Using a Computer Safely
Good Posture at the Computer 260
Safety on the Internet 261

Being Safe at Home
When Home Alone 262

Bicycle Safety
A Safe Bike 264
Your Bike Helmet 265
Safety on the Road 265

Safety in Emergencies
Fire Safety 266
Earthquake Safety 267
Storm Safety 267

First Aid
For Choking 268
For Bleeding 269
For Nosebleeds 270
For Burns 270
For Insect Bites and Stings 271
For Skin Rashes from Plants 271

Understanding Life Skills

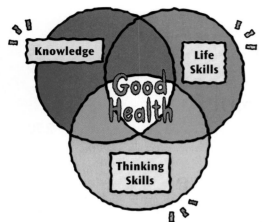

Knowledge

Life Skills

Good Health

Thinking Skills

Having good health isn't just a matter of knowing the facts about what to eat or how to stay well. It's also thinking critically about those facts and knowing how to apply them to your daily life. The Life Skills presented in this program can help you do just that. When you think through and use the skills to apply your growing health knowledge, you can attain the goal of good health.

Make Decisions

When you make decisions, you think about a group of choices and decide the wisest thing to do in order to avoid risky situations or health risks.

Steps for Making Decisions

1. Find out about the choices you could make.
2. Imagine the possible result of each choice.
3. Make what seems to be the best choice.
4. Think about the result of your choice.

Manage Stress

Everyone feels stress. Knowing how to manage your stress can help you get through tense or exciting situations.

Steps for Managing Stress

1. Know what stress feels like and what causes it.
2. When you feel stress, think about ways to handle it.
3. Focus on one step at a time.
4. Learn ways to reduce and release tension.

Communicate

In order to communicate well, you need to explain your ideas, needs, or feelings. You also need to listen to what others have to say, and try to understand their feelings and needs as well.

How to Communicate

1. Understand your audience.
2. Give a clear message.
3. Listen.
4. Gather feedback.

Refuse

Knowing what to say **before** you are asked to do something you don't want to do can keep you moving toward good health.

How to Refuse

1. Say **no** and say why not.
2. State your reasons for saying **no**.
3. Suggest something else to do.
4. Repeat **no**; walk away.

Other Ways to Say *No*

- Use humor to make your point.
- Say that the drug doesn't taste good, or that the activity suggested is no fun.
- Say that it's against the law.
- Say that you don't want to become ill.
- Say it is against your family rules.

Set Goals

When you set goals, you must decide a change you want to make, and then take action to make that change happen.

Steps for Setting Goals

1. Set a goal.
2. List and plan steps to meet that goal.
3. Check your progress toward the goal.
4. Evaluate the goal.

Resolve Conflicts

To resolve conflicts, you must choose and use strategies to communicate and compromise in order to find solutions to problems or to avoid violence.

Steps for Resolving Conflicts

1. Use I-messages to tell how you feel.
2. Listen to each other.
3. Think of the other person's point of view.
4. Decide what to do.

Other Ways to Resolve Conflicts

- Ask for a mediator.
- Use humor.
- Walk away.

The Food Guide Pyramid

No one food or food group supplies everything your body needs for good health. That's why it's important to eat foods from all the food groups. The Food Guide Pyramid can help you choose healthful foods in the right amounts. By choosing more foods from the groups at the bottom of the pyramid and fewer foods from the group at the top, you will eat the foods that provide your body with energy to grow and develop.

Fats, oils, and sweets
Eat sparingly.

Meat, poultry, fish, dry beans, eggs, and nuts 2–3 servings

Milk, yogurt, and cheese
2–3 servings

Fruits
2–4 servings

Vegetables
3–5 servings

Breads, cereals, rice, and pasta 6–11 servings

Estimating Serving Sizes

Choosing a variety of foods is only half the story. You also need to choose the right amounts. The table below can help you estimate the number of servings you are eating of your favorite foods.

Food Group	Amount of Food in One Serving	Some Easy Ways to Estimate Serving Size
Bread, Cereal, Rice, Pasta Group	1 ounce ready-to-eat (dry) cereal	large handful of plain cereal or a small handful of cereal with raisins and nuts
	1 slice bread, $\frac{1}{2}$ bagel	
	$\frac{1}{2}$ cup cooked pasta, rice, or cereal	ice cream scoop
Vegetable Group	1 cup of raw, leafy vegetables	about the size of a fist
	$\frac{1}{2}$ cup other vegetables, cooked or raw, chopped	
	$\frac{3}{4}$ cup vegetable juice	
	$\frac{1}{2}$ cup tomato sauce	ice cream scoop
Fruit Group	medium apple, pear, or orange	a baseball
	$\frac{1}{2}$ large banana or one medium banana	
	$\frac{1}{2}$ cup chopped or cooked fruit	
	$\frac{3}{4}$ cup of fruit juice	
Milk, Yogurt, and Cheese Group	$1\frac{1}{2}$ ounces of natural cheese	two dominoes
	2 ounces of processed cheese	$1\frac{1}{2}$ slices of packaged cheese
	1 cup of milk or yogurt	
Meat, Poultry, Fish, Dry Beans, Eggs, and Nuts Group	3 ounces of lean meat, chicken, or fish	about the size of your palm
	2 tablespoons peanut butter	
	$\frac{1}{2}$ cup of cooked dry beans	
Fats, Oils, and Sweets Group	1 teaspoon of margarine or butter	about the size of the tip of your thumb

Fight Bacteria

You probably already know to throw away food that smells bad or looks moldy. But food doesn't have to look or smell bad to make you ill. To keep your food safe and yourself from becoming ill, follow the steps outlined in the picture below. And remember—when in doubt, throw it out!

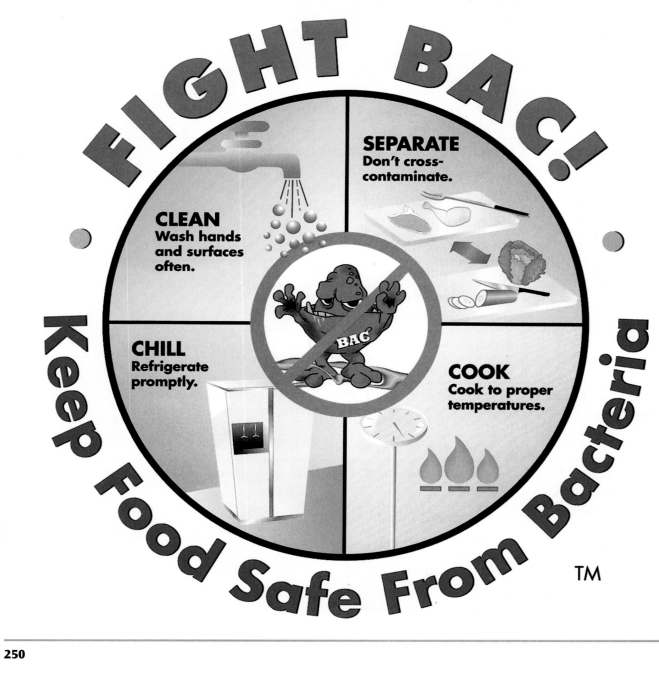

FIGHT BAC!

Keep Food Safe From Bacteria

CLEAN
Wash hands and surfaces often.

SEPARATE
Don't cross-contaminate.

CHILL
Refrigerate promptly.

COOK
Cook to proper temperatures.

TM

Food Safety Tips

Tips for Preparing Food

- Wash hands in warm, soapy water before preparing food. It's also a good idea to wash hands after preparing each dish.
- Defrost meat in the microwave or the refrigerator.
- Keep raw meat, poultry, fish, and their juices away from other food.
- Wash cutting boards, knives, and countertops immediately after cutting up meat, poultry, or fish. Never use the same cutting board for meats and vegetables without washing the board first.

Tips for Cooking Food

- Cook all food completely, especially meat. Complete cooking kills the bacteria that can make you ill.
- Red meats should be cooked to a temperature of 160°F. Poultry should be cooked to 180°F. When done, fish flakes easily with a fork.
- Never eat food that contains raw eggs or raw egg yolks, including cookie dough.

Tips for Cleaning Up the Kitchen

- Wash all dishes, utensils, and countertops with hot, soapy water. Use a soap that kills bacteria, if possible.
- Store leftovers in small containers that will cool quickly in the refrigerator. Don't leave leftovers on the counter to cool.

Planning Your Weekly Activities

Being active every day is important for your overall health. Physical activity helps you manage stress, maintain a healthful weight, and strengthen your body systems. The Activity Pyramid, like the Food Guide Pyramid, can help you choose a variety of activities in the right amounts to keep your body strong and healthy.

The Activity Pyramid

Sitting for more than thirty minutes at a time: Only Once in a While

Light Exercise: Two to Three Times a Week

Flexibility and Strength: Two to Three Times a Week

Twenty-plus minutes of continuous aerobic activity: Three to Five Times a Week

Stay active: Every Day

Guidelines for a Good Workout

There are three things you should do every time you are going to exercise—warm up, work out, and cool down.

Warm-Up: When you warm up, your heart rate, breathing rate, and body temperature increase and more blood flows to your muscles. As your body warms up, you can move more easily. People who warm up are less stiff after exercising, and are less likely to have exercise-related injuries. Your warm-up should include five minutes of stretching, and five minutes of low-level exercise. Some simple stretches are shown on pages 254–255.

Workout: The main part of your exercise routine should be an aerobic exercise that lasts 20 to 30 minutes. Aerobic exercises make your heart, lungs, and circulatory system stronger.

Some common aerobic exercises are shown on pages 256–257. You may want to mix up the types of activities you do. This helps you work different muscles, and provides a better workout over time.

Cool-Down: When you finish your aerobic exercise, you need to give your body time to cool down. Start your cool-down with three to five minutes of low-level activity. End with stretching exercises to prevent soreness and stiffness.

Warm-Up and Cool-Down Stretches

Before you exercise, you should warm up your muscles. The warm-up exercises shown here should be held for at least fifteen to twenty seconds and repeated at least three times.

At the end of your workout, spend about two minutes repeating some of these stretches.

▶ **Hurdler's Stretch** HINT—Keep the toes of your extended leg pointed up.

▲ **Shoulder and Chest Stretch** HINT—Pulling your hands slowly toward the floor gives a better stretch. Keep your elbows straight, but not locked!

◀ **Sit-and-Reach Stretch** HINT—Remember to bend at the waist. Keep your eyes on your toes!

▲ **Upper Back and Shoulder Stretch**
HINT—Try to stretch your hand down so that it rests flat against your back.

▼ **Thigh Stretch** HINT—Keep both hands flat on the ground. Lean as far forward as you can.

▲ **Calf Stretch** HINT—Keep both feet on the floor during this stretch. Try changing the distance between your feet. Is the stretch better for you when your legs are closer together or farther apart?

Tips for Stretching

- Never bounce when stretching.
- Hold each stretch for fifteen to twenty seconds.
- Breathe normally. This helps your body get the oxygen it needs.
- Do NOT stretch until it hurts. Stretch only until you feel a slight pull.

Building a Strong Heart and Lungs

Aerobic activities cause deep breathing and a fast heart rate for at least twenty minutes. These activities help both your heart and your lungs. Because your heart is a muscle, it gets stronger with exercise. A strong heart doesn't have to work as hard to pump blood to the rest of your body. Exercise also allows your lungs to hold more air. With a strong heart and lungs, your cells get oxygen faster and your body works more efficiently.

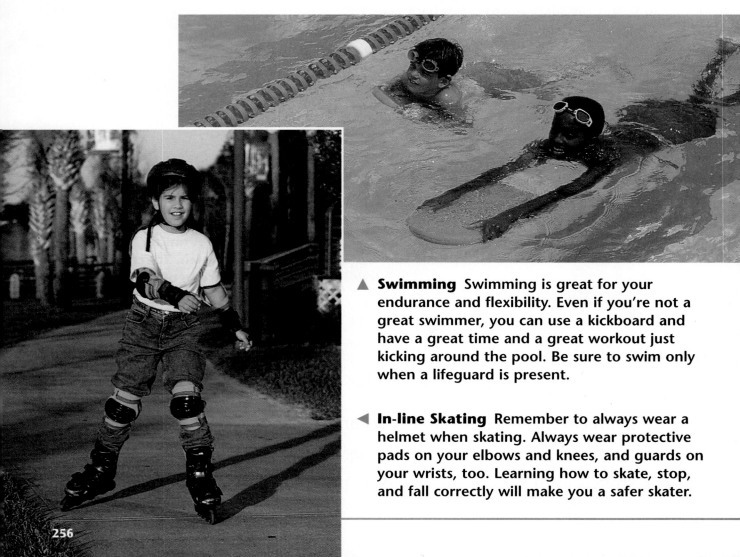

▲ **Swimming** Swimming is great for your endurance and flexibility. Even if you're not a great swimmer, you can use a kickboard and have a great time and a great workout just kicking around the pool. Be sure to swim only when a lifeguard is present.

◀ **In-line Skating** Remember to always wear a helmet when skating. Always wear protective pads on your elbows and knees, and guards on your wrists, too. Learning how to skate, stop, and fall correctly will make you a safer skater.

▼ **Walking** A fast-paced walk is a terrific way to build your endurance. The only equipment you need is supportive shoes. Walking with a friend can make this exercise a lot of fun.

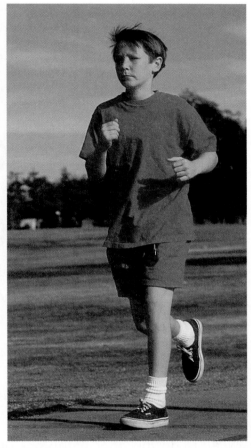

▲ **Jumping Rope** Jumping rope is one of the best ways to increase your endurance. Remember to always jump on an even surface and always wear supportive shoes.

▼ **Bicycling** Bicycling provides good aerobic activity *and* a great way to see the outdoors. Be sure to learn and follow bicycle safety rules. And *always* remember to wear your helmet!

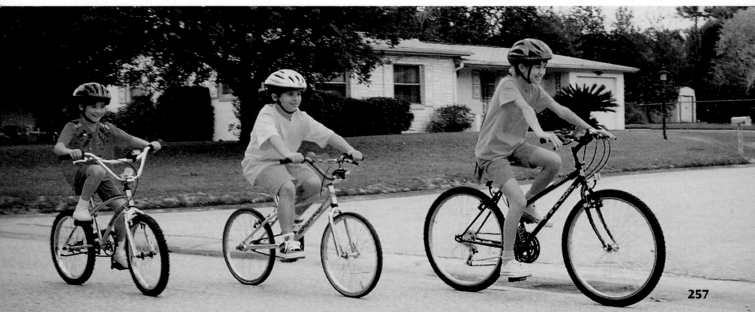

The President's Challenge

The President's Challenge is a physical fitness program designed for students ages 6 to 17. It's made up of five activities that promote physical fitness. Each participant receives an emblem patch and a certificate signed by the President.

The three different awards:

 Presidential Physical Fitness Award—presented to students scoring in the top 15 percent in all events.

 National Physical Fitness Award—presented to students scoring in the top 50 percent in all events.

 Health Fitness Award—awarded to all other participants.

The Five Activities

1. Curl-Ups or Sit-Ups measure abdominal muscle strength.

- Lie on the floor with your arms across your chest and your legs bent. Have a partner hold your feet.
- Lift your upper body off the ground, then lower it until it just touches the floor.
- Repeat as many times as you can.

2. Shuttle Run measures leg strength and endurance.

- Run to the blocks and pick one up.
- Bring it back to the starting line.
- Repeat as many times as you can.

3. One Mile Run or Walk measures leg muscle strength and heart and lung endurance.

- Run or walk a mile as fast as you can.

4. Pull-ups measure the strength and endurance of arm and shoulder muscles.

- Hang by your hands from a bar.
- Pull your body up until your chin is over the bar. Lower your body again without touching the floor.
- Repeat as many times as you can.

5. V-Sit Reach measures the flexibility of your legs and back.

- Sit on the floor with your feet behind the line. Your feet should be shoulder-width apart.
- Reach forward as far as you can.

Good Posture at the Computer

Good posture is important when using the computer. To help prevent eyestrain, stress, and injuries, follow the posture tips shown below. Also remember to grasp the mouse lightly and take frequent breaks for stretching.

top of screen at or just below eye level

shoulders in line with ears and hips

neck and shoulders relaxed

arms at sides, bent as shown

wrists straight

feet flat on floor

Safety on the Internet

You can use the Internet for fun, education, research, and more. But like anything else, you should use the Internet with caution. Some people compare the Internet to a real city—not all the people there are people you want to meet and not all the places you can go are places you want to be. Just like in a real city, you have to use common sense and follow safety rules to protect yourself. Below are some easy rules to follow to help you stay safe on-line.

Rules for On-line Safety

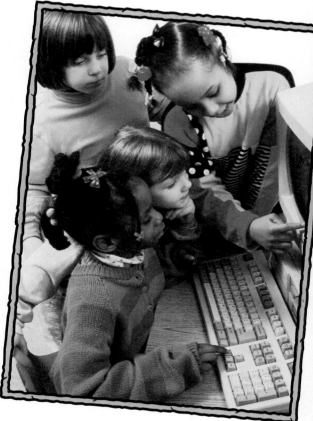

- Talk with an adult family member to set up rules for going on-line. Decide what time of day you can go on-line, how long you can be on-line, and appropriate places you can visit. Do not access other areas or break the rules you establish.

- Don't give out information like your address, telephone number, your picture, or the name or location of your school.

- If you find any information on-line that makes you uncomfortable, or if you receive a message that is mean or makes you feel uncomfortable, tell an adult family member right away.

- Never agree to meet anyone in person. If you want to get together with someone you meet on-line, check with an adult family member first. If a meeting is approved, arrange to meet in a public place and take an adult with you.

When Home Alone

Everyone stays home alone sometimes. When you stay home alone, it's important to know how to take care of yourself. Here are some easy rules to follow that will help keep you safe when you are at home by yourself.

Do These Things

- Lock all the doors and windows. Be sure you know how to lock and unlock all the locks.

- If someone calls who is nasty or mean, hang up. Your parents may not want you to answer the phone at all.

- If you have an emergency, call 911 or 0 (zero) for the operator. Describe the problem, give your full name, address, and telephone number. Follow all instructions given to you.

  - If you see anyone hanging around outside, tell an adult or call the police.

  - If you see or smell smoke, go outside right away. If you live in an apartment, do not take the elevator. Go to a neighbor's home and call 911 or the fire department immediately.

- Entertain yourself. Time will pass more quickly if you are not bored. Try not to spend your time watching television. Instead, work on a hobby, read a book or magazine, do your homework, or clean your room. Before you know it, an adult will be home.

Do NOT Do These Things

- Do NOT use the stove, microwave, or oven unless an adult family member has given you permission, and you are sure about how to use these appliances.

- Do NOT open the door for anyone you don't know or for anyone who is not supposed to be in your home.

  - If someone rings the bell and asks to use the telephone, tell the person to go to a phone booth.

  - If someone tries to deliver a package, do NOT open the door. The delivery person will leave the package or come back later.

  - If someone is selling something, do NOT open the door. Just say, "We're not interested," and nothing more.

- Do NOT talk to strangers on the telephone. Do not tell anyone that you are home alone. If the call is for an adult family member, say that they can't come to the phone right now and take a message. Ask for the caller's name and phone number and deliver the message when an adult family member comes home.

- Do NOT have friends over unless you have gotten permission from your parents or other adult family members.

A Safe Bike

You probably know how to ride a bike, but do you know how to make your bike as safe as possible? A safe bike is the right size for you. When you sit on your bike with the pedal in the lowest position, you should be able to rest your heel on the pedal. Your body should be 2 inches (about 5 cm) above the support bar that goes from the handlebar stem to the seat support when you are standing astride your bike with both feet flat on the ground. After checking for the right size, check your bike for the safety equipment shown below. How safe is *your* bike?

headlight

horn

white front reflector

red rear reflector

clear reflector

pedal reflectors

clear reflector

Your Bike Helmet

About 400,000 children are involved in bike-related crashes every year. That's why it's important to *always* wear your bike helmet. Wear your helmet flat on your head. Be sure it is strapped snugly so that the helmet will stay in place if you fall. If you do fall and strike your helmet on the ground, replace it, even if it doesn't look damaged. The padding inside the helmet may be crushed, which reduces the ability of the helmet to protect your head in the event of another fall. Look for the features shown here when purchasing a helmet.

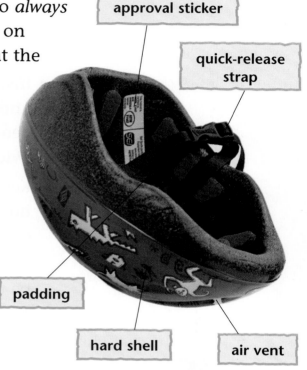

approval sticker

quick-release strap

padding

hard shell

air vent

Safety on the Road

Here are some tips for safe bicycle riding.

- Check your bike every time you ride it. Is it in safe working condition?

- Ride in single file in the same direction as traffic. Never weave in and out of parked cars.

- Before you enter a street, **STOP. Look** left, then right, then left again. **Listen** for any traffic. **Think** before you go.

- Walk your bike across an intersection. **Look** left, then right, then left again. Wait for traffic to pass.

- Obey all traffic signs and signals.

- Do not ride your bike at night without an adult. Be sure to wear light-colored clothing and use reflectors and front and rear lights for night riding.

Fire Safety

Fires cause more deaths than any other type of disaster. But a fire doesn't have to be deadly if you prepare your home and follow some basic safety rules.

- Install smoke detectors outside sleeping areas and on every other floor of your home. Test the detectors once a month and change the batteries twice a year.

- Keep a fire extinguisher on each floor of your home. Check them monthly to make sure they are properly charged.

- Make a fire escape plan. Ideally, there should be two routes out of each room. Sleeping areas are most important, as most fires happen at night. Plan to use stairs only, as elevators can be dangerous in a fire.

- Pick a place outside for everyone to meet. Choose one person to go to a neighbor's home to call 911 or the fire department.

- Practice crawling low to avoid smoke.

- If your clothes catch fire, follow the three steps shown here.

1. STOP

2. DROP

3. ROLL

Earthquake Safety

An earthquake is a strong shaking or sliding of the ground. The tips below can help you and your family stay safe in an earthquake.

Before an Earthquake	During an Earthquake	After an Earthquake
• Attach tall, heavy furniture, such as bookcases, to the wall. Store the heaviest items on the lowest shelves.	• If you are outdoors, stay outdoors and move away from buildings and utility wires.	• Keep watching for falling objects as aftershocks shake the area.
• Check for fire risks. Bolt down gas appliances, and use flexible hosing and connections for both gas and water lines.	• If you are indoors, take cover under a heavy desk or table, or in a doorway. Stay away from glass doors and windows and from heavy objects that might fall.	• Check for hidden structural problems.
• Strengthen and anchor overhead light fixtures to help keep them from falling.	• If you are in a car, drive to an open area away from buildings and overpasses.	• Check for broken gas, electric, and water lines. If you smell gas, shut off the gas main. Leave the area. Report the leak.

Storm Safety

- **In a Tornado** Take cover in a sheltered area away from doors and windows. An interior hallway or basement is best. Stay in the shelter until the danger has passed.

- **In a Hurricane** Prepare for high winds by securing objects outside or bringing them indoors. Cover windows and glass with plywood. Listen to weather bulletins for instructions. If asked to evacuate, proceed to emergency shelters.

- **In a Winter Storm or Blizzard** Stock up on food that does not have to be cooked. Dress in thin layers that help trap the body's heat. Pay special attention to the head and neck. If you are caught in a vehicle, turn on the dome light to make the vehicle visible to search crews.

For Choking . . . ◆ ◆ ◆

The tips on the next few pages can help you provide simple first aid to others and yourself. Always tell an adult about any injuries that occur.

If someone else is choking . . .

1. Recognize the Universal Choking Sign—grasping the throat with both hands. This sign means a person is choking and needs help.

2. Put your arms around his or her waist. Make a fist and put it above the person's navel. Grab your fist with your other hand.

3. Pull your hands toward yourself and give five quick, hard, upward thrusts on the choker's belly.

If you are choking when alone . . .

1. Make a fist and place it above your navel. Grab your fist with your other hand. Pull your hands up with a quick, hard thrust.

2. Or, keep your hands on your belly, lean your body over the back of a chair or over a counter, and shove your fist in and up.

For Bleeding . . .

If someone else is bleeding . . .

Wash your hands with soap, if possible.

Put on protective gloves, if available.

Wash small wounds with soap and water. Do *not* wash serious wounds.

Place a clean gauze pad or cloth over the wound. Press firmly for ten minutes. Don't lift the gauze during this time.

If you don't have gloves, have the injured person hold the cloth in place with his or her own hand.

If after ten minutes the bleeding has stopped, bandage the wound. If the bleeding has not stopped, continue pressing on the wound and get help.

If you are bleeding . . .

- Follow the steps shown above. You don't need gloves to touch your own blood.

- Be sure to tell an adult about your injury.

For Nosebleeds . . .

- Sit down, and tilt your head forward. Pinch your nostrils together for at least ten minutes.
- You can also put an ice pack on the bridge of your nose.
- If your nose continues to bleed, get help from an adult.

For Burns . . .

Minor burns are called first degree burns and involve only the top layer of skin. The skin is red and dry and the burn is painful. More serious burns are called second or third degree burns. These burns involve the top and lower layers of skin. Second degree burns cause blisters, redness, swelling, and pain. Third degree burns are the most serious. The skin is gray or white and looks burned. All burns need immediate first aid.

Minor Burns

- Run cool water over the burn or soak it in cool water for at least five minutes.
- Cover the burn with a clean, dry bandage.
- Do *not* put lotion or ointment on the burn.

More Serious Burns

- Cover the burn with a cool, wet bandage or cloth. Do *not* break any blisters.
- Do *not* put lotion or ointment on the burn.
- Get help from an adult right away.

For Insect Bites and Stings . . .

- Always tell an adult about bites and stings.
- Scrape out the stinger with your fingernail.
- Wash the area with soap and water.
- Ice cubes will usually take away the pain from insect bites. A paste made from baking soda and water also helps.
- If the bite or sting is more serious and is on the arm or leg, keep the leg or arm dangling down. Apply a cold, wet cloth. Get help immediately!
- If you find a tick on your skin, remove it. Crush it between two rocks. Wash your hands right away.
- If a tick has already bitten you, do not pull it off. Cover it with oil and wait for it to let go, then remove it with tweezers. Wash the area and your hands.

▲ deer tick

For Skin Rashes from Plants . . .

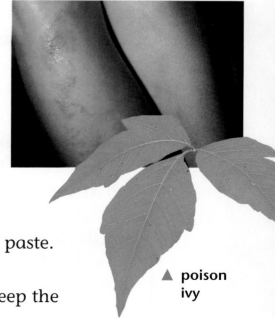

Many poisonous plants have three leaves. Remember, "Leaves of three, let them be." If you touch a poisonous plant, wash the area. Put on clean clothes and throw the dirty ones in the washer. If a rash develops, follow these tips.

- Apply calamine lotion or a baking soda and water paste. Try not to scratch. Tell an adult.

▲ poison ivy

- If you get blisters, do *not* pop them. If they burst, keep the area clean and dry. Cover with a bandage.
- If your rash does not go away in two weeks or if the rash is on your face or in your eyes, see your doctor.

GRADE 3

Glossary

Numbers in parentheses indicate the pages
on which the words are defined in context.

PRONUNCIATION RESPELLING KEY

Sound	As in	Phonetic Respelling	Sound	As in	Phonetic Respelling
a	bat	(BAT)	oh	over	(OH•ver)
ah	lock	(LAHK)	oo	pool	(POOL)
air	rare	(RAIR)	ow	out	(OWT)
ar	argue	(AR•gyoo)	oy	foil	(FOYL)
aw	law	(LAW)	s	cell	(SEL)
ay	face	(FAYS)		sit	(SIT)
ch	chapel	(CHAP•uhl)	sh	sheep	(SHEEP)
e	test	(TEST)	th	that	(THAT)
	metric	(MEH•trik)	th	thin	(THIN)
ee	eat	(EET)	u	pull	(PUL)
	feet	(FEET)	uh	medal	(MED•uhl)
	ski	(SKEE)		talent	(TAL•uhnt)
er	paper	(PAY•per)		pencil	(PEN•suhl)
	fern	(FERN)		onion	(UHN•yuhn)
eye	idea	(eye•DEE•uh)		playful	(PLAY•fuhl)
i	bit	(BIT)		dull	(DUHL)
ing	going	(GOH•ing)	y	yes	(YES)
k	card	(KARD)		ripe	(RYP)
	kite	(KYT)	z	bags	(BAGZ)
ngk	bank	(BANGK)	zh	treasure	(TREZH•er)

abdominal muscles (ab•DAH•muh•nuhl MUH•suhlz): body muscles located in the area of the stomach (6)

abstinence (AB•stuh•nuhnts): avoiding a behavior that harms health (139)

addiction (uh•DIK•shuhn): something that makes people keep using a drug even when they want to stop (174)

aerobic exercises (air•OH•bik EK•ser•sy•zuhz): exercises that strengthen the heart and lungs by making them work harder (82)

air pollution (AIR puh•LOO•shuhn): dirt and harmful materials in the air (226)

alcohol (AL•kuh•hawl): a drug found in beer, wine, and liquor (173)

alcoholism (AL•kuh•haw•lih•zuhm): a disease in which a person can't stop using alcohol (181)

allergy (A•ler•jee): the body's reaction to a substance (132)

anger (ANG•ger): a feeling of being very mad (26)

apologize (uh•PAH•luh•jyz): to say a person is sorry (35)

arteries (AR•tuh•reez): blood vessels that carry blood away from the heart throughout the body (11)

asthma (AZ•muh): a disease that causes people to have difficulty breathing (134)

bacteria (bak•TIR•ee•uh): living things that are so tiny they cannot be seen without a microscope (70, 124)

balanced diet (BA•luhnst DY•uht): a diet in which foods from each food group are eaten each day (105)

biceps (BY•seps): front upper arm muscles (6)

bloodstream (BLUHD•streem): the blood flowing through the body (178)

blood vessels (BLUHD VEH•suhlz): arteries, capillaries, and veins that carry blood throughout the body (11)

body language (BAH•dee LANG•gwij): how the body shows feelings (21)

brain (BRAYN): main organ of the body's nervous systems; control center of body's activities (15)

bully (BU•lee): someone who hurts or frightens others, especially those who are smaller or weaker (200)

caffeine (ka•FEEN): a drug that speeds up the heart (156)

cancer (KAN•ser): a disease that makes cells grow wildly (175)

cavity (KA•vuh•tee): a hole in a tooth (74)

cell (SEL): the smallest working part of the body (58)

chewing tobacco (CHOO•ing tuh•BA•koh): moist tobacco used for chewing (174)

clavicle (KLA•vih•kuhl): collarbone (4)

clinic (KLIH•nik): a place where people get health care (225)

cocaine (koh•KAYN): an illegal drug made from the leaves of the coca plant (161)

communicate (kuh•MYOO•nuh•kayt): to share information (34)

community (kuh•MYOO•nuh•tee): a place where people live, work, play, and go to school (222)

compassion (kuhm•PA•shuhn): the ability to feel what others feel (34)

cool-down (KOOL-down): slow exercise and stretching done for five minutes after hard exercise to help prevent muscle soreness later (89)

deltoid (DEL•toyd): shoulder muscle (6)

dental floss (DEN•tuhl FLAHS): a special thread to remove plaque from between teeth (75)

diabetes (dy•uh•BEE•teez): a noninfectious disease that prevents the body from using sugar properly (135)

diaphragm (dy•uh•FRAM): partition that separates the chest and abdomen (12)

diet (DY•uht): the foods a person usually eats and drinks (99)

disease (dih•ZEEZ): something that causes the body not to work normally (122)

divorce (duh•VORS): when a couple is no longer married to each other (49)

drug (DRUHG): something other than food that changes the way the body works (148)

ear canal (IR kuh•NAL): part of the outer ear where sound enters (2, 78)

eardrum (IR•druhm): located at the end of the ear canal; is moved back and forth by sound waves (2, 79)

emergency (ih•MER•juhnt•see): a situation in which help is needed right away (204)

emotions (ih•MOH•shuhnz): strong feelings (22)

environment (in•VY•ruhn•muhnt): everything, living and nonliving, around you (226)

environmental tobacco smoke (in•vy•ruhn•MEN•tuhl tuh•BA•koh SMOHK): smoke that fills an area when someone is smoking (176)

esophagus (ih•SAH•fuh•guhs): tube made of muscle that squeezes food into stomach (9)

exercise (EK•ser•syz): any activity that makes the body work hard (82)

family (FAM•lee): the group of people with whom a person lives (44)

fear (FIR): the feeling of being scared (24)

feelings (FEE•lingz): the way a person reacts to people and events (18)

femur (FEE•mer): upper leg bone (4)

fever (FEE•ver): a body temperature that is higher than normal (126)

fiber (FY•ber): the woody part of plants; important part of a healthful diet (99)

fibula (FIH•byuh•luh): the outer and smaller of the two bones between the knee and the ankle (4)

first aid (FERST AYD): caring for small injuries (214)

flexors (FLEK•serz): muscles that help bend body parts such as limbs (6)

fluoride (FLAWR•yd): a nutrient the body needs in small amounts that helps keep teeth strong and hard (76, 104)

Food Guide Pyramid (FOOD GYD PIR•uh•mid): a tool to help choose foods for a healthful diet (102)

food label (FOOD LAY•buhl): found on packaged food; gives information about how nutritious a food is (111)

grief (GREEF): a deep sadness (27)

groundwater (GROWND•waw•ter): water that sinks into the soil and fills cracks and spaces buried in rocks (232)

growth rate (GROHTH RAYT): how quickly or slowly a person grows (60)

hazard (HA•zerd): a danger that could lead to an injury (195)

health department (HELTH dih•PART•muhnt): a group of health workers that works for the government and serves the community (222)

heart (HART): organ that pumps blood and keeps it moving through the body at all times (10)

honest (AH•nuhst): truthful (19)

hospital (HAHS•pih•tuhl): a place where hurt or ill people get medical treatment (224)

humerus (HYOO•muh•ruhs): upper arm bone (4)

immune (ih•MYOON): to be protected against a pathogen that causes a disease (129)

infectious disease (in•FEK•shuhs dih•ZEEZ): a disease that can spread from one person to another (124)

ingredients (in•GREE•dee•uhnts): the things that go into a food (110)

inhalants (in•HAY•luhnts): substances that give off fumes (158)

injury (INJ•ree): harm done to a person's body (195)

iris (EYE•ruhs): colored part of the eye that changes size to adjust the amount of light coming into the pupil (2)

large intestine (LARJ in•TES•tuhn): hollow tube in the lower part of the digestive system in which wastes are stored until they leave the body (8)

life cycle (LYF SY•kuhl): four stages of growth people go through (54)

limit (LIH•muht): a point at which a person must stop doing something (195)

littering (LIH•ter•ing): dropping trash on the ground or in water (236)

lungs (LUHNGZ): large, spongy organs used for breathing, located in the chest (12)

marijuana (mair•uh•WAH•nuh): an illegal drug that comes from the hemp plant (160)

medicine (MEH•duh•suhn): a liquid, powder, cream, spray, or pill used to treat illness (130)

mouth (MOWTH): opening through which food passes into the body (8, 12)

mouth guard (MOWTH GARD): a protective plastic shield worn in the mouth (208)

nasal cavity (NAY•zuhl KA•vuh•tee): main opening inside the nose (3)

nerves (NERVZ): bundles of cells that carry messages to and from the brain (14)

nicotine (NIH•kuh•teen): the drug in tobacco (173)

noise pollution (NOYZ puh•LOO•shuhn): disturbing or harmful sounds made by human activities (228)

noninfectious diseases (nahn•in•FEK•shuhs dih•ZEE•zuhz): diseases that are not spread by pathogens and cannot be caught from or spread to other persons (132)

nose (NOHZ): the part of the face between the mouth and eyes that has two openings for breathing and smelling (3)

nostril (NAHS•truhl): opening to the nose (3)

nutrients (NOO•tree•uhnts): the parts of food that help the body grow and get energy (98)

nutrition (nu•TRIH•shuhn): the study of food and how it affects the body (98)

olfactory bulb (ahl•FAK•tuh•ree BUHLB): contains nerves that carry information about odors (3)

olfactory tract (ahl•FAK•tuh•ree TRAKT): part of the nose that carries information from the olfactory bulb to the brain (3)

optic nerve (AHP•tik NERV): part of the eye that transmits nerve signals to the brain (2)

organ system (AWR•guhn SIS•tuhm): organs that work together (59)

organs (AWR•guhnz): groups of tissues joined together, such as the heart (59)

over-the-counter medicine (OH•ver-THUH-KOWN•ter MEH•duh•suhn): a medicine an adult can buy without a doctor's order (150)

passenger (PA•suhn•jer): someone riding in a car or bus with a driver (196)

pathogens (PA•thuh•juhnz): germs that cause disease (115, 124)

peer (PIR): a friend within the same age group (33)

peer pressure (PIR PREH•sher): when friends want someone to do something just because "everyone is doing it" (33)

pelvis (PEL•vuhs): hipbone (4)

plaque (PLAK): a sticky coating that is always forming on teeth (74)

poison (POY•zuhn): a substance that causes illness or death when it gets in the body (206)

pollution (puh•LOO•shuhn): harmful material in the air, water, or land (226)

pollution control technician (puh•LOO•shuhn kuhn•TROHL tek•NIH•shuhn): a person who tests water, air, or soil for harmful substances (227)

pores (POHRZ): tiny holes in the skin (70)

prescription medicine (prih•SKRIP•shuhn MEH•duh•suhn): a medicine that must be ordered by a doctor (151)

private (PRY•vuht): belonging only to a specific person (63)

pupil (PYOO•puhl): hole in center of eye through which light enters the eye (2)

quadriceps (KWAH•druh•seps): front thigh muscles (6)

radius (RAY•dee•uhs): the bone on the thumb side of the forearm (4)

recycle (ree•SY•kuhl): to collect used things so they can be made into new things (238)

reduce (rih•DOOS): to make less of something (238)

refuse (rih•FYOOZ): to say *no* (162)

relationship (rih•LAY•shuhn•ship): the way one person gets along with another person (30)

respect (rih•SPEKT): belief in someone (19)

responsible (rih•SPAHNT•suh•buhl): when a person acts so other people can count on him or her (19)

retina (REH•tuh•nuh): tissue at the back of the eyeball which contains cells that turn images into nerve signals (2)

reuse (ree•YOOZ): to use something again (238)

rib cage (RIB KAYJ): the bones that protect the chest, including the ribs and the bones that connect them (5)

safety gear (SAYF•tee GIR): clothing or equipment worn to protect players from injury (208)

safety rules (SAYF•tee ROOLZ): rules that help protect people from injury (195)

self-control (SELF-kuhn•TROHL): power over emotions (22)

serving (SER•ving): the amount of a food probably eaten during a meal or as a snack (102)

sibling (SIH•bling): a brother or sister (49)

side effects (SYD ih•FEKTS): unwanted changes in the body caused by a medicine (155)

skull (SKUHL): the connected bones that protect the brain (4)

small intestine (SMAWL in•TES•tuhn): hollow tube between the stomach and the large intestine through which the body absorbs digested nutrients (8)

smokeless tobacco (SMOHK•les tuh•BA•koh): powdered or shredded tobacco people put between their cheeks and gums (174)

snacks (SNAKS): food between meals (106)

spinal cord (SPY•nuhl KAWRD): bundle of nerves that relays messages between the brain and the rest of the nerves in the body (14)

spine (SPYN): backbone (4)

spoiled (SPOYUHLD): unsafe to eat (114)

stomach (STUH•muhk): organ between the esophagus and the small intestine that squeezes and mashes food (8, 9)

stranger (STRAYN•jer): someone not known well (198)

stress (STRES): a feeling of pressure (25)

sunscreen (SUHN•skreen): a lotion or cream that can protect a person from the sun's harmful rays (73)

symptom (SIMP•tuhm): a sign that something is wrong with the body (122)

tar (TAR): a dark, sticky substance that coats the lungs and air passages of people who breathe in tobacco smoke (175)

taste buds (TAYST BUHDZ): tiny nerve cells on the tongue that pick out tastes and send signals to the brain (3)

tibia (TIH•bee•uh): the inner and larger of the two bones between the knee and the ankle (4)

tissues (TIH•shooz): cells that work together to get a job done (59)

trachea (TRAY•kee•uh): tube that lets air go from the nose and mouth into the chest; also called the windpipe (12)

triceps (TRY•seps): back upper arm muscles (6)

trusted adult (TRUHS•tid uh•DUHLT): a grown-up known well or an adult in a responsible position (198)

ulna (UHL•nuh): the bone on the little-finger side of the forearm (4)

vaccine (vak•SEEN): a substance given to keep someone from getting a certain kind of disease (129)

values (VAL•yooz): strong beliefs, such as honesty and caring about others (44)

veins (VAYNZ): blood vessels that carry blood to the heart (10)

virus (VY•ruhs): a tiny pathogen that causes disease (125)

warm-up (WAWRM-uhp): stretching and slow exercises done for about five minutes that get muscles ready for hard exercise and help prevent pulled muscles (89)

water pollution (WAW•ter puh•LOO•shuhn): harmful materials in lakes, oceans, or rivers (230)

Boldfaced numbers refer to illustrations.

Abdominal muscles, 6
Abdominal thrust, 268
Abstinence, 139
    from drugs, 162
    from tobacco use, 139
Achilles tendon, 7
Activity Pyramid, 252, **252**
Addiction, 174
Aerobic exercise, 256–257
    biking, 257
    effects on cardiovascular
        system, 82–83
    in-line skating, 256
    jumping rope, 257
    swimming, 256
    walking, 257
Air pollution, 226–227
Alcohol, 173, 178–181
    effects on body, 178–181
    as a harmful drug, 172–173,
        178–181
    labels, 182
Alcoholics. See Alcoholism.
Alcoholism, 181
Allergy, 132–133
Anger, 26
Animal control, 223
Antibiotics, 152
Apology, 35
Arteries, 10–11, **10–11**
Aspirin,
    harmful effects of, 131, 152
Asthma, 134

Bacteria, 70, **125**
    as cause of disease, 124–126
    fighting, 70–71, 128–130,
        250–251
Bad breath, control of, 3
Balanced diet, 102, **103,** 105
Basic needs, 44
Biceps, **6–7**
Bicycling, 257
Bicycling safety, 210, 211,
    264–265
Bike reflectors, **264**

Blood,
    safety around, 11, 215, 269
Bloodstream, 178
Blood vessels, 10–11, **10–11**
    effects of nicotine on, **175**
Body language, 21
Body parts,
    effects of alcohol on, 174–181,
        175, 179
    effects of caffeine on, 156
    effects of cocaine on, 161
    effects of exercise on, 82–83
    effects of inhalants on, 159
    effects of marijuana on, 160
    effects of tobacco on, 174–177
    protection for by wearing safety
        gear, 208–209
Body proportions, **61**
Body systems
    circulatory system, 10–11,
        10–11
    digestive system, 8–9, **8–9**
    muscular system, 6–7, **6–7**
    need for water, 104
    nervous system, 14–15, **14–15**
    organ systems, 1–15, 59
    respiratory system, 12–13,
        12–13
    sense organs, 2–3, **2–3**
    skeletal system, 4–5, **4–5**
Body temperature, 126, 130, 131
Body weight,
    percentage of water in, 104
Bottled water, 104
Brain, 15, **15**
    cells, 61
    effects of alcohol on, 178–181,
        179
    effects of tobacco on,
        174–177, **175**
    See also Nervous system.
Breathing, 13, **13**
Brushing teeth, 76
Bully, 200–201

Caffeine, 148, 156–157
Cancer, 175
    caused by ETS, 177
    caused by marijuana use, 160
    caused by smoking, 139

caused by tobacco, 139, 175
Capillaries, 11, **11**
Cardiovascular system, effects of
    aerobic exercise on, 82–83,
    256–257
Cartilage, 5, **5**
Cavity, 74
Cell, 58, **59**
    functions of, 59
    growth because of, 61
Changes in families, 48–49, 51
Chemical dependency, 161, 181,
    183
Chest protector, 209
Chewing, 9, 74
Chewing tobacco, 172, **172,** 174
Chicken pox, 129
Cigarettes, 172, **172**
    See also Smoking; Tobacco.
Cigars, 172, **172**
    See also Smoking; Tobacco.
Circulatory system, 10–11,
    10–11, 59
    effects of tobacco on, **175**
Clavicle, **4**
Clean water, 230–233
Cleated shoes, 208, **208**
Clinic, 225
Coca plant, 161
Cocaine, 158, 161
    effects on the body, 149, 161
Colds, 122, 124, 126
    treatment of, 130
Collarbone, 4
Communicable diseases.
    See Infectious disease.
Communicate, 34–35, 246
    See also Communication; Life
        skills.
Communication, 34–37
    for conflict resolution, 36–37,
        247
    with family members, 51
    of feelings, 20–21
    about first aid, 214
    skills for home health nurses,
        135
    See also I-messages; Life skills.
Community, 222
Community health care, 222–223,
    225
Community improvement,
    234–235
Compassion, 34

Computer, safe use of, 260–261
Conflict resolution,
    with friends, 36–37, 247
    verbal communication, 51
    See also Life skills.
Consumer safety, 155
Cool-down, 88–89, 253–255
Cooperation, 30–31
Crack cocaine, 161
Crown, **74**
Cutting boards, 115, 251

Dangerous substances
    alcohol, 172–173, 178–181
    cocaine, 149, 160–161
    inhalants, 158–159
    marijuana, 149, 160
    tobacco, 172–177
Decision making
    affected by alcohol use, 178
    protection for teeth, 77
    safe choices, 212–213
    steps for, 213, 246
Deltoids, **6**
Dental floss, 74, 75
Dentin, **74**
Diabetes, 132, 135
Diaphragm, 12
Diet, 99, 102–107
Digestive fluid, 9
Digestive system, 8–9, **8–9**
    alcohol in, 178
Diphtheria, 129
Disabilities
    people with, 123
Diseases, 122–123
    infectious, 124–126
    noninfectious, 132–135
    prevention and treatment of,
        128–131, 136–137
Divorce, 48, 49
Doctor
    and health care, 224, 225
    and medicine, 151
    pediatrician, 55
Drinking water
    bottled, 104
    sources of, 232
Drugs, 147–165
    alcohol and tobacco as,
        172–173

harmful effects on the body,
    148–149, 152, 154–156,
    158–161, 172–181
as medicines, 148, 150–155
illegal substances, 149,
    160–161
illegal use, 161
saying *no* to, 162–165,
    182–187

Ear canal, 2, **2,** 78, **78,** 80
Eardrum, 2, **2, 78,** 79, 80
Ears, 2, 78–80
    caring for, 2, 78–80
    effects of loud noise on, 79
    effects of noise pollution on,
        228–229
    parts of, **2, 78**
    protection for, 80
Earthquake safety, 267
Eating,
    effects of, 98, 105
Electricity,
    safety rules, 206
Emergency, 204
    calling 911 for help, 205, 214
Emotions, 20–29
Enamel, tooth, **74**
Energy,
    from foods, 98, 105
Environment,
    keeping a healthful,
        226–239
Environmental tobacco smoke
    (ETS), 176–177
    laws against, 182
Esophagus, **8–9,** 9
ETS. See Environmental
    tobacco smoke.
Exercise, 82–83, 138
    aerobic, 82–83, 256–257
    body fitness, 252–259
    effect on circulatory system,
        11, 256
    as a family activity, 45
    injuries, 90
    and muscular system, 7
    safety, 88–90, 208–213
    use of water with, 89
Exhaust,
    as air pollution, 226–227

Eyes, 2
    parts of, **2**
    protection for, 73

Face guard, **208**
Family, 44–55
    activities, 45
    and basic needs, 44
    changes, 48–49, 51
    communication, 31, 45, 51,
        52–53
    and feelings, 23
    help against strangers, 198
    jobs within, 46–47
    for protection from harm, 194
    relationships, 30–31
    responsibilities to, 31, 46–47,
        50–51
    right to privacy, 63
    rules, 50
    and peer pressure, 33
    working together, 31, 46–47,
        50–51
Family support, 31, 48–51
    with refusing alcohol and
        tobacco, 185
    with refusing drugs, 162–163
Family values, 44, 50
Farm operator, 100
Fear,
    dealing with, 24
Feelings, 18, 20–29
    communication of, 21, 23, 27,
        34–35
    compassion, 34
    control of, 22–23
    effects of exercise on, 23, 83
    expressing through actions, 21
    dealing with, 24–27
Femur, **4**
Fever, 126, 130, 131
    as symptom of disease, 122,
        131
Fiber, 99
    fight against disease, 137
Fibula, **4**
Fight Bac, **250**
Fire,
    escape plan, 204–205
    staying safe in, 204–205, **205,**
        266, **266**

Fire drills, 204
First aid, 214–215, 268–271
  for bleeding, 269
  for burns, 270
  for choking, 268
  for insect bites or stings, 215,
    271
  for nosebleeds, 270
  for skin rashes from poisonous
    plants, 271
First-aid kit, **215**
Fitness, 82–91, 252–259
Flexors, **6**
Flossing teeth, 75, **75**
Flu, 122, 126
Fluoride, 76
  as a nutrient, 104
Food,
  allergies to, 133
  safe handling of, 114–115,
    250–251
Food choices, 98–99, 102–103,
  106–109, 136–137
  for energy, 98, 105, 136
  importance of, 98
  making healthful, 110–111
  snacks, 106–109
  sources, 100–101
  for water, 104, **104**
  variety of, 99
Food Groups, 102, **103, 248**
  bread, cereal, rice, and pasta
    group, 102, **103, 248**
  fats, oils, and sweets, 102,
    103, 248
  fruit group, 102, **103, 248**
  in the Food Guide Pyramid,
    102
  meat, poultry, eggs, and nuts
    group, 102, **103, 248**
  milk, yogurt, and cheese
    group, 102, **103, 248**
  vegetable group, 102, **103, 248**
Food Guide Pyramid, 102, **103,**
  105, 137, **248,** 248–249
Food labels, 110–111, **111**
Food processing,
  wheat, **100–101**
Food safety tips, 251
Food storage, 114–115
Football safety gear, 80, 208, **208**
Friendship, 32–33
  communicating, 35
  conflict resolution, 36–37
  sharing emotions, 23
Friends' support,
  with refusal of drugs, 162

Glue
  safe use of, **158**
Goal setting. See Life skills.
Grief, 27, 49
Groundwater,
  pollution of, 230–233
Growth and development, 54–57,
  60–61
  affected by alcohol use, 180
  cell division, 58
  need for sleep, 85
  self-awareness, 60–61
  understanding varying rates of,
    58–61
  X rays of, **60**
Gums, **74**

Haemophilus Type B (Meningitis),
  129
Handwashing, 71, 128, 251, **251**
Harmful substances
  alcohol, 172–173, 178–181
  caffeine, 148, 156–157
  cocaine, 149, 160–161
  home cleaning products, 149
  inhalants, 158–159
  marijuana, 149, 160
  tobacco, 172–177
  See also Drugs.
Hay fever, 133
Hazard, 195
Head lice, 127, **127**
Health care, 222–225
  pediatrician, 55
Health clinics, 225
Heath departments, 222–223
Health habits, **62**
Health records, 223
Health screening, 225
Health spokesperson, 183
Healthful activities, 162, 184–185
Healthful choices,
  avoiding tobacco or alcohol,
    182–187
  caring for self, 62
  choosing snacks, 106–107
  dealing with unpleasant
    feelings, 24–29
  eating for good nutrition, 105
  getting rest, 84–87

  using a mouth guard, 77
Healthful diet, 98–99, 102–109,
  136–137
  Food Guide Pyramid, 102, **103,**
    248
Healthful lifestyle, 136–139
Hearing protection, 228–229
Hearing problems
  and loud noises, 79, 229
Heart, **10–11**
  building a strong, 256–257
  effects of alcohol on, **179**
  effects of caffeine on, 156
  effects of tobacco on, 139, **175**
  See also Cardiovascular
    system.
Heart disease
  caused by ETS, 177
  caused by smoking, 139, **175**
Helmets,
  for bicycle safety, 210–211,
    210–211, 265, **265**
  buying, 211
  football, 208, **208**
  hockey, 208
  parts of, **211**
  softball, **209**
Hemp plant, 160, **160**
Hepatitis B, 129
Hockey safety gear, 208
Home alone,
  safety while, 262–263
Home health nurse, 135
Home safety, 204–207
Honesty, 19
Horn, bike, **264**
Hospitals, 224
Household products,
  and groundwater pollution, 233
  as poisons, 207, **207**
Human body,
  organ systems, 1–15, 59
  See also Body systems.
Human life cycle, 54–57
Humerus, **4**
Hygiene. See Personal Hygiene.

Illegal drugs, 160–161
  See also Cocaine; Marijuana.
I-messages,
  in communication, 34
  in conflict resolution, 36, 247
Immune, 129

Infectious disease, 124–126
Ingredients, 110–111
Inhalants, 158–159
    effects of abuse of, **159**
    warning labels, 158
Inhaler, **134**
Injury, 195
    treating, 90, **90**
Injury prevention
    exercising safely, 88–89
    following rules of sport, 209,
        210
    following safety rules, 195–197
    safety gear, 77, 80, 208–211
Inner ear, **2**, **78**
International choking sign, 268
Internet safety, 261
Iris, 2, **2**

Jaw, **5**
Jobs
    family responsibilities, 46–47
Jumping rope, 257

Knee pads, **208**

Labels
    to help choose healthful foods,
        110–111, 137, **157**
    to identify dangerous
        substances, **149**
    on over-the-counter medicines,
        150–151
    as warnings, 158, 182
Large intestine, **8**, 99
Laws
    about alcohol, 182
    against pollution, 227
    about tobacco use, 182
Lens, 2, **2**
Lice, head, 127, **127**
Life changes, 54–57
Life cycle, 54–57
Life skills, 246–247
    communicate, 127, 163, 176,
        233, 246

    when angry, 26
    with family members, 52–53
    about feelings, 35, 56, 200
make decisions, 77, 85, 186,
    237, 246
    about diet, 102, 105,
        108–109
    about safe choices, 212–213
manage stress, 246
    to control disease, 140–141
    at school, 28–29
refuse, 247
    alcohol, 183
    alcohol and tobacco,
        186–187
    ETS, 139
    inhalants, 164–165
    unsafe medicines, 154
resolve conflicts, 247
    with family members, 51
    with friends, 36–37
    using negotiation, 202–203
set goals, 86–87, 234–235, 247
Lifestyle
    healthful, 136–139
Listening, 34, 36, 45, 51, 53
Litter, 236–237
Liver,
    effects of alcohol on, 179, **179**,
        181
Loneliness, 22–23
Loss of loved one. See Grief.
Love, 44
Lung disease
    caused by ETS, 177
    caused by tobacco, 139, 175
Lungs, 12–13, **12–13**
    building strong, 256–257
    effects of asthma on, 134
    effects of tobacco on, 175

Make decisions. See Life skills.
Manage anger, 26
Manage stress. See Life skills.
Marijuana, 149, 160, 161
Measles, 129
Meats,
    as food source, 101
    on Food Guide Pyramid, 102,
        103, 248
Medicine, 130–131, 148, 150–153
    alcohol in, 173
    consumer safety, 155

    forms of, 153
    safe use of, 154–155
    for treatment of asthma, 134
    for treatment of diabetes, 135
    in treatment of disease, 130
    uses from long ago, 148
Middle ear, **2**, **78**
Mouth, **8, 9, 12,** 13
    effects of alcohol on, **179**
    effects of tobacco on, **175**
    protection of, 77, 208–209
Mouth guard, 77, **77**, 208, **208**
Mumps, 129
Muscle pairs, 7, **7**
Muscular system, 6–7, **6–7**
    and exercise, 82

Nasal cavity, 3, **3**
Needs, basic, 44
Nerves, 14, **14**
Nervous system, 14–15, **14–15**
    cells of, 59, **59**
    protection for, 208–210
    sense of smell, 3
Nicotine, 173
    effects of on brain, 174
Noise pollution, 228–229
Noncommunicable diseases,
    132–135
Noninfectious diseases, 132–135
Nonsmokers,
    and ETS, 176–177, **176**
Nose, 3, **3, 12,** 13, 81
Nosebleed, 3, 81, 270
Nostril, **3**
Nutrients, 98, 102, 104, 105, 106,
    107
Nutrition, 98, 101
    body needs, 98
    and diabetes, 135
    effects of on circulatory
        system, 11
    effects of on skeletal system, 5
    facts, on labels, 111
    good health habits, **62**

Olfactory bulb, **3**
Olfactory tract, **3**
Optic nerve, **2**

Organ systems, 1–15, 59.
   circulatory system, 10–11, **10–11**
   digestive system, 8–9, **8–9**
   muscular system, 6–7, **6–7**
   nervous system, 14–15, **14–15**
   respiratory system, 12–13, **12–13**
   skeletal system, 4–5, **4–5**
   See also Body systems.
OTC. See over-the-counter medicine.
Outer ear, **2**, **78**
Over-the-counter medicine (OTC), 150–151

Pain relievers, 152, 153
Parents. See Family.
Passenger, 196
Pathogens, 115, 128
   as cause of disease, 124–125
   good uses of, 129
   use of medicine against, 130, 152
Pediatrician, 55
Peer, 33
Peer pressure, 33
   and refusing alcohol and tobacco, 183, 186–187
Pelvis, **4**
Personal hygiene
   bathing, 70, 71
   brushing and flossing, 74–76, **75**, **76**
   head lice, 127, **127**
   preventing infectious disease, 128
   washing hands, 70, 71, 251
Personality changes,
   result of alcohol use, 180, **180**
Pertussis (whooping cough), 129
Pets, 46
Pharmacist, 151
Physical fitness, 82–85, 138, 252–259
Physical therapist, 90–91
Plants,
   as a food source, 100–101
Plaque, 74
   removal, 75–76
Poison, 206–207
Poison Control Center, 214
Poison safety rules, 207

Polio, 129
Polluted water. See Water pollution.
Pollution, 226–233
   See also Trash; Water pollution.
Pollution control devices, 227
Pollution control laws, 226, 227, 228
Pollution control technician, 227, 231
   check for noise control, 228
Pores, 70
Power cords,
   safe use of, 206
Preparing foods safely, 114–115, 250–251
Prescription medicine, 151
President's Challenge, 258–259, **258–259**
Preventing disease, 128–129
   through a healthful lifestyle, 136–139
Privacy, 63
Public health nurse, 222–223
Public health officers, 223
Pulp, **74**
Pupil, **2**

Quadriceps, **6**

Radius, **4**
Recycle, 238
Reduce, 238
Refuse. See Life skills.
Registered nurse, 224
Relationships, 30–32
Remarriage, 48
Resolve conflicts. See Life Skills.
Respect, 19
   communication, 34
   showing, 30–31
Respiratory system, 12–13, **12–13**
   asthma, 134, **134**
   effects of ETS on, 177, 256–257
   effects of exercise on, 13, 256–257

   effects of inhalants on, **159**
   effects of tobacco on, 139, 175
Responsibility, 19
   family cooperation, 50
   for safety, 194–197
   verbal communication and, 35
Rest, 84–85
Retina, **2**
Reuse, 238–239, **239**
Rib, **4–5**
Rib cage, **4–5**, 5
Root, tooth, **74**
Rubella, 129
Rules,
   family, 50
   for using medicines, 154–155
   See also Safety rules.

Sadness,
   making it go away, 22–23
   See also Feelings; Grief.
Safety, 194–201
   bicycle, 210, 264–265
   around bullies, 200
   computer, 260–261, **260**
   earthquake, 267
   with electricity, 206
   while exercising, 88–89, 253–255
   fire, 204–205, 266
   gear, 2, 15, 77, **77**, 80, **80**, 208–211, **208–211**
   when handling food, 114–115, 250–251
   at home, 204–207
   with household products, 158, 206–207
   making decisions about, 212–213
   responsibility for, 194
   to and from school, 196, **196**
   for sports, 208–210
   storm, 267
   around strangers, 198–199
   in using medicines, 152, 154–155
Safety rules,
   for biking, 265
   with bullies, 201
   around electricity, 206
   when home alone, 262–263
   with household products, 207
   on Internet, 261

for riding in vehicles, 196
  at school, 197
  to and from school, 196
  with strangers, 198–199
  when walking, 196
Say *no,*
  to alcohol, 182–185
  to drugs, 162–163
  to inhalants, 164–165
  to strangers, 198–199
  to tobacco, 182–187
Self-awareness, 18, 20–21
  growth and development, 58, 60–61
Self-control, 21–23
  and peer pressure, 33
Self-forgiveness, 23
Self-impressions, **18–19**
Self-knowledge, 18, 20
Self-respect, 19
Sense organs, 2–3, **2–3**
Setting goals. See Life skills.
Severe storm safety, 267
Sewage treatment, 230–231, **230–231**
Shin guard, 209, **209**
Shopping for food, 110–113
Sibling, 49, 50
Side effects,
  caused by medicine, 155
  of inhalants, **159**
Skateboard safety gear, 210, **210**
Skating, 256,
  safety gear, 210, **210**
Skeletal system, 4–5, **4–5**
  cells of, 59, **59**
  See also Body systems.
Skin, 3, **3**
  bacteria on, 70
  cells, **59**
  care, 3, 70–73
Skin cancer,
  protection from, 72–73
Skull, **4–5**, 5, **15**
Sleep, 84–85
Small injuries, 214–215, 269–271
Small intestine, **8**
  effects of alcohol on, **179**
Smoke alarm, 205, 266
Smokeless tobacco, 172, **172**, 174
Smoking,
  abstinence from, 139
  effects of, 139, 174–175, **175**
  See also Tobacco.
Snacks, 106–107
  making decisions about, 108–109

Snuff, 172, **172**, 174
Soccer safety gear, 209, **209**
Softball safety gear, 208, **209**
Sore throat, 122, 126, 130
Spinal cord, **14**
Spine, **4**
Spoiled food, 114, 250
Sports rules, 209
Spread of disease, 122–126
Spread of germs, 70, 71
  preventing, 71, 128
Stages of growth, 54–56
Sternum, **5**
Stomach, **8**, **9**, 9
  effect of alcohol on, **179**
  effect of caffeine on, 156
  effect of inhalants on, **159**
Strangers, 198–199
Strep throat, 126
Stress, 25
Stress management, 25, 28–29
  exercise, 25, 138
  through time management, 25
  See also Life skills.
Stretching, 88–89, 254–255
Sugar in blood,
  diabetes, 135
Sunburn,
  protection from, 72, 73
  and skin cancer, 72
Sunscreen, 73
Sweat, 70
Swimming, 256

Tar, 175
Taste buds, 3
Teeth, 74–77, **74**
  brushing of, 76, **76**
  flossing of, 75, **75**
  fluoride, 76, 104
  protection for, 77
Temperature, body, 130–131
Tendons, 7, **7**
Tension. See Stress.
Tetanus, 129
Throat,
  effects of smoking on, **175**
Tibia, **4**
Tobacco, 139, 172–177, 183
  in advertisements, 183
  types of, **172**
  warning labels, 182
  See also Smoking.

Tongue, 3, **3**
Tooth. See Teeth.
Touching,
  unwanted, 24, 63
Trachea, **12**
Traffic,
  and bicycling safety, 210
Transmission of disease,
  preventing, 128–129
Trash, 236–238
Treating disease, 130–131, 133–135, 152
Triceps, **6–7**
Trusted adult, 198

Ulna, **4**
Unpleasant feelings, 24–27
  changing, 22–27
Using a computer safely, 260, **260**
Using medicines safely, 154–155

Vaccine, 129
Veins, **10–11**, 11
Viruses, 125, **125**

Walking, 257
Warm-up, 88–89, 253
  stretches, 254–255
Washing hands, 70–71, 251, **251**
Water,
  in diet, 104
  during exercise, 89
  sampling of, 231
Water pollution, 230–233
Water sources, 231, 232
Water treatment, 230–231, **230–231**
Windpipe, **12**
Workout, 253, 256–257
  planning a, 252
  See also Exercise.

Great

Good
job

THE
SEEKER

Books by Ann H. Gabhart

The Scent of Lilacs

Orchard of Hope

Summer of Joy

❖

The Outsider

The Believer

The Seeker

THE
SEEKER

A NOVEL

ANN H. GABHART

Doubleday Large Print
Home Library Edition

Revell

a division of Baker Publishing Group
Grand Rapids, Michigan

© 2010 by Ann H. Gabhart

Published by Revell
a division of Baker Publishing Group
P.O. Box 6287, Grand Rapids, MI 49516-6287

Printed in the United States of America

ISBN 978-1-61664-641-7

Scripture used in this book, whether quoted or paraphrased by the characters, is taken from the King James Version of the Bible.

This book is a work of fiction. Names, characters, places, and incidents are the product of the author's imagination

Page 239–243: "The Rock" (From "A Collection of Hymns, Selected from different parts. Improved in our General Worship. Written by Elizabeth Lovegrove, 1822." New Lebanon)

Page 245: "Hop Up and Jump Up" (From one of Mary Hazzard's hymnals, New Lebanon, 1847)

Page 362: "O the Simple Gifts of God" (From one of Mary Hazzard's hymnals, New Lebanon. Song originated in North Union, Ohio—date unknown)

To my family
for their unfailing love and support through
the years

A NOTE ABOUT THE SHAKERS

American Shakerism originated in England in the eighteenth century. Its leader, a charismatic woman named Ann Lee, was believed by her followers to be the second coming of Christ in female form. After being persecuted for those beliefs in England, she and a small band of followers came to America in 1774 to settle in Watervliet, New York, and there established the first community of the United Society of Believers in Christ's Second Appearing, more commonly known as Shakers.

When religious fervor swept the Western frontier at the turn of the nineteenth century, the Shakers, whose communities in New England were flourishing, found the spiritual atmosphere in Kentucky perfect for expanding their religion to the west. By the middle of the nineteenth century the Shakers had nineteen communities spread through the New England states and Kentucky, Ohio, and Indiana.

The Shaker doctrines of celibacy, communal living, and the belief that perfection could be attained in this life were all based on revelations that Mother Ann claimed to have divinely received. The name *Shakers* came from the way they worshiped. At times when a member received the "spirit," he or she would begin shaking all over. These sorts of "gifts of the spirit," along with other spiritual manifestations such as visions, were considered by the Shakers to be confirmation of the same direct communication with God they believed their Mother Ann had experienced.

Since the Shakers believed that work was part of worship and that God dwelt in the details of that work, they devoted themselves to doing everything—whether farming or making furniture and brooms or developing better seeds—to honor the Eternal Father and Mother Ann. Shaker communities thrived until the Civil War, which proved to be a very difficult time for the Shaker communities, partly because they never refused to feed those who came hungry into their communities and partly because their normal trade routes to the South were disrupted by the war. On one day after the Battle of Perryville in Kentucky, the Shakers at Pleasant Hill saw ten thousand troops march through their village and they served fourteen thousand meals.

After the war, much change came to the nation. Factories began producing brooms, furniture, preserves, and other products the Shakers had made, and these were sold at prices that pushed the Shakers out of the market. Jobs were easier to find, fewer and fewer young people were willing to accept the strict, celibate life of the Shakers, and the sect gradually died out. The few remaining Shakers reside at the last active Shaker village, Sabbathday Lake in Maine.

In Kentucky, the Shaker villages of Pleasant Hill and South Union have been restored and attract many visitors curious about the Shaker lifestyle. These historical sites provide a unique look at the austere beauty of the Shakers' craftsmanship. The sect's songs and strange worship echo in the impressive architecture of their buildings. Visitors also learn about the Shakers' innovative ideas in agriculture and industry that improved life not only in their own communities but also in the "world" they were so determined to shut away.

1

"The Shakers! Have you taken leave of your senses, Edwin? You can't seriously be considering joining the Shakers?" The words came out harsher than Charlotte Vance intended, and Edwin Gilbey stepped back from her until the budding branches of the lilac bush behind him had to be poking holes in his dinner jacket.

"Please, Charlotte. Calm yourself. You know I can't abide a scene." He sounded alarmed as he shifted his eyes away from her face to look longingly over her shoulder toward the veranda door.

Charlotte's irritation grew as she stared

at Edwin in the light of the nearly full moon. He didn't even like social gatherings. Behind her the door opened, and laughter mixed with the music of the string ensemble she'd hired from Lexington flowed out into the garden. The party seemed to be proceeding well in spite of the charged emotions in the air.

When her father first sent word from Frankfort that he wanted her to arrange a grand gala for his return home to Grayson Farm after completing his business in the capital city, she'd doubted his sanity. Surely as a senator in the state legislature he was more than aware the country was teetering on the brink of destruction after Mr. Lincoln had taken the oath of office and moved into the White House last month. Half a dozen Southern states had already followed South Carolina out of the Union. That's all anybody was talking about. Whether they could do that. Whether the government should allow them to do that. Whether there would be armed conflict to preserve the Union.

How in the world did her father expect them to have a civil party with half the guests waving the Union flag and the other half shouting states' rights and favoring secession? She'd sent a message back to him saying they might as well lay the dueling pistols on the table in the front hall and let the men take turns out on Grayson's front lawn. But he had made light of her worries and on return post had insisted he had news to announce that required the finest party she'd ever arranged. Astounding news.

Charlotte had surmised he was bringing word back to Grayson that the Constitutional Union Party had pegged him as their next candidate for governor. Certainly reason enough to dare entertaining in spite of the political climate. But no, that hadn't been his news. Instead he had handed a woman dressed to the nines in silk and jewels down out of the carriage and introduced her as his wife.

Not wife-to-be. Wife. A woman from the North. Selena Harley Black. A widow with a young son somewhere still in the North, or so Betty Jamison had whispered in Charlotte's ear while her father escorted his bride from group to group to introduce her. Of course, after the death of Charlotte's mother, Betty had entertained the improbable notion that she might eventually catch Charlotte's father's eye.

When the veranda door closed again and muffled the sound of the party, Charlotte was relieved. She couldn't think about her father and that woman right now. Not with Edwin talking this ridiculous Shaker talk. One problem at a time. She turned her attention back to the man pinned against her mother's favorite lilac bush. He shifted uneasily on his feet and glanced over his shoulder as though considering an escape under the lilac's branches, even if it meant spoiling the knees of his trousers.

"But Edwin," she said as sweetly as she could under the circumstances. "Unless I am greatly mistaken, the Shakers have a ban on matrimony."

Edwin straightened his shoulders and almost looked at her face again before he let his eyes slide down to the ground at their feet. "You are not mistaken. It is one of their strongest tenets. The avoidance of such unions allows them to live in peace and harmony. Hence the name of their village, Harmony Hill."

"I am well aware of the name of their

village." The irritation in her voice sounded
a bit strident even to Charlotte's ears. Not
the way to win arguments. She attempted
to pull in a deep, steadying breath, but with
the tight lacings of her corset constricting
her breathing, she simply ended up light-
headed. She fought the feeling. She refused to have the vapors. She could control
this. She could control Edwin. Hadn't she
done so ever since they were toddlers playing together in the nursery?

He threw up his hand to ward off her
anger as he hurried out his words. "Yes,
yes, of course you are. At any rate, I have
become well acquainted with an Elder
Logan in their village. He has found great
peace among the Believers there. A peace
I envy." Edwin peeked up at her and went
on in a tremulous voice. "You know yourself how unsettled I've felt ever since my
dear grandmother departed this world last
spring."

"I do understand how difficult the loss
has been for you. For all of us. She was a
fine lady." It took effort, but she managed
to sound sympathetic as she spoke the oft-
repeated words. What she actually wanted
to tell Edwin was that Faustine Hastings

had been well along in years and that no one could live forever. Or grieve forever. Charlotte had resigned herself to a year of mourning before their marriage, even though that would make her nearly twenty when they spoke their vows in May. A mere month from now.

Edwin knew they were to marry in May. He had agreed to the date. Charlotte's dressmaker was putting the finishing touches on her wedding dress. The last time she had tried it on, it had taken Mellie almost a half hour just to fasten its many pearl buttons down the back and from the elbows on the sleeves. Of course part of the reason for that was Mellie had something unfavorable to say about Edwin with every button she fastened.

Charlotte's familiar words of sympathy seemed to allay Edwin's apprehension, and he eased a bit away from the bush closer to her as he said, "Elder Logan thinks Grandmother would have understood and approved of my search for peace in my life."

"Does he? And how can he know that? Did he get a vision as he was doing his worship dances?"

Edwin frowned at her mocking tone. "You needn't try to disparage Elder Logan. He's a fine man and their worship dances are often very sedate and orderly. At least the ones I have witnessed."

"But isn't it so that they spin and at times fall prostrate on the floor in odd fits? That hardly sounds sedate to me." Charlotte's head was spinning every bit as wildly as she'd heard the Shakers did in their worship dances. How could both of the men in her life lose their senses at the same time? First her father and now Edwin.

She tried to block from her mind the vision of her father's beaming face as he presented that woman as the new mistress of Grayson. He hadn't even glanced toward Charlotte, who had been running Grayson with Aunt Tish's help even before her mother's untimely death four years ago. He had without a doubt lost his mind. Proof was surely in how he had sounded almost proud when he said he'd met the woman only six weeks earlier. Charlotte would be surprised if he had even checked into her family lineage. Or given the first thought to why a woman her age would consider marrying a man his. She had to be twenty years younger than him. Perhaps thirty to his fifty.

Charlotte reached up to smooth out the furrows of a frown forming between her eyes. A lady could not chance developing grimace lines to mar her appearance. It was bad enough that she had a too-generous sprinkling of freckles across her nose which no amount of cream could fade. Her mother had laid the fault of that on Charlotte's red hair and her Grandmother Vance back in Virginia, who neither she nor her mother had ever laid eyes on. But her father said his mother's hair was the color of new bricks, and while Charlotte's was lighter than that, more like ginger spice, nobody in the Grayson family line had ever been born with such a flamboyant hair color.

"You have to be among them to truly understand," Edwin was saying. "When the spirit comes down on the Believers, it takes control of their bodies and demonstrates its ecstasy in myriad ways. Not always by shaking as is commonly believed by those of the world."

"Those of the world," Charlotte echoed

softly. This was more serious than she had thought. He already sounded like one of them.

Of course Charlotte knew Edwin had been visiting the Shaker village. Aunt Tish had heard as much through the servant grapevine that delivered news between their adjoining plantations faster than a crow could fly between the two great houses. But who would have ever thought Edwin would seriously consider joining with them?

Even Mellie, who held Edwin in considerable disdain, had never suggested that. Just last week while she'd been pinning up Charlotte's hair, Mellie had told her, "That Mr. Edwin, you best stop countin' on him comin' courtin' you any time soon, Miss Lottie."

"He doesn't have to court me, Mellie. We've known we were marrying ever since we were six," Charlotte told her.

"You might be knowin' it, Miss Lottie, but that Mr. Edwin ain't a knowin' it. If ever I did see a man afraid of lovin', it's him." Mellie had twisted Charlotte's hair in a tight roll and jabbed a pin in it as she added, "And you ain't no way lovin' him neither."

"What do you know about loving?" Charlotte spoke shortly as she stared at Mellie's face in the mirror.

"Enough to know it's something a slave like me had best avoid like the plague. 'Fore I find myself on the auction block like my mammy and pappy with me goin' one way and whoever I was fool enough to fall in love with goin' the other."

Charlotte turned on the dressing stool to touch Mellie's arm. "You know I'd never let Father put you on the block. Never. You and Aunt Tish are family."

"I know you wouldn't want to. And I know we as close to sisters as a black slave girl and a rich white girl can be, seein' as how we took turns suckling at my mammy's breast, but things change. That's somethin' we can count on, and if we ain't ready for it, we're gonna get knocked down and trampled into the dirt. Mammy warns me about that all the time, and she knows about them kind of changes."

Mellie mashed her lips together and shook her head a little as she placed her long slender hand over Charlotte's and went on. "And I guess as how you know about them too, what with your mama dyin' how she did. Just steppin' out in her garden and fallin' down there by her red rosebush. I can still see her layin' there with that rose in her hand like as how she'd pricked her finger and fell asleep like some princess in one of them fairy tales."

Charlotte slowly shut her eyes and pulled in a breath. She would never forget the sound of her mother's gasp as she collapsed on the garden path and how she had run to kneel by her mother's side, but it was already too late. Her mother was gone. Charlotte blinked her eyes to keep back her tears as she said, "Except she wasn't asleep."

"Except that," Mellie agreed sadly as she squeezed Charlotte's hand, then pulled it away to start pinning up Charlotte's hair again. "Things changed then and things is sure to change again."

Charlotte had turned back to the mirror and said, "Some things won't." She hadn't looked at Mellie's reflection in the mirror but instead had stared into her own eyes as if making the promise to herself. She would see that no changes upset their lives at Grayson.

Now she studied Edwin's face as he

went on and on about what this man, Elder Logan, had told him. How a person needed to pick up the cross of purity and bear it no matter how heavy it might be in order to find that peace he needed. How at the Shaker village, men and women lived as sisters and brothers without the thorn of marital relationships to disturb their peace. How they owned everything in common, and how, when he joined with them, he would turn his land, Hastings Farm, over to the Ministry there at Harmony Hill. With each word his voice got stronger and bolder until he didn't even sound like the Edwin she knew. The Edwin who had always done whatever she said.

"But, Edwin," she interrupted him. "We are to wed next month."

He did have the grace to look uncomfortable, but he didn't back away from her. "That was more your decision than mine, Charlotte. While I regret disappointing you, Elder Logan assures me a man should not allow himself to be pulled into an unwanted and sinful union simply to avoid a bit of embarrassment. Not when his eternal salvation is at stake."

"Marriage is not sinful," Charlotte said.

"I fear you have been listening to bad advice from those who simply want to gather your land in with theirs."

Edwin stiffened at her words, and in the moonlight, the lines of his face looked chiseled out of stone as he stared down at her. The man in front of her little resembled the Edwin she had grown up with. That Edwin had hidden behind his grandmother's skirts until he was well out of knickers. That Edwin had been afraid of his shadow when she pulled him out into the garden to play hide-and-seek. That Edwin listened without argument to her plans for their lives.

When he finally spoke, his voice was harsh. "And why have you always said we must wed, Charlotte? Isn't it to join our properties? Hasn't that always been your primary purpose? To do your father's bidding and make his holdings the largest in Mercer County."

"Not his holdings, Edwin. Ours. Grayson and Hastings farms together." She pushed the words at him. "We've talked of nothing else for years."

"*You've* talked of nothing else. Perhaps it is time you listened for a change," he said shortly.

Then without waiting for her to say more, he stepped off the path to go around her as if even the touch of the ruffles on her hooped skirt must be avoided. She stared after him, astounded by his rudeness. And by the determined set of his shoulders. That old Shaker elder with his insidious words of peace was the cause of this, but she wouldn't let it be the end. Edwin would marry her. Of course he would. He'd come to his senses and crawl back to her, begging to carry out the plans they had made. She'd find a way to see that he did.

When he opened the veranda door, the noise of the party drifted out. He stepped inside and snapped the door closed behind him, clipping off the sound, but through the glass door and window she could see the guests milling about. Her guests. She was neglecting her hostess duties. Edwin could wait. She touched the pile of hair elaborately styled on top of her head to be sure no strand had escaped its pins and started back toward the house.

A man's deep voice stopped her before she had gone a dozen steps. "He must be an extremely foolish man to turn his back and run from such beauty."

2

Charlotte whirled to face the man who stepped up on the path behind her. He must have been sitting out of her view on the stone bench in the shadow of the dogwood that reached its limbs toward the veranda.

"Forgive me," he said. "It wasn't my intention to startle you."

In the moonlight it wasn't hard to see the amused smile playing across his lips under his mustache that gave lie to his words. That had been exactly what he'd intended, Charlotte thought as she stared up at him with no pretense of demurely lowering her

eyes. He was tall, even taller than Edwin,
but while Edwin slouched to try to keep
from towering above his companions, this
man stood straight, completely at ease with
his height. He was quite handsome with
thick dark hair brushed back from his forehead and a strong profile. She had no idea
who he was.

"I don't think we've met," she said in her
most reserved, yet still civil voice. He could
be a new political friend of her father's
who had arrived at the party late and un-
announced. Best to be polite until his
importance was determined. He wore a
dinner jacket, so surely he was a guest
and not just a passerby attracted by the
lights and music.

His smile was full now. "My introduction
got a bit overlooked after the presentation
of the new Mrs. Vance. It's very like her to
do a little grandstanding, but your father
could have extended the courtesy of letting you in on their little surprise prior to
the carriage's arrival. That way you could
have been prepared with your smile."

"I smiled."

"That you did," the man said with a half
nod of agreement. "Bravely. Staunchly. In

spite of the way the color drained from your face and you looked faint."

"I have never felt faint," Charlotte said tersely. She didn't know why she was continuing to talk to this man who was assuming entirely too much about her without the first bit of knowledge, but something about his eyes held her there. Even in the soft light of the moon, they looked sharp and piercing, able to see past shadows, past pretense. Suddenly she wanted to hurry out of sight of those eyes before they stripped away her every defense and laid bare her soul. She was poised to flee up the veranda steps when his next words stopped her.

"Then you are an unusual young woman. Our Selena certainly has never hesitated to feign a swoon if such an action fit the occasion and achieved her end."

Our Selena. Instead of a political acquaintance, he must be a friend or even relation of this woman who had captured Charlotte's unwary father, perhaps by feigning a great deal more than a swoon. Charlotte studied the man a moment before she said, "So are you related to my father's new wife?" She managed to get out the word "wife" without it choking her. She would get used to it. What other choice did she have?

"Oh no. I fear I am just a hired artisan." The man laughed out loud and bowed at the waist toward Charlotte. "Adam Wade at your service, Miss Vance."

"And for what purpose have you been hired, if I may be so bold to ask? A cupola here in my mother's garden?"

"Perhaps artisan is not the proper word. Artist. Although my grandfather's practical side shudders every time I claim the title. But that is what I am. An artist. A curse I fear I was born with. And I have been commissioned—or a better word might be coerced—to paint a wedding portrait of the lovely Mrs. Vance."

"Coerced? By whom? Our Selena?" She carefully emphasized the last two words.

"Oh no." He laughed again. Easily, without inhibition. "I barely know the woman."

"Neither does my father."

"You have a point, but not one, I am relieved to say, that can poke me. My sister, Phoebe, knew our Selena back home in Boston, and she is the one whose coercion I cannot ignore. Not and maintain any sort of familial peace. I've oft explained to her how I detest doing portraits, but my sister thinks one can slap a few dobs of paint on a canvas, make the subject look beautiful whether they carry beauty or not, collect the commission, and everybody's happy. To Phoebe, one picture is like any other and a brother's duty is to do as she says. Or else." With a rueful smile, he chopped his hand down through the air in front of him before he looked at her with something akin to sympathy as he continued speaking. "I fear you will find the new Mrs. Vance has some of the same characteristics. I will be much relieved to have the portrait finished and hanging over your mantel."

"Where Mother's hangs now."

He raised his dark eyebrows at her. "You can hardly expect her portrait to remain there. Lovely though it is."

"No, I suppose not." Charlotte sighed, surprised at how she was stepping into acceptance of the change coming to Grayson. Change she was beginning to see she could not hold at bay. Her father was married. That would change everything. Perhaps even more than Mr. Lincoln's inauguration.

She mentally shook her head at her foolish thought. A house changed couldn't compare to a country torn asunder.

"I'm sorry," Adam said with honest sincerity in his voice.

She shivered slightly, feeling the chill of the night air for the first time since she'd followed Edwin out without grabbing a wrap, but now her anger had drained away, leaving her vulnerable to the cold and a kind word. She pulled herself together and smiled at the man in front of her, determined to be the proper hostess again and not even let her mind consider how much of her conversation with Edwin he might have overheard. It was of no concern to him. But he was a guest to be treated as such.

"Then if you don't generally do portraits except under coercion, what sort of art do you do?" she asked, as if they had just met inside in the double parlor and weren't standing in the shadowy chill of her mother's garden while the party played on with no notice of their absence.

"I daresay you've read *Harper's Weekly* and perhaps leafed through some of the other northern newspapers and magazines your father must bring home on occasion." He didn't wait for her to answer. "If so, you may have seen my work. The illustrations."

"Adam Wade. Of course. I have seen your work in *Harper's*." She stared at the man with fresh eyes. "I should have recognized your name."

"Don't pretend," Adam said. "I liked you better when you were too upset to trot out your manners."

"A lady always remembers her manners."

"Tell your young man that."

Charlotte ignored his words, refusing to let him bait her. He was the guest. She was the hostess. "No, really. A few months back, in a January issue I think, there was a man on horseback somewhere in the Western regions. He was hunched down in the saddle trying to escape the snow and wind. Just thinking about it now makes me cold." Charlotte wrapped her arms around her middle and shivered.

"Quite a compliment to have you shiver just at the thought of the illustration. Believe me, it was every bit as cold as I was able to make it look. But I think your chill now may have more to do with the night air." He slipped off his jacket and stepped closer to drape it around her.

He let his hands linger on her shoulders. She told herself to step back from him, but she didn't move as she soaked up the warmth of his jacket and breathed in his scent. An outdoors odor mixed with a light trace of manly sweat and linseed oil. She wished she could just stay wrapped in his jacket there in the garden until all the guests had gone home. Then she could sneak in the back door and creep up the servants' stairway to Aunt Tish's room. Aunt Tish would help her see what to do. There had to be a way to keep her world from crumbling.

"I'd like to paint how you look right now here in the moonlight. So winsome. So pure." He moved his right hand off her shoulder and rubbed his thumb down her nose and across her cheek, measuring her face for his painting. The pad of his thumb was rough against her skin, but still she didn't pull away. "So beautiful."

"No one has ever told me I was beautiful. No one but Aunt Tish." Her voice was barely above a whisper.

"Not even the young man who was with you in the garden?"

"Especially not Edwin. I frighten him."

"Then he's not much of a man."

"I'm going to marry him." Charlotte didn't know where the words were coming from or why she was saying them. She felt mesmerized by his eyes on her, measuring her, seeing past her façade, doing what she had most feared he could do. Seeing into her soul.

"I think not. That would surely be a waste." His fingertips walked across her face gently probing the shape of her cheekbones.

"That's what Mellie says."

"A true friend if she tells you the truth."

"Do you tell the truth?" Charlotte peered up at him. She thought she would be able to see on his face if he lied.

"Always. If I know it."

"That's the trouble, isn't it? Knowing it. Recognizing the lies."

"And has your Edwin lied to you?" His voice was soft, insistent.

"No. It might be better if he did."

"And why would that be better?" His eyes didn't waver on hers.

"He could tell me he loved me." She couldn't believe she spoke the words out loud. What kind of spell was she letting this man's eyes put on her?

"Sometimes that is spoken in actions better than words." He brought his finger over to trace around her lips. "Has he kissed you? Surely he's kissed you."

She just looked at him without saying anything. She couldn't answer that.

His eyes pierced straight through her as he waited for her to speak. At last he said, "Then have you ever been kissed, my beautiful Miss Vance? Really kissed."

Without giving her a chance to respond, to consider his words, to recognize the alarm rising in her as she thought of her position there in the shadows with a man she didn't even know, he stepped closer and dropped his mouth down to cover hers. And she let him kiss her. Not only did she let his lips touch hers without protest, but her lips reached for his. Sought the touch.

It was as if somebody else had taken over her body. As if she had given up control and now was drifting without thought, without sense, toward disaster.

The yearning swelled up inside her to step into his embrace, to slip her arms around his back, to touch his dark hair, to surrender completely to the feelings his lips were pulling up from deep inside her. Even her toes in her dancing slippers felt warm.

His hand moved from her shoulder to slide down her back to pull her closer, to swallow her completely in his strength. She'd be powerless to do anything but lay her head on his shoulder and surrender to his will. There would be no more arranging, no more shaping events, no more making sure things happened as they should. As she planned. As they must. She'd turn into one of those fine ladies who sat in sunny windows, pulling bright-colored threads through flat squares of cloth as they let life drift past them without ever raising a finger to change their circumstances. She would be her mother waiting, always waiting.

The thought was like a dash of cold water and she jerked back to free herself from his embrace. She put her fingers over her lips as her face burned with the ignominy of allowing a stranger such an intimate kiss. A man she'd just met.

The man looked amused at her embarrassment. "Go ahead. Slap me if it will make you feel better."

"Then I would have to slap myself as well." Charlotte dropped her hands to let them hang limply down under his jacket still around her shoulders. Perhaps he had taken advantage of her unsettled spirit and the moonlight, but that hadn't been reason for her to melt into his embrace as she had. She was as much to blame as he was.

He surprised her by laughing. "I don't think I've ever met a Southern belle with such refreshing candor."

She did not allow a smile back on her face. She would not let him charm her again. "If you are a gentleman as well as an artist, I will expect no mention of this. If not, then my refreshing candor will force me to reveal how you startled me and kept me in the shadows against my will."

"Never fear, milady. I may not be a high-ranking gentleman like the scared rabbit you chased back inside, but I don't kiss and tell."

"Thank you." She slipped his jacket off her shoulders and held it out to him. She ignored the shiver chasing up and down her back that was not entirely due to the chill of the night air as she said, "It was kind of you to loan me your jacket. Now I must see to my guests."

"I have no complaints about your fine hospitality." He took the jacket with another infuriating smile.

She turned and lifted her skirts to hurry away from him toward the veranda steps. Behind her, she heard him chuckle, and she hoped he would remain in the garden the rest of the evening. Even better, that he might stop worrying about what his sister said for him to do and instead ride to the West to paint some cacti or sagebrush and take her reason for shame with him.

How could she have surrendered to his kiss so willingly? The evening's events had surely unbalanced her thinking. Something she could not allow to happen again. She was Charlotte Mayda Vance, the daughter of Senator Charles Vance and the granddaughter of Richard Grayson, strong men who knew what they wanted and made it happen. That was the blood flowing through her. And she knew what she wanted. It was more than a casual kiss in the shadows of her mother's garden. Much more.

She paused on the veranda to look out over the land stretching away from the house. She couldn't see past the copse of trees at the edge of the grounds, but she knew how it rolled gently across the horizon. All good fertile land. Grayson land. Her land. Her father speaking a few vows with that woman couldn't change that. Nor could a kiss. Or the lack of one.

3

Adam Wade couldn't keep from laughing softly as the pretty red-haired girl lifted her hooped skirts to race up the veranda steps with no outward show of concern about revealing her well-turned ankles. Her guests would think she'd come across a snake in the garden. His laughter faded. Perhaps she had. One who had entranced her as surely as the serpent in that first garden had Eve.

When she paused on the veranda, he expected her to glance back at him, perhaps with another blushing appeal to not sully her reputation and give her young

man more reason to weasel out of his prom-
ises to her. But she didn't turn toward him.
Instead she became still as a statue as she
looked out over the grounds. For what he
didn't know or even care, but his fingers
itched for his pencils and sketchpad.

Since he didn't have so much as a scrap
of paper in his pocket, he traced her figure
there on the edge of the veranda in his
mind. The ginger-colored hair elaborately
curled and piled on top her head, the graceful neck flowing into soft, creamy shoulders bare above the satiny dress the color
of emeralds. Just a shade deeper than the
green of her eyes. He couldn't see those
eyes now as she stared into the distance,
but the lift of her head, the set of her shoulders made him believe it was more than
trees and fields she saw. Although she
gazed outward, it was something within
that she sought, and that's what pulled
at the artist in him. The image of yearning.

Then she turned, smoothed the skirts bil-
lowing out from her slender waist made
even more slender by one of those tortuous
corsets women seemed compelled to wear.
Even his sister Phoebe wore one, though
she had long since passed the possibility of

slender no matter how tightly the lacings of her corset were pulled. She claimed such an undergarment was a necessity for the current fashions. So it was little wonder the young ladies who peeked at him from behind their elaborate fans at social gatherings were always so breathless.

Charlotte Vance hadn't seemed at a loss for breath or to fear facing the truth. Even after her father's unwelcome surprise. He had obviously given his daughter's reaction to his new wife no thought at all. He was a man wrapped up in himself. Adam had seen that from the first handshake a week ago in Frankfort. A politician through and through with his eye constantly on how to broaden his base of support in the state.

It was hard to understand how the man leaned in the current civil strife. He claimed to support the Union, but a slaveholder and a Unionist didn't seem to go together to Adam, who had spent most of his years in Massachusetts where abolition seemed the only policy for a man of morals. But here abolitionists were looked upon with suspicion and distrust by all, Union or Secessionist. So much so that most of them

worked under the cover of darkness or has-
tened to the friendlier climes of the North to
do their campaigning for the end of slavery.
That wasn't a problem for Adam. His art
trumped his political leanings every time,
and he had no trouble observing and re-
cording without revealing his inner thoughts.

At least he knew what those thoughts
were even if he didn't bother trying to bring
others around to his way of thinking. A man
should not be able to own another man.
States did not have the right to withdraw
from the Union. The federal government in
Washington, D.C., had to make that absolutely clear. The Union must be preserved
by whatever means necessary.

But the politicians and perhaps the
whole populace in Kentucky seemed in a
state of denial as they entertained the idea
that if war came—and few doubted Lincoln
could avoid some sort of armed conflict—
then their state, their people could remain
neutral without declaring support for the
North or South. They were dreamers who
were trying to erect a fence of words around
their borders. Senator Vance had explained
it to Adam at great length in the carriage
ride from the train station to the party in

spite of the obvious boredom of his new wife at his political talk.

"Kentucky is a Union state. We believe in the Union first and foremost. That goes back to Henry Clay, our greatest son. The Great Compromiser." His face puffed up with pride. "I knew him well."

"What about President Lincoln? Wasn't he born in Kentucky?" Adam had asked, already knowing the answer, but sometimes he couldn't keep from trying to stir a bit of fire into a conversation.

"While I can't deny Mr. Lincoln was born inside the borders of our great state, I regret to say he shows little evidence of being a Kentucky son now. Illinois seems to have stamped her mark upon him," Senator Vance answered with feeling. "They report he only got one vote in the whole of Lexington even though his wife was born and raised there. That surely tells you something about the man."

"Or Kentucky," Adam said.

The senator glowered at him as if thinking of stopping the carriage to put such a nettlesome Northerner out. But his bride wanted her portrait finished, and she was well practiced in the art of changing the atmosphere around her when change was desired.

She put a gloved hand on her new husband's cheek and spoke to him with the hint of a pout. "Now, Charles, you know how your political blathering wears me down and I do so want to look fresh and lovely for your guests. Can we not find a more amusing topic than the state of the political world?" She flashed her eyes toward Adam with a bright smile that was meant to charm him into submission. "I'm sure our famous young artist didn't mean to raise your dander or bore me into an unladylike frown. Now did you, Mr. Wade?"

"Of course not, Mrs. Vance," Adam agreed with an answering smile that was as empty as her own as he settled back in the corner of the carriage seat with his sketchbook.

The lady lifted her chin and turned her profile to its most flattering side, sure he was practicing his strokes for her portrait. He let her think what she wished even as he began sketching his memory of the village they'd just passed through where a blacksmith had been ringing his hammer down on an anvil while a barefoot black boy had stared at their carriage, his eyes wide and hungry. Adam had come to Kentucky to capture its citizens' confusion of thought in pictures. The senator's wife's portrait was simply a bothersome side venture to placate his sister.

Now he had unwisely complicated the life of the senator's daughter. He had told her the truth when he said he didn't kiss and tell, but he also never kissed and lingered. Often not even long enough for a second kiss no matter how delightful the first had been. And Charlotte Vance's lips had been soft and yielding. While he would not look with disfavor on a second or third such encounter, he had no intention of settling down to one hearth and home. Something the senator's daughter seemed quite anxious to establish in her own life even to the point of browbeating a most unwilling and, to Adam's eyes, unlikely candidate into meeting her at the altar of matrimony.

That was not a trap Adam was about to fall into no matter how delightful the lady's lips. He needed to be free of ties. Even though he'd already been all the way to California and back looking for the father who had disappeared in search of gold when Adam was a child, there was much of the country out there yet to see. He didn't know what scenes awaited him, but he did know he planned to capture the spirit of the country with his artist pencils and brushes so that those who never left the stuffy confines of their sitting rooms could feel the majesty of the country's wide-open spaces. He considered himself more than an artist. He was a reporter.

Still, it might be interesting to get to know the senator's daughter better. She seemed to be as much a contradiction of feelings as her state of Kentucky. Speaking of marrying one man while quite willingly surrendering her lips to another. The strong lift of her chin contrasting to the soft line of her cheek. Her determination in the face of the impossibility of her dream of marriage if the young man fleeing her was serious about joining with the Shakers.

Adam rubbed his fingertips and thumb together in anticipation at the thought of the Shakers. Their village just a few miles from where he stood in the senator's garden—another reason he was not sorry to be in Mercer County. Sam Johnson, the editor at *Harper's Weekly*, was eager to see sketches of their buildings and the graceful winding staircases that so amazed all visitors.

While Adam was ready to supply whatever illustrations the editor requested, he was more curious about the peculiar people who would choose such a life. Men and women who had turned against all that was natural between a man and woman as if they believed the Lord had changed his mind about his initial command to Adam and Eve to be fruitful and multiply.

With a reputation as peaceful, honest, and industrious, the Shakers nevertheless were generally depicted as being dour and exceedingly plain in appearance. Especially the sisters whose uniform white caps and shapeless dresses obscured any hint of feminine charm.

Adam had once visited a Shaker village in the East, but had not been free to wander among the Believers, as they called themselves. Here in Kentucky, he'd heard the public road went straight through the village so a man could surely see much of the Shakers' way of life without being invited into their midst. He wanted to see them when they weren't presenting a face to the world they took such pains to shut away. He wanted to watch the children and see if they looked glad to be in the village or if they were uneasy captives. He wanted to sketch their likenesses when they weren't aware of his pencil strokes, perhaps even sketch them whirling in their worship dances. He liked the challenge of capturing the illusion of movement in a drawing.

Perhaps this Edwin Gilbey who had fled from the beautiful Charlotte could be his ticket into the village. Adam left the quiet of the garden behind with a bit of regret. Parties could be tiresome with too many young ladies concocting ploys to get his attention. Then as he climbed up the veranda steps, he thought of the senator's daughter and how even now he could taste her sweet innocence on his lips. He knew which young lady his eyes would be seeking as the music continued to play into the night.

His time in Kentucky stretched before him with much promise. In spite of the threat of a civil confrontation. Or perhaps because of it. What better place to be than in the middle of a divided state where it would be easy to sketch the faces of both sides.

On the veranda, he paused where Charlotte had stood so motionless, but all he could see was the graceful lift of tree limbs not yet bedecked with leaves as they cast moonlit shadows over the long lane up to the house. His gaze lingered on the road as he wondered if her yearning had been to follow that road away from the life she knew. If so, she shared kinship with him. He'd never seen a road he wasn't eager to travel.

4

It was past midnight when the last guests finally called for their carriages and the door shut behind them. Charlotte was left alone in the entryway with her father and his new wife.

The silence that fell over them beat against Charlotte's eardrums, but she didn't trot out any polite words to ease the tension as she faced this woman who was going to climb the stairs and lie down in her mother's bed. The woman returned her look with the hint of a smile that held little warmth. She wasn't worried about winning

Charlotte's approval. She had the approval of the Vance who mattered.

Beside her, Charlotte's father yawned, obviously with no awareness at all of the strained air between the two women, or perhaps simply not caring. "A good gathering, Charley." He clapped a hand down on her shoulder and gave it a squeeze.

The praise and his use of her pet name almost softened her anger at him, but then he went on. "Send Mellie up to help Selena do whatever it is you ladies have to do to retire for the evening." His sleepiness fell away and his eyes brightened as he turned to Selena. "You were especially lovely tonight, my dear Selena. I was, without a doubt, the envy of every man here."

"Thank you, my love." Selena smiled up at him with practiced charm. She turned from him to lay her hand lightly on Charlotte's arm. It was all Charlotte could do to stay still and not jerk away from the woman's touch. "Your father and I do appreciate all you did to make my welcome here at Grayson so fine. I'm sure you have been invaluable to Charles in seeing to so many details of the household, and I'm even surer you will be greatly relieved to have that burden lifted from your young shoulders so that you can pursue the more lighthearted activities suited to a young lady." She raised her perfectly shaped eyebrows at Charlotte. "I hear you plan to wed next month. We shall have to host a dozen parties for you before the big event."

Charlotte stared at the woman in front of her and was unable to push even the corners of her mouth up to fake a smile. The woman might as well have put both hands against Charlotte's back to shove her out the front door behind the last guest. "Yes, well, Edwin is not extremely fond of social gatherings, and it's not the best time for entertaining with the country so precariously divided." Charlotte shifted her feet just enough to move out from under the woman's hand.

Selena pretended not to notice as she actually laughed. A sound as practiced as her smile. Lilting and feminine. Everything about her was lovely, from her rich brown hair swept up in the latest style to her soft white hands with perfectly shaped nails that showed no evidence of ever being used for anything other than fluttering a fan in front of her beautiful china doll face. Charlotte hid her own hands in the folds of her skirt. The woman in front of her would probably shrink back in horror if she knew how only that morning Charlotte had buried her hands wrist deep in dough to help Aunt Tish get the many tarts prepared for the party.

"Oh, but my dear child, that is the very best time for light entertainments to help take our minds off such unpleasantness," Selena was saying. A look of sympathy pulled down her lips. "And I do understand your Edwin's reluctance, but sometimes a man only needs to be convinced of what he truly wants." She glanced up through dark eyelashes at Charlotte's father. "Isn't that so, my love?"

He laughed down at her. "I took little convincing." His eyes drank her in and his voice was husky as he went on, "It's late. Time to retire. You and Charlotte can discuss the need for such feminine wiles on the morrow." He took Selena's arm and ushered her toward the stairs. He didn't even glance back at Charlotte as he said, "Tell Mellie to be quick, Charlotte."

Rooted to her spot, she stared after

them and wanted to yell that Mellie was not his new wife's to order about. Charlotte wanted Mellie to come to her room to help her pull the pins from her hair and undo her stays while they talked about the party. That's how it had always been. Mellie helping her get ready for bed. But there was nothing for it but to do as her father said.

"Don't you be worrying, Miss Lottie. I'll have that woman tucked under the covers 'fore she blinks twice," Mellie promised when Charlotte delivered her father's message. "I can see to the both of you. Come tomorrow maybe he'll be bringin' somebody else up to the house for her."

"He'll dance to whatever tune she decides to play." Charlotte didn't try to keep the disgust out of her voice.

"Ain't no need gettin' your dander up, Miss Lottie." Mellie patted her shoulder. "That's how he was with your mama too. You remember that. Whatever Miss Mayda wanted, that's what we done. He'd a give his fortune to keep her happy."

"It was her fortune," Charlotte muttered, but she knew Mellie was right. Her father had doted on her mother even after she withdrew from life with a multitude of health complaints. Charlotte had always thought the complaints were more in her head than her body, but then she'd been struck down in her garden. Charlotte sighed. "It's all right, Mellie. You see to the new Mrs. Vance and keep everybody happy. I can take down my own hair."

"I ain't hearin' none of that. You best wait on me. You'll get it all in a tangle for sure. And ruin that fine dress tryin' to unbutton it."

In her room at last, Charlotte managed to reach a few of the tiny buttons up the back of the skintight bodice, but Mellie was right. To undo them all, she'd have to be a contortionist or rip them loose. She sat on the dressing stool and stared at her face in the mirror in the flickering lamplight. It was surely the most ridiculous thing in the world to wear a dress—no matter how lovely—that one could not put on or take off without aid.

Of course Mellie had been helping her dress since they were both children, and Aunt Tish before that. Her mother said it was the only way for a lady to live. Cosseted and pampered. Waited on while engaging in refined activities such as poetry reading and that detested needlework. A lady couldn't even lean down and pluck a stray weed out of her own flower garden.

She had people for that. People for cooking and cleaning. People to open the door to guests and usher them into the parlor. People to empty the chamber pots and fill the lamps. People to drop the dresses over a lady's head and fasten the buttons. People to work the fields and bring in the crops that made life in the big house so fine for the ladies and gentlemen who lived there. Her mother claimed it was how things were meant to be and that it was their Christian duty to take care of their people.

The word *slave* never crossed her mother's lips. Those who did her bidding and kept Grayson running were their *people*. But Charlotte knew the word from her father and from Aunt Tish and from Willis, the gentle black man who brought her pony out to her and taught her how to ride. Still, she was going on ten before she understood, really understood, what being a slave meant.

At a festival in the town, she had gotten separated from her mother, and after wandering down the wrong street, came upon a crowd of mostly men, some dressed rough like her father's overseer, Perkins, and others in gentlemen's coats. A white man stood at a podium like a preacher, and to his side black men wore chains on their wrists and ankles that clanked when they moved.

Charlotte stopped in her tracks and knew instinctively the scene before her was something her father would think unfit for her eyes. One part of her wanted to run from the sight, but another part of her couldn't stop staring as a couple of men prodded a boy in chains up on the block. A black boy surely only a year or two older than Charlotte.

He stared over the heads of the men eyeing him straight at Charlotte. She had expected to see fear on his face or perhaps dismay, but instead there was smoldering anger. Somehow she knew without a word passing between them that he hated her. Not because of anything she'd done, but because she had no chains to keep her from going where she willed. She looked straight at him, hoping he would see how sorry she felt, but he jerked against his chains as his look grew fiercer. Later she decided it must have been the same as hot coals dropping on his heart to think about her walking away in freedom he would never know.

"Keep your eyes down, boy," the man behind him had shouted as he hit the boy so hard he fell to his knees under the blow.

Charlotte whirled and ran back up the street the way she had come until she found her mother shopping for parasols while Willis sat in the carriage and waited.

She didn't tell her mother what she'd seen. She didn't tell anyone, not even Mellie. Especially not Mellie. The raw hatred in the boy's eyes haunted her sleep for weeks until Aunt Tish took her aside.

"What's the matter with you, chile? My Mellie says you ain't sleepin' hardly none at all. That you toss and turn till the sheets is all a-tumble on your bed. You best be comin' clean to your Aunt Tish with whatever is tormentin' you."

And so she let the words come out to say what she'd seen.

Aunt Tish got too quiet as she sat beside her at the kitchen table. Charlotte couldn't remember her ever sitting so quietly for so long.

Finally Charlotte said, "I did see it. I'm not lying."

"I knows you did, chile. You don't have to do no explainin' what it looked like to me. I been there. Me and my Mellie both, though she was just a babe with no sense of nothin' but her mammy's arms. The Massah bought me off the block so's I could wet-nurse you."

Charlotte looked at Aunt Tish. She'd always been part of her life, warm and kind. Full of wisdom and sometimes laughter. There was no laughter now. "Did you hate him?" Charlotte whispered. "The way that boy hated me."

"I didn't think it would help anythin' for me to let hatred build up in my innards. But I had to fight against it when he stopped shoutin' out bids on Jonah. We'd done jumped the broom before Mellie was born. I thought then right at first maybe he didn't have the money and as how I ought to be glad enough me and Mellie weren't goin' downriver. Little babies die goin' down the river. That's what Jonah told me. Not to worry none about him. He could take whatever they threw at him on those cotton plantations."

Charlotte had no words to say as Aunt Tish looked away at the wall as if she could see beyond it to the south where her Jonah might still be picking cotton. "But then when we got here and I saw the Massah had a mess of slaves, I had to fight powerful against the bitter gall that wanted to poison me. It still rises up to smote me at times."

Tears pooled in Charlotte's eyes and dripped down her cheeks. And she felt the boy she'd seen was right to hate her. She choked out the words. "Do you hate me too, Aunt Tish?"

"Now, now, chile. You's like my own." Aunt Tish laid her calloused black hands on Charlotte's cheeks. "You knows my heart could never hate you. And that poor boy you saw wasn't hatin' you either. He was hatin' how life is. And fact is, I can see it in your eyes. You'd a turned him free as you be right now if you coulda done it. That's what you got to 'member, chile. You'd a set him free if'n you coulda."

Charlotte stared at the black woman's loving face. "But Aunt Tish, I can't even set you free, can I?"

"No, chile, you can't. Not now, but maybe someday. And then I knows you'll do the right thing by me and Mellie."

Charlotte hadn't thought about the slave boy for a long time. She had blocked him from her mind, blocked it all from her mind. Things were the way they had to be. The way her mother and father had always told her they were meant to be. Why the memory came sneaking back to unsettle her thoughts on this night, she had no idea.

Perhaps because everything was different, thrown up in the air to land who knew where. Certainly not as she'd ordered or planned. Edwin standing up to her. That artist, a man she didn't even know, kissing her. Her own wantonness to allow such a happening. Her father lying down beside that woman in her mother's bed. A woman young enough to perhaps bear him the son he'd always wanted. Mellie not there to unfasten her buttons. Grayson slipping out of her hands and with it the power to do that right thing by Aunt Tish and Mellie the way she had promised in her heart as she sat beside Aunt Tish at the table that day so many years ago.

Now there were those who said the country was going to war because Lincoln seemed poised to do what she had not had courage or strength to ask her father to do already.

5

Charlotte was still staring in the mirror when Mellie slipped into the room to help her out of her dress. "You done had to try, didn't you, Miss Lottie?" she fussed as she pulled the rest of the buttons loose with quick fingers.

"I don't like being captive to a dress."

Charlotte stood up to let Mellie untie the top of her hoops. They fell to the floor with a soft clatter as the silky skirt collapsed against her legs. She pulled her arms out of the sleeves and stepped out of the piles of emerald fabric. Mellie gathered up the dress quickly and spread it out on the bed before it could get too rumpled.

"How about squeezed half in two with a corset?" Mellie said as she pulled loose the ties on Charlotte's stays. "It ain't no easy thing bein' a lady. Same with that Miss Selena. She had her stays pulled so tight it took me five minutes to work the lacings loose enough to get her out of the contraption. It's a wonder she wasn't faintin'."

"I've heard she does at times." Charlotte rubbed her sides and pulled in a deep breath that felt wonderful as she sat back down at the dressing table in her camisole and pantalettes.

"I ain't surprised," Mellie said as she began pulling the pins out of Charlotte's hair and brushing it out. "You want me to massage your feet, Miss Lottie?"

Charlotte took the brush from Mellie and began pulling it through her hair herself as she said, "You're every bit as tired as I am, Mellie. You need to go on to bed and massage your own feet."

"I didn't have to dance with ever' man in the state," Mellie said, but she didn't try to take the brush away from Charlotte. Instead she sat down on the bench at the end of Charlotte's bed, slipped off her shoes, and held her feet out in front of her to wiggle her toes inside her black stockings. "I was watchin'. How many times did that old Mr. Robertson step on your toes?"

"Too many." Charlotte groaned at the memory. "But he's always generous whenever Father needs funds for his campaigns."

"Then let that new woman your daddy brung home get her toes stepped on."

"I don't want to talk about her tonight, Mellie. Please." Charlotte put down the brush and began plaiting her red hair in a thick rope.

"Fine with me." Mellie stood up and pushed Charlotte's hands aside to finish the job quickly and efficiently. "Then how about we talk about that Mr. Wade what come with them? Now, he is one fine-lookin' gentleman. And did I hear somebody say he was paintin' that woman's portrait?"

"You did, and I don't know about gentleman." Charlotte's cheeks warmed at the memory of her lack of control. How could she have been so wanton?

Mellie leaned back and eyed Charlotte in the mirror. "Sounds like you must have run up on him in your mama's garden. I did note you looked a mite breathless when you come in from outside."

"Nobody can breathe with those stays squeezing your ribs in a vice." Charlotte pointed toward the corset she'd shed moments before.

"Then it didn't have naught to do with Mr. Edwin chasin' in like some storm had hit out there and then you runnin' in all aflush some minutes later followed by that painter feller with a grin like as how he'd just eat the last of Mammy's dried apple tarts."

"You see entirely too much," Charlotte said.

"What else I got to do but look, and you know you like hearin' about what I see. Like that Janie Preston. You'd think that girl would figure out yellow makes her look like yesterday's leftover gravy, but it didn't seem to bother Mr. Matthew. I think he's about to get caught." Mellie was always a fountain of information after any party on who was making eyes at who or which men were plotting political alliances. "'Course tonight most all the young ladies were findin' ways to sashay up to that new man. The 'no gentleman' from the garden."

"He's famous," Charlotte stared down at her hands. "Has illustrations in *Harper's Weekly* all the time."

"You don't say? On top of bein' so fine lookin'." Mellie tied off Charlotte's braid and sat back down on the bench. She folded her white apron in pleats for a minute before she said, "Fact of the matter is, you might not be the only one the likes of him is gonna cause trouble for."

"What do you mean, trouble?" Charlotte turned on the dressing table stool to study Mellie.

"I kept my eyes down, Miss Lottie. I swear I did. I didn't even take a peek up at him, but he talked to me." Mellie glanced up at her and then down at the pleats she was folding and unfolding with nervous fingers. "I mean like I was a person. Not a slave. Like you talk to me. Like I matter."

"What did he say?"

"He asked me if I liked it here. Like I was one of the party ladies instead of a servant there holdin' a tray of tarts." Mellie reached up and yanked off the cap she'd been wearing for the party and ran her hand through her black curls. "I didn't know what to say—he just stood there till I had to say somethin'."

"And did you tell him you liked it here?" Charlotte kept her eyes on Mellie's face, but she was seeing the boy on the block again. She held her breath as she waited for Mellie's answer.

Mellie didn't look at Charlotte. Instead she stared at the flickering light of the gas lamp beside the door for a moment before she said, "You know I wouldn't want to be nowhere 'cept with you and Mammy. But . . ." She let her voice trail off as she looked back down at her apron and began folding it in pleats again.

"But what?" Charlotte reached over and touched Mellie's arm. "You know you don't have to worry about what you say to me. I want you to talk to me."

Mellie finally looked straight at Charlotte. Her dark brown eyes looked sad. "I do know that, Miss Lottie. Mammy says that's part of my problem. How you've been more sister than mistress. Mammy says it's give me ideas I might be better off forgettin' about. That slave girls ain't supposed to know how to read like you taught me. And I taught Mammy. She says I'd best never be lettin' on about none of that. Or lettin' myself fall in love with no long-legged field hand. She understands how I might want to, bein' all of twenty now, but she says that would set my feet on a sure path to sorrow."

Charlotte searched for something to say to make Mellie feel better, but nothing came to mind. There was truth in what Mellie said. They sat there in silence a minute before Mellie went on.

"But not ever knowin' about lovin', that's reason for sorrow too, ain't it, Miss Lottie?"

Finally Charlotte said, "I don't know, Mellie."

Mellie shook her head as her mouth hardened into a thin line. "You speakin' the truth there, Miss Lottie. That's sorrow you gonna know too if you settle on Mr. Edwin. There ain't never gonna be no lovin' between the two of you. It ain't in the man." She stood up and carefully gathered up the dress. "You sure did look pretty tonight," she said as she hung the dress on a padded hanger in the wardrobe. She laid out Charlotte's nightgown before she started toward the door. "If you don't need nothin' else then."

"Wait, Mellie." Charlotte stopped her before she could turn the knob.

Mellie looked back at her, ready to do whatever she asked. Her training from childhood on. Take care of Miss Lottie. Charlotte was relieved to see no hint of the hate she remembered in the slave boy's eyes, but she could still see the sorrow there like the glint off water down a deep well. "Did you ever think maybe love is glorified too much?"

"I don't know, Miss Lottie. Could be won't neither one of us ever find out for sure unless'n we try it for ourselves. But the Good Book that Mammy is always after me to read speaks highly of it."

"But that's love for God. Or for your neighbor. Not love between a man and a woman."

"He made Eve for Adam and told them to have babies. He put the want to for that kind of love in a body's heart too. And you know if you'll think on it, there ain't all that much difference between folks no matter what color their faces is when it comes to thinkin' on love. That's how come Mammy still looks to the south and wonders about my daddy even all these years after they carried him off."

Charlotte shifted uneasily on the dressing table stool. Of course she'd thought about being in love the way Mellie meant. Her imagination had tingled as she read great love stories, but real life didn't often mirror the fantasy of stories. In real life a person had to be practical. A person had to do what was expected. She looked at Mellie and sighed a little before she said, "I guess I've always thought there were more important things than love. The kind of love you're talking about."

Mellie's face softened. "That might be a good thing if you stay fixed on Mr. Edwin. I heard him talkin' last night. About goin' to them Shakers what don't think the Lord intended no Adam and Eve lovin' the way I'm thinkin' on it."

"I know. Everything's turned upside down tonight. Everything."

"You'll figure it out, Miss Lottie. You just need to get some sleep so's your head can think up the ways. Come mornin' you'll find a way to turn things back right."

Come morning. Charlotte echoed Mellie's words in her head as she pulled on her nightgown and crawled under the covers Mellie had turned back for her. And she did always find a way. This wouldn't be any different. She could turn things back right. Come morning.

But the morning sun didn't ease Charlotte's worries. For the first time in her memory, she felt out of place in her own house as she got out of bed and dressed for the day. Mellie had slipped in while she slept and filled her pitcher and washing bowl and laid out her clothes, but she'd probably been ordered to the new Mrs. Vance's aid.

Charlotte ran her hands along the cherry banister as if absorbing the familiar feel of it as she went down the stairs. She loved Grayson. She knew every corner, every floorboard squeak, every angle of sunlight through the windows. It was her house, warm and loving and home. But now a stranger was going to be climbing Grayson's stairs and inspecting all the rooms and wardrobes not as a guest but with permanence in her step.

Plus the other stranger, the artist, was somewhere under the roof. She might turn a corner, open a door, and encounter him face-to-face at any moment with the truth of her shamelessly allowing him to kiss her vibrating in the air between them. So it was a relief when she went into the kitchen and Aunt Tish told her the man had been up at first light and gone from the house as the sun was rising.

"But he'd best be back here by half past noon or it'll be his head," Aunt Tish added with raised eyebrows as she looked up from taking three of the leftover dried apple tarts out of the warming oven and arranging them on a plate for Charlotte. "Miss V done been askin' where he be when I carried a tray of coffee up to her and the Massah. She done told your papa in my hearin' that he'd best be tellin' that man he weren't to go off paintin' some lowdown field hand's face instead of her own. Like as how such might spoil the man's brush."

"Unless I miss my guess, Mr. Wade will be painting whatever he likes," Charlotte said as she sat down at the table. She always ate breakfast in Aunt Tish's kitchen when her father wasn't at Grayson, and this morning he'd hardly note her absence with Selena filling his eyes. She liked it in the kitchen with the bacon sizzling in the skillet and the pots boiling on the stove. To Charlotte, it felt like the center of Grayson,

where she could see the whole of whatever might be happening.

"Here you are, Miss Lottie. I saved you
the ones with the most apples." Aunt Tish
set the plate of sweet tarts in front of Charlotte and poured them both a cup of tea.
She wiped her face with her apron, but
Charlotte saw the smile that sneaked up
from her lips to her eyes.

"Sit down and tell me what's so funny."

Aunt Tish lowered herself into the chair
opposite Charlotte with a little groan. She'd
put on a few extra pounds around her
middle over the last years and had trouble
with rheumatism in her back. "That Mr.
Wade, he ain't doing nothin' with a brush."

"How do you know that?" Charlotte
peered at her over the rim of her cup.

"He done been in here drawin' the likes
of me. Can you believe that? Had this great
big pad of paper and some pencil sticks.
Had me sit right here while he sat there
wheres you are. Stared holes plum' through
me, and when I looked down 'fore I got in
a mess a trouble for starin' bold at his white
face, told me to keep lookin' at him. You
shoulda seen how he moved his hand
fast as anythin' over that paper." A look of

wonder came over Aunt Tish's face as she drew quick lines on the tabletop with her fingertip. "Then he turned over the page and did it all ag'in."

"Did he show you what he drew?" Charlotte was wishing more and more that the kiss in the garden had never happened. Adam Wade sounded like someone she might enjoy getting to know better, but she could hardly stay in his company now without him thinking she was chasing shamelessly after him.

"He done better than that. He give me one of 'em." Aunt Tish reached under her apron to pull a folded sheet of paper out of a hidden pocket. "I hated to fold it up, but I couldn't leave it layin' out where anybody might see it." She smoothed it out on the table between them.

Aunt Tish stared up at Charlotte from the paper as if Adam Wade had lifted the likeness of her face out of a mirror. And while the sketch was bare bones, just a few lines, there was more to it than just the image of Aunt Tish. In those few strokes he had captured a look in her eyes. One Charlotte had seen often enough herself when Aunt Tish stood out on the back steps and looked beyond at the horizon.

"And he did this in just a few minutes?"

"Ten, fifteen at the most." Aunt Tish lightly rubbed her flat palm over the paper. "He caught me, didn't he now?"

"He did." She thought of him measuring her face with his thumb and fingers the night before, and she wondered what the sketch would have shown about her if he'd drawn the lines. Maybe she was just as glad he hadn't had a pencil in his hand. "I think there are some old frames up in the attic if you want to get Mellie to climb up there and look for one."

"I might just do that," Aunt Tish said as she folded up the paper to slide back in her pocket with great care.

"Where is he now? Do you know?" Charlotte asked before she bit into one of the tarts.

"That weren't none of my bus'ness." Aunt Tish stood up to fork the bacon out of the pan.

Charlotte eyed her broad back. "But you know."

Aunt Tish didn't say anything for a long

moment as she stirred a pot of grits and lifted the lid on the coffeepot. Charlotte didn't ask her again. She just waited, and finally as if Aunt Tish could feel Charlotte's eyes on her, she sighed and turned around. "I don't know if'n that's where he really went or why he would want to." She hesitated again.

Charlotte lifted her shoulders in a show of unconcern. "It doesn't really matter to me where he went. I was simply curious about what he might be sketching next."

"Uh-huh," Aunt Tish said with one peaked eyebrow that showed she was seeing right through what Charlotte was saying. "Looks to me like as how he done caught your eye. Guess that's why it's so odd him askin' the way to Mr. Edwin's place."

"Edwin's?" Charlotte didn't even attempt to hide her surprise. She shifted uneasily in her chair. He'd promised not to kiss and tell.

"I couldn't figure him wantin' to be drawin' Mr. Edwin's long skinny face, but then I couldn't figure him wantin' to draw my round black one neither. I overheared him talkin' to Willis as he was leavin'. He was wantin' a horse. Course when Willis come in later for his breakfast, he was tellin' how the man was full of questions on how to get to the Shakers' town too. Askin' all manner of questions about what Willis knew about them and the way they lived and such."

"What'd Willis tell him?"

"Well, you know Willis. He ain't much for talkin' to white folks. Says the less said, the better. He just tol' him all he knew was they had some mighty fine workhorses."

Charlotte played with one of the tarts on her plate, breaking edges off it but not putting them in her mouth.

Aunt Tish sat back down and reached across the table to touch her arm. "Somethin' botherin' you, Miss Lottie?"

"Edwin says he wants to go to the Shakers."

"I knowed it. Mattie tol' me so some weeks ago. Says that Shaker man is in and out of the house over there like as how it was his."

Mattie was Edwin's longtime housekeeper. "What's she think about it?"

Aunt Tish pulled her hand back and wrapped it around her cup. "She ain't upset." She stared straight at Charlotte. "No way she could be. Folks join the Shakers, they has to set their people free. Them Shakers don't abide with slaveholdin'."

"Or marrying either."

"You speakin' the truth there."

The bell in the dining room tinkled and Aunt Tish pushed herself up out of her chair. "Sounds like the Massah's wantin' his bacon. You goin' out there with 'em?"

"Not today, Aunt Tish. If Papa asks, you can tell him I've already eaten."

"There's little truth in that," Aunt Tish said as she eyed the tarts still on Charlotte's plate. "You gonna waste away to nothin', chile."

6

Edwin Gilbey wasn't home. Off to the Shaker village, according to the servant who met Adam in the driveway to hold his horse. The man had the biggest smile on his face as any Negro Adam had seen since he got to Kentucky. When Adam asked if he could sketch his picture holding the horse's head, the man's smile got even wider. He was missing a couple of teeth.

"Ain't nobody ever wanted to use up no pencil markings on the likes of me." The man ran a hand through the fuzz of gray hair on his head as the horse snuffled his shoulder. "You any good at it?"

"No Michelangelo, but I do a fair like-ness." Adam opened his pad to the sketch of the senator's cook and turned it around where the man could see it.

"Well, I'll be if Latisha Sparrow ain't a-starin' up at me off'n that paper plain as day. I reckon if she let you draw her, won't be no harm in you drawin' my old face too." He tilted his chin up a bit the way he'd surely seen white men's portraits posed.

Adam turned over to a blank page and made some quick marks. "What's your name?"

"Redmon."

"Last name or first?" Adam asked.

"Last name, first name. All the name I needs."

"Well, tell me, Redmon. Are you always this happy?"

"Ain't no good lookin' like you got hold of a sour persimmon. No sir. Best to keep on grinnin' cause that's what ever'body wants to see."

"Your smile's looking pretty genuine this morning, Redmon. Is it because Mr. Gilbey's gone?"

"You done tryin' to get me in trouble, Mr. Sir. But no sir, I've known Massah Edwin since he was in knickers. Taught him to ride a horse. Now that was a task, let me tell you." Redmon chuckled a little. "Young Massah Edwin was some timid as a boy. But he done seems to be growin' out of it. What with wantin' to learn them Shaker twirls and spins."

"I met him last night, and to tell the truth he didn't look like the dancing type." Adam looked up at the black man and then quickly back down as he sketched his hand on the horse's bridle. The man's fingers were bony but strong.

"You got that right. But them Shaker dances is different. We's all hopin' he might take to them."

"Oh, why's that?" Adam had the sketch done, but he added a little shading here and there just to keep the man talking.

"Them Shakers set a ton of store by their folks keepin' their rules. Not marryin' fer one, but they got another one that matters more to us'n around here. No ownin' nobody. We's thinkin' on breathing some free air."

"What would you do, Redmon?" Adam glanced up at him. "Join up with the Shakers too?"

"I ain't thinkin' on that. No sense tradin' one massah for another no matter how kindly they might be. And I wouldn't be wantin' to give up my Mattie. We jumped the broom long time back." He looked off to the north. "No sir. Me and Mattie, we'd go north. They say a man like me can get a job up there holdin' horses and such."

"You could get a job here too, couldn't you? As a free man."

Redmon looked down at the ground. "It ain't all that easy. They has this law about freed slaves leaving the state or so I been told. Besides, around here, some scalawag might grab my free papers away from me and make him some money sellin' me south. That kind a thing wouldn't be worth noticin' here, but they tell me it's different in the North." The man peered up at Adam and his smile faded away. "You sound Northern. Is it true we're gonna go to war? The North agin the South?"

"It looks that way."

The black man shook his head. "We best pray the good Lord has mercy on us all."

"Guess I'll have to depend on your prayers, Redmon. I've never been much of a praying man," Adam admitted with a smile.

"Ever' man is a prayin' man if times is bad enough, and could be times is gonna be bad enough for a bunch of folks soon if shots start firin'."

"You could be right." Adam turned the pad around for Redmon to see, and the man's smile came back.

"I do declare, Mr. Sir, you done grabbed old Redmon's face and put it down on that paper. And the horse ain't bad neither. My Mattie ain't gonna be believin' it."

Adam turned the pad back around and scribbled Phoebe's address on the bottom of the drawing. She owed him after pushing him into the unwelcome task of painting Selena Vance's portrait. He tore off the drawing and held it out to the black man. "Here. You take this and show Mattie. Then she'll believe you."

"Oh no sir, Mr. Sir. I couldn't take that from you." Redmon held up his free hand with his palm toward Adam and stepped back a couple of paces. The horse danced backward with him.

"Sure you can, Redmon. I'm giving it to you. Just fold it up and put it in your pocket."

He pointed to the address he'd scribbled on the bottom of it. "And if you get your free papers and go north as far as Boston, you go to that address there and show them this picture. They'll hire you on to handle horses just like you do here. That's a promise."

Adam folded the drawing a couple of times and handed it to Redmon, who took it from him as though he thought the paper might ignite in his hand. The man stared at the folded paper a few seconds before he slipped it out of sight in his pants pocket.

"That's mighty generous of you, Mr. Sir." He flipped his eyes up to Adam's face and then back at his feet. "You makin' a promise to old Redmon, I'll be makin' one back. Seein' as how you ain't on familiar terms with the good Lord, I'll do some prayin' for you. Just in case things start goin' bad."

"Thank you, Redmon. A man would be foolish to turn down a believing man's prayers." Adam smiled and took the reins to his horse. "And you say Mr. Gilbey's over at the Shaker village. Can you point the way?"

The sunshine was warm on Adam's

shoulders as he rode along the road past cattle grazing on the spring grass in the rolling pastures. In the plowed fields, black men with hoes walked in an up-and-down wave across the smooth dirt, planting seeds. In the distance the redbud blooms brightened up the tree line of woods. All in all, a day to make a man glad to be out riding a horse down a sunny Kentucky road.

A dozen times, Adam wanted to stop and get out his sketchpad. But the morning was speeding past and he'd told Selena Vance he'd be back to work on her portrait that afternoon. For the hundredth time he wished he hadn't let Phoebe talk him into such a tiresome task. The woman was not a pleasure to paint. Full of vanities and not the least interested in a portrait that revealed her nature. She wanted something pretty. Her comfortable image of herself. He could do it, but it was tedious, uninteresting brushstrokes to paint flattering poses that he had no pleasure signing his name to. He liked stripping away a person's pretenses and drawing the stark lines of truth. But there was nothing for it but to make her as beautiful as artistically possible and move on to more interesting subjects. Like Redmon or the senator's cook. Or perhaps the senator's lovely redheaded daughter.

He'd like to try to capture the spark in those green eyes. He'd never known a girl quite like her, although he did have to admit a quick kiss in the garden was hardly enough to claim knowing her. But sometimes he could watch a person and guess much about them. His artist eye, his grandmother told him. She'd had an artistic bent. As a young lady she had tried her hand at painting delicate wildflowers, which she told Adam was one of the few acceptable subjects a young lady might try to capture with brushstrokes.

Later she taught art to inept young ladies to supplement the income of Adam's grandfather, headmaster of a school that touted itself as preparing the best young gentlemen for Harvard and Yale. A respectable profession and one that supplied their needs, but few extras. Especially after Adam's father left to seek their fortune in California and was never heard from again. Adam's mother had no choice but to take her three sons and daughter and move back in with her parents.

While she had been greatly relieved to be back in the urbane society of Boston instead of stuck in the uncivilized area of Louisville where Adam's father had run a store, there was always a shortage of funds to keep up proper appearances. Satisfying her need for the luxuries of life was probably the primary reason his father had been lured away from his family by the siren of gold panned from creeks. If she could have been satisfied with a storekeeper's clerk as a husband, then all of their lives might have been different. But she had been raised on the cusp of society in the East and wanted her children to climb up to a higher rung on the social ladder.

Phoebe, Adam's elder by three years, had grabbed the higher rung with great enthusiasm and married well some years back before producing an appropriate number of offspring for her contented husband. Adam, on the other hand, cared nothing for social standing. That had been knocked out of him in his grandfather's private school where all the true gentlemen's sons had peered down their noses at the lowly headmaster's grandson. It didn't matter to them that his mind had been quicker than many of theirs, or perhaps that was the reason for their disdain. A disdain that he learned to return in spades.

His grandfather had often caned him for posting irreverent sketches of this or that student. Or perhaps not for the irreverence but just for the sketching. His grandfather wanted to beat the artistic dreamer out of him, but some things can't be altered in a man's spirit. Art was one of those things for Adam. That and his streak of independence that made him say no when his grandfather tried to force him into Yale to spend four more years being the charity case of the school. He didn't need Yale. He only needed his pens and his brushes.

When he had told his grandfather he would not enroll in college, that instead he would concentrate on improving his art, his grandfather had almost spit out the word. "Art." His voice was full of contempt, and his hands curled as if he were wishing for the headmaster's cane to attempt one more time to bring Adam into line. "You're as much a fool as your father before you. Chasing off after some dream that will never come to fruition."

Adam braced his shoulders as though

expecting a blow from the old man, but he didn't back down. "I am an artist." Those were words he'd practiced for just that moment, and he spoke them with conviction.

His grandfather had once been tall, like Adam, but years of studying and bending over students to instruct them had rounded his shoulders until he had to peer up at Adam through gray eyebrows that grew in wayward paths. But his light blue eyes were as sharp and as accusing as ever. "Artists starve in garrets."

Adam had lived in the man's house since he was twelve years old, but little affection had grown between them. He had realized early on that his grandfather saw Adam's father whenever he looked at him and that he could never be good enough, smart enough, or pliable enough to override the anger his grandfather still carried for the man who had ruined his daughter's life. So Adam never tried. He didn't try that day either as he answered his grandfather's near curse. "Then I will starve."

He had not exchanged a word with his grandfather since. His grandmother had written him encouraging letters that caught up with him occasionally as he traveled to the West searching for his father. He still carried regret that he had not returned to Boston when his grandmother fell ill. He hadn't thought she would die so quickly.

By the time he received word of her death, she'd been underground for days. He saw little need to rush to Boston then. His mother had Phoebe and the boys, his two younger brothers, to hold her hand and pull her through. As for his grandfather, the man needed nothing from Adam. He would simply shut himself away in his library and hardly notice the good woman's passing.

The truth was, Adam didn't have the money for the trip to Boston and to New York both. And it was to New York he had finally been summoned. To interview with *Harper's Weekly*. He didn't believe in angels, but sometimes he wondered if his grandmother had whispered his name in Sam Johnson's ear as she passed through the air on her way to heaven. He had not looked back since except to send his mother money to help pay the younger boys' tuition.

Jake was in his first year at Harvard. A hothead who didn't have art to turn to. Instead he had fought his way through their grandfather's school with his fists and had earned a measure of respect from the gentlemen's sons that allowed him a more accepted place in their society. That had carried through for Harry, who at sixteen was almost ready to matriculate at the college of his choice. He had a love of books and the feeling that teaching was a calling. His calling. Phoebe wrote that Grandfather Tyler was a changed man when he was around Harry.

Perhaps the old man was changed with Harry, but there was no change that could bridge the rift between him and Adam. Adam had proved him wrong, and that was something he could never accept.

Adam shook away the thoughts of his grandfather as the landscape alongside the road changed. Stones stacked on stones with no masonry to hold them in place kept the cows in the lush green fields. Even the cattle seemed different, fatter with little sign of having just come through a hard winter. The sturdily built barns had wide doors that slid back on long iron rods attached to the barn instead of swinging open. But perhaps the most telling difference was that, among the many workers in the fields, he spotted only two black faces under the straw Shaker hats.

Adam didn't stop. Up ahead, the buildings of the Shaker village rose up into the sky. The main houses were every bit as large as the manor houses he'd just come from but built without the first curling bit of ornamental trim work that adorned the local gentry's mansions. Yet somehow the straight, simple lines of the Shaker structures lent them a kind of natural elegance Adam's artist eye admired.

As he rode into the village, a bell sounded, and men and women in uniform dress began filing out of the various buildings to make their way to the large stone building in the center of the village. None of the people seemed to be engaged in conversation as they walked, and few even cast a curious glance toward him riding past them. He was part of the world and so of little interest.

Adam glanced up at the sun straight over his head. The bell had evidently summoned them to their midday meal. He slid off his horse and held the reins while he pulled out his sketchpad. He didn't see

Edwin Gilbey. Or any person who stood out. They were all as alike as ants trailing into an anthill as they filed past him. The women wore white caps and large white collars lapping over their bosoms to tuck down in their aprons, covering their plain dresses. The men wore straw hats with wide brims and suspenders to hold up their butternut brown or gray pants.

As he began to sketch them flowing into the white stone building in front of him, one young girl peeked over at him curiously before an older sister shot her a stern look. The girl quickly lowered her eyes to the path once more.

"I mean no harm," he said with a winning smile as the older sister looked at him with suspicion.

She made no response except to narrow her eyes on him with evident distrust before she shooed the young women with her past him like a farm woman trying to pen up a gaggle of geese.

Before his eye could forget the two women's faces, he turned a page and drew the young Shaker girl with the bloom of youth in her cheeks and the older woman drained of cheer. He was still filling in the details on the three sketches when the Shakers began coming back out of the building to return to their duties.

With a look up at the sun, Adam reluctantly put away his sketchpad and mounted his horse.

It was two hours past noon before he got back to Grayson. Selena Vance was not pleased.

In the days that followed, Charlotte felt as if she had been tossed into a spinning vortex with no way to break free. She had no control in her own house. Her father's new wife wasted little time in assuming her role as mistress of Grayson. All sweetness and light disappeared with Selena's party dress on that first day as she settled at Charlotte's mother's writing desk in the morning room and began handing out orders.

The house would be scrubbed from top to bottom. Wardrobes were to be emptied out to make room for her things that would be arriving in trunks in the coming days.

The Grayson china with its delicate rose pattern would be packed away and replaced with a pattern of her choice as soon as she had the opportunity to travel to Boston to purchase it. Work on redoing rooms for her son, Landon, who would be arriving with his governess at the end of the month, would begin in earnest at once.

Charlotte felt as if she should run up the stairs and bar the door to her room to at least keep the woman's changes from it. Her father may have felt the same, because each day as soon as breakfast was over, he retreated to his library. The library with its great cherry desk was his sanctuary and the place where he plotted his political campaigns and curried favors from influential visitors and backers. His political strategy room.

He cared little for the books filling the shelves from floor to ceiling on one side of the room. That had been her Grandfather Grayson's passion when the library had been his retreat before her father. Grandfather Grayson claimed to have read every book on the shelves, some over and over until those books fell open to his favorite passages when Charlotte pulled them from the shelves to read. As she curled in the chair in front of the library's fireplace, Charlotte often imagined the old gentleman reading over her shoulder.

After her mother died, Charlotte had free access to the books as there was no one to tell her which books were proper fare for a young lady and which were not. Her father certainly didn't know. He had little time for literature or even history. He claimed to be too busy making history to worry about dwelling on the mistakes of the past.

Charlotte had no argument with that. She also shared her father's passion for politics, and some of her best times with her father were spent in the library listening to the political news from Frankfort. She saw no need to give up these talks just because he had brought a wife home. If Selena's strained look was any indication whenever Charlotte's father began talking of the necessity of preserving the Union at all costs, the woman had little interest in politics.

But Charlotte was eager to know her father's thoughts on whether the Southern states could be wooed back into the Union.

President Lincoln hadn't been able to do so in his first month in office, but diplomacy took time. Or so her father always told her. Coaxing an opponent back to your side could be more difficult than doing so by force, but the extra effort was well spent.

However, from what Charlotte read in the newspapers, the South didn't seem to look with favor on any sort of compromise. Even before President Lincoln took office, the Secessionist states had already established their own government—the Confederate States of America. Charlotte had read about their meeting in Alabama, but surely saner heads would prevail as they had in crises of the past. Those in positions of power would want to find a way to heal the breach without picking up arms.

Charlotte was anxious to hear her father say as much. Plus she was eager to know his plans for the next campaign. That was more than a year away, but a man who wanted to be re-elected couldn't wait too long to get his name on the right people's lips. While it was unseemly for a candidate to go out begging for votes for himself, it was vital to have a great many supporters who would. Even more, she wanted to laugh with him about the ridiculous bills some of his fellow senators at times tried to push through the Kentucky legislature.

She wanted to feel his hand patting her head and hear him saying, "Charley, you should have been a boy. You could have been the next governor. Right after me. We could have kept it in the family for years." Even though he always said it as if he'd made a big joke, she knew that thinking about running for the governor's office wasn't a joke to him.

But Selena managed to steal those times with her father from Charlotte too, for now when she carried coffee to him after breakfast, he wanted to talk of nothing but Selena. Selena this. Selena that.

It didn't seem to matter what the woman did. On the very first day, she ordered Gibson, their butler, to carry Charlotte's mother's portrait to the attic, and her father didn't protest. On the second day, she demanded access to the account books not just for the household but for the whole farm, and he handed them over with a smile. Charlotte began to fear that if Selena asked him to burn down the house and build it back to her specifications, he might strike the match on his boot. As long as she kept calling him "my love" and flashing her ingratiating smile at him.

It was almost beyond bearing. But Charlotte had never spent much time pretending. Not since she was twelve and her mother had handed over the keys to the pantry and linen cabinet. She had never pretended her mother would rise up off her couch and take control of the household again. She had never pretended that her father would notice and appreciate the way she, Charlotte, kept the household running. She had never pretended that she loved Edwin or that he loved her. Love had nothing to do with the agreement between them.

And now she didn't pretend that she could stop Selena's onslaught on Grayson. Not without her father's help, and he was so enamored with the woman it was obvious he thought she could do no wrong. Charlotte saw little choice but to bide her time and carry on as if her life wasn't getting turned upside down. She wasn't exactly pretending that things hadn't changed or that her carefully arranged future wasn't slipping out of reach, but with time, she was sure she could step out of the vortex. She could take control of her future again. Just as soon as her head stopped spinning.

Meanwhile, it didn't help that she often caught Adam Wade's much-too-perceptive eyes on her as she put forth a polite front at the dinner table each evening. It didn't help that the only news she received from Hastings Farm was of Edwin visiting the Shaker village. It didn't help that her father began talking of six-year-old Landon, whom he hadn't even met, as if he was the son he had always wanted. It didn't help that Selena began to speak of the dowry Charlotte would take with her when she married in May, when it was becoming more and more apparent that there might not *be* a wedding in May.

It especially didn't help that Charlotte's father told her Selena thought she spent an inappropriate amount of time in the kitchen with Aunt Tish and had suggested Charlotte should go visit his Virginian relations for a few months to broaden her horizons beyond Grayson. When Charlotte asked which relatives, since the redheaded grandmother had passed on years since, her father said there was a cousin but he would have to find out her name. Even so, he was sure Charlotte would be quite welcome as a houseguest.

Charlotte felt as if she had been bowled over by a runaway horse, and every time she tried to stand up and get her bearings, the same thing happened all over again. Selena was outflanking her at every turn. And all with a too-sweet smile and the claim that she only had Charlotte's best interests at heart.

On the third day, she summoned Charlotte to her while she was sitting for the portrait. If it hadn't been her father delivering the message, Charlotte would have ignored Selena's summons. Not forever. Just until after the sitting because of how assiduously she had been avoiding the artist except at the evening meal when she could hardly be absent from her place without a good excuse. Cowardice would not be an acceptable reason or one she would like to explain to her father. Nor could she come up with a reasonable excuse to delay talking to Selena when her father found her in the garden.

"Charley, I've been looking for you." He

sat down on the stone bench beside her and shifted his weight from side to side with a little groan. "These things need some padding." He was a man who liked his comfort.

"But the sunshine is nice." Charlotte smiled as she dropped her book to her lap, keeping her finger on the page to mark her place. The extra weight her father had put on in the last few years had aged him. He was barely past fifty, but he winded easily and preferred his easy chair to any sort of sporting activity. At least before Selena.

Charlotte hadn't seen him for several months, since he had been staying in Frankfort. With the country in such a state of turmoil, she had not thought his extended absence from Grayson odd. He had to keep abreast of legislative issues and work for his constituents. But it seemed this year there had been time for more pleasurable pursuits as well.

He glanced up at the cloudless sky as if he hadn't noticed whether the sun was even shining until she mentioned it. "So it is," he said.

The bright light in the garden made it easy to see how thin his hair was getting on the top, even though Ruben, his long-time valet, had carefully combed his remaining hair over the balding spot. Gray was creeping back from his temples and taking over his eyebrows. His moustache was almost completely gray. A light sheen of perspiration moistened his forehead even though the air was cool enough that Charlotte had considered going back inside for her shawl.

"Are you feeling all right, Father?" Charlotte asked with a worried frown.

"Now don't you be worrying about me." He patted her arm. "I've never been better."

"You look tired."

"Well, things were busy in Frankfort what with the current unrest in our country, and of course once I met Selena, things started hopping. Not much time for relaxation. Not that I'm complaining," he said with a little laugh. "Most certainly not. Selena's the best thing to happen to me in a long while. And to Grayson too, or I miss my guess."

Charlotte had no words to answer that, but her father didn't need her words as he went on. "You can't know how very glad I am that you and Selena are getting along so well. She thinks of you as a favored younger sister, you know."

"Does she?" Charlotte stared down at her book as she carefully marked her place with a ribbon before she closed it. "Not a daughter, then."

Her father laughed. "You can hardly expect that, since she's only a few years older than you."

"That's good anyway. I had a loving mother." Charlotte looked up at him as if the next question just came out of thin air. "How old is Selena anyway?"

He raised eyebrows that Ruben must have forgotten to comb that morning before he said, "I haven't been a politician these many years not to know there are some questions a man dares not ask, and a woman's age is one of those."

"What do you know about her?" Charlotte looked directly at her father. When the color rose in his cheeks, she wasn't sure if it was due to anger or embarrassment.

He frowned a little. "I know enough and I should think you know enough not to be disrespectful to your father."

"I'm sorry. I didn't mean to sound disrespectful, Father." She stared down at her book a moment. *The Scarlet Letter* by Nathaniel Hawthorne. A story of impropriety. "I was merely curious about her. And her son, Landon. Have you met him?"

"No, no, but I am anxious to have him here at Grayson. Selena planned to send him to Georgia to spend some time with relations there, but I've talked her out of that. He needs to be here with his mother. And me. He's only six, but Selena says he's smart as a tack." Her father's good humor returned as he looked up and off across the garden. "It will be good to have a boy running about the house."

"Georgia? I understood Selena was from Boston."

"That's where she was living when her late husband made his tragic departure from life. Some sort of wasting sickness, she says. All very sad. But her extended family owns a plantation in Georgia. Very well-to-do, I surmise. That's why she's so capable of looking at Grayson and seeing where we might have been neglectful over the last few years in managing our people.

A soft heart is fine in church but can get you in trouble on the farm."

Charlotte sat frozen on the bench, almost afraid to breathe, but she had to ask the question pushing at her lips. "What does she suggest? For our people?"

"We have to cull them out the same as we would our horses. She's already talked to Perkins about it and he's giving her names."

"You're going to sell them?" Charlotte's voice sounded wrong in her ears. "To the South?"

"That's where the best market is. Selena says the plantations down there are always anxious to get Kentucky-bred Negroes. And with Mr. Lincoln's abolitionist leanings, who knows what might happen. A person has to protect his investments."

"President Lincoln hasn't put forth a plan to free the slaves, has he?"

"Not as yet, but there are many who think it could be in the offing if a compromise isn't reached with the Secessionist states. I don't know what those governors and representatives down there can be thinking." He rubbed his hands up and down his thighs as his voice got a little louder. "Just because the President spoke against allowing slavery in new territories in the West doesn't mean he planned to ban it in states where it already existed. He won't do that. Not if he wants to keep Kentucky in the Union."

"Would you vote for secession?"

"No, no. I can't imagine any situation where Kentucky wouldn't stay with the Union." He pulled his eyebrows together in a frown just thinking about it. "But at the same time I can't see surrendering my property to the federal government without proper recompense. It's better to leave things status quo. And not keep stirring things up like those copperheads up north with their abolition talk."

"I wish we could just set all our people free."

"My dear girl, you don't know what you're saying." Her words obviously shocked her father. "No, no, my dear, that would be the ruin of us all. Perhaps them even more than us. What would become of them without us to feed and clothe them?" He shook his head at her as his look turned from indignant to indulgent. "Being so young, you can hardly be expected to understand all the ramifications of freeing the slaves, and it is something you shouldn't concern your pretty head about. What you need to remember is that our people are well cared for."

Charlotte wanted to argue with him, but she knew it would be useless. Better to pick her fight. "Is Mellie mine? Mother always told me so. That Aunt Tish was hers and Mellie was mine."

"She did say that."

Charlotte opened the book in her lap and tore out the blank page at the back of the book. "Would you write that down for me? That Mellie belongs to me. And Aunt Tish too. It can be an early wedding present."

"Not Aunt Tish," he said. "We have to have a cook here at Grayson."

"Then Mellie," Charlotte insisted.

He looked at the paper she handed him. "I don't have pen and ink."

Charlotte reached under the bench where she'd laid her writing tools when she started reading. "I was making a list earlier. Of things I need to do before the wedding." It wasn't exactly true, but close enough. It was actually a note to Edwin to try to ensure there was a wedding. She dipped the pen nib in the ink and handed it to her father.

He held the pen in the air above the paper as he hesitated. "I don't know about this, Charlotte."

"You were going to let Mellie go with me when I married, weren't you?"

"Well, yes, I suppose so, but that was before Selena. I really should speak to her about this. Besides, isn't there some doubt of the wedding going on as planned in May?"

"Even if I don't wed in May, I will wed eventually. And Mellie was promised to me by Mother." Charlotte spoke the words with quiet firmness.

"Yes, your mother was always senti-mental about the servants. Something Selena says we can't be. She says it could be we should have found a new place for Mellie years ago when it was apparent you were getting too attached to her." He frowned as he stared down at the paper while the ink dried on the pen's nib.

Charlotte's heart went cold inside her. How could her father even listen to such a suggestion? That woman had spun a spell over him. Charlotte moistened her lips and managed to keep her voice soft and insistent without letting the panic she was beginning to feel leak through. She had to protect Mellie. She had given Aunt Tish her word. "Mother didn't think I was too attached. She said it was good to have servants we could depend on. You do remember that she promised Mellie to me, don't you? A promise she had no doubt you'd keep."

He stared across the walkway at the dogwood tree whose buds were already showing white. "I did so love your mother. I planted that tree for her with my own hands on our first anniversary to prove how much. She sat on this very bench and laughed when I showed her the dirt under my fingernails. She had just felt the stirrings of the first child she tried to carry for me." He smiled at the memory, but then the smile slipped off his face. "She lost that baby two weeks later. You and our poor little baby boy were the only two she carried past the first five months. And then the baby boy never drew breath."

"I remember," Charlotte said.

"Yes, I suppose you do. What were you four, five?"

"Almost six," Charlotte said. "He was born in May before my birthday in June."

"So many years ago and yet even now I can close my eyes and see that round little face, so perfectly formed. So silent and still. Mayda held him to her breast and whispered the name she'd planned for him as if at the sound of her voice he might yet gasp and begin to breathe. Charles Grayson after me and her father. I didn't want to use the names. I wanted to save them for the baby son we might yet have, but she would not hear of naming him anything else." Her father let out a breath heavy with the sadness of his memories. "I had to peel her hands from his tiny body to let Aunt Tish prepare him for burial. Mayda was never the same after that."

"But she kept loving us." Charlotte needed to hear him affirm that.

"Yes. As much as she was capable. She put too much on you when you were little more than a child, and I suppose I did as well. We should have let you go away to school."

"I never wanted to leave Grayson. Grandfather taught me to read and write before he died," Charlotte said. "And I went to Miss Lucinda's school in town. I'm not uneducated."

"Not in history and letters, but there is an art to being a lady and rules that must be observed by young women in your position."

"I have observed the rules." Charlotte pushed her words at him. "Haven't I always managed to show Grayson in the best light whenever you wanted to entertain here? You have never had reason to be ashamed of me."

His eyes came away from the tree back to Charlotte. "Oh, my dear girl, I didn't mean to make you think that. You've always been a very dutiful daughter."

Dutiful. Is that how he thought of her? As only dutiful. She let her eyes fall shut a moment as she composed herself. She didn't want to lose her focus. Not until he wrote the paper giving her Mellie. She opened her eyes and smiled at him. "And you a loving, caring father. That's why I know you will honor Mother's promise to me."

"Promise?" He had gone so far back in

memory that he seemed to have forgotten what promise she meant as he looked down at the pen in his hand with a little frown.

"Mellie. Mother's promise to me." Charlotte held the little pot of ink out toward him. "My wedding present." She wanted to ask for Aunt Tish again, but feared pushing him too far.

"Oh, Mellie. Well, I suppose you're right. I should honor your mother's promise." He dipped the pen into the ink and wrote the words on the paper. He handed it to her.

She read his writing. "This is legally binding?"

"It is. You are now a slaveholder."

"Yes," Charlotte agreed as she stared at the paper. "Thank you, Father." She reached over to kiss his cheek before she carefully folded the paper and slipped it down into her pocket.

After that, she could hardly refuse to obey his request to heed Selena's summons to the parlor. She had Mellie's promised freedom in her pocket.

8

Adam Wade mixed the paint on his palette as quickly as possible. Time was wasting while he stood in the senator's parlor painting the senator's wife as scores of better subjects were going undrawn. He would have even preferred sketching the lines of the senator's florid face. Sam would probably welcome that, along with a few of the senator's words stating his seemingly sincere belief that his state could remain a neutral buffer zone if the confrontation between the states escalated. And the senator would be happy to have the notoriety of being in *Harper's Weekly*. The man had ambitions. Beyond senator in the Kentucky Senate.

Governor, the new Mrs. Vance claimed, which perhaps explained why she was the new Mrs. Vance. Adam doubted love had much to do with it, even if she did liberally sprinkle her conversations with the senator with words of devotion. Plus the senator was old money or at least had inherited such from his first wife. The wife whose portrait had been removed, leaving behind a darker square of forest green striped wallpaper over the mantelpiece behind Adam. Across the parlor the new wife sat by the window in a shaft of afternoon light.

Adam hadn't warmed to her. Something he generally did when he was painting someone. Perhaps his reluctance to do the portrait was the cause, or perhaps it had more to do with the way the woman ordered him about like one of her husband's servants as he stood behind the easel and wielded his brush. Twice he'd had to wipe away his brushstrokes depicting her eyes because of the hard glint he kept letting the paint on the canvas reveal. He wished he was back at the Shaker village painting the old sister whose suspicious glower had wiped away every trace of feminine beauty from her face. At least there he could be honest with his brush.

Selena Vance hadn't seen her painted eyes. He knew better than to let a subject see a portrait in progress. Especially someone like the woman in front of him. She seemed—if that could be possible—even wearier of the whole process than he was. She came to each sitting wearing a cream-colored dress with an edging of delicate lace around the plunging neckline. Her skin was very white, almost too white, but it contrasted nicely with the pink of her cheeks, which she kept pinching to give them color whenever she thought he wasn't watching.

He could have told her he could paint in the color without her resorting to the painful pinches, but he didn't. Her dark hair was piled high on her head in an elaborate style that had to take an hour to pin and arrange. So he supposed it was no wonder the woman was tired of sitting still even before she came to the parlor to perch on the Victorian chair and, with a bare word of greeting, demanded he begin.

Paint her pretty and get it over with, he told himself every ten minutes. It didn't matter that the more he looked at her, the less attractive she seemed to him in spite of her perfectly aligned features. He had an imagination. While he had never used that imagination to intentionally change the looks of one of his subjects, that didn't mean he couldn't this time. For his mental sanity he needed to think of Selena Vance as beautiful and portray that on the canvas. He needed to be free to get back to drawing subjects that mattered. The nation was boiling and he was stuck inside a parlor painting lace on the bodice of a dress.

The finer points of the lace might be missing in the portrait, for he planned to be gone from the senator's house by the end of the week. If the senator wasn't pleased with the finished portrait, he had plenty of resources to contract another artist who might be as captivated by the new Mrs. Vance's beauty as the senator was.

Of course Adam would miss Aunt Tish's cooking. Plus he had entertained a few hopes of coming across the senator's daughter alone in the garden again. While a repeat of their earlier encounter wouldn't be unwelcome, it was not likely the way she had avoided him since. The only time he'd seen her was at the dinner table, where she seemed a pale shadow of the girl in the garden who had met his eyes so brazenly in the moonlight and spoken so honestly. She let no honest words brighten the dinner conversation as she kept her eyes on her plate and only perked up if the senator began talking politics.

From memory, he had sketched the senator's daughter gazing off her veranda into the darkness. He thought Sam might print it with a caption saying something like, "With war on the horizon, a Southern belle ponders her future." Sam was a genius with captions.

Adam wasn't worried about the senator's daughter not wanting her picture in the newspaper. Truth be known, she might not even recognize herself, since the illustration would lack color to show her red hair. But he hoped to find a time to show her the drawing before he left Grayson so she'd know in case the newspaper eventually found its way into her hands. It was like a gift he could give her to perhaps make up for taking advantage of her at a vulnerable moment. Although he was hardly averse to catching her in another such moment or too much of a gentleman to seize the advantage if it did happen again.

So he was surprised when the daughter appeared at the parlor door in the middle of the afternoon's sitting. By command, it turned out. Selena had been browbeating the butler, an old black gentleman named Gibson who seemed totally overwhelmed by the new Mrs. Vance's stream of orders. There was little doubt he was going to forget most of them before he got out of the room.

Adam had tried to help by telling Selena how important it was that she sit quietly for him to capture the best image on the canvas.

She glared Adam's way for a brief moment. "I sat quietly yesterday. Today you will have to find a way to work around my words. This is all taking much too long. I've had my portrait done before without the need for so many sittings."

If only she had called on that artist again, Adam thought as he had to stay his brush from turning the jeweled combs in her elaborate hairstyle into horns. He sent Gibson a sympathetic look, but the butler kept his eyes on the floor. Adam's fingers itched to capture his dejection. The old fellow had probably been accustomed to opening the door to guests and ushering them into the receiving parlor, to making sure the stair spindles and furniture were properly dusted, and to seeing that fires blazed in Grayson's hearths if the weather turned cool.

While that might have satisfied the senator's daughter, he had a new mistress in residence now, one who was changing things too rapidly for Gibson to take in. Each new word from the woman in the chair by the window seemed to bend his shoulders a little more, as if she were loading bricks into a sack on his old back while he mumbled, "Yes'm."

When the senator's daughter came in the room, the old man's face brightened. Something his new mistress noted with evident displeasure.

"This is useless." Selena heaved an elaborate sigh of disgust. "You're dismissed, Gibson. Send that other girl in here. The one who does my hair. She at least seems to have a memory."

"Mellie," Charlotte told Gibson as he looked at her. "Tell Mellie Mrs. Vance wants her." Her voice was soft and kind with none of the sharp edges in Selena's commands.

"Yes, miss. Right away, miss." The old fellow started out of the room, but stopped to ask, "Do you want her to bring tea?"

"Just . . . get . . . her." Selena spoke the words one at a time with force.

"Yes'm."

Adam was surprised at how fast the old man got out of the room. He wished he could follow on his heels, and he thought the senator's daughter would have been right behind them if she could have done as she wanted. But then she seemed to find some courage as she looked directly at Selena and said, "Gibson has been with the family for many years."

"Perhaps too many years." Selena didn't bother to hide her annoyance whether with Gibson or the senator's daughter or life in general.

Without thought Adam painted in the frown lines between her eyes and then had to smooth them away with his brush. Paint her pretty and quickly, he reminded himself. Neither woman was paying the least bit of attention to him.

"He's a great favorite of many of Father's political friends," the younger woman said.

Selena mashed her mouth together in a thin line. "Politics can't rule everything."

"Elections are won by a thousand little things."

"More like a few thousand votes. But I didn't call you in here to discuss political maneuvering. I get an overabundance of that from your father, you can be sure."

"Father is committed to serving his state as best he can. A difficult charge now with all the divisions."

Selena's eyes narrowed on Charlotte. Adam was pleased to see the girl didn't wilt under her glare. "Are you attempting in your clumsy way to take me to task?"

"Oh no. I do beg your pardon if such seemed the case." She sounded sincere as she turned to bring Adam into the conversation. "I certainly wouldn't want Mr. Wade to think there was any kind of ill feeling between us. Forgive me, Mr. Wade, if my words appeared uncharitable."

Adam twisted his mouth a little to the side to keep from smiling. "Don't mind me. I'm just the portrait painter."

"How is it coming? May I look?" Charlotte took a step toward his easel.

"No." Selena stopped her in her tracks. "Our dear Mr. Wade claims he can't allow anyone to see the portrait until it is finished. Not even me."

Adam let the smile leak out to his face as he made a few brushstrokes. "You know how artists can be. Temperamental about their work."

"Of course," Charlotte said and stepped back. "But I've heard you are very good with portrait sketches."

"Sketches of whom?" Selena's eyes were sharp on Adam.

"I've seen his work in *Harper's Weekly.*" Charlotte didn't really answer the woman's question as she turned back to her. "I've been going through some of our old newspapers, and every illustration Mr. Wade has done is quite remarkable. I'm surprised Father was able to convince him to take time out from such work to do your portrait."

"Charles had little to do with it. I am a friend of Mr. Wade's sister."

"How fortunate for you," Charlotte said.

She acted as if Adam hadn't already told her the same thing in the garden.

Perhaps she had wiped that encounter out of her mind. Perhaps he should do the same. He pretended to turn his full attention back to the canvas in front of him.

Charlotte continued to stand in the middle of the floor instead of settling in one of the chairs which she surely had a right to do even if the senator's wife didn't ask her to sit. After a brief and uncomfortable silence, Charlotte said, "My father said you wished to speak to me."

"Yes, so I did." Selena's voice sounded almost as superior as it had moments ago when she was speaking to the old butler. "The servants have been packing up your mother's things. Something that should have been done years ago."

"I suppose you're right, but there never seemed any urgency." Charlotte's voice held a whisper of sadness. "Until now. Do you want me to go through the things?"

"No need," Selena said with a wave of her hand. "We've already disposed of them."

"Disposed of them?" The color drained from Charlotte's face. "Without consulting me?"

"Really, Charlotte, those dusty old clothes would have done nothing but make you sneeze. I had them sent to a charitable group." Selena swept her eyes up and down Charlotte from her shoulders to her toes. "You certainly could never tighten your stays enough to fit into any of those garments. Your mother must have been stylishly slender."

"Please, Selena, this hardly seems proper conversation in mixed company." Red bloomed in Charlotte's face as she glanced sideways at Adam.

Selena laughed at her innocence. "Never you fear about Mr. Wade. I'm sure he's quite familiar with the workings of corsets."

Adam looked up from his paints and searched for a way to ease Charlotte's humiliation. Humiliation Selena was relishing. It was becoming obvious that she was as ready to pack up the senator's daughter and ship her off as she had been the first Mrs. Vance's dresses. He pushed out a little laugh. "You've got me there, Selena. My first paying job was drawing corsets for a catalogue advertisement." He mixed some colors on his palette and told himself to forget about painting her pretty. Just finish the job. He hadn't promised satisfaction to her. Or to Phoebe. He cleaned his brush. "Perhaps I should leave so you can continue your talk in private."

"That won't be necessary, Adam. Charlotte and I are almost through here." Selena pointed to a small wooden box on the table beside her. "Your father says that was your mother's jewelry, and he insisted you would want it even if there is little of worth in the box. Nothing but a few old tarnished pieces."

"Mother preferred books and flowers to jewelry," Charlotte said as she swooped up the box.

"So Charles has told me. And that's another thing." Selena looked out the window. "The garden needs major renovation. Everything has been sadly neglected here for too long."

"Grayson has its own unique charm," Charlotte said.

"But all charms can be enhanced. Isn't that so, Adam?"

"In a perfect world perhaps," Adam said.

"There are no perfect worlds. Or are there, Charlotte?" Selena turned her sharp eyes back to Charlotte, who halted her backward edging toward the door but stayed silent as she stiffened her posture and waited for the woman to go on. "Your young Mr. Gilbey seems to disagree with me there. The night of the party he was telling me all about this Shaker village nearby where he seems to feel a perfect life might await him. Have you heard any more from him on the status of your planned wedding? Will it be a Shaker wedding?"

Charlotte's face lost all pretense of a smile. "No. The Shakers don't believe in marriage."

"I thought that was the case." From the smug look on Selena's face, it was obvious she had known that all along but had merely been baiting Charlotte. "Then, my dear, don't you think it is time to look in a new direction? Find a new plan for your future? I'm sure your father shared with you the opportunity of going east for a while. That would save you the embarrassment of being the subject of many whispered conversations at all the spring gatherings."

"Grayson is my home," Charlotte said.

"Of course it is. I certainly don't mean to imply any differently." Selena's voice was honey-coated but underneath was steel. "But you do have to realize it is no longer your home only. Your father has a new family now. I'm sure he's told you about his plans for Landon."

"Plans? It was my understanding he'd not yet met the child."

"That's true, but I've naturally enough shared a great deal about Landon, and your father has generously offered to adopt him. He says my son is his son. Just as his daughter is my daughter. And of course we have hopes of having a child of our own." Selena smoothed her hands down over her midsection and raised her eyebrows knowingly at the girl.

Two bright red spots burned in Charlotte's cheeks as she looked down at the floor and spoke barely above a whisper. "Of course."

Selena let out a short burst of unladylike laughter at Charlotte's evident discomfort. Adam was sorry he hadn't left the room earlier in spite of the woman's orders to the contrary. He could have simply walked out. He wasn't her slave. It was painful watching the calculating woman attempting to dismantle the world of the girl in front of her. A few days ago the girl had been the senator's beloved daughter with all of Grayson at her feet. Now all she could claim as her own was the box of jewelry clutched so tightly against her side the wooden corners had to be digging into her ribs. Ribs that were obviously free of the type of tortuous corset Selena had immodestly mentioned earlier.

Charlotte had no need of the slimming stays. She had no need of any beauty enhancements. In her everyday blue flowered dress flowing about her legs without multiple petticoats and her red hair falling free down on her shoulders, she easily outshined the polished woman he was painting. Even with no hint of a smile on her face.

He suddenly wanted to cross the room and put his arm around her. To protect her from the hard truths of life. He wanted to see her smiling, embracing life. Embracing him. The thought pulled him up short. He couldn't let himself get carried away by a pretty face. He didn't need those sorts of complications in his life. What he needed to do was paint faster and get away from this house. He needed to be back searching out the scenes to capture the truth of the country's current upheaval. He needed no upheaval in his own life. Especially not the kind a girl like Charlotte Vance could bring him.

When the girl mumbled some words of thanks for the box and almost ran out of the room, he told himself that was good. With her out of sight, he could concentrate on finishing the loathsome portrait and be gone from the senator's house. He was no knight in shining armor ready to rescue every damsel in distress he met. Especially not when the dragon in question was only the damsel's stepmother. It wasn't as if her life was in danger. Merely her immediate happiness.

9

Selena was right. Most of the tangled pile of necklaces and brooches were old and tarnished and of little value other than to Charlotte's heart. She remembered playing with some of them when she was a child. She fished out an emerald ring and a strand of pearls that had belonged to her Grandmother Grayson and held each of them for a long moment as if testing their weight and value.

Then she carefully freed a locket on a fine gold chain from the other strands of jewelry in the box. Inside was a wisp of baby hair clipped from her baby brother's head before he was laid in his tiny casket. Her mother had never taken the locket off after that day. Charlotte thought her mother had worn it to her grave, but now here it was tossed aside in a box and forgotten. Charlotte shut the locket and held it tightly in her palm.

Be strong. Miss Mayda would want you to be strong. Aunt Tish's words echoed in Charlotte's mind. And that had been easy for Charlotte to do in spite of her mother's sudden death, because everybody had helped her. Everybody knew Grayson would be hers. In time. Even if she had thought about her father remarrying, she would have never considered Grayson passing to someone who didn't carry Grayson blood. Her whole life centered around that belief.

But now she'd been betrayed. By her own father. They were going to ship her off to Virginia and do what they willed with Grayson and their people. No, not what they willed. What Selena willed.

She couldn't let it happen. But what could she do? She had sent the letter to Edwin demanding to know his intentions. Willis had carried it to Hastings manor house at noon. She had to know. She couldn't just hide in the shadows and hope without knowledge. If Edwin stayed true to their agreement, then she could wait out Selena. The flattery of the woman's attention had obviously blinded her father, but his eyes would clear and he would see through the woman's pretense in time.

Meanwhile. That was the problem. Charlotte had never been one to sit on the side and simply let things happen. Not the way her mother had. Charlotte made things happen. But now nothing was working. She closed her eyes and held the locket against her cheek. Perhaps she should pray about it. Ask the Lord to make things come out right, but that hadn't worked for her baby brother. His life had ended on the day of his birth. It hadn't worked for Aunt Tish. Her husband had been sold down the river.

Charlotte had no doubt Aunt Tish prayed then. Aunt Tish believed in prayer. She had taught Mellie and Charlotte to pray over their food as soon as they could sit at the table. She had prayed over Charlotte's mother. She probably covered Charlotte with prayers every morning now. But that didn't mean things were going to turn out right. Aunt Tish told her once that a person couldn't expect God to hand out favors on a silver tray.

"Then why pray if you don't think the Lord is going to answer?" Charlotte had asked.

"I never said the good Lord don't answer. He always answers. That don't mean his answers is gonna match up with the answers you think you're wantin'. But the one thing a child of his can count on is that, no matter the answer, the Lord is right there with you. Walkin' through them valleys right along 'side you. Liftin' you up when you fall. Helpin' you bear up under the trials." Aunt Tish had put her work-roughened hand on Charlotte's cheek. "And we all, ever' last one of us, has trials and tribulations."

"But is that any reason to collect them like charms and gather them close and moan over them without trying to do something about them?" Charlotte said.

"No, I guess not, child. You ain't much a one for moanin'." Aunt Tish had smiled at her as she patted her cheek. "The good

Lord done give you a fightin' spirit and the freedom to use it."

A fighting spirit. That's what she needed now. Charlotte opened her eyes and stood up. There was a time for praying and a time for doing. This was the time for doing. Edwin had her letter. She had her mother's jewelry. And Mellie's path to freedom. She slipped her hand in her pocket and felt the paper. She hadn't given up. It might have seemed that she had lost the battle in the parlor. She was sure Adam Wade thought so. She'd felt him looking at her with pity. But she didn't need pity. Pity or prayers. There'd be a way. She just had to find it.

She'd make her father see that Grayson was meant to be hers. The same as he had realized Mellie was hers. Of course, if he had known her plans to free Mellie, she doubted he'd have given her the paper. He claimed freed slaves did nothing but foment trouble and unrest if not made to leave the state. That was why he'd supported the Kentucky Colonization Society that up until a couple of years before had worked to buy passage back to Africa for emancipated slaves.

Mellie wouldn't want to go to Africa. Her

home was here at Grayson the same as Charlotte's. That shouldn't mean she couldn't be free to decide her own fate. Free to fall in love as she wanted. Actually Charlotte was beginning to suspect it wasn't only a dream of falling in love for Mellie. She'd been volunteering to carry the leftover food from their dinner to the slave quarters nearly every night before Selena began to demand so much from her. And hadn't Charlotte caught a worried look in Aunt Tish's eyes more than once when she looked at Mellie?

One thing at a time. She had the paper. She'd figure out the rest eventually. First there was the locket warm in her hand. Charlotte pulled the top off a nearly empty powder tin and dropped the locket down inside. It should have been buried with her mother. She would rectify that first thing in the morning.

She slipped the emerald ring on her finger. She'd never seen her mother wear it. It would have been too large for her mother's dainty fingers. She had favored an opal ring in a ruby setting. Charlotte searched through the jumble of jewelry. That ring wasn't in the box. So perhaps she had worn it to the grave.

Charlotte stuffed the box of jewelry up on the top shelf of her wardrobe. She started to hide Mellie's paper under the box, but changed her mind. It was too important to let out of her sight.

When Mellie came in a few minutes later to help her dress for dinner, Charlotte slipped the paper out of her pocket and down into the top of her camisole when Mellie had her back turned. She couldn't show it to her yet. Not until she had a plan, and before Charlotte could make a plan, she had to know her future with Edwin.

If she didn't get an answer from him by noon tomorrow, she would ride over to Hastings Farm. She'd make him state his intentions. But tonight she would go down to the dining room and listen to Selena's false chatter at the table. She would pretend there wasn't a battle drawn up between them. Just as many in the North and South were pretending the same thing. It was better to keep the illusion of peace as long as possible.

❧

Even as they ate their dinner that night with a pretense of good humor and fine manners, the illusion of peace for the country had already been shot down at Fort Sumter in South Carolina.

A messenger brought the news the next morning. Charlotte didn't see the messenger ride up. After breakfast she had stopped in the kitchen and hid a heavy stirring spoon in the folds of her skirt before going out the back door to the family cemetery. She didn't want help from anyone for the job at hand.

The ground was soft from a late afternoon shower the day before, and she had no trouble cutting out a circle of the greening grass and scooping out a hole at the base of her mother's stone. She pushed the metal powder box down into the hole and tamped the dirt back in around it before carefully replacing the bit of grass sod. When she stood up and looked down, the disturbed ground was barely noticeable.

Charlotte ran her hands over the carved letters in the stone. MAYDA GRAYSON VANCE. BELOVED WIFE AND MOTHER. AUG 5 1816–MAY 24 1857. Her baby brother's small tombstone was beside her mother's. In behind were the stones for her grandparents and her mother's sisters, Alice and Emma, taken by cholera in 1833. Another stone that towered higher even than her grandparents' stone bore the name of their one son, Richard Grayson III, in deeply chiseled granite letters. He had gone west to seek adventure and broken his parents' hearts by getting killed in an Indian skirmish. His body wasn't actually under the stone but was instead in an unmarked grave somewhere on the prairie.

Charlotte thought how different her life might have been if her uncle Richard had lived to come home and marry. His family would be living in the Grayson manor house. His son the descendant to carry on the Grayson name and tradition. But there were no Grayson sons. No sons at all. Up until now.

She raised her head to look out between the tall oaks that shaded the graveyard. Grayson land stretched as far as she could see in every direction. Good land. Her land. She could almost feel the roots attaching her feet to the ground as strongly as the roots holding the towering oaks around her. It would take a mighty storm to break her free.

She was so immersed in her thoughts

that she didn't notice the artist walking up behind her until he spoke.

"I've been looking for you," he said.

She whirled to face him.

"I must beg your forgiveness once again, my lady," he said with a smile as he stopped a couple of paces away from her. "I really didn't intend to startle you. This time. I should have whistled a tune or something to warn you I was coming."

"Can you whistle a tune?" Charlotte asked to give herself time to recover her poise. She hid her hands in her skirt so he wouldn't see the dirt under her fingernails.

"Of course," he said and began whistling "Yankee Doodle Dandy."

She couldn't keep from laughing even as she wondered if such joviality was proper in a graveyard. "You are a man of many talents, Mr. Wade."

"So I've been told." His eyes settled on her face. "But don't you think we've shared enough familiar moments for you to call me Adam?"

Her cheeks warmed and her lips tingled at the memory of some of those moments with him. She fixed her eyes on the blades of grass at her feet and tried to ignore her heart thumping in her chest as she said, "I daresay some familiar moments are best not remembered."

He stepped closer to her and put his fingers under her chin to tip her face up to look at him. It was a replay of the moments in the garden, except this time the sun was shining brightly and there was no chill in the air to necessitate him offering her his jacket. But he seemed to be offering something more. Understanding, or perhaps compassion. Why, she didn't know. He couldn't read her thoughts.

"Don't say that, Charlotte. I quite enjoyed the moments of which you speak."

She told herself to step away from him. To look away from the blue gray eyes that were probing her soul. But she stayed still as she said, "And how many times have you enjoyed like moments in other gardens?" Her voice was barely above a whisper.

"I won't deny there have been other gardens, but no girl so lovely. Or lips so enticing." He moved his fingers from under her chin to trace her lips.

She pulled herself together and stepped back from his touch. It was colder there but safer. Much safer. "We're not in a garden now, Mr. Wade."

"Adam, please." He kept his hand in the air reaching toward her face for a moment before he dropped it to his side and looked around. "And you're right. I do have to admit I've never enjoyed such a moment in a graveyard." He nodded toward the stone behind her. "The beautiful first Mrs. Vance, I assume."

"She was very pretty," Charlotte said as she glanced back at the stone. "I don't look anything like her."

"Did you want to?"

His unexpected question brought her eyes back to him. "What?"

"Look like her. Be like her." His eyes were probing her again.

"No. I always thought her too fragile." Her words sounded disloyal in her ears, but she didn't stop talking. "At times she seemed almost afraid to leave her couch. As if she feared the day would be too difficult to face."

"Are you afraid of your tomorrows?"

She looked at him, not sure how she should answer, but his eyes demanded honesty. "I don't know," she said at last.

"Last week I would have said not, but now if not afraid, then I do admit to being unsure of my future." She stared straight at him with wanton disregard of proper behavior, but a graveyard seemed a place to pitch aside social conventions and reach for the truth. "What about you?" She hesitated before she added, "Adam."

The corners of his lips lifted in a brief smile at the sound of his name. Then he grew solemn again as his eyes shifted color to more gray than blue. "I don't entertain fear. Instead I seek opportune possibilities."

"But there are oftentimes reasons for fear."

"Unfortunately you're speaking truth even not knowing the news that's come to us this morning."

"What news?" Dread woke inside her. The news couldn't be good.

"The Confederates fired on and forced the surrender of Federal forces at Fort Sumter. War is now inevitable."

"War," she echoed. She looked away from him out toward the horizon once more and now she couldn't keep from picturing cannons lining up against cannons. Perhaps even eventually on this very ground.

"The dark war clouds will no longer hang back. The storm is upon us," he said as if he too was imagining what war would bring to them. "But I didn't follow you out here just to deliver that unhappy news. I wanted a private moment with you to say goodbye before I left Grayson."

Her eyes came back to him. "Are you off to fight the South, then?"

"No, I'm not a soldier. I see other possibilities. I will go but only to draw the scenes to break the hearts of those far from the battlefields."

"Surely there are no battlefields as yet."

"Battles rage in many places. People will be choosing sides. In the legislatures. Village streets. Drawing rooms."

His look sharpened on her with the last, but she pretended not to know his meaning. "So Selena's portrait is finished?"

"I plan to add the final strokes to it this afternoon and be on my way come morning."

"Then you could have said goodbye in the morning."

"Perhaps, but you seem to lose a bit of that honesty I find so enchanting when others are in our company." A smile was back in his eyes.

She let his words slide past her. She had no answer for that. Instead she shifted the subject. "I'm sure Father will be leaving too. Back to Frankfort to be in the middle of the decision making for our state."

"He was ordering his servant to begin packing when I left the house."

"I do hope Selena plans to accompany him." Charlotte mashed her mouth together. She shouldn't have spoken that aloud.

Adam's smile reached his lips. "Your father said the same, but in a much different tone of voice." His smile faded as he peered at her with a good deal of sympathy. "Unfortunately for the happiness of you both, she feels she has too much to do here at Grayson to return to Frankfort at this time."

"She has many plans." Charlotte kept her voice as free of expression as she could.

"Many plans," Adam agreed. "Sometimes all a person can do is get out of the way of a woman like Selena."

"I can hardly pick up and leave the way

you can." She looked at him with a bit of envy even as she thought of poor dead Richard who had done that and never come home. If there truly was war between the North and the South, how many more gravestones would rise in the family grave-yards around them?

"What about your gentleman friend?" Adam's eyes were sharp on her again.

"The one going to the Shakers?" Something about this man kept her from pretending even to herself.

"I suppose that does present some dif-ficulties."

"Certainly few of your opportunities." She wanted to keep her voice strong and sure, but the way his eyes were try-ing to swallow her was taking her breath away. She stepped back and felt the cold edge of her mother's gravestone against her legs.

"Opportunities can pop up in the most unlikely places, but sometimes you need to know the right opportunity to pursue." He stepped closer to her. "It's good Edwin Gilbey is going to the Shakers. That sets you free."

"Free to do what?" Charlotte's voice fell

almost to a whisper again. She tried to back up and put more distance between them, but the gravestone stopped her.

"Live your life." Adam softly traced the curve of her cheek with his finger. "Enjoy the moment. This moment."

A tremble swept through Charlotte at his touch. Not of fear but of desire. She couldn't move. She didn't want to move. His eyes had her mesmerized.

"Seize the opportunity." His voice deepened and sounded husky as he bent his head down toward her, but he stopped before he touched her lips. She could feel his breath against her face as he went on. "Do you have the courage to do that, my beautiful Charlotte?"

It took all her strength to keep from melting against him and raising her lips to meet his. He was going to be gone from Grayson in the morning. She'd likely never lay eyes on him again. What good purpose could there be in yanking her heart out of her chest to throw at his feet, even if that was what she wanted to do? And yet what could one kiss hurt? A kiss she could remember and treasure no matter what happened in the days ahead.

Surrendering to his embrace would take no courage. The courage was in putting her hands flat against his chest and turning her head away from his lips as she pushed him back from her.

"I don't think you have honorable intentions, Mr. Wade," she said as she scooted to the side to put a bit of space between them and immediately wondered if she'd made the biggest mistake of her life. Even with the sun warm on her shoulders, she felt as cold inside as the gravestone behind her.

A look of regret to match her own flashed across his face before he said, "You surely didn't expect a proposal for a harmless farewell kiss."

"I expected nothing. Except the goodbye you claimed to seek me to deliver."

He shut his eyes for a moment before he made a sound that was somewhere between a sigh and a laugh. "Then I suppose your expectations will not be disappointed." He reached out and touched her cheek. He was smiling again now. "Goodbye, my beautiful Charlotte. If only we had met at a different time with no war on the horizon."

She didn't pull away from his touch even as she said, "There would always be those possibilities on the horizon for you."

"I think my eyes might be feasting on a possibility now. One I may regret turning away from." His eyes were swallowing her again. "Perhaps our paths will cross again someday."

"There's always that possibility."

"Tonight?" He raised his eyebrows at her. "In the garden?"

"Goodbye, Mr. Wade." She softened her implied refusal with a smile as she moved away from him. "I will look forward to seeing your illustrations in the news. Stay safe." She didn't wait for him to say any more as she turned and began walking in measured strides toward the house. She'd have to come back later to retrieve Aunt Tish's spoon. But now it was time to remember who she was and not be carried away by a handsome face and smooth words. The only possibility Adam Wade held out to her was the possibility of trouble.

When she got back to the house, Edwin's return letter was waiting for her on the table in the hallway.

She carried it to the privacy of her room before she pulled the letter free of its envelope.

Dear Charlotte,

You are quite within your rights to demand the truth of my intentions and I am now ready to reveal such to you and to the world. I am going to the Shakers at Harmony Hill for a month's trial. Elder Logan thinks that an excellent way to test my determination and spirit. I myself feel no need of a trial period. I have no doubt that at the end of those thirty days I will feel unchanged and will at that time commit completely to the Society's rules and be ready—nay, not simply ready but eager—to shut away the evils of the world, accept the true salvation they offer, and begin walking the path of the true Believer. I feel such peace in the village as I see the order there and the brotherly love just as the Good Book teaches.

I do realize you had other

expectations and I regret disappointing you by denying you those worldly desires. However we can still join together in a meaningful and spiritual way if you want to join with me in the Society of Believers as a sister. That is the sort of love more than anything of romantic nature that we have always known for each other. I have spoken of this possibility with Elder Logan and he gives me his assurance the Shakers would welcome you into their midst even as they welcome me. I know we could both attain a level of happiness there that would never be possible in a common marital union as the world knows it.

If you wish to respond to this message, please forward your answer to me at Harmony Hill.

Ever your loving <u>brother</u> in Christ,
Edwin Gilbey

Charlotte stared at the underlined word *brother* written in Edwin's neat script for a long moment before she looked up and met her eyes in the mirror. What was it Adam Wade had asked her? Did she have the courage to face the possibilities awaiting her?

She stared at her image in the mirror until it seemed as if she were looking at a girl she'd never met as she considered the possibility Edwin offered her. She didn't flinch from the truth. Selena was taking control of Grayson. She already had Charlotte's father dancing to whatever tune she wished to hum into his ear. Hadn't he already spoken of Charlotte being sent away? Her place here at Grayson and in her father's heart was being crowded out. At least at the Shaker Village she would be standing on land adjacent to her land and not hundreds of miles away in Virginia.

And she would have thirty days to convince Edwin he was making a mistake. Something she would have no way of doing if he was there and she was here or in faraway Virginia at the home of some unknown relative. Perhaps it might even open her father's eyes to the truth of his betrayal of her mother's trust. Of the Grayson trust.

Best of all, she could take Mellie with

her. Charlotte reached into her pocket and touched the paper there. Shakers required converts to free their slaves. Did she have the courage to step through the Shaker door long enough to assure Mellie's freedom?

10

"Miss Lottie, you has done gone and lost your mind." Mellie plopped down on the bench at the end of the bed and stared at Charlotte with wide eyes. "You go to those Shakers? That's crazy talk."

"Aunt Tish doesn't think so. She thinks it will work."

"Then my mammy's done lost her senses too. Work is a good word for you to think on, Miss Lottie. The' ain't no ladies over there in that Shakertown. Just women more like me than you that them preachers put to work makin' hats and cookin' jams." Mellie frowned. "What could Mammy be thinkin'?"

"What's best for me the way she always has. And for you."

"Then she's done mixed up on that. How's you goin' to those Shaker people gonna be any kind of good for you or for me? I better go talk sense to her."

Mellie stood up, but Charlotte put a hand out to stop her. "First you have to listen, Mellie."

Mellie sank back down on the bench. "All right, Miss Lottie. You tell me what's got you and Mammy thinkin' on this crazy stuff."

Charlotte rubbed her forehead as she looked at Mellie and wondered where to start. "It's not crazy. Aunt Tish wouldn't tell us to do anything crazy. But this is the best way. I think it may be the only way."

It had been an eventful day from the moment they had assembled in the parlor for the unveiling of the portrait that morning. Her father had made a big deal of pulling off the cover sheet, but Adam Wade had stood to the side as though completely bored with the whole production. Selena was pleased, clapping her hands like an excited little girl as she moved to view her painted face first from one perspective, then another.

Charlotte moved back to get a better look. She had expected it to be better. It was a flattering likeness of Selena's face, but yet the portrait seemed lacking in some way.

"You're frowning." Adam stepped up close behind her and spoke the words in her ear.

"Not a frown of displeasure, you can be assured. I was merely concentrating on your work." Charlotte smiled at him even as she ordered her heart not to start beating faster just because his arm grazed hers. Her heart wasn't obedient. "It's lovely."

"A good word for it. A lovely painting of a lovely face." He lowered his voice even more. "But rather dull and lifeless. A cardboard image."

"Perhaps if you'd had more time." Charlotte kept her voice as low as his, but it hardly mattered. Her father and Selena were busy celebrating the empty loveliness of the portrait.

"Or a better subject." Adam moved even closer to her until she could feel the heat of his body before he said, "I went out to the garden last night."

"It was a pleasant spring evening for a walk." Charlotte kept her eyes on the portrait, but she was no longer seeing Selena's painted face. She was imagining what might have been if she had succumbed to the temptation to go out into the garden the night before.

"But very lonely."

"I'm sure you'll find other gardens more populated."

"That could be." She could hear the smile in his voice even though she didn't look back at him. "But I will always be left to wonder if I might have gone down on one knee to capture that kiss I so wanted to carry away with me."

"I doubt there would have been much chance of that." She bit the inside of her lip to keep an answering smile off her face. She knew he was toying with her, but at the same time she thought she caught the hint of wistful truth in his voice.

"I don't know. Redheads have a way of making a man do unexpected things."

She finally turned a bit to look at his

face and let her smile appear. "You live for the unexpected, Mr. Wade."

"So I do." He laughed softly. "I think you may be the first woman I've ever met who understood that." His smile faded. "And what are you going to do, Miss Vance, in the face of the conflict before us?"

She wasn't sure if he was speaking of her personal or their national conflict. It didn't matter. Her answer was the same. "The unexpected."

He looked straight into her eyes. Neither of them was even aware of Charlotte's father and Selena in the room any longer. "Perhaps you will. I left something for you in the garden last night. I was going to give it into your hand, but that was not to be." He lightly grazed her hand with his fingers. "Please seek it out else the little field mice may carry it away to line their burrows."

When they left the parlor, Willis had been waiting in the carriage to take him and Charlotte's father to the train station. Charlotte didn't follow them out. She had no desire to witness her father and Selena's fond farewells. Instead she went out the veranda door into the garden.

The sketch was anchored against a stray wind by a couple of rocks on the bench near where they had shared the first of those familiar moments Adam had referred to in the graveyard. The paper felt a bit soft from being out in the dew as she unfolded it to stare straight into her own eyes. At the bottom, he'd written, "Your face will add beauty to a thousand scenes."

"Now there is a portrait with some sparkle," he spoke behind her. "Even only in pen and ink."

She couldn't keep from jumping. "Do you ever give a girl some warning?"

"No." He smiled.

"I thought you left."

His smile got broader. "I had to come back for my favorite sketching pencils. I thought I remembered leaving them here in the garden." He reached down under the bench, picked up a couple of pencils, and held them up in the air. "And here they are."

She laughed. "You'll miss your train."

He waved his hand in a gesture of unconcern. "They'll delay its leaving a few minutes for the senator. But I forgot something besides my sketching pencils.

Something I couldn't leave without." His eyes fastened on her face.

"What's that?" When he reached for the sketch, she surrendered it with regret.

"Never fear. You can have it back, but we wouldn't want it to get crumpled." He dropped it on the bench beside them before he said, "Always expect the unexpected."

Then without another word to warn of his intent, he grabbed her and pulled her close in an embrace. His lips were on hers before she had time to utter a word of protest. And she was glad. She let herself be swallowed up in his embrace and gave the response his lips demanded. As the ground seemed to shift beneath her feet, she didn't worry about what was going to happen next. She simply surrendered to the joy of the moment.

But the moment ended. He raised his lips from hers. When he spoke, he sounded as out of breath as she felt. "And that is what I couldn't leave without."

Then just as suddenly as he had appeared, he was gone. Running away from her to his future. Leaving her behind to find hers.

That future is what she and Aunt Tish had worked out in the kitchen that afternoon after Selena had gone to visit a new acquaintance in the town and what Mellie couldn't believe she was serious about now. She was staring at Charlotte as though she had sprouted an extra head. "I ain't knowin' how you tryin' to turn into one of them dried-up old Shaker crones can be the best anything."

"Those old crones dance. Or so I've heard," Charlotte said. "They can't be too dried up. Or all old. They have a school there. So there must be children."

"None of their own making. Them people don't hold with the general Bible beliefs on the matter of Adam and Eve."

"Their beliefs do sound strange, but maybe that's just because we haven't tried to understand them." Charlotte hadn't expected Mellie to argue with her. She'd thought she'd agree to do whatever Charlotte said. Whatever Aunt Tish said.

"Ain't no understandin' how they live. Or worship. Rollin' around on the floor in fits."

"They don't always do that. I've been told that sometimes they simply dance in up-and-back marches. Not a lot different from a cotillion except the men and women stay separate."

"Separate for sure." Mellie shook her head a little, resisting Charlotte's every word. "What's got this in your head? That Mr. Edwin goin'? You's done better off without him anyhow, Miss Lottie. You need to latch on to the likes of that artist man."

Charlotte couldn't keep the color from rising in her cheeks. "He's gone, Mellie. I doubt I'll ever see him again. And getting Edwin to change his mind is my only chance to save Grayson."

Mellie frowned at her. "How's that gonna save anythin'? Mr. Edwin don't own Grayson. Massah Charles does."

"Father will come to his senses and see Selena for what she is. But I can't be off in Virginia when that happens. I need to be here close by."

Mellie leaned over to touch Charlotte's hand. "Even if you had to go to Virginia, it would just be for a little while and you might meet some other fellers like that artist gentleman. Somebody better'n poor Mr. Edwin who lacks any kind a starch in his makeup."

Charlotte hesitated. For some reason

she'd been reluctant to tell her what Willis had told Aunt Tish. What Charlotte had confirmed in an ugly confrontation with Selena that afternoon. "It's not just Grayson I'm trying to save," she said finally. "It's you."

"Me?" Mellie jerked back from Charlotte. "What? Has Mammy done tol' you I been makin' eyes at Nate?"

When Charlotte just looked at her without saying anything, she went on. "I love him, Miss Lottie. And he loves me. He done ask't me to jump the broom with him. You ain't wantin' to say no to that, are you?"

Charlotte sighed. "It doesn't matter what I want to say, Mellie. Selena's the one that matters now here at Grayson. She's put your name on the list Perkins is making. She aims to sell you."

"She can't do that." Mellie looked shocked and her next words were barely above a whisper. "Not send me down the river."

That's what Charlotte had told Selena just a couple of hours before. "You can't do that."

Selena had pretended a look of concern. "I certainly understand your reluctance to part with a servant you've had for so many years, but our Mellie is very pretty. She'll fetch a high price and help to stabilize Grayson's somewhat precarious financial position in the face of the looming war. Such is sure to disrupt the markets for our crops. Charles has been understandably, but regretfully negligent in his business matters what with the political crises he's had to deal with in Frankfort, but it can't go on. Grayson has more people than the land can support. This is an opportune time to remedy that before Mr. Lincoln finds a way to confiscate and steal our property."

Charlotte stood stiff with her hands clenched at her sides. She could barely speak through her anger. "You can't sell Mellie."

"What are you going to do? Tell your father on me?" Selena arched her eyebrows a bit. "I think we both know who'd win that battle. Besides he agrees with me that you have allowed Mellie to grow much too familiar with you. She is not your sister. She is a servant."

Charlotte kept her voice controlled. "Did you tell Father your plan?"

"He was much too concerned with more important matters to bother with which slaves might be culled from our holdings. He has entrusted me to do what needs to be done."

Charlotte took a deep breath and made herself uncurl her fists in spite of the way she was trembling with anger. "Then I suppose in his hurry to be off to Frankfort he must have neglected to let you know that he gave me Mellie. She belongs to me. Not to him. Or to you."

Selena looked at her for a long moment before she smiled a little and said, "And how do you propose to feed and clothe your slave?"

"She has a place here at Grayson the same as I do. Grayson is not yours."

"Are you so sure? I am your father's wife. And while your father and I will certainly always feel bound by charity to see that your needs are met, we might not extend that charity to your servant. A slave must earn her keep. Having been raised on a plantation, you are surely aware of that." Selena paused a second to let her words sink in before she went on. "But your Mellie is strong. She can probably learn to work fast enough in the fields to stay away from the whip."

"Father would never let you send Mellie to the fields."

"Your father is not here, Charlotte." Selena spoke each word slowly and distinctly as though Charlotte were a child with limited understanding. "I am here. Perkins has been told to take orders from me. Not you."

Charlotte stared at her a moment before she could push the words out. "Why are you doing this?"

"My dear Charlotte, this is all for your own good. Your father and I are in complete agreement. It is past time that you learn the proper behavior of a lady and stop consorting with the help." As the woman kept talking, the fake look of concern on her face made Charlotte feel ill. "I daresay much of this comes from your father letting you read so many improper books and newspapers. It's well known a young female brain can't stand up under the strain of too much education except, of course, in the finer arts. The sort a proper finishing school will teach you so that we can hope you won't chase away the next young gentleman who calls on you as you did young Mr. Gilbey."

"You cannot sell Mellie. She is mine." Charlotte kept her voice ice cold in spite of the way the hot knot of anger was burning in her chest. "And I am not going to Virginia. You will never take Grayson from me."

Now Selena's laughter dismissing her words rang in Charlotte's ears as she looked at Mellie. "We don't have a choice, Mellie. Either of us. It's the only way we can keep you safe. And maybe Grayson too."

When Mellie simply kept staring at her as if she knew no words to say, Charlotte went on. "We won't have to stay with the Shakers forever. Just for a while until Father sees through that woman's pretense or we find another way."

"What about Nate?" Mellie sounded ready to cry.

"I don't know, Mellie. But you'll be safe as soon as we enter the village. And free. I promised Aunt Tish that I'd set you free years ago. As soon as I could." Charlotte reached over to squeeze Mellie's hands. "This is the only way I can keep that promise now."

"Once I'm free I can go wherever I take a mind." Mellie pulled her hands free and lifted her chin with a hint of defiance.

"I guess so. You might make your way across the river to Indiana where it's safer to be a free Negro. But what if one of those horrible slave trackers grabs you? They might not listen if you say you're free. They could just tear up your papers and take you wherever they wanted."

"Massah Charles wouldn't let them do that."

"He wouldn't know. He doesn't know what's happening here in his own house." Her voice sounded shrill in her ears. Charlotte sat back and pulled in a slow, deep breath to calm herself. She had to convince Mellie. "You'll be safe with the Shakers. With me. We'll be sisters."

"We's already sisters, Miss Lottie."

"Free sisters." Charlotte stared into Mellie's eyes. "Please. I don't think I can do this without you."

Mellie mashed her mouth together a moment before she blew a burst of air out her nose and gave in. "All right, Miss Lottie. When do we leave?"

"At daylight."

"Sneakin' away like a couple of runaways."

"I don't want to have to see her again." They both knew who Charlotte meant.

"I don't know, Miss Lottie. This done feels like you's givin' up and that ain't like you."

"I'm not giving anything up. I'll be back. We'll both be back."

"I always believed most everythin' you ever tol' me, but this time I don't have no certain feelin'." Mellie sighed as she stood up. A frown creased her face. "What about Mammy?"

"I tried, but Father wouldn't give me her papers. Said Grayson needed a cook. And it does. She wouldn't dare bother Aunt Tish."

"We better pray that's true," Mellie said right before she slipped out Charlotte's door.

Pray. Charlotte shut her eyes, but no prayer words came. Instead her thoughts jumped from here to there and back again. She was feeling Adam Wade's arms around her. She was remembering the words in Edwin's letter. She was hearing Selena's words pushing her out of Grayson. She was wondering exactly how one did join with the Shakers. Edwin said he was going to the Shaker village to find peace. And the Shakers prayed about everything, or so she'd heard. Perhaps if she gained nothing else in the weeks ahead, she'd learn how to pray to find her own kind of peace.

Finally she whispered, "Give me courage to face tomorrow."

She sat there for a long moment with her eyes closed, listening to the steady ticking of her clock as she waited for some kind of answer. Nothing happened except that she became even more aware of the hard knot of fear inside her chest. She opened her eyes and stared at her face in the mirror. She was going to have to come up with her own answers for the morrow. The way she always had.

Maybe that was her answer.

11

Charlotte's heart began thumping in her ears and her hands grew stiff on the reins of the mare as the large stone and brick buildings of Harmony Hill rose up in front of them. Mellie's grip on Charlotte's waist tightened until Charlotte worried the buttons on her riding jacket would pop off. Mellie had been terrified ever since Charlotte made her climb up behind her on the mare. She'd never been on a horse.

Now she whispered in Charlotte's ear, "Where has we come to, Miss Lottie? I done feel like Jonah about to get swallowed by that big fish."

Charlotte knew what she meant. They were entering a different world. One where the buildings had no porches for sitting to catch the evening breezes or even a decorative gable to please the eye. Everything was plain and solemn. Including the people. Men and women walked between the buildings, but Charlotte caught no sound of talk or laughter. It was as if they were on the way to somebody's funeral except nobody was wearing black. The women were dressed in like blue or brown dresses with large white collars that lapped across the front of their bosoms above a white apron. White caps covered their hair.

Of course Charlotte had seen Shaker women before. She'd ridden carriages through Harmony Hill on the way to Lexington on occasion, but then she'd just looked upon them as an oddity. She'd never given the first thought of someday being one of them.

Even now, riding her mare with Mellie behind her, it still seemed an impossible thought. A laughable thought. Her in Shaker dress, meekly walking to some task she'd been ordered to do. She wasn't concerned about the idea of work in spite of how Mellie had looked at her when she first talked of going to the Shakers. Charlotte could work. She wasn't a vapor-prone Southern belle who could barely manage to raise a glass of tea to her lips without a servant's help.

At the same time, she had never had tasks imposed on her. She was the one who ordered her life. That was the reason she was ready to pretend to be a Shaker for a few weeks. To get her life back. She could learn some new ways to make that happen.

The new ways had begun that morning when she had eased open the stable door to keep it from creaking as night began to give way to the first gray light of dawn. She hadn't wanted anyone to see them leaving. Not even Willis. She was afraid Selena might find a way to hold it against him and add his name to her list for Perkins.

When she had held the lead rope out toward Mellie to hold while she got the saddle, Mellie had stepped back. "I can't hold no horse."

"Of course you can. All you have to do is stand still and hold this rope." Charlotte grabbed Mellie's arm and placed the end of the lead in her hand before she turned to get the reins and saddle. She had never saddled the mare without help from Willis, but she knew how. Willis had taught her. He'd said a person shouldn't be riding if that person didn't know how things worked on a horse.

Mellie stared at the mare with evident fear, ready to give up their plans. "This ain't gonna work, Miss Lottie. I can't ride no horse. I'll fall off and break my head for sure."

"I won't let you fall off," Charlotte said as she pulled the cinch tight. She hadn't picked the sidesaddle because she didn't see how Mellie could ride with her on that. Sometimes when her father was in Frankfort and she wanted to ride across Grayson's fields jumping fences, Charlotte got Willis to bring out a regular saddle for her mare. It was far too easy to get unseated making a jump in a sidesaddle. Nevertheless it was highly improper for a lady to ride astride a horse even if her riding habit skirts were sufficiently full to modestly drape all the way to her ankles. Proper or improper didn't seem to matter today.

"I knows you won't aim to, but there's some things even you can't make happen, and me stayin' on this horse might be one of them." When Charlotte just looked at her across the mare's back without saying anything, Mellie went on. "And what about Massah Charles? What's he gonna think when he hears you've run off from Grayson?"

"I don't know," Charlotte answered honestly. She'd left a letter with Gibson to be posted to her father explaining where she was without dwelling on the reasons why. Right now with his total infatuation with Selena, he'd refuse to believe anything bad about the woman anyway. He'd think she was doing this because of Edwin, and she supposed there was some truth in that. Just not the truth her father would assume. Certainly she had no broken heart. Only ruined plans. Not ruined, she corrected herself. Sidetracked. She didn't mention Mellie at all in the letter. There was no need.

Here in the heart of the Shaker village, Charlotte thought about her father opening her letter, and she worried that she might not have chosen the best words. Or made the best plan. Still, she had no choice now but to see it through. For Mellie's sake if nothing else. By the time

Gibson gave the letter to Perkins to post and then it made its way to her father in the Capital City, Mellie would be free with nothing Selena could do to change that. Charlotte could bear a week or two of captivity here with these strange people to assure that.

Even so, when she stopped to ask one of the Shaker men how to go about joining with them at Harmony Hill, her voice trembled, and the mare, sensing her unease, danced to the side. The man looked to be quite old, but his movements were quick as he reached out to take hold of the bridle and calm the horse with a soft-spoken command before he answered Charlotte.

"We welcome all who would live the perfect life, my sisters," he said with solemn kindness. "Let me take your horse and I will call one of the sisters to help you."

Charlotte's hands tightened on the reins for the barest moment before she pulled in a deep breath and forced a smile as she surrendered the reins to him. She expected him to step up to help them off the mare, but instead he pulled his hat down low on his forehead and turned his back on them.

"I'll lead you to a block where you can dismount." He kept his face straight forward as he led the mare to a round wooden block in front of a large brick building.

Charlotte slid out of the saddle down onto the block and then helped Mellie dismount. The man kept his eyes averted as he promised to send someone to help them before he led the mare away.

Mellie sank down on the wooden block as though her legs would no longer hold her up. She looked up at Charlotte. "You sure we's doin' the right thing, Miss Lottie?" Her voice carried the same tremble Charlotte's had a moment earlier.

"As sure as I can be." Charlotte tried to sound sure as she sat down beside Mellie and took her hand, but inside she felt anything but confident. She stared down at her fingers clasped around Mellie's dark hand and wished Aunt Tish were there with them. She would tell them they were doing the right thing. The only thing.

The next mornig when Charlotte had given up on sleep, she climbed out of bed in the pre-dawn darkness and pulled on her riding habit. She hadn't allowed herself to think about what she was getting ready to do. She simply eased her bed-room door shut and crept down the stairs to the kitchen where Mellie and Aunt Tish waited. Shadows cast by the lone candle Aunt Tish carried hovered on the wall be-hind them and then seemed to leap and dance after them when without a word they moved toward the door. A lump formed in Charlotte's throat at the sound of Grayson's back door clicking shut behind her, but she refused to cry. There was no reason for tears. This was all temporary. She'd be back soon enough.

But Mellie had fallen on Aunt Tish's neck and wept as she begged her, "You'll tell Nate where I am, won't you, Mammy? You'll tell him I didn't have no choice. I don't, do I?"

"No choice but freedom, Melana." Still holding the candle, Aunt Tish stepped back and grabbed Mellie's chin with her free hand to raise her face up until she was looking straight into Mellie's eyes. "You keep that in the front of yo' mind and think on it."

"Yes'm." Mellie choked back a sob be-fore she went on. "But what's the good of bein' free without you? Or Nate?" Mellie's voice trailed off as she pulled away from Aunt Tish's hand to look toward the slave quarters.

"I'll be next." Aunt Tish let her eyes slide over to Charlotte. "And then who can know what might be happenin' after that? What with ever'body saying a war is comin' 'cause of how Mr. Lincoln talks 'bout freedom for the people."

Freedom. That's what Charlotte felt like she was giving up as she and Mellie followed two Shaker sisters up the steps into the brick building and down a broad hallway with polished wood floors. Lines of blue pegs on both walls held candle sconces, cloaks, and hats. The room they were shown into was small and bare except for a lone table. Two chairs were suspended on the blue pegs that lined this wall too, but nobody offered to lift down the chairs for anyone to sit.

Charlotte fought the urge to run back out the door as she waited for someone to speak. Both women looked to be well past their middle years, and as they solemnly studied Charlotte and Mellie, Mellie's old crone description wormed into Charlotte's thoughts. She couldn't imagine either of these women ever dancing or singing. In worship or not.

Sister Altha spoke first. She was tall and thin with angular features. The few strands of hair that peeked out around her white cap were steel gray. She looked at Mellie and then settled her sharp eyes on Charlotte as she said, "You are not our usual novitiate. What has made you consider this choice? Are you concerned for the condition of your soul?"

Charlotte searched for words to say that wouldn't be false without giving the real reason she had come knocking at the Shakers' door. She had the uneasy feeling the woman in front of her would know immediately if she spoke lies. Finally she said, "All right-minded people should surely worry about their souls, especially in these uncertain times with war on the horizon."

Sister Altha moved her hand in a dismissive gesture. "We have no part in wars. Our testimony is for peace now and always. No Christian can use carnal weapons or fight, and so we have separated ourselves from such conflict and live in peace with all."

"Peace seems a good way, but how will

you keep the cannons from your land if the armies decide to come?" Charlotte asked, truly curious about how they planned to maintain peace in the midst of war.

"Mother Ann and the Eternal Father will protect us. But you will have time to learn of our ways of peace if you decide to stay among us."

"That's why I'm here. Why we're both here." Charlotte looked over at Mellie, who seemed poised up on her toes as though any second she might break for the door. Charlotte reached over to lay her hand on Mellie's arm.

Sister Altha's frown deepened. "You must be aware that none come among us with slaves. Such must be set free to make their own decision to live among us or not." Her eyes shifted from Charlotte to Mellie, and a bit of regret came into her voice. "Nor can we take in runaway slaves against the laws of the land, no matter how wrong those laws may be."

Mellie spoke up. "I'm not a runaway. I belong to Miss Lottie."

Sister Altha's face softened. "That will no longer be, my sister, if you choose to stay among us here at Harmony Hill. We belong only to the Eternal Father and Mother Ann." Her eyes came back to Charlotte.

"I have her papers." Charlotte reached into her pocket and pulled out the folded paper. "I am ready to do whatever is required to set her free."

"That is good." Sister Altha's eyes narrowed on Charlotte again. "You say the right words, but are you truly prepared to give up your place in the world, your life of ease, to work among us?"

"I am here to find out about the Shaker life. We both are." Charlotte spoke the words as if coming to the Shaker village was something they'd been planning for months instead of a desperate midnight plan. She squeezed Mellie's arm to give her courage before dropping her hand back to her side.

"Once more the proper words, but I hear an unspoken undertone." Sister Altha frowned. "Here in our Society of Believers we do not hide our wrongs, but confess them in order to receive forgiveness. If you have some sin you are running from, my sister, you must reveal it. Have you done some wrong that has compelled you to come among us?"

Both sisters watched Charlotte intently while waiting for her to speak and explain why a young woman of her position would be presenting herself to the Shakers. Beside her, Mellie was as still as the sisters, as if afraid to breathe. Somewhere in the building outside the room, a clock gonged out the time. Charlotte counted. Nine strikes. The clock fell silent and the same sort of silence seemed to seep out of the very walls of the room where they were standing. She had no doubt that the clock could strike its next hourly total before either woman broke the silence if she did not answer Sister Altha's question.

Charlotte swallowed and opened her mouth to tell as much of the truth as she thought wise, but Mellie, spooked by the women's silence, jumped in front of her words. "Miss Lottie's doin' it for me. To save me. That woman Massah Charles married was gonna sell me down the river."

Sister Altha frowned. "How could that be if Miss Lottie owns you?" She looked at the paper Charlotte had handed her. "As appears to be the case. Melana, isn't it?"

"I don't know." Mellie sounded ready to cry. "But Miss Lottie thought it might happen. And if you knew Miss Selena, you might think so too. "

"Who is this Selena?" Sister Altha looked at Charlotte.

"Perhaps I should explain," Charlotte said.

"That would be well," Sister Altha said.

"Selena is my father's new wife. As you may know, my father is a state senator."

Sister Altha inclined her head a bit. "Is your father aware that you have come to Harmony Hill seeking admittance?"

"I wrote him of my intentions," Charlotte answered truthfully. The truth or at least part of the truth seemed the best story to tell. "He is very involved with the political situation of our state right now, and it may be a while before he can respond to my letter. In the meantime, his new wife and I have not seen eye to eye, and I thought it best if Mellie and I left. That it would be a way to keep peace in our family."

She used the word "peace" purposely, since the Shakers claimed such a fondness for peaceful living, but Sister Altha only lifted her eyebrows a bit as if she knew Charlotte was merely attempting to sway her opinion with words and not with honest feelings. After a slight hesitation, Charlotte went on. "I also had planned to marry Edwin Gilbey who has come among you, and he suggested, since he seeks to follow your way and thus will no longer consider marriage, that I might think about joining him here." Sister Altha's eyebrows shot up a little higher and Charlotte rushed on. "As a sister, of course. Plus I wanted Mellie to be safe from those who hoped to do her harm in order to injure me."

While Sister Altha continued to look doubtfully at Charlotte, the other sister, the one named Cora, moved forward with the touch of a smile that gentled the lines of her face. "We do not turn those away who come to us seeking peace. So we welcome you among us as long as you both abide by the rules we set forth. There is no consorting with the opposite sex. All work at the duties assigned by the Ministry, and you must open your minds and attend to the telling of the Believers' way to salvation."

"We are ready to do as you say," Charlotte said.

"Each must answer for herself," Sister Cora said quietly as she looked at Mellie.

"Are you ready to bend your will to our way, sister?"

Mellie shot a look at Charlotte, but Charlotte stayed silent. They were right. If Mellie was to be free, she would have to answer for herself.

"Well, sister, do you have an answer?" Sister Altha demanded without the gentleness of the other sister.

"I can do what you want," Mellie finally said as she lowered her eyes to the floor.

"That is a good beginning. Now we will find you a place and proper clothing." Sister Cora reached for Mellie's hand. "Come, Sister Melana."

When Mellie sent another panicked look at her, Charlotte pushed confidence into her smile and her voice. "It's all right, Mellie."

"But who will take care of you, Miss Lottie?"

Sister Altha's frown deepened while Sister Cora was kind in her answer as she ushered Mellie out of the room. "Have no concern for your sister. Sister Altha will summon another sister to introduce her to our way the same as I am doing for you."

"I thought we'd be able to stay together,"

Charlotte said after the door closed behind Mellie and Sister Cora.

"Nay, you both need to find your way on your own. If that is what you truly want." Sister Altha gave her another suspicious look. "If you have doubts of the path you've chosen, you may stay in a visitor's room for a few days while you dwell on the matter more fully."

"I have no doubts," Charlotte lied.

"That is good." For the first time Sister Altha lifted the corners of her lips up in a small smile. "First you must sign Sister Melana's manumission papers. Then you will begin your journey on the true way. The simple life and salvation await those who come to us with expectant hearts." She motioned Charlotte toward the door. "Come, my sister. For as we learn in Mother Ann's teachings, we must not waste one moment of time, for we have none to spare."

Charlotte wasn't sure who this Mother Ann was, but she had no problem agreeing with that teaching. She had no time to spare. Somehow she would have to find Edwin and convince him that he was wasting time here. They both were.

As she followed Sister Altha down the

hallway once more, they stopped between a matching pair of winding stairs that curled along opposite walls up three floors with little visible means of support. She had never seen anything to compare with them in any manor house. No outward decoration adorned the cherry handrails or steps, but even so the stairs rose upward in such a graceful spiral that surely no eye could gaze upon them without admiring their beauty.

"What lovely stairs," Charlotte said before she thought better of breaking the silence between her and the stern sister.

Sister Altha looked at the staircases and then back at Charlotte. "Many of the world say the same, but to us their beauty is in their usefulness. That is where true beauty resides."

Whoever built this stairway had more in mind than utility, Charlotte wanted to insist, but she bit her lip and remained silent. She wished Adam Wade was there to see it with her. She could almost hear his words echoing her own marvel in her ears.

She shook away the thought. Adam Wade was gone. He was not part of her future. He had never been part of her future

in spite of the way her heart leaped up inside her just at the thought of him and the
memory of his lips on hers. While she was
here among the Shakers, she would practice the discipline and plainness of the
woman beside her. She would push his
memory completely from her mind.

Yet in spite of her determined thoughts,
she slipped her hand in her pocket and felt
the corners of the folded sketch. His lines
drawing her face. That and her grandmother's ring and pearls were all she had
brought from Grayson.

12

Charlotte tried to quell her growing trepidation as she followed Sister Altha outside and along the walkways. She hadn't thought they would separate her and Mellie, for she had spoken the truth when she'd told Mellie she didn't think she could do this alone. And now they were both alone. Both being swallowed up by this strange group of people. At her request.

They stepped from the sunshine on the steps into the deep shadow of the brick building behind them. The morning air felt immediately cooler, and a shiver crawled up Charlotte's back. What was she doing here, trailing after this unsmiling woman in her plain brown dress? Maybe Mellie was right. It could be she had abandoned her senses.

She had told Adam Wade that she was going to do the unexpected. She'd certainly done that in the last couple of days. Allowing a near stranger to kiss her without the slightest hint of resistance. Riding away from Grayson and leaving her home to the clutching designs of that woman. Pretending to want to be one of these unsmiling Shaker women. Imagining that such a crazy plan would bring back the expected life she longed after.

As the shadow enveloped Charlotte, her prayer from the night before echoed in her head. *Give me courage.* A prayer that was not being answered if the tremble inside her was any indication. Perhaps courage wasn't one of the blessings the Lord doled out. The Bible spoke of forbearance and longsuffering, gentleness and meekness, joy and love as gifts of the Spirit one should seek. But what of courage? Surely Daniel had been gifted with courage when he continued to say his prayers in full sight of his enemies even though he knew he might be thrown into a den of hungry lions.

But she wasn't Daniel. She hadn't spent all that much time in prayer or reading the Bible. She had little reason to believe the Lord would shut the mouths of any hungry lions ready to devour her. *Be strong and of a good courage.* The words popped into her mind, and while she knew not where they came from, she was sure they were Bible words.

She pulled in a deep steadying breath and looked ahead. Sunlight splattered the path only a couple of steps in front of her. She had done the unexpected. She had left Grayson. She had freed Mellie and kept at least part of her promise to Aunt Tish. She wasn't giving up on her future. She was fighting for it even if she was walking a very strange path to achieve her aim. Perhaps the Lord did attend to her prayers. Courage didn't mean the absence of fear. Courage meant walking forward through whatever shadows lay across her path toward the future she had to find a way to make happen.

Ahead of them, the sun bounced off the

windows and stonework of the large white building in the center of the village and lent it a special glow that made Charlotte hope it might be their destination. But when Sister Altha paused in front of her, she didn't even glance over at the stone building. Instead she pointed to the frame building opposite it. "Our meetinghouse," she said.

Without waiting for any sort of reply, the woman turned and began walking again. Sister Altha kept her capped head bent with her eyes down and her hands tucked under her apron, but now with her new-found courage, Charlotte saw no need to copy her. She wanted to see it all. If she was being swallowed into the belly of the whale as Mellie had suggested, at least she could be familiar with each rib that made up her new home.

The paths between the houses were mostly deserted. When she dared to ask Sister Altha why no one was about, the sister looked back at her with evident irri-tation before she answered, "The brethren and sisters are attending their duties."

"All of them?" Charlotte asked.

Sister Altha frowned slightly. "You will

discover the answers to your questions in due time without the need for idle conversation on the walkways."

So Charlotte bit back her questions as they walked on through the village past smaller buildings with open windows that let out the peck of hammers, the sweep of brooms, and numerous other sounds of industry. Now and again, she spotted a man's head or the white cap of one of the sisters through the windows. In the gardens between the buildings, several sisters dressed in like fashion to Sister Altha were bent over or on their knees raking leaves and debris away from the roots of the herbs and other plants. Only a couple of the women looked up at them when they passed, and even those two quickly lowered their eyes back to their work.

Sister Altha finally stopped in front of a three-story brick house with separate stone steps up to two identical front doors. The sister led the way up to the door on the left of the house.

"You will be given a bed here at the Gathering Family House. Those who come among us live here while being instructed on the true path to salvation. There will be much for you to learn. Such as always using the proper door to go in and out of our houses. Sisters use the west doors and the brethren use the doors on the east."

"The church my father and I attend has two doors, one for the women and one for the men."

"Yea, it is a common custom, but where worldly worshipers fail is in thinking that such is only necessary for their Sabbaths. We pick up the cross of purity of body and soul and carry it every day of the week." Sister Altha paused inside the door and peered over at Charlotte. "It is a cross that is oft too heavy for many who come to us."

"What happens then?" Charlotte looked straight at her face. "If they are unable to follow the Shaker way?"

"They go back to the world. We force no one to stay with us who finds the true way too intolerable. But we mourn their return to the miry pit of worldly sin when they had every opportunity to walk the way of peace and love."

"Do many leave?"

Sister Altha looked grieved as she said, "Yea. Few can walk the narrow road. I will pray to Mother Ann that your feet will not wander from the path to salvation while you learn our ways."

A young sister came down the hall to meet them. Her face looked as opposite of Sister Altha as was surely possible. While she wore the solemn Shaker expression, her brown eyes sparkled with friendliness and the bloom of youth was in her cheeks.

Even Sister Altha's face brightened as she looked at her. "Ah, Sister Cora has sent Sister Gemma to be your guide to the more physical elements of our lives. She will instruct you on proper Shaker dress and explain your work duties, Sister Charlotte." A hint of a frown returned to Sister Altha's face. "I would not wonder if you might need a great deal of instruction in how to perform some such duties, but all who are able-bodied labor with their hands here at Harmony Hill. The Lord intended us to be useful, and you will discover it is a gift to so work for the good of all."

"Yea, laboring with our hands increases the strength of our spirits," Sister Gemma said. "And gives us good sleep at night. Never fear, Sister Altha. I will take good care of our new sister. Charlotte, did you say?"

"Yea. She can go with you to your work duty after the midday meal," Sister Altha said.

"I am helping to package the seeds for the brethren's selling trips next week."

"An easy task. That will be a good beginning for her."

"What about Mellie?" Charlotte asked as Sister Altha turned toward the door.

Sister Altha looked back, a frown deepening the furrows between her eyes again. It was clear she did not like being questioned. "She is no longer your slave," she said sternly. "She is your sister now."

"She has ever been my sister," Charlotte said quietly. "I was only concerned for her because she was so nervous on the way here and not sure what to expect. She has always depended on me."

"You need not worry. Your sister will blossom like a flower in the sun in the warmth of the freedom you have rightly given her." A fleeting look of approval softened Sister Altha's face for just a second. "Sister Cora will see to her needs. It will be good for you to learn that decisions of the elders and eldresses cannot be questioned. Obedience is necessary for the peace of our society."

Sister Gemma waited until the door shut behind the older sister before she let a smile lift the corners of her lips. "Don't fret. It's not near as hard as Sister Altha makes it sound, Sister Charlotte. Come, we will begin." She moved toward the left staircase. "This is the west stairs, the sisters' stairs. You must always use them and not the ones on the east side of the room. Those are for the brethren." She stopped at the bottom of the stairs. "And always step up on the first stair with your right foot first."

Charlotte did as instructed and followed the woman who appeared to be near Charlotte's own age up the stairs stepping with her right foot first, but she couldn't keep from asking. "Why?"

The question seemed to surprise Gemma, who paused in the middle of the flight of stairs to look around at Charlotte. "Because the Ministry decided it should be so many years ago. Long before I came to be here."

"When was that?"

"I was eight. My father brought me here to go to school."

"And he never came back to get you?" Charlotte thought of her own father and wondered what he would do when he got her letter. Would he come storming through the Shaker gates and demand to talk reason to her?

"Yea, he so intended. I'm sure of that. But he and my mother succumbed in the cholera epidemic of '51. My baby brother too. My uncle took in the other two boys, but it seemed to be the sensible thing for me to stay here where I could keep going to school and learn other useful occupations. The Believers have always been kind to me. And with my folks gone, it felt more like home here than anywhere else I could imagine going." She turned to climb on up the stairs.

"So you like it here." Charlotte made it part question, part statement of fact as she followed the sister. After all, Gemma looked happy, as if she'd found that peace Edwin talked about seeking for himself.

"I am content. There is much love between the sisters and brethren. And when the spirit comes down in meeting, I sometimes feel light as a feather with no concerns or worries. I often simply float away on the joy of the moment." At the top of the stairs, Gemma turned to smile at

Charlotte. "Sister Altha says that's a spirit gift. Have you ever felt such a gift of the spirit in your worship times?"

"Nothing that made me think I was floating away. Joyful or not." The only time Charlotte had felt anywhere near that way was in the garden with the artist's lips touching hers, but that was hardly something to reveal to these odd people who considered such joy shared between a man and woman sinful.

"Spirit gifts can be much different. Many feel they receive fruit from heaven to eat and enjoy. Others are gifted with song or a gift of whirling. Some draw spirit pictures."

"You mean a picture of a ghost?"

The girl actually laughed out loud. The sound was so unexpected after Sister Altha's solemn attitude that Charlotte jumped a little. Gemma put her hand on Charlotte's arm. "Nay. Of a surety, nay. Have you been told ghost tales about us here? I have heard that those of the world tell many wild stories about us Believers, but I don't think I've been told of any such that claim our village is haunted." Suddenly she looked more solemn. "Of course, there are those spirits of our departed brothers and sisters who come back to deliver messages to us from Mother Ann at times."

Charlotte looked behind her at the stairs and wondered if she should go back down them to search out her mare and ride back to Grayson. She'd done what she intended and set Mellie free. But she hadn't accomplished her other aims. She hadn't seen Edwin. She hadn't given her father time to regret letting Selena push her out of Grayson. But people who got messages from spirits and ghosts might be more than she had bargained for.

Gemma tightened her hand on Charlotte's arm. "Don't look so concerned, my sister. It will become clear to you after you learn more of our ways. Trust me, there are no ghosts to fear. The gifts of the spirit bring joy, not fear. And so it is with the spirit drawings as well. A special gift that can bless us all. You will see in the days ahead and gain understanding of our ways."

Gemma led the way into a room that held five narrow beds that looked hard and uncomfortable with little room for even a shift in position while sleeping. Nothing at all like Charlotte's soft featherbed under its ruffled, white lace bedspread at Grayson.

A tall narrow chest sat against the outside wall. It had many drawers but absolutely nothing upon it. No flower, no pot of cream or box for hair ribbons or combs. Not even a speck of dust. Three chairs were suspended on the blue pegs that seemed a fixture in every Shaker room.

"How do you comb and arrange your hair with no mirrors?" Charlotte asked.

"We only have the need to adjust our caps, and there is a small mirror in the bathhouses and dressing rooms for that purpose." Gemma touched her cap and then smiled as she reached over to touch Charlotte's curls. "Your hair looks as cheerful as a candle flame on a dreary winter night. It does seem a shame to cover it, but it is our way for the sisters to cover their hair. You will grow accustomed to the cap, and if your hair proves to be a bother Sister Melva is good at clipping it short."

Charlotte's hand went instinctively to her hair in a protective gesture. She had not considered submitting to a shearing.

"Your hair will grow less important to you in time, but until then Sister Melva will not force her scissors upon you." Gemma laughed again.

"That's a relief," Charlotte said as she lowered her hands and studied Gemma a moment. "Are more sisters like you or Sister Altha?"

Gemma looked puzzled. "I'm not sure of your meaning."

"Sister Altha seemed so . . ." Charlotte hesitated as she searched for an acceptable word. "So solemn. I cannot imagine her laughing."

"She has many duties and little time for frivolity," Gemma said. "Plus it is only fitting to maintain an even and solemn countenance so one does not disturb the peaceful air around one with an overabundance of chatter or laughter. Both sins I find need to confess much too often."

She pulled open one of the drawers in the chest and lifted out a dress and underclothing. "And now is a time for solemn attention to the task at hand so we won't miss the midday meal." She handed Charlotte the clothes. "If you need assistance with your collar and cap, I can supply that after I fetch you some shoes."

"Why can't I wear these?" Charlotte lifted her skirt to show her feet clad in the sturdy side-laced shoes she wore when riding.

"You will feel better wearing the same as all the sisters."

"Can I keep these here in my room?"

"Nay, such would only be undesirable clutter. Those of the Ministry will store them for you if you feel an attachment to them. It is the Shaker way." She spoke kindly, but there was no room for argument as she pointed Charlotte toward a small dressing room that opened off the sleeping room. "I will gather up your worldly clothing after you change."

Charlotte stripped off her gray riding habit and laid it aside with some regret. She was tempted to leave on her own underclothing, but she had agreed to abide by their rules. She untied the ribbons around her waist and let her pantalettes fall to the floor in a soft cloud of silk before quickly pulling on the plain white cotton drawers with no bit of lace anywhere on them. She had not worn a corset over her camisole, and she was relieved to see there was none in the clothing Gemma had handed her. At least she'd be able to breathe while pretending to be a Shaker. She shed her camisole with its lace and ribbons and pulled the shiftlike undershirt over her head.

The fabric of the dress was sturdy but soft and faded to a light blue from many washings. It was too large for her, but once she lapped the white collar across her front and tied on the apron, it didn't much matter that several inches of the waistline were folded under. A mirror not much bigger than her hand hung on the wall. She peered into it as she stuffed her hair up into the cap.

When she was finished, she stared at her reflection a moment longer as though staring at someone she didn't know. Had she lost her identity so easily? Just by shedding a few clothes the way a butterfly broke out of a cocoon? But this was not a transformation to beauty. Rather in the opposite direction. From the active pursuit of beauty in every facet to plainness. There would be no party dresses she could not unbutton here. No jeweled combs in her hair. No glittering necklaces or rings. No one would care if freckles appeared on her nose or if her hair curled or hung straight. No one would see more than a glimpse of hair under the cap.

She suddenly smiled as she spoke to the reflection in the mirror. "Good morning,

Sister Charlotte. I do hope I can learn to get along with you for a few weeks."

Then she laughed softly as she thought that Adam Wade would have little desire to steal a kiss from the new Charlotte. But it wasn't the artist she needed to think about. It was Edwin. Perhaps this plain sister would not be so intimidating to him. Perhaps he would look at her and regret the thought of giving up their plans. It was beyond her understanding how he could even consider surrendering the Hastings land to the Shakers. Land passed down from his grandparents. Whatever that Elder Logan had told Edwin, it certainly wasn't true that Faustine Hastings would have approved of that. She was no doubt turning over in her grave.

As surely Charlotte's own mother was. Charlotte took one last peek in the mirror and twisted her mouth to the side to hold back another smile at the glimpse of Charlotte Mayda Vance as a plain and simple Shaker sister. Not the heiress to Grayson. Not the senator's daughter. A Shaker sister.

The thought wasn't nearly as distressing as she might have supposed it would be. Of course it was only temporary. She ran her hands down the long white apron so like Aunt Tish's, tucked a stray hair up into her cap, and pushed open the door just as Gemma came back in the sleeping room carrying Charlotte's new shoes. They bore little resemblance to any dancing shoes she'd ever seen, but everyone knew the Shakers danced in worship. A dance she was prepared to learn.

13

"It won't last three months. Once a few shots are fired, those Johnny Rebs in the South will see the futility of their position and come back into the Union like whipped dogs with their tails between their legs." Sam Johnson sounded sure of his words.

Adam watched Sam pace in front of him as he spoke. Tall with a bony frame, the man was rarely still in spite of an old knee injury that caused him to limp badly. He claimed to be able to think better on his feet. The pain of movement was incidental. Actually sharpened a man's thinking, Sam claimed. A mind lacking agility, that's what should worry a man. Not a crippled knee. Sam had no problem carrying dozens of story ideas for *Harper's Weekly* in his head all at once, and he often jumped between them without warning.

Something he did now—to the chagrin of his secretary whose charge it was to record whatever was said if Sam deemed it important. The only problem for the long-suffering man with the pen and paper sitting across the room at a little desk was that Sam never indicated which words he might later deem important enough to recall. So his aide found it necessary to record everything.

Sam stopped in front of the table where Adam's sketches were spread out for his view. As he pushed them to and fro searching through them, Adam had to force himself not to lean forward to rescue them from the man's impatient hands. Sam had summoned Adam to meet him in Washington, D.C., and hear his new assignments now that war clouds were looming on the horizon. That didn't mean he'd forgotten Adam's old assignments.

"Where's that Shaker staircase? I told you we needed that."

"You want a staircase? Now? With war breaking out?"

"Not any old staircase. The one that people say rises straight up in the air curling around the wall like it's attached with glue or something. They say if you stand at the bottom and stare straight up that it's a good chance you'll get dizzy from those stairs telescoping away from you." Sam made a telescope shape with his hands and looked through them toward the ceiling. "Up. Up. A marvel of engineering. Shaker engineering. I've heard people say they were almost afraid to step on the risers since they didn't see how the whole contraption held to the wall. Didn't trust the glue, I guess. What about you?" Sam lowered his telescoped hands to peer through them toward Adam. "Did you climb up it?"

"No, I didn't even see it."

"Didn't see it? That's why you went down there." Sam's voice cranked up a couple of levels as he dropped his hands and frowned at Adam.

Adam didn't bother pointing out to Sam that he hadn't gone to Kentucky on assignment for *Harper's Weekly*, but on his own. The Shaker staircase had simply been a suggested side venture, but it never did to contradict Sam. Instead he mumbled, "Sorry, boss."

Sam waved away Adam's apology as if he no longer cared about any of it and turned his attention back to the sketches. "Whew! Guess Dickens was right if all the women look like her. He visited one of their communities in the East when he came to America, you know." He snatched up the sketch of the old sister Adam had seen on the pathways at Harmony Hill and held it out away from him for a better look. "No feminine charms, he said. Not one. And very few red-blooded men are beyond wanting to see a few feminine charms. Right, Adam?"

"Absolutely, sir." Adam pushed the words out quickly before Sam took off on a new tangent. The secretary scribbled frantically on his pad of paper. Adam shifted to a more comfortable position on the settee in the editor's hotel suite. At first it had bothered him to be seated when the editor was pacing and ranting, but he'd grown used to it. Now he just listened and tried to pick out the directions the editor most wanted to travel in his weekly newspaper.

The editor turned to pin Adam to the brocaded back of the settee with his sharp eyes. "I haven't been hearing about any female problems about you now, have I?" He didn't wait for Adam to answer. He threw the sketch back down on the table and began pacing again. "You've got to keep your mind on business. No time for women. Leastways the kind who want to tie the knot and commence to having a pack of children. You'll have to wait for that pleasure, my boy. Especially with those Secessionist states stirring the pot. Of course a little bit of war is sure to up circulation. If you find the pictures we need. People like pictures. Nothing but words bores them to tears."

"Pictures can bring them to tears too," Adam said.

"But those are the tears we want, my boy. Pictures that yank on their heartstrings and open up their purse strings. Open purse strings. That's what we're after." He paused a moment and shot Adam a look. "That and that staircase. Didn't you say you were within a stone's throw of the place? There's that atrociously ugly woman to prove it." He threw out his arm to wave at Adam's sketches. "And who's the girl?"

He pulled the drawing of Charlotte on her veranda out of the pile, pausing his pacing for a moment to give it consideration. "Why didn't you draw her face? Nobody cares about a woman's backside when it's hidden under all those hoop-de-doops. Looks like an upside-down mushroom." He peered closer at the sketch. "Can't even be sure there is a backside under there but the shoulders and neck are quite enticing." The older man turned back to Adam with a grin that hinted of lechery. "What about it, boy? Can you vouch for her backside?"

"Now, Sam, she was a lady."

"When did that ever stop you? I hear you've left a string of broken hearts from here to California and back."

"I just draw their pictures, Sam. That's all."

The old man laughed and shook the sketch at him. "Then draw their front sides."

"But I wanted you to see the posture of her pensive longing for peace. Can't you sense her worry about whether the war is going to tear apart her world?"

"You're making that up on the spot," Sam said with another laugh. "That's why I like you, Adam. You're quick on your feet. You're going to have to be to stay out of the fray and bring home the scenes we need. Lincoln's plan to blockade the Southern ports has got them stirred up if their newspapers are any indication. The gentry down there are equipping regiments. Out of their own pockets. Got to have some deep pockets for that, but what is it they say? Cotton is king. Pockets might empty out if they can't get around Lincoln's ships. Rich men's soldiers won't get that cotton to the English factories. Their army will turn out to have a thousand arms flailing against the wind with no head. Probably end up shooting each other instead of us Yankees."

"That sounds good for us."

"For me. But you'll have to duck bullets to draw it happening. And no yearning backside pictures." He flipped his fingers against the picture of Charlotte Vance before he dropped it back on the table. It slid off on the floor, but he didn't lean down to pick it up. "We want to see the gritty truth. If men are fighting, men are going to be dying. Our readers will want to see it all."

"I think I'd rather do the yearning for peace ones." Adam leaned forward and rescued the picture before Sam could step on it.

"Dead men don't move. They'll lay right there and let you draw them however you want." Sam had the grace to let a flash of sorrow cross his face as he slowed his pacing and sighed deeply. "I'm not saying I'm glad for this, but it's going to happen. We're going to have to march an army down there into Virginia, take Richmond back, and let those Rebels know they can't just up and leave the Union whenever they take a notion. The President never once said he was going to take their slaves away even if that's what he should have said. No place for slavery in this modern-day world. Those old boys down south are jumping to conclusions without the first thought of wanting peace. So it's history in the making, my boy, and our job is to capture that history and send it out to the people."

"Yes sir." Adam wasn't exactly sure what he was agreeing to, but those were the words Sam expected to hear. And he did want to be there to record history in the making while drawing down pay for it. He stood up to leave. He had learned to sense when Sam was through even if he didn't always know what Sam was through telling him.

"Best get to it, Adam," Sam said. When Adam reached down to straighten his sketches and put them back in the portfolio holder, Sam waved him away from the table. "James will pack those up. Some of them might do."

"Good to hear," Adam said. He was still holding Charlotte's veranda picture. He didn't seem to want to drop it down on top the others and surrender it to Sam's careless hand.

He had other sketches of her back in his hotel room. He must have drawn her from memory at least a dozen times since he'd left Kentucky to come to the capital. Every time he drew a crowd scene, he put her face there. But this was the very first time he'd captured her likeness. He could almost feel the soft curve of her shoulder under his hand when he looked at it. He turned toward the hotel room door carrying the sketch with him.

Sam stopped him. "Where do you think you're going with the yearning backside picture?"

Adam turned back toward him. "You said you didn't like it."

"Artist ears! Always perked up for criticism in everything a man says." Sam shook his head. "What I like don't matter a penny's worth. It's what our readers like."

When Sam reached for the picture, Adam surrendered it reluctantly.

"Who is she?" Sam asked.

"A Kentucky senator's daughter. There's no need to print her name."

"Protecting her, are you?" Sam looked up from the picture at him. "From what? Most young ladies would be thrilled to see their picture in *Harper's*."

"Without a name she can represent a hundred Southern belles."

Sam looked back down at the sketch. "True enough." Then he was eyeing Adam with a knowing smile. "I think this Southern belle's charms caught your eye, young Adam."

Adam smiled back to try to negate the bit of color climbing into his cheeks. "She was very pretty. Red hair and green eyes. Not your usual fainting belle."

"I knew a redhead once. Quite a woman.

Would have married her except she found a man with more money."

"A mistake I'm sure she rues to this day," Adam said.

"He invested in railroads, so I doubt it. She was dripping in diamonds last time I saw her, but the red had turned gray. Old gets us all."

"If a bullet doesn't get us first," Adam said, turning toward the door again.

"You stay out of the crossfire, boy. We need pictures, not dead illustrators."

"I'll do my best."

He was almost out the door when Sam called after him. "No bullets are flying yet, so go on back down there and get that staircase. You keep dragging your feet, somebody's going to beat us to it. I'll print it right beside the old Shaker cow you drew. Make a good contrast. Heaven knows why, but readers want to know about those crazy Shakers. But do it fast. Armies are gathering and you don't want to miss the war."

That's how everybody in the capital was talking. As if the war might only last a few days, weeks at the most. While men were lining up to volunteer to preserve the Union, nobody thought it was going to take much effort. A show of cannons. A few rounds of ammunition. Adam had sketched some of the new recruits gathering in the Army of the Potomac. Young. Fresh. With no idea of what they were heading toward.

Adam didn't know either. He'd never been in a war. But he'd read history. His grandfather had insisted that the only way to be ready for the future was to know the past. Plus Adam had talked to Mexican War veterans. Some of them were lining up to volunteer again alongside the fresh-faced kids. The old warriors had a different look. While they weren't shying away from the conflict, they were going into it with a stoic knowledge that fighting and dying went hand in hand in a war. And this time the face of the enemy wouldn't be foreign. This time they would be fighting their brothers and cousins and some of the men who had lined up beside them to fight the Mexicans.

That was the story he needed to be finding. Not some winding staircase at a Shaker village in Kentucky. His interest in the Shakers had been shoved aside. They'd be there living their strange beliefs after the conflict ended. Now he needed to be where the armies were massing. Where men were choosing North or South.

Then again it might be good to be back in Kentucky. If ever a state was divided, Kentucky was. Their governor leaned toward Secessionist, but most of the other political leaders waved the Union flag even while they had nothing good to say about President Lincoln. They wanted to ignore the war. Keep trading with the North and living like the South with slaves working their land. Governor Magoffin saw no problem with sitting on the fence. Something it seemed both sides were willing to go along with as long as they could set up their recruiting camps just across the borders to the north and south. The last news report Adam had read said plenty of Kentucky men were walking out of the state in both directions to sign up to fight.

So maybe Kentucky wouldn't be a bad place to be. There would be scenes aplenty to keep him busy while the armies were gathering. And he could do that ethereal staircase Sam was so determined to show his readers. It was good to keep Sam happy. Or as happy as was possible.

Adam smiled a little. A side trip to Grayson might not be out of the question on his way to the Shaker village. Another stolen kiss before he went off to war. He couldn't remember a girl so haunting his thoughts, but the senator's daughter was different. He might consider propping his feet up in front of a fire that she was tending. He hoped that pantywaist from next door had gone to the Shakers so Charlotte would forget the asinine idea of marrying him.

Not that Adam was ready to propose or anything. The word even surfacing in his mind was enough to bring him up short on the street outside the hotel. His sudden stop caused the man walking behind him to bump him a little before he veered to the side to pass him with some angry words. Adam muttered an apology without really hearing what the man said.

What was the matter with him? Charlotte Vance was a mere diversion. That was all. So what if her lips had been sweet? So what if he couldn't stop drawing her face and seeing her in his dreams? That didn't mean anything. Nothing except the artist in him admired a perfectly aligned face.

It was the war. That was what had made him consider the unthinkable. A man faced with the prospect of being in front of a bullet with his name on it wanted to leave something behind. Wanted to know someone would grieve his passing. Wanted to leave his seed so that a child might carry his spirit forward. The sound of war drums gave Cupid a whole quiver full of arrows. That's all it was.

He'd have to rein in his emotions and not get carried away. He hadn't ever seriously considered proposing to Charlotte Vance or any other girl, no matter how entrancing. Of course it wasn't just beautiful women who posed a danger when the sabers were rattling. Many men and boys jumped into the recruiting lines to prove their courage.

Adam touched the pocket of his coat where he'd stuck Phoebe's telegram. Her words were to the point. *Jake dropped out of school. Joining the Potomac Army. Too young. Do something.*

So before he could head to Kentucky to

draw Sam's staircase, he'd have to search through the Potomac Army to send Jake home. The boy had always been ready to fight at the slightest provocation. No sense of self-preservation at all. Phoebe was right about this one. Adam did need to do something. And Sam would take the army scenes and sell more newspapers with them than with any staircase.

But first Adam wanted to go back to his room and sketch that picture of Charlotte on her veranda from memory. The same as he'd done the first time. He assured himself it wasn't because he wanted to keep the picture of Charlotte necessarily. It was the idea of yearning for peace. That was what he wanted to keep.

14

Once Charlotte had put on the Shaker costume, the pretense was easy. It was as if, along with the new clothes, she donned a new identity. The other Charlotte, the real Charlotte, was hovering somewhere in the shadows of her mind waiting for the right moment to step back into her life, while this new Charlotte—Sister Charlotte—was following after Sister Gemma meekly, learning to say yea and nay, to bend her head and watch the path in front of her instead of the sky. At least some of the time.

The new Charlotte was acting a role in a play. One that she had set in motion herself, for she had come voluntarily to this place. But once at Harmony Hill, the next act wasn't as easy as she'd imagined. No matter how she searched the pathways, furtively peering up from under her cap at each Shaker brother who came near, she saw no sign of Edwin. He was there. She was sure of that, but she could hardly search through the men's quarters for him. Not with Sister Gemma or Sister Altha constantly by her side to teach her the Shaker way. So as the week passed, the ending began to stretch far in the distance. At the same time, she saw no way to step out of the role and go back to Grayson. For her or for Mellie.

She missed Mellie. Not because of the way she'd helped her dress back at Grayson. It was a welcome novelty not having to be concerned about what she wore or how she looked. She certainly didn't miss the constricting stays squeezing her waist fashionably small for the party dresses or the hoops that had to be scooted sideways through doors. But she did miss Mellie plaiting her hair at night. Not because she couldn't weave the plaits herself, but because that was when she and Mellie had talked and laughed.

While the Shakers spoke of being loving sisters, idle chatter among these sisters was frowned upon. Silence allowed one to concentrate on one's duties. A loose tongue was reason for confession, Sister Altha instructed before she pinned her sharp eyes on Charlotte as if waiting for her to voice that confession. Not because she gossiped but because she couldn't keep from questioning the why behind the Shakers' many rules. So Charlotte did ask forgiveness for her curiosity, then could not keep from following it up with another question. "But shouldn't a person try to make sense of rules?"

"Understanding is not necessary. Obedience is necessary. That is what the Eternal Father asks of us. Obedience." And then she had looked at Charlotte as though she should make another plea for forgiveness.

Perhaps that was why Sister Altha saw to it that Charlotte and Mellie were separated. To make obedience to the rules come easier for both of them. When Charlotte had asked about Mellie, Sister Altha frowned and said, "Worldly relationships are the cause of much stress and loss of peace. Especially that of husband and wife or slave and master. The Scripture clearly states, 'Be not ye servants of men.' For Sister Melana's spiritual growth and for yours, it is best if you break loose from the sinful ties of the world."

Charlotte bit back the arguments that sprang to her mouth. While she was playing this role, she had little choice but to do as Sister Altha said. Her pretense of obedience didn't keep Charlotte from looking for Mellie among the Shakers with the same diligence as she searched for Edwin. Relief swooshed through her when she finally spotted Mellie on a pathway between the buildings on the third day and saw that she no longer looked frightened. Instead Mellie raised her eyebrows high and shrugged her shoulders the barest bit before flashing a smile as if this whole thing with the Shakers was some kind of farce they had planned together as an escapade of sorts. Then without the chance to exchange a forbidden word on the silent walkways, she had rushed off to keep up with her Shaker guide, Sister Cora.

When Charlotte had taken a step after her, Gemma placed a restraining hand softly on Charlotte's arm. "Come, my sister. Our work duties lie in another direction."

"But I only wanted to speak with Mellie for a moment."

"Sister Melana," Gemma corrected.

"Sister Melana then," Charlotte said looking after Mellie. "I just want to ask her if she's all right."

"She appears in good health," Gemma murmured before she turned and began walking again the opposite direction toward the workshop where they were filling the seed packets. Charlotte had no choice but to follow her. She had no idea what they had Mellie doing.

So it was with some surprise she found herself actually seated beside Mellie in the meetinghouse on Sunday morning. A bell had summoned them to meeting. Bells were always ringing in the village, summoning the Shakers to do something—get up, go to work, take meals in total silence in what to Charlotte's amusement the Shakers called the biting room, go to bed. It seemed every moment of the day was regimented by the ringing of bells.

Charlotte hadn't known what to expect when the bells sounded to call them to meeting. They had returned to their sleeping rooms after the morning meal for a time of meditation that Gemma said would properly prepare their spirits for meeting. Charlotte had been on her knees more in the few days she'd been with the Shakers than her whole life. A Shaker knelt in silent prayer upon rising. A Shaker knelt in silent prayer before and after every meal. A Shaker knelt in silent prayer before lying down at night on the narrow, uncomfortable bed.

Each time Charlotte knelt, bowed her head as instructed, and listened to the silence. She could almost feel the devout prayers rising from the sisters around her as her own thoughts jumped hither and yon from prayer words she'd learned as a child to the sweet memory of Adam Wade pulling her close against him for a kiss before he raced out of her life.

With effort, she would push thoughts of Adam aside and dwell only on the plans she'd made that were the reason she was kneeling among the Shaker sisters. She'd find Edwin and convince him of the error of his ways. With proper remorse, he'd come away from the Shakers with her. Or her father would see the terrible mistake he had made marrying Selena and beg Charlotte to return to Grayson so everything could go back to the way it used to be. Then she would remember Fort Sumter and despair would darken her thoughts. Nothing was happening as it should. And she didn't know what to do except to keep walking this strange path she had chosen until a better way presented itself.

With the bell still tolling, Gemma led Charlotte out into the hallway to line up with the other sisters for the march down the stairs, out the door, and to the meetinghouse. The brethren were making a parallel line down their own set of stairs. Outside one voice began and then others joined in singing what Gemma said was a gathering song as they walked. The unity of spirit was palpable as the streams of Shaker men and women converged on the meetinghouse from all directions.

Each person fell silent as they entered

the white frame building, while outside the voices continued, growing less clear as more of the Shakers came inside. The sisters and brothers silently found their seats on backless wooden benches arranged in two sections facing one another, the men on the east side, the women on the west. Charlotte was ushered over to sit beside Mellie on the end of the front sisters' bench so Eldress Sadie, who seemed to be filling the role of preacher for the morning, could introduce them to the assembly. Charlotte couldn't imagine what a stir a female preacher would cause in the church she normally sat in on a Sunday morning.

Sister Altha had spent much time in the days Charlotte had been at Harmony Hill in trying to open Charlotte's mind to the truth of the Believers. "The Eternal Father created both man and woman in his own image, and how can that be if there is no feminine form of God?" She hadn't expected Charlotte to answer, only to listen. "I assure you such cannot be. That is why it was necessary for Mother Ann to come into the world. Doesn't the Scripture speak of a bride coming? Not in the physical sense of the world, but in a spiritual sense.

The Eternal Father revealed that truth to Mother Ann, and because she accepted the truth of his calling for her to be the Second Coming, she was persecuted and maltreated. There is much evil in the world. So those who sought and embraced the truth withdrew from that world to establish our islands of peace and harmony onto which we invite all to come and share in the true way."

Sometimes after a couple of hours of Sister Altha's words beating down on her, Charlotte had no idea what she actually believed. She had always attended church faithfully when her father was at Grayson and occasionally when he was not if the weather was favorable for a carriage ride. And Aunt Tish had preached Jesus to her ever since she was big enough to remember Bible words.

She knew what Aunt Tish believed. Now she heard the belief in Sister Altha's voice, even though much of what she said seemed contrary to words Charlotte had heard preached from the pulpit in the town church. But when she peered down into her own spiritual heart, she knew not what was there. Perhaps nothing. Perhaps that was why her prayers only circled around her own head and never rose to heaven.

She could speak the words, *Our Father who art in heaven*, but as Aunt Tish had often told her, it wasn't the words that mattered. It was the feeling behind the words. "You got to lean on Jesus, chile. Once you does that, everything comes clear."

But Charlotte saw no need to lean on anybody. It was up to her to make things happen the way she wanted them to. Didn't everybody say the Lord helped those who helped themselves? So what if those words weren't actually written in the Scripture. They were still true. Even the Shakers seemed to believe so, or else why would they go about their assigned duties with such diligent industry? Charlotte had heard as much about the work of the village as the spiritual beliefs in the days she'd been there.

Sister Altha spoke one line so often that it echoed in Charlotte's head like a tune caught there sounding over and over. *Put your hands to work and give your heart to God.* The older woman told her with great assurance that if she managed to do that, all else at the village would be easy.

"All can believe who so will," Sister Altha said before she shook her head a bit and fastened her eyes on Charlotte. "It is a sorrow that not all wish to pick up the cross and carry it. In many there is a lacking of proper spirit."

It was obvious she judged Charlotte to be one of the unwilling ones in spite of Charlotte's best efforts to do all she was told. Under Gemma's kinder guidance, Charlotte had carefully counted the bean seeds and sealed them into the packets. She had hung the chairs on the blue pegs and swept the bare wide-planked floors. She had pretended to bend her spirit while continually watching for some sight of Edwin.

She hadn't seen him until the Sunday morning meeting. Then he looked so different lined up with the other brethren, dressed in his gray trousers and round-collared cotton shirt with his hair combed in bangs across his forehead that she almost didn't recognize him.

But it was more than the clothes. Something else was different. Something she couldn't quite put her finger on until she realized he was sitting without a slouch even

though he was a head taller than the two
men on either side of him. She had never
seen him sit so tall. His posture didn't
change when Eldress Sadie spoke Charlotte's name. If anything, he appeared to
square his shoulders even more, almost
as if with pride as he looked directly at
Charlotte with something akin to joy on his
face. It wasn't a look that gave Charlotte
any hope he was regretting his decision
to come to the Shakers. Rather it was a
look celebrating her joining him there. As
a sister.

Charlotte and Mellie returned to their
places on the bench as Eldress Sadie
continued to talk. She was a little woman,
barely taller than a half-grown child, but
she seemed to radiate energy as she
moved about in front of the Shaker believers perched on the hard benches.

There were no adornments in the building that might suggest this was a house of
worship. Instead, ringing the walls were
hats and cloaks hung on the same sort of
blue pegs as in every other Shaker building. There was no pulpit for a preacher to
place his Bible or pound out a warning of
damnation, no offering plates, not even a

table for the Holy Communion cups and unleavened bread. To Charlotte, the large open room more resembled a barn than a house of worship.

That didn't seem to matter to those gathered in the building as they listened to Eldress Sadie's words with rapt attention and hushed reverence, even though she was speaking more of the business concerns of the village than of any spiritual matters. With each of her words, a feeling of anticipation trembled a bit more vibrantly in the air. Charlotte studied the faces around her and decided it wasn't what the woman was saying but rather what her words were leading up to that was exciting the congregation. They wanted to dance.

At last Eldress Sadie spoke the words the assembled Shakers had obviously been waiting to hear. "Let us go forth and labor a song to bring down the joy of the spirit upon us."

The men and women stood in unison and began carrying the benches to the ends of the room in an orderly fashion. Charlotte and Mellie moved awkwardly out of the way. Sister Altha appeared in front of them to lead them to the benches where a few older Shakers were sitting.

"In a few weeks, you might be practiced enough to take part in laboring the songs, but for now it will be well for you to watch and open your minds and hearts to the words of the songs." She let her eyes settle on Charlotte's face. "I asked the singers to do this first song for your ears, Sister Charlotte. It's an old hymn of humility."

Charlotte bent her head and studied her hands in her lap. Silence was often the easiest answer. Beside her, Mellie's surprise at her submissive posture was almost tangible. Charlotte waited until Sister Altha turned away and the singers began their song before she peeked over at Mellie with a sideways grin. Mellie covered her mouth quickly to hide her answering smile.

One of the sisters had stepped forward to begin the song.

> I want to feel little.
> I want to feel small.
> The last of my Brethren,
> The least of them all.

Other voices joined her clear voice.

That I may inherit that pure gospel spirit.
The spirit of Christ and of Mother.

Charlotte scooted closer to Mellie. She glanced behind her, but none of the older Shakers were paying any attention to them. All eyes were on the singers, and then others began to move out into the middle of the floor to form lines to begin the dance. She didn't look at Mellie as she said, "I don't think Sister Altha believes I can humble my spirit."

"You appears to be humbler than I ever thought to see you." Mellie's voice was not much above a whisper, but there was little chance anyone would hear them now, with the dancers shuffling back and forth across the wooden floor while the singers continued. There was no music except the sound of the voices in unison.

I want to feel humble
And simple in mind.
More watchful. More careful.
More fully resigned.

That I may inherit that pure gospel spirit.
The spirit of Christ and of Mother.

"I'm trying, Mellie," Charlotte said.

"It ain't so bad, Miss Lottie. You just do whatever they tells you. Instead of Mammy or you doin' the tellin', it's Sister Cora." Mellie frowned a little as she studied Charlotte's face. "Course I guess as how it's harder for you. You ain't never had nobody tellin' you what to do all that much. You sorry you came?"

"Things aren't happening the way I planned," Charlotte admitted.

"You had a chance to talk to Mr. Edwin?"

"No, I was never alone to look for him," Charlotte said. "Only laid eyes on him just now."

"He don't look the same in them Shaker clothes. That's for sure." Mellie looked toward the men dancing in front of them. Edwin moved past them in step with the other Shaker brothers. He didn't look their way but kept his eyes on the floor as if searching for something. Mellie's voice held a touch of wonder. "Can you believe that? Mr. Edwin never even liked to dance, did he?"

"I guess worship dances are different,"

Charlotte said as she watched Edwin shuffle away from them across the floor. The dances were precision forward and backward motions and turns such as a company of soldiers might practice. "Everything is different. We probably look as different as he does."

"Ain't that the truth. What with these long-eared caps." Mellie pulled on the flap of her cap that hung down by her left ear. "Especially for you with your pretty hair covered up. But Mr. Edwin looked right happy to see you."

"In Shaker dress. As his sister."

"Better his sister than his wife. I've been tellin' you that forever. You just need to get out of here and be glad to be shuck of the likes of him. You need a real man. Somebody like that artist feller."

The singers started in on a new verse.

> I want to be holy.
> More perfect in love.
> I want to be gentle
> And meek as a dove.

Meek as a dove. Was that what she was becoming? Charlotte Mayda Vance.

No, the meek as a dove Charlotte was the new Sister Charlotte. Not really her at all. Just a role she was playing while she figured out how to make things happen the way they had to. And in spite of the way her heart jumped at the thought of Adam Wade, he played no part in her future. None at all.

"He's gone," she whispered to Mellie.

"For now. But could be I was just happenin' to be lookin' out the upstairs window when he come back to tell you goodbye in the garden. A man kisses a woman like that, he's intendin' on comin' back."

"Even if he did, he wouldn't find me now." Charlotte wasn't quite able to keep the tremble of sadness out of her voice.

Mellie scooted her hand over under their skirts to squeeze Charlotte's hand. "You don't have to stay here, Miss Lottie. Go on home. It ain't a far walk even if they don't let you have your horse back."

Charlotte stared out at the Shakers moving back and forth in orderly formations. The men stayed in their lines as they passed through the lines of sisters. No one touched shoulders or hands. Then as if on a signal only they could hear, the lines turned and began marching in the opposite direction. The singers were repeating the words of the song, but the tune was getting livelier. The dancers began stepping higher and quicker until their feet on the floor were like the beating of drums.

All at once all the dancers and singers clapped and the sound exploded like the blast of a gun. Both Charlotte and Mellie jumped. The singers changed songs. Some of the dancers continued the orderly marching while others began leaping and jumping as the singers sang.

Hop up and jump up and whirl round.
Gather love, here it is, all round.

All the dancers began to jump and whirl until Charlotte thought they would surely fall from dizziness. Several young girls hopped up and down while holding hands. Some of the women began to reach up into the air as though plucking fruit from a tree. Sister Cora came over to where Charlotte and Mellie watched.

"Have some pomegranates, Sisters.

Mother Ann has sent them down to us." There was a glow on the older sister's face as she held out her cupped hands toward them. "Eat these and love will flow through you like a river."

They both just stared at her. She pushed her hands toward them. "Take it. You'll be glad you did."

Mellie lifted her eyebrows, but she reached out and pretended to take something from the woman's empty hands. Charlotte did the same while all around them the other Shakers were whirling and chattering and laughing. It was hard to hear the singers.

"I ain't never ate a pomegranate. They ain't poisonous, are they?" Mellie said as she frowned down at her hand as if she actually saw something there.

"Oh no, my sister. Mother Ann only sends down good gifts. The fruit she sends us is sweet as honey and like none you will ever taste anywhere else," Sister Cora assured them.

Mellie and Charlotte lifted their hands up and pretended to take a bite. Sister Cora smiled and spun away back to pick more fruit.

"These people done crazy as loons." Mellie shook her hand as if getting rid of the remains of the imaginary fruit.

Charlotte couldn't deny that as the Shakers began to form lines and march in orderly fashion again. "Sister Altha says we should be open to the spirit."

"The' ain't nothin' real wrong with that, but Mammy would say you'd better be sure you isn't lettin' in no wrong spirits. We'd best keep our eyes fastened on Jesus till we know more about this Mother Ann and her spirit fruit." Mellie warily watched the dancers as if worried some other Shaker was going to spin away and offer her fruit she didn't want to eat. "And you need to just go on back to Grayson before that Miss Selena messes everythin' up."

"Have you heard something?" Charlotte turned her head to look at Mellie.

"Best look back out toward them dancers. Sister Cora told me nobody was supposed to do no talkin' much at meeting. They's apt to move us apart."

Charlotte looked forward quickly, and they both sat in silence as they tried to see if anyone had noted their inattention.

"Nobody's watching," Charlotte said after a moment.

"Sister Cora says they has watchers that you don't never see. Peephole watchers." She barely moved her mouth as she went on. "Nate says that woman is gonna sell them all down the river."

"Father won't let her do that."

"Not in his right mind, but that woman has done spun his head around like these here Shakers were spinnin' a couple minutes back. Besides, Nate says Massah Charles ain't even there. He's still in the capital tryin' to stop the war a comin'."

"You saw Nate? When? And how?"

"Ever'body's got to go to the necessary room from time to time. Sometimes right in the middle of the night. But it don't matter all that much when I saw him. Just what he tol' me."

"But what can I do? She said Father gave her full rein to do whatever she wanted at Grayson."

"She said. You ain't knowin' for sure what he said or what he might know or not know about what's goin' on."

Mellie was right. Her father did need to know. "I'll write my father in the morning."

"A letter?" Mellie seemed to forget her worry about the watchers as she turned and looked directly at Charlotte. "What's the matter with you, Miss Lottie? I ain't never seen you act scared. That woman can't send you down the river. Grayson is your home."

"Nothing's working out the way I thought it would," Charlotte whispered. "The way I planned."

"Then maybe it's time to think on a new plan."

An old sister whose back was bent from years of work appeared in front of them. Her wrinkled face was not condemning, but rather full of kindness. "If we cannot dance or sing, we must meditate and ask the spirit to fill our souls with love and joy. Let me sit with you to help you properly meditate on the gifts of the spirit."

"Yea, Sister." Charlotte used the Shaker yes to try to make up for her and Mellie's lack of proper behavior as she scooted over to let the woman sit between them.

"I'm Sister Martha." The woman groaned softly as she lowered herself to the bench, and then lightly patted both of their legs. "Forgive me. My spirit is willing. Would that

I could still get out there and dance down glory, but the old bones are weak."

"Is that what they're doing? Dancing down glory?" Charlotte asked.

"I suppose that sounds strange to you," Sister Martha answered with a gentle smile. "Never fear, you will learn our ways. But first you must free yourselves from thoughts of the world. Whatever worries you had there are no longer important. You have left that life for a better life here with us where there is only peace and harmony."

Peace and harmony. Charlotte wondered if such was even possible with the nation split and shots already fired at Fort Sumter. The news received at the Shaker village since then didn't hold out much hope for peace with the threats of blockades of the Southern ports and the call to arms by both sides. The situation seemed to be totally out of control. The same as Charlotte's life.

A few days ago it had seemed reasonable to follow Edwin to the Shaker village to convince him he was wrong to want to be a Shaker. A few days ago she had believed she would be able to hang on to

Grayson. To go home again and sit in the peace of Aunt Tish's kitchen. Her kitchen.

But now she was sitting in a church without an altar, watching men and women whirl until they collapsed from the effort, eating imaginary fruit while people watched from peepholes to be sure she was obedient. Reason was lost.

15

It took Adam the better part of the afternoon to find Jake. Rows of tents were popping up on any bit of open ground in and around Washington, D.C., as regiments and companies from all across the Union answered President Lincoln's call for troops to enforce the laws of the land. Some of the volunteer companies came in with proper supplies and like uniforms, but others showed up with no hint of military bearing or dress, carrying hunting guns that had probably never been fired at anything bigger than a raccoon.

Just outside the city across the Virginia

border, the same mustering in was going on as reports came in that men of the South were navigating to Richmond, the new capital of the Confederate States. When Fort Sumter fell, taking with it the last faint hope of a peaceful compromise between the two sides, Virginia, Arkansas, North Carolina, and Tennessee had seceded to join their sister Southern states. It was also being bandied about that Robert E. Lee had been offered command of the whole Union army, but instead of answering the President's call, he had resigned his commission and gone south to line up against the Union.

Sam Johnson had already offered Adam a bonus if he could get a sketch of Lee in his Confederate gray leading his troops into battle. When Adam asked how he was supposed to keep the Rebels from shooting him as a Yankee spy while he was doing such a drawing, Sam had waved his hand in airy dismissal. "You'll find a way. You always do."

And Sam was right. He would find a way. If it was a face or scene that mattered, Adam wanted his name to be the one scribbled at the bottom of the illustration.

While it might not be the best time to be a Northerner in the South, that didn't mean it couldn't be done.

Adam pushed that problem aside to concentrate on the task at hand as he rode his horse slowly through the camps, pausing now and again to ask if any companies from Massachusetts had marched in. Everywhere he turned, patriotic feeling was at a fever pitch. The soldiers nearly to a man carried a spirit of revelry as if the whole idea of war was some kind of frolic the President had organized for their sole enjoyment.

Adam left his pencils in his bag and didn't pull out his sketchbook even though scenes all around him begged to be captured. On one side a baby-faced soldier who didn't look a day over fifteen caressed the barrel of the Springfield rifle just handed him by his captain. Down the block a plump lady in a feathered hat climbed down from a carriage to offer a basket of food to a circle of soldiers around a campfire. A mournful-looking black and tan hound rested his head on his master's leg as the man read a letter from home.

But Adam wasn't on a work mission. He

was on a Phoebe mission. Something he seemed to be doing way too much in the last few weeks. First Selena Vance. Now Jake. But Phoebe was right about this mission. Jake shouldn't be here straining at the bit to go to war. He was only nineteen and a young nineteen at that. It would destroy their mother if something happened to him. She doted on Jake and William.

"I'm almost twenty," Jake said with fire in his eyes when Adam at last found the 5th Massachusetts Regiment and confronted him. "Besides, who are you to tell me I'm too young? You left school even younger."

"But not to play at going to war."

Red flooded Jake's face as he balled up his fists. Adam stared him down before he could swing a punch. Adam was still the big brother, the one who had always bested Jake in any confrontation and then cleaned up his bloody nose before their mother could see. Adam wasn't sure if it came to it that he could best Jake anymore, but luckily for both of them, Jake wasn't anxious to take the chance there in front of his fellow recruits that Adam might still be able to whip him.

The boy had grown another inch or two taller since Adam had last seen him, and his shoulders were broad under the blue Massachusetts Regiment uniform. There was no mistaking he and Adam were brothers, but where Adam tamped down his emotions and rarely let anybody know what he was thinking, Jake hid nothing. He did everything to the fullest, whether it was fighting or racing horses or loving. He'd already suffered a severely broken heart thanks to Phoebe, who claimed if not for her diligent watch and timely action, Jake would have been trapped in a disastrous marriage that would have brought nothing but embarrassment to the family.

But an unfortunate marriage might be less dangerous than a battlefield. Embarrassment was rarely fatal. A battlefield could be. That's why Adam had tracked him down. To try to slow Jake's headlong rush into yet another disaster.

Adam threw his arm around his brother's stiff shoulders and tried to defuse his anger. "Sorry, Jake. I shouldn't have said that. It's just that Phoebe is worried about you." He didn't add that so was he. Better for Jake to feel the two of them were taking sides against Phoebe as they had so often in their younger days. "You know how Phoebe is."

Jake's muscles relaxed as he uncurled his fists and shook his head. "I should have known she would sic you on me."

Adam guided him away from the curious eyes and ears of the other men lolling about. They had been eager for the diversion of a fight to break the monotony of the camp. "She sent word you had signed up."

Jake hung his head a little. "Yeah, she isn't very happy with me. Says Mother weeps every time anybody mentions my name. I feel bad about that, but I still had to sign up. What else could I do?" He looked back up at Adam. "A man has to step up for his country at a time like this. You're joining up too, aren't you?"

"I'm not planning on it anytime soon."

Jake stared at him with wide open eyes that were a truer blue than Adam's. His never faded off to gray. "You're joshing me, aren't you?"

"Sorry to disappoint you, little bro, but no, I'm quite serious. I'll be there but not carrying a government-issued rifle."

"Drawing." Jake spat on the ground in disgust. "What good will that do?"

"More good than being cannon fodder." Adam stared straight at Jake until his brother shifted uneasily on his feet and looked down. "No need in you being cannon fodder either. Go back to school and finish out the year. Then you can be commissioned an officer if you're still determined to go to war."

"The fighting could all be over by then."

"We can hope," Adam said. *And pray.* He heard Edwin Gilbey's servant's words echoing in his head. Redmon. That was the man's name. If Adam went back to Kentucky and saw him again, he'd tell him to forget about those prayers for him and just pray for Jake. And others like him. Young. Foolish. Too ready to die for their country. Or maybe too sure they couldn't die.

Adam was only five years older than Jake, but in some ways he'd been older than Jake was now since he was twelve and their father left to seek his fortune. With his father gone, Adam had no choice but to leave boyhood behind. If he wanted something done, then it was Adam who had to do it. Nobody was going to step in and be a buffer between him and the realities of the world. But Jake and Harry had Adam ready to step in the gap for them and protect them as much as he was able.

Now it appeared Jake was determined to break through the gap and be his own man as he planted his feet on the ground and stretched up to his full height. His eyes were level with Adam's. "I won't leave the regiment. I'm not sitting on the sidelines. If you try to make me, you might as well just shoot me between the eyes right now, because I couldn't live being branded a coward." Jake's voice rose with each word until a couple of the men back at the camp lifted their heads to look out toward them.

Adam kept his voice quiet, almost pleasant. "Is that the iron you're branding me with, Jake? A coward's brand?"

Another flush reddened Jake's cheeks before he dropped his eyes to the ground. After an uncomfortable few ticks of silence, he mumbled, "You know I don't think that, Adam. Not really. You just look at things different than me. The artist in you, I guess. You've always been an observer. A watcher. But that's not me. I can't sit on the side and watch. I've got to be in the middle of making it happen." He raised his eyes back up at Adam. "It's time you and Phoebe realize that and let me be my own man." He was the little brother again beseeching Adam for permission to do something that would horrify their mother or Phoebe.

Adam stared at him for a long moment before he let out a sigh and shook his head. "I don't know what I'm going to tell Phoebe. Or Mother."

Jake smiled like a kid getting a puppy on Christmas morning as he bounced up on his toes and down again. "You can tell them you think I'm a man now. You do, don't you?"

Adam frowned at him. "I think you're headstrong and foolish." He let his frown fade away as he put his hand on Jake's shoulder. "But way too big for me to knock any sense into. Just remember it's war, Jake. Real bullets. Be brave but don't be stupid."

He went back over to the campfire with Jake and let him introduce him around to his buddies. All young. All burning with the war fever. He sat with them until dark fell, sketching their faces, hearing their blustering talk, wondering what he was going to tell Phoebe.

He took the easy way out and didn't go back to Boston before he caught a train to Kentucky. He sent a telegram. *Jake won't listen. Matter of honor. Pray war short.*

Adam could only hope Phoebe's response wouldn't find him until after the shooting stopped and Jake was safely home. As he watched the colors of spring bursting forth in the fields outside the train window, it seemed impossible that American men were gathering to shoot at other American men and that the only difference in the enemy would be the color of their uniforms. There'd even been stories in the papers about brothers shaking hands and marching off in opposite directions. To his chagrin, some other artist had beaten him to that illustration, but who knew what the coming weeks would bring? Cannons might be exploding in these very same green fields rolling so peacefully away from the train tracks, or the trains themselves might be derailed. If so, commerce in the nation could grind to a halt. That's what President Lincoln was hoping would happen in the South when he ordered the blockade of their ports.

Adam felt as ambivalent about it all as Kentucky was. It hadn't bothered him that Jake thought he lacked courage. He wasn't a coward. He had no need to prove himself on a battlefield except to draw the scenes that would tell the battle's story. That was the greater need. To record the conflict for history.

It seemed a waste of time heading back to the Shaker village in Kentucky just to draw a staircase. Sam had to be losing all sense of what was important. But Sam was the boss, and like he said, no cannons had lined up yet. As best Adam could tell from what he had heard in Washington, as many battle plans as there were regiments were being bandied about. If Lincoln didn't find a way to pull all the units together, who knew what might happen or when? So he supposed there was time for Sam's staircase. Plus time to swing by Grayson first. A slaveholding landowner trying to straddle the fence while waving a Union flag had to be a picture Sam Johnson could use. And could be he might convince the senator's daughter to pose for him in the garden. That would be one to add to his private collection.

But the senator wasn't there. Nor was the senator's daughter, according to the very proper black butler who answered the door and escorted him to the receiving parlor before going to inform the senator's wife she had an unexpected guest. Gibson, the old butler who had quaked so visibly under Selena's tirade in the parlor that day, had obviously been replaced. After cooling his heels in the small room for the better part of an hour, Adam decided to go see who he could find on his own to tell him when the senator's daughter might be in.

The house was being transformed. The sound of hammering drifted down from the upstairs floor while in the main parlor two black men were scraping paint off the woodwork. They paid scant attention to him as he stepped into the room and looked around. The furniture was covered in sheets and all the paintings removed from the walls, so at least Adam's eyes didn't have to be assaulted by his too-pretty portrait of the new Mrs. Vance. Outside the window the garden was no longer a peaceful retreat as a swarm of workers was cutting and trimming and tearing out the old plants and bushes. No chance of a quiet encounter with the beautiful Charlotte there now, even if she had been home.

He turned toward the kitchen. The cook had been friendly to him when he was here before. What was her name? Something odd. Aunt Tish. Latisha, according to Redmon when he saw the sketch Adam had drawn of her. Adam still had that sketch, along with the one he'd redrawn from memory of Redmon holding his horse. Someday Adam hoped to find a backer to help him publish a book of the many faces of America.

"Who are you?" a young voice asked as Adam stepped into the dining room that as yet was untouched by the bevy of workers.

Adam looked around the empty room. "Am I talking to a Grayson ghost?" he asked. "If so, I demand you introduce yourself."

A boy of five or maybe six poked his head out from under the table and giggled. "I'm not a ghost."

"What a relief." Adam put his hand over

his heart and let out an exaggerated breath. "But if not a Grayson ghost, who are you?"

"I asked you first."

"So you did. Adam Wade at your service." Adam bowed a little from the waist and then crouched down to be eye level with the child. He surmised the boy must be Selena Vance's son, even though his small round face little resembled his mother as it shone with an innocence quite foreign to hers. "Is some sort of attack imminent? Should I ask you to make room for me under there with you?"

The boy giggled again, his dark eyes dancing under a mop of curly hair. "You're too big to hide under here, but I doubt you need to. Miss Pennebaker won't be chasing you to make you form your letters on the slate until your fingers won't uncurl from the chalk." He flexed his fingers as his smile disappeared. "Miss Pennebaker has no fondness for fun. If she catches me, I'll have to stand with my nose in a circle on the schoolroom wall for hours."

"How irksome for you, young sir. Can your mother not intercede for you, Master . . . ? I don't believe you gave me your name."

"Landon. Landon Black, and Mother gets even angrier than Miss Pennebaker when I run off and hide." The boy's eyes got bigger as he shrank back under the table a bit. "The last time she said she was going to tell my new father to give me a whipping. But he hasn't come back from wherever he works. Do you know him?"

"I do know him."

"Is he very mean?"

"He didn't seem so, but perhaps you should do what Miss Pennebaker tells you so you won't have to find out about that."

"I suppose I will just have to take my punishment then." The little boy sighed heavily. "A whipping is better than staying in the schoolroom all the day long. Mother says I have to learn to be a gentleman, but I don't want to."

"What do you want to learn to be?"

"A sea captain. I want to smell the sea air and harpoon whales." The little boy crawled the rest of the way out from under the table. He stayed on his knees but stretched his head up in the air. He was so thin that Adam thought a stiff sea breeze would surely bowl him over. The child peered at Adam and asked, "Have you ever seen a whale?"

"Only in drawings."

"Drawings." Landon frowned. "That sounds like schoolwork."

"Not to me. To me it's an adventure every day as I chase the unexpected the way a sea captain chases whales."

"But you can't harpoon whales unless you're a sea captain. Harpoons are heaps more fun than drawing pencils." The boy raised his arm and pretended to throw a harpoon before he shook his head sadly. "But Mother says I have to be a gentleman because all this will be mine someday."

"What about Charlotte? Where is she?"

"Charlotte. That's my new father's daughter. Mother says I'm my new father's son, so that would make Charlotte my sister, wouldn't it?" The child didn't seem to expect Adam to answer him as he went on. "But she's not here. She's somewhere in Virginia. Mother says she had to go there to learn to be a lady before I came here."

"Virginia?"

"That's a state. Miss Pennebaker says they seceded from the Union, and we'll be shooting people from Virginia now, so I might never get to meet her. My sister, I mean. I had a father." The boy's lip trembled as he went on. "He had to go to heaven to see God. So I don't need a new father even though Mother says I do, but I've never had a sister. A sister might be fun. If she knows about seas and such, but Mother says to forget about having a sister."

"Oh? Why is that?"

Landon started to answer, but the sound of female heels clicking on the wooden floor and coming closer stopped his words. "Mother's coming. I'll harpoon you if you tell her I'm under here." He scooted back out of sight under the tablecloth.

16

Adam stood up and stepped away from the table a bare second before Selena Vance came into the room. He pushed his lips up in a smile as he greeted her.

Her return smile looked every bit as fake as his felt. "Adam, how delightful to see you again. But James said you were waiting in the receiving parlor."

"So I was," Adam said. "But it was a long ride here and the day was warm. I hoped to impose on your housekeeper for a drink of water."

"You poor man." She pulled her mouth down in a sympathetic look. "I should have had refreshment sent to you at once. What a regretful lapse of proper hospitality! I fear I've been in quite a spin trying to correct years of neglect here and simply got distracted. Let me ring the bell for tea."

She hardly seemed dressed for work, with her waist pinched small as a wasp's above the shimmering rose-colored skirt, fashionably plumped out by multiple petticoats. As she brushed past Adam toward the sideboard, the skirt's silky material rustled softly against his legs.

"That's kind of you, but you don't have to bother with tea on my account," he said. "A glass of water, then I'll be on my way. I only stopped by to have a few words with the senator, but your servant says he's not here."

"No, I fear he's still in Frankfort. The war news is causing so much division that he doesn't know when he might be able to return. Plus of course, the election looms next summer." She studied Adam as if trying to figure out why he would need to speak with the senator. "Was there some difficulty with your payment for the portrait? I have come to realize that sometimes mundane business matters very often escape Charles' notice when he is up to his ears in political maneuvering."

"No, no difficulty. Actually it was politics that brought me here." Adam told the partial truth. "I hoped to speak with him about the local political mood. And to see if he might be willing to allow me to do a sketch of him for the newspaper. A Kentucky senator trying to hold on to the peace here in the state." Adam held his hands up as if framing the caption.

Her face changed, became more welcoming. "I'm sure he'd look on that with favor. You really must stay for tea so that we can chat about your work." She picked up a small bell off the sideboard and rang it.

"Will Charlotte be joining us?" Adam asked as if the butler and the child hiding under the table hadn't already told him she wasn't there. "I do hope she is well."

"I'm sure she is quite well." Selena carefully set the bell down to keep it from tinkling again and ran her fingers along the tatted lace edge of the cloth on the sideboard before she turned to look at Adam. "But Charlotte's not at Grayson right now. She's gone to Virginia."

"Virginia? With war imminent, do you think that is wise?"

"Charlotte is a very determined young woman. What she decides to do, she does." Selena held out her hands in a gesture of helplessness. "Charles warned me she was thus before we married."

"I'm surprised she would decide to leave Grayson. She spoke so fondly of her home here." Adam watched Selena. Something seemed amiss in what she was telling him.

"Young women can be quite unpredictable." Selena shook her head slightly with a look of amused wonder. Then her eyes sharpened on Adam. "She is very attractive in spite of those unfortunate freckles. Were you smitten by her?"

A young female servant answered the summons of the bell and saved him from having to come up with a suitable response.

"We'll take tea in the receiving parlor," Selena told the girl.

"Your offer of tea is very kind, but I really must be on my way," Adam said quickly. He had no desire to be trapped into an extended visit with this woman. But he had pretended thirst, so he added, "However, a glass of water and perhaps one of Tish's apple tarts would be more than welcome."

Selena shooed the servant girl back to the kitchen with no change in her orders before she turned to smile at Adam. "We have a new cook now. One I brought down from Boston. Unfortunately a skill for finer cooking seems to escape our Southern Negroes."

"Oh. And where is Tish? I had the feeling that she had long been part of the household."

"So she had, but you needn't dredge up any of your Northern sympathies for her. I haven't sent Tish away, merely moved her to the slave quarters to cook there. Perkins says she's quite happy. How altruistic of you to be concerned for her." Selena's bland smile grew even wider.

"None of my business, of course," he said in what he hoped was a pleasant tone. "I was just a bit surprised to hear the senator would agree to change cooks. He seemed fond of Tish."

"My dear Adam, all things change. You surely know that. Think of how our Charlotte found it necessary to make new plans after the disappointment of her broken

engagement. You did know of her disappointment, didn't you?" She pulled a sorrowful face and went on with no pause for
him to answer. "And so we all find it necessary to make changes. Grayson was sinking under my husband's misguided kindness
and distracted management. That is being
corrected."

"I see." Adam gave up on pretending
politeness.

His frown seemed to make her smile
more genuine. "Perhaps you do," she said
as she once more picked up the bell. "I'll
have James show you out."

"Don't bother," Adam said before she
could ring it. "I can find my way back to the
door."

"I daresay you can." Her smile didn't
waver as she replaced the bell without letting it make a sound. "Would you like me
to send your regards to Charlotte when
next I write?"

"Certainly. *If* you write."

"Oh, I have written her. It's the least I
can do for Charles, since he is much too
busy himself to worry with such correspondence."

She reminded him entirely too much of Phoebe, who continually arranged and ordered the lives of everybody around her, but at least he could usually believe Phoebe was driven by love to push her family to do whatever she determined was best for them. In Selena Vance, Adam glimpsed no redeeming core of love. Marriage to the senator had given her position, prestige, and power, and those were the whips she was using to bring the world around her to its knees. There would be no peace at Grayson for a long while. As Adam turned to go out, he felt a rush of gratitude that he'd never allowed himself to be caught by such a woman.

He was almost to the door when a frazzled-looking middle-aged woman passed him in the hall without seeming to note or perhaps care that he was a stranger. "I have lost young Landon again. If you've seen a small boy of six, I would count it a great favor if you would point me in his direction."

Adam was saved from answering by Selena's firm voice in the dining room. "Landon Harley Black, come out from under that table at once and go do as you're told by Miss Pennebaker. There are consequences to pay."

As if the consequences were payment due from her instead of Landon, the unfortunate Miss Pennebaker looked near tears as she hurried on toward the dining room.

Poor Landon had little chance of ever harpooning his whales. Not with Selena calling the shots. He would be a gentleman or else. Then again, the same might have once been said about Adam's chance of being an artist with his grandfather so set against it. Of course Adam hadn't had the added burden of being a gentleman on his shoulders. The son of a shopkeeper and the grandson of a schoolmaster didn't have quite as much to live up to. No Graysons in his future. Thank the merciful heavens.

And what of Charlotte's future? She had seemed so set on coercing her young gentleman friend into marriage. As he had eavesdropped on her and Gilbey in the garden the night of the party, she had shown signs of Phoebe's and the new Mrs. Vance's determination to shape life to suit them. That should have been enough to make him run from any contact with her, but instead he had stepped out of the shadows to confront her. He still wasn't sure why. Perhaps because of the innocent vulnerability he'd glimpsed behind her smile when the senator had escorted his new wife into the house. Perhaps simply because he was a man and she was a woman. He had thought to merely offer her a few kind words, but she was so lovely and her lips so inviting.

Even now as he rode away from Grayson, he could shut his eyes and bring up the exact image in his mind of how she had looked in the moonlight. Her skin soft under his touch, her eyes brimming over with fearful desire, her lips begging to be kissed. He had drawn her face many times since then, but not that image. If he kept it only in his head, then he might still convince himself that she was only another beautiful woman who had allowed him to steal a kiss from her in a weak moment. He could forget his disappointment when she pushed him away in the graveyard and assure himself that the kiss before his leave-taking the next day was nothing more than the last move in a game they had been playing with their emotions. His winning move.

But if that was true, why did he feel so much the loser now that he hadn't found her at Grayson? He had expected her to be there. He had pictured her there, if not exactly waiting for him, at least remembering him the way he was remembering her. As some unexpected twist in the road with entrancing possibilities glimmering in the distance. Obviously her plans with young Gilbey had gone awry. Perhaps that had been a disappointment she had run from as Selena Vance had suggested. But into the direct path of the war? The senator should have known better than to let her go to Virginia where both armies were lining up to fire the first salvos of the conflict. Each thought to take the other's capital and end the war in one brilliant maneuver.

Adam wished he had asked where in Virginia. But if Charlotte had gone to a finishing school as Landon said, Adam could find her. It wouldn't be that much of a challenge. The challenge would be in not getting shot as a Yankee spy.

He reined in his runaway thoughts as up ahead he caught sight of the buildings of the Shaker village rising into the sky. It was better that he didn't know where Charlotte was. He had no time to be chasing after her, no matter how she haunted his thoughts. Her father would undoubtedly send for her before the war advanced to any place near her. She wasn't Adam's responsibility. So what if she had touched something deep inside him that no other girl had ever even come close to touching. That didn't mean it was something that wouldn't fade into forgetfulness after a few months in spite of how memories of her pulled at his heart now. He had pictures to capture, and the first one was this confounded staircase Sam Johnson was so determined to have.

But since he was there, he might as well look around for more faces and scenes to draw. The next day was Sunday. Perhaps they would allow him to attend their morning meeting to observe the Shakers' dancing worship that sounded so odd to him. Dancing had no place in the religion his grandfather had shoved down his throat. In his grandfather's place of worship, a person sat on hard benches and listened in total silence as a dark-clad preacher threatened the Lord's punishment on any man, woman, or child who let his thoughts wander away from the preacher's words.

While the Lord had never sent down a lightning bolt to strike Adam down as the preacher sometimes warned might happen to those who didn't take the message of the Lord seriously enough, Adam's grandfather had been more than ready to pick up the rod on the Lord's behalf to keep Adam's spirit in check. Adam hadn't been in a church building since he left his grandfather's house.

It wasn't that he didn't believe there might be a God. The beauty of this very spring day seemed to suggest some higher power had set the world in motion. Even more than the beauty of nature, Adam couldn't dismiss the strong belief of a man like Redmon who offered to pray for a white man he barely knew while enslaved to another white man. And the man clearly believed his prayer would be heard and attended to. Yet if that was so, why was Redmon still a slave? If what the Bible said was true and nothing was impossible with the Lord, why hadn't that most powerful God set Redmon, a man who loved him, free?

While Adam hoped Redmon's prayers brought him comfort, he couldn't imagine a most high God leaning down to pay attention to any petitions he, Adam, might offer up. Perhaps the Lord had lent his ear to the first Adam in the garden or helped the disciples catch fish the way the Bible said, but a lot of years had passed since then.

And now soldiers were lining up to go to war, and on both sides men were praying to God for victory. What happened then? Wouldn't it be better if the prayers of men of peace were answered and there was no war?

The Shakers believed in peace. They had shut out the world in order to establish a community of perfect peace. A few days immersed in their peace might be good before he had to go back east where the armies were massing and the voices of those calling for peace had been drowned out by the beat of war drums.

17

The letter from Grayson came the first week of May. Spring had spread its blooms from one end of the village at Harmony Hill to the other, but when Charlotte paused to admire the white clouds of apple blossoms in the orchard, Gemma had mildly taken her to task.

"We don't look at the fleeting beauty of the bloom. It is the beginning of fruit that we see," Gemma told her.

"But what is the wrong in enjoying the flowers first? Don't you think the Lord created such beauty for the eye to behold?"

Charlotte was trying to understand the

Shakers. Not because she planned to stay with them, but merely as a puzzle she needed to figure out. She had asked so many "why" questions that Sister Altha finally forbade Charlotte to speak the word in her presence. A novitiate's place was to listen and learn and not to question why. Sister Altha said the why had been answered many years ago by Mother Ann through the visions she had received from the Eternal Father. There was no need to question the Believers' truths given in such a sacred manner nor should one doubt the decisions of the Ministry who were even now led by Mother Ann's precepts and spirit.

More patient with Charlotte's questions, Gemma stared out at the blooming trees as she explained, "The beauty in anything is in its usefulness. It is wrong to celebrate beauty for beauty's sake, but with our bees' help, these blossoms will become apples to supply our needs for nourishment and for produce to sell to the world. That is what we celebrate. We can ever be thankful for the bounty of nature."

But the whys still sat on Charlotte's tongue. Why couldn't they breathe in the beauty of the blossoms and still celebrate the apples? Why? Why? The questions circled in her head and always ended with the same ones sitting down to stay with her. Why was she still here? Why hadn't she gone back to Grayson the way Mellie had told her she should on that first Sunday?

Perhaps she needed to forbid her mind from thinking the word *why*, for she had no answers. She had always had answers. From the time she was a small child, she'd been able to see the path of her life clearly before her, but now the path she'd been so sure of was fading from sight. Selena had taken over her beloved Grayson, and Edwin showed no inclination to return to the "world," as the Shakers called all that lay outside the borders of their villages. He was cut from the same cloth as the most devout of the brethren.

When at last she had been able to speak with him face-to-face, she had never seen him so animated as he told her how anxious he was for his birthday in December when he would be of the proper age to officially sign the Covenant of Belief and hand over Hastings Farm to his new family. She stared at him and did not know him. Arguments rose in her mind, but she couldn't seem to bring them to her lips with Sister Altha beside her and Elder Logan beside Edwin as they supervised their meeting.

She had been surprised when Sister Altha suggested she talk with Edwin. Charlotte hadn't requested to do so, even though she had almost given up meeting Edwin in some unsupervised place. There were no unsupervised places at Harmony Hill. Even the shadows seemed to have eyes and ears.

Very aware of Sister Altha's stern eyes upon her, she looked at Edwin and finally got out the weak question. "Are you sure?"

"I have never been surer of anything in my life, Charlotte." When he forgot to call her "sister," Sister Altha frowned and he quickly amended his words. "Sister Charlotte. The brotherly love here surrounds me until I feel as if I'm resting on a pillow of peaceful purity. This is the way the Lord wants us to live. Staying pure of worldly sins of the flesh, listening to him and working to make his way our own. Mother Ann instructed us to let such be our inheritance, our treasure, our occupation, our daily calling. Isn't that right, Elder Logan?" He looked to the man by his side for approval. They sat in two chairs facing Charlotte and

Sister Altha with a good distance between, as if even the air the brothers and sisters breathed should not be mixed.

"It is as you say, Brother. Our sister may come to know the same treasure if she bends her will and opens her heart to the teachings." Elder Logan's face was lined with wrinkles that seemed to speak of kindness and understanding. His hair was as white as the stones that made up the impressive exterior of the building they were in. He sat straight in the chair with his open hands resting lightly atop his knees. Edwin sat exactly the same, a head taller than the elder.

"I have often told her so in the time she has been among us," Sister Altha put in. "Have I not, Sister Charlotte?"

"Yea," Charlotte agreed, using the Shaker word. She was tempted to add that Sister Altha always made it sound as if it was a treasure Charlotte had scarce hope of finding, but she held her tongue. That hardly mattered, since the Shaker way was not a treasure she had ever thought to seek. It certainly wasn't the reason she was sitting in a Shaker room looking across at Edwin, who had donned the Shaker spirit along with his Shaker clothes. The Hastings land no longer mattered to him. He had found his place among the brethren. Perhaps for the first time ever, he looked comfortable in his own skin.

Charlotte had never been one to hide from the truth. Hadn't she knelt by her mother's body on the garden path and looked death in the face without pretense? She had looked on her arrangement with Edwin with the same direct honesty. She had realized early on that the two of them might never share any sort of bond other than the love for their land, but she had believed that would be enough. Now she knew it was not. And yet she stayed hidden among the Shakers, waiting for some word from her father that she could come back to Grayson. She needed the loving assurance that, even with Selena attempting to push her out the door, he—her father—would always make a place for her there.

She had sent a letter to her father on that first Monday with the Shakers the way she had promised Mellie she would. Gemma told her she was free to write what she willed to her father, but that the Ministry would read her words before the letter was posted to be sure she had written nothing too worldly or improper. So she had carefully considered each word she penned.

Dear Father,

Please forgive me for leaving and coming here to Harmony Hill without talking to you first. I tried to explain my reasons in the letter I wrote to you before I left Grayson, but sometimes it's hard to tell everything in words on paper. As you may already know, Edwin has decided to join with the Shakers and become a Believer. Thus there will be no wedding in May and no joining of the Grayson and Hastings farms as we had once hoped and dreamed.

I followed Edwin here at his invitation in hopes of finding a new plan for my life. I brought Mellie with me and she is now a free sister among the Shakers. She has heard some disturbing news from Grayson that Selena has no awareness—as is understandable since she is so new to our home—of our commitment to our people. Our Negroes have long

been loyal to us at Grayson. I know
you feel the same sort of loyalty back
toward them and will want to protect
them from the great sorrow of being
forced to leave the only home many
of them have ever known. I can't
believe you would approve of such a
course of action and trust you will do
what needs to be done to make
things right again. For all of us.

**Your loving daughter,
Charlotte**

As Sister Altha read through the letter,
the frown lines deepened between her
eyes. But she made no comment for or
against any of Charlotte's words when she
handed the sheet of stationery back to
Charlotte. "Address the envelope," she ordered. "I will have to post it for you."

Charlotte dipped the pen nib in the ink-
pot and stared at the blank envelope, not
sure which address to write. She could
post it directly to Frankfort, but then what
if her father had returned to Grayson? It
had been her experience in the past that
letters sent to him in Frankfort often were

lost if he wasn't still in the capital city to receive them.

"You surely know your own address, Sister Charlotte." Sister Altha blew out an impatient sigh as she tapped her toe against the wood floor.

"Yea, of course, Sister Altha."

"Then let's be done with this. We cannot neglect our duties overlong."

Finally Charlotte wrote her father's name on the letter and sealed it with a bit of wax before slipping it into the envelope. Quickly she addressed the envelope to Perkins, the overseer at Grayson, with instructions on the back to forward her letter to Frankfort if her father wasn't expected home. Perkins might be taking orders from Selena, but his first loyalties would surely be to Grayson and her father. He would see that the letter was delivered into her father's hand.

"I hope you are not planning on writing many letters, Sister." Sister Altha snatched the envelope from Charlotte before the ink had time to dry. "Now Sister Gemma is waiting to take you to your work duties. It is good to dwell on the truth that a Believer has no time to waste."

Days passed and became weeks as

Charlotte anxiously awaited an answer, while at the Shaker village she continued the mind-numbing cycle of work and listening to Sister Altha's instruction in the Shaker way. With the seed packets all sealed and ready to be marketed in the world by the Shaker traders, she followed Gemma to a new duty in the pressing room on the third floor of the Gathering Family House.

It promised to be hot and tedious work. A fire in the small round stove in the center of the room kept the irons hot—and also the workers, whose faces glistened with sweat in spite of the windows open to the spring breeze. As she followed Gemma into the too warm room, Charlotte longed to fling off the worrisome cap and let her head feel the air, but she knew Gemma would simply fetch the discarded cap and pleasantly tell her to put it back on. Nothing she did upset Gemma, who seemed to float on a peaceful sea with no storm waves ever. But at the same time, she never allowed Charlotte to lag.

When she noted Charlotte eyeing the overflowing basket of bedclothes beside the ironing board assigned to her, Gemma laughed. "We have need of many beds for our sisters and brothers, but do not despair, my sister. We also have many hands to get the work done. You are not expected to do more than your share."

"That is good to hear, but you'll have to show me how," Charlotte said as she watched one of the sisters pick up an iron from the stove and moisten the tip of her finger to give its flat side a quick touch. Obviously satisfied with the heat she felt, she moved back to her board and began smoothing the skirt of one of the Shaker dresses. "I've never used an iron."

"Never?" Gemma looked surprised. "Did you wear your clothes wrinkled?"

"Oh no." Charlotte almost laughed at the idea. Her mother had taught her that a lady had to maintain the proper appearance at all times. "That wouldn't have been allowed."

A sister plain of face and looking to be in her middle years looked up from her steady pressing strokes. "Our new sister was a lady, Sister Gemma. Remember? Ladies have servants to do such common chores. I've even heard they have servants to dress them. That all they do is hold up their arms and turn and stand like a china doll while a servant tightens their corsets and does up their buttons. Is that true, Sister Charlotte?"

The other sisters in the room held their irons up away from the fabric spread on their ironing boards and looked at Charlotte as they waited for her to answer. None of them had probably ever had a servant do up their buttons or tie the laces on their pantalettes, but Charlotte sensed no animosity, only interest in what her answer might be.

"At times," Charlotte said. "For fancy dresses and such. A lady's waist must be fashionably slender and so the stays must be pulled as tight as possible. Tighter than one can do on her own. And then the buttons are completely out of reach on those dresses and they have no wiggle room. Not like these dresses at all." Charlotte smiled and pulled the loose fabric of her dress out away from her waist.

The other women looked at her with unbelieving eyes as if hardly able to imagine such a life where somebody else fastened one's buttons. One of the older sisters returned her iron to the stove and picked up a new one. When she spat on it, her spit sizzled on the hot surface before she turned toward Charlotte. "Did you not like being a lady, young sister? Or did your family's fortunes change?"

The woman's look was sharp, and Charlotte thought that, not only would she know if Charlotte did not speak the truth, she would be sure to report such a lapse of honesty to Sister Altha. So she simply said, "At times I felt trapped in dresses I could not unbutton."

She might have said more, but one of the younger sisters spoke up. "I wore such a dress once. My wedding dress had tiny pearl buttons with fabric loops to hold them. My dear mother fastened them for me. She'd worn the dress when she married my father years before."

"And did you feel trapped in it the way our new sister says?" the older sister asked.

"Nay. I felt beautiful and happy on my wedding day." The girl's face softened as if she could still see herself the way she had looked on that day.

"Such feelings of vanity are a sin, Sister Dulcie," the older sister warned.

"Yea, Sister Erma." The young woman lowered her eyes to the floor. "I will confess my sin at the first opportunity."

"You are married?" Charlotte looked at

the girl in surprise. "I understood marriage was not allowed among you here."

Gemma answered before Dulcie could. "Many come among us with the need to shake free from the sin of matrimony before they can begin living the true way."

"And how does that happen?" Charlotte asked. "Aren't the vows of marriage sacred? Doesn't the Bible speak of forsaking all others and cleaving to your husband or wife?"

Gemma smiled. "Sister Altha is right. You do have many questions and little understanding of our ways. Here in our community we demonstrate the practical love that is asked of believers in the Scripture. 'By this shall all men know that ye are my disciples, if ye have love one to another.' The selfish love of husband and wife and children cannot satisfy that commandment of the Lord. Such selfish unions bring naught but sin and stress into one's life. But the peaceful, all-encompassing love we practice here for all our brethren enables us to live the perfect life at Harmony Hill. Is that not right, my sisters?" Gemma swept her eyes around the other women in the room.

"Yea," they echoed one another, but Charlotte noted some of the voices sounded less enthusiastic than the others. Dulcie's yea was barely above a whisper.

"Good, we are all agreed as how it should be. We have no ladies here, only sisters," Sister Erma said with another sharp look toward Charlotte before she began plying her iron again. "Now it will be best if we stop our chatter and attend to our labor. The irons do not smooth the wrinkles without our arms pushing them."

Again the sisters answered with a chorus of obedient yeas as they turned back to their ironing boards. Dulcie stepped over in front of Gemma. "If it pleases you, Sister Gemma, let me show our new sister how to iron the sheets. I have not learned much well enough to teach it while I have been here at Harmony Hill, but I know well how to do this duty. And there is an open ironing board here beside me."

"That would be good, Sister Dulcie. Sister Altha has asked me to write some letters for her since her arthritis is making writing difficult, so this will give me the opportunity to tend to those duties. Plus I must confess ironing is not my favorite duty." Gemma flashed them her smile before she headed for the door.

18

Dulcie watched Gemma leave and then shook her head slightly. "Sometimes you want to pinch Sister Gemma just to be sure she is a flesh-and-blood sister and not an angel in Shaker dress. Have you ever seen her the least bit perturbed?"

Charlotte thought a minute before she said, "Not that I can remember. Even my many questions don't seem to bother her. She always answers me kindly. Unlike Sister Altha who tells me such mindless curiosity will surely lead me down the devil's path."

Dulcie made a sympathetic face. "Yea,

Sister Altha does greatly desire to keep us off that path. But engaged in our duties, we won't be tempted to stray. Come, let me show you how to do this ironing duty."

She pulled the basket of sheets over to the side and showed Charlotte how to sprinkle water over them and then roll them up tightly so the fabric would be damp enough for the irons to smooth more easily.

The hiss of the heated irons against the damp cloth, the clank of cooling irons being set back on the stove, and the rustle of the fabric being shifted and straightened on the ironing boards made it impossible to hear any words spoken except by someone standing very near. Charlotte peeked over at Sister Erma to be sure she wasn't looking their way before she asked Dulcie, "So how come you to be here if you were married?"

Dulcie kept her voice as low as Charlotte's. "My husband was converted by a Shaker brother selling garden seeds. Our farm was rocky and the ground so poor we could barely grow enough corn to feed our children."

"Children?" Dulcie looked too young

and too slight to have ever borne a child. "You have children?"

"We had three. Two girls and a wee boy. Then the wee one, our sweet little Willy, got a fever and died. I could have overcome the sadness, but my William felt it was a direct punishment from the Lord for what he called our sins of lust." Dulcie kept her eyes on the tightly rolled dampened sheet as she placed it back in the basket. "Brother Joseph, the Shaker man, said the Lord had revealed that truth to William, and the only way to protect our girls was to come to Harmony Hill. So we did." She stood up and together they carried the basket of dampened bedclothes back to the ironing board.

Charlotte shook out a pillowcase and laid it on the board as she saw a sister doing across the room. "Are you sorry to be here?"

"We don't go hungry and Shaker children rarely get fevers." Dulcie handed Charlotte an iron. "Careful. You can burn yourself," she warned as Charlotte set the iron down on the pillowcase. There was a slight hiss as steam rose up around the hot iron.

"Keep it moving or you will scorch the fabric." Dulcie took the iron from Charlotte and moved it back and forth with just the right pressure to smooth out the wrinkles. "A very hot iron works best, so when this one cools you must put it back on the stove in the iron holder and take a newly hot one. When you need to adjust the material, you can set the iron down on its heel." She propped the iron up on the end of the ironing board.

"It looks easy when you do it," Charlotte said as she picked the iron up to give it another try.

"I've had much practice. My mother had me ironing pillowcases by the time I was six."

While not as quick as Dulcie, Charlotte managed to smooth the wrinkles out of the rest of the case. She ran her hand over the warm cotton with satisfaction at its smoothness.

"Now fold it over and do the other side," Dulcie instructed. "We have no time to admire our work. There are many pieces to iron." She watched as Charlotte pressed and folded the pillowcase into a square that matched all the other Shaker pillowcases.

Uniformity was desired in all they did. "Now lay it aside on the finished table and begin another until your basket is empty."

Charlotte looked at the basket heaped with sheets and pillowcases. "I have to do them all? Today?"

Dulcie smiled. "I will take from your basket too and we will be finished before the midday meal. Sisters help one another here. That is a good thing." Then her smile faded as she reached down to lift a sheet out of the basket and hold it up against her bosom as if the bundle held a baby. "But I do miss holding my children against my heart."

Charlotte spread another pillowcase on the ironing board. "Where are they?"

"In the Children's House. They are well cared for and go to school."

"But does anyone hold them as you wish to?"

"Not like a mother. Only as a sister." Dulcie unfolded the sheet and spread it on her ironing board. She kept her voice low, barely loud enough for Charlotte to hear. "But they are not unhappy. They don't cry for me, and I manage to only weep on the inside when they call me Sister Dulcie."

She ran her iron over the sheet for a moment before she said, "I shouldn't have burdened you with my words. Sister Altha will tell me it is a sin to speak of my unhappiness or even to feel such."

"Don't worry. I am far from perfect enough to share all I hear with Sister Altha. Our words are only about the ironing." Charlotte matched her quiet tone.

"Then, my lady sister, why are you here if you aren't searching for the perfect way?" Dulcie asked.

Charlotte looked across at the other sisters. None seemed to be paying the least attention to them. Even Sister Erma. "I thought to marry Edwin Gilbey before he came here."

"And you were so in love with him that you followed him here rather than live your life of comfort without him."

Dulcie looked at her with such dreamy eyes that Charlotte almost laughed. Put that way it sounded quite ludicrous, but was her way any less so? "I'm not in love with him."

A frown wrinkled Dulcie's forehead. "Then why would you think to marry him?

And why did you follow him here? I don't think I understand."

"It seemed a good plan at the time."

"And now?"

"Now I don't know."

"You could leave the village and go back to your life as a lady, couldn't you?" Dulcie asked.

"I suppose, but there are complications. I'm waiting to hear from my father."

Dulcie paused in her ironing and looked at Charlotte a long moment before she asked, "Do you fear he is angry with you for following Brother Edwin here?"

"Perhaps." Charlotte carefully doubled over the pillowcase and pressed the iron down on it before she went on. "Or perhaps I am more worried that he might not care. Whichever it is, I seem to need his words telling me to come home before I can do so."

Charlotte smoothed the last fold of the pillowcase and laid it with the first one she'd done. With only a moment's hesitation, she pulled out a sheet and went to get a hot iron off the stove. Dulcie smiled at her courage to try the bigger piece and showed her how to fold the sheet to make it fit on the board. When Charlotte finally had the sheet ironed and folded and on the finished table with the other pieces, she felt a moment of pride. She had a blister on her thumb and a burn on her arm, but she had done it. She was capable. She wasn't a helpless young female who couldn't do up her own buttons or boil her own water for tea.

She'd read history books and studied politics at her father's knee. Such pursuits had not injured her mind as some were wont to think would happen when a young woman was interested in learning more than which flower denoted forgiveness or other such useless drivel. And now the Shakers had proven to her that she could accomplish necessary tasks. Her body was as strong and capable as her mind. She could go back to Grayson and begin her life anew.

Then Sister Martha brought her the letter after the evening meal during their time of rest before the families gathered to practice their songs and dancing.

"I have something for you." Sister Martha was so out of breath she could barely get out the words, and Charlotte quickly lifted down a chair from the pegs for her to sit. The old sister eased down on it gratefully as she put her hand over her heart and pulled in a few deep breaths before she was able to say any more. "The stairs get more difficult for me every day. Regrettably my advanced years render me incapable of performing most duties, but I can still help with the delivery of letters, though the task is easier if there are not so many steps to climb." She blew out a puff of air and reached into her pocket to pull out a letter. "This one is from your family in the world."

Charlotte took the letter from her. It wasn't her father's writing. She turned the envelope over to see that its seal was already broken. "It's open."

"Yea, the Ministry must be sure the words in any letter coming to those in our Society are not improper," Sister Martha said.

"Oh." She stared down at the neat, concise letters forming her name. The envelope had been addressed by Selena. Of course she could still believe the letter inside might be from her father as long as she didn't pull it out to see proof otherwise. "And so the words in this one were acceptable?"

"I so assume. I was not the reader. I was simply given the duty of carrying the epistle to you." Sister Martha sat quietly for a moment before she said, "If you have no wish to read it, I can carry it back unread. Some who come among us have no desire to glance backward at the world they left behind, and that serves them well."

"Nay." The Shaker word came easily to her lips as she sat down on the edge of her narrow bed. "I must read it."

"I always think that's best. To read and know instead of wondering. I did much wondering in my younger years."

"How old are you now, Sister Martha?" Charlotte looked over at her. The letter was almost burning her fingers, but still she delayed pulling it out to read. She had the unsettled feeling that reading it might be just another step to change her life forever.

Sister Martha didn't try to rush her even as a bell sounded to summon those in the Gathering Family to the upper room for their meeting time. The other sisters in the room began to file out, but Sister Martha made no move to rise from her chair. So Charlotte stayed seated as well.

Sister Martha waited until the room was

empty except for the two of them before she answered. "I am well into my eighties. Perhaps as much as ninety. It's hard to keep an exact count of so many years. What are you? Seventeen?"

Charlotte smiled. "Not so young. I will turn twenty next month. I had planned to be married by then."

"Yea, it has been told us. You and Brother Edwin had such an arrangement. The sin of matrimony can cause many problems. It is good the two of you turned from such transgression and came to us unsullied."

Something in her voice made Charlotte curious. "Were you ever married? Before you became a Believer."

"I rarely bring to mind the early years of my life, but it is true that I was guilty of the sin of matrimony before I joined with the Believers when they first came to this place. My husband had left me and I thought him dead, but our worldly ties had caused us much misery. I have grown greatly in spirit since I came to Harmony Hill. As you can as well if you will put worldly desires behind you. Peace and love are the rewards of a faithful Believer."

"So you are happy here?"

"Happiness." The word was a soft sigh on Sister Martha's breath. She studied Charlotte before she asked, "Is that the reason you delay reading the letter? Because you fear it will not bring you happiness?"

Charlotte looked down at the envelope, then back at Sister Martha's kind face. "Perhaps."

"Ah well, then it is time you learned one of our teachings. Happiness does not so much depend on circumstances as we think. Within our souls the foundations must abide."

"How do I build such a foundation?"

"Alas, it is not a foundation we can undertake to build ourselves. We must offer the building stones of faith and obedience to the Master Builder so that he can put that foundation in our souls." Sister Martha pushed up out of her chair and hung it back on the pegs before she turned back to Charlotte. "Now read your letter, my sister. You can overcome whatever it says with the help of the Master Builder."

Sister Martha lightly touched Charlotte's cheek before she smiled and shuffled out the door. Charlotte let the silence of the room fall around her. Above her head she could hear the sound of the other sisters and brothers in the house practicing their dances. There was no fury to the sound. The fury of the spirit seemed only to come in the meetinghouse on Sunday. Everything was disciplined and sedate in the practice hours.

She stared once more at Selena's writing on the envelope, and the one prayer she had been able to pray before she came to the Shakers whispered through her mind. *Lord, give me courage.* She took a deep breath, slipped the sheet of stationery out of the envelope, and unfolded it with trembling fingers. The letter was not from her father. At least not directly.

Dearest Charlotte,
    It pains me to write this letter on behalf of your father, but he has demanded I do so and as a devoted wife I can do no less than honor his wishes. Charles cannot understand why you would leave the home where he has always attended to your every need as he has never had anything but your best interests at heart. Your irresponsible and

ungrateful behavior in the face of
that devoted caring has wounded
him deeply. In time I feel sure he may
be able to look upon this whole silly
affair with more sympathy but until I
am able to help him understand that
young women sometimes make rash
and foolish decisions they come to
regret and persuade him to look
more favorably upon you once more,
he has ordered me to inform you that
he has no desire to see you or
correspond with you at this time. He
feels you have deserted him and
Grayson and so has washed his
hands of you and states he no
longer has a daughter.

Perhaps I should not have written
that last, but I thought it best for you
to realize the extent of the injury you
have done him. And at a time when
he needed your unfailing support as
his staunch Unionist beliefs are
causing some problems here at
Grayson. It appears this area is quite
overrun with those who sympathize
with the South and do not see the
same need to preserve the Union at

all costs as Charles does. It is good he is not up for re-election this summer. Being cloistered in that strange village, you may not be aware of the division happening in families all around us. But at least you should be safe and I hear well fed.

Be assured I will so inform you when I have convinced Charles to soften his stance. I trust young Edwin is well.

Your ever loving stepmother, Selena

Charlotte folded the letter and slid it back in the envelope. She sat without moving on the edge of the narrow Shaker bed and let the darkening air of the evening gather around her. Above her head the thumps of the Shakers' feet continued. She pulled off her Shaker cap and stared at its whiteness in her hand. What had she done? It had seemed the only way at the time, but now she could see no way.

What was it Sister Martha had told her? That the foundations of happiness had to reside in one's soul. But her foundations lay

in ruins. The other Charlotte, the one waiting to pick up her life at Grayson, was lost. If
only she could find Mellie. Mellie would tell
her the other Charlotte could yet be found,
but Mellie was the same as lost to her too.

All she had left was this Sister Charlotte. Safe and well fed.

She crumpled the cap in her hand, but
then very carefully smoothed it out again
and put it back on her head before she
stood up and went to the chest to pull the
bottom drawer all the way out. She anchored a corner of the letter in the crack
where the side and the back of the chest
joined above the paper she had wedged
there on the first day she was at Harmony
Hill. Her fingers caressed that paper before she pulled it out. It was too dark to
see now, but she unfolded the paper anyway and stared down at it. She knew the
lines that were there. The lines of her face,
the other Charlotte, drawn by the artist. By
Adam. And instead of her face, she saw
his as she wondered where his unexpected roads had taken him.

19

The double Shaker staircases were incredibly beautiful as they rose seemingly without support to the two upper floors. One side of the risers kissed up against the curve of the wall as the stairs wound up in a spiral, but the other side with its curling wooden railing seemed suspended in air. One stairway was for the men and the other for the sisters, stated the old elder with Adam. To Adam's surprise, the Shakers had not shown the least bit of hesitance to have part of their village featured in *Harper's*.

"We wish all to know the peace and

serenity of our village, and if that peace can be felt by gazing on a drawing depicting our spiral staircases, then we have no desire to withhold sight of it from those of the world. Yea, we must do all the good we can in all the ways we can as often as we can to all the people we can," Elder Logan said as he stood back to allow Adam clear view of the stairways.

"Sounds like a good creed to have," Adam said.

"Not a creed. Simply our duty as Believers," Elder Logan corrected him mildly.

Adam went to the stairs and ran his hand gently along the curving cherry handrail. Sam was going to be happy. "Who came up with the design?" he asked.

"Some years ago, a young man in our Society, Micajah Burnett, demonstrated a gift for design. The Ministry sent him to school to develop his gift, and his dedicated work brought much good to Harmony Hill and to other Shaker villages as well. It is his design that allows the air to flow freely through our buildings and lets the unhealthy stale air escape through our roofs. Our rooms are full of light because he designed them so. That saves lamp oil and candles and improves our efficiency."

"But whoever designed these stairways surely had beauty in mind," Adam said as he stared up through the spiraling stairs to get their lines in his head.

"Not beauty. Utility and proper conservation of space. True beauty lies in an object's usefulness."

"Do the other buildings have such stairways too?" Adam asked.

"Nay. The more common staircases well serve the purpose in our family houses. If you desire to see them, I will take you there."

"Not right now." Adam stepped back and opened his sketchbook. "It's best I complete the task at hand, but before I leave I would greatly appreciate having a tour of your village." Adam looked over at Elder Logan as he added, "And I would like to also attend a worship meeting if outsiders are allowed to do so."

"At times in the summer we have open meetings for those of the world. While the spirit rarely comes upon our gatherings at those times, the watchers show great curiosity as we go forth to labor the dances. We once thought such open worships might be a way to bring converts into our Society, but history has shown that rarely to be the case. Most watchers from the world are simply curious. I doubt we will open our services to any this year with the unsettledness of the country and the threat of war." Elder Logan studied Adam for a moment. "And why do you wish to watch? Do you have an interest in learning the true Shaker way?"

"No. Only the same curiosity that you spoke of others having." Adam answered with honesty. "And the desire to draw your worship for others who might be curious as well."

"Is everything a drawing to you, Mr. Wade?"

"It is my work," Adam said.

"That is an answer we as Believers can understand. Work is as much a part of our worship here as the dancing that seems to so amuse the world. We believe the Eternal God is a part of any work we do, and therefore it is a grievous sin to do that work in a slipshod manner." Elder Logan peered over Adam's shoulder at the beginning lines of the stairway on his sketchpad. "You have been blessed with talent. Do you allow the Lord to guide your hand?"

Adam smiled and answered without looking up at Elder Logan. "I've always guided my own hand."

"And you prefer that thought?" Elder Logan asked but didn't wait for an answer. "I much prefer the idea of our heavenly Father guiding our occupations as Mother Ann taught us to believe."

"Is she still among you? Your Mother Ann. Would she allow her likeness drawn?"

"Nay, she only lives among us in spirit now, but perhaps you are capturing something of her likeness in the lines of our staircase."

"A Shaker sister might be a better avenue to capturing her spirit," Adam suggested. "Perhaps one who is young and fair of face? Too often I have seen Shakers portrayed in an unflattering light."

"That matters naught to us insofar as our outward looks are concerned. Beauty as the world judges it is not important to us. Only the inward peace and love that shines through from the windows to our souls." The elder pointed to his eyes. "That is the desire of a Believer."

Adam looked up from his sketch pad at the elder. While the man's face was deeply lined from years of living, his light brown eyes sparkled with the energy of a much younger man, and he seemed to radiate a calm acceptance of the world around him. "I do see peace in your eyes."

The elder stared back at him. "I fear I cannot say the same of your eyes, my brother."

"What do you see?" Adam asked with an amused smile.

"You ask that question in some jest, but I will answer with none." The elder looked at him with gentle kindness as he said, "I see someone forever seeking."

"Seeking what?" Adam's smile faded as he waited for the elder's answer. Somehow the conversation had been turned from him trying to understand the Shakers to trying to understand himself. When Elder Logan kept looking at him and didn't speak right away, Adam tried to rush his response. "Truth? Fame? Success? Love? What?"

The elder smiled now with a tinge of sad understanding as he finally answered, "That is a question only the seeker can answer. We here at Harmony Hill know the answers we seek, and we guide those who come into our village to live in such a way that true and worthy answers may be found for each of them."

"Do you try to convert all who come into your village?" Adam laughed to cover up his unease.

"Only those who might be seeking our answers."

"That's not me. I'm just here to do some illustrations of your buildings and perhaps some of your people if you agree to it. Maybe I could draw you." It was easier to think of lines on a paper than questions of the soul.

Before the elder could answer, a young Shaker sister came in the door. Even before she spoke, Adam was shaping the lines of her face. The cap hid most of her dark hair except for a few tendrils along the side of her face. Her skin was fair and her eyes even bluer than his brother Jake's. She wore nothing to enhance her beauty, but there was a pureness to her face that made jewels or lace unnecessary. She almost glowed with innocence. With little thought of what he was doing, he turned the page on his sketchpad and began capturing her face. She was the perfect Shaker sister he had asked to draw.

She turned her eyes downward at his blatant stare and spoke to Elder Logan. "Forgive me for interrupting. I seek Sister Altha. I thought she asked me to find her here, but I must be mistaken." She eased backward toward the door as she spoke.

"Nay, you are in the proper place, Sister Gemma. Sister Altha asked that you wait here for a moment while she spoke with Eldress Susan. And that is well, since our visitor was seeking one such as you to draw. Do you mind if he captures your image on his paper?"

"Nay, I do not mind," the young sister said with a quick smile toward Adam. "Not so long as such is not improper and I don't have to stand motionless overlong. A posture of silent stillness is not a gift I have attained as yet."

"I sketch very quickly," Adam assured her and was rewarded with another smile.

He drew with fast strokes of his pencil. "What are your gifts then, Sister?"

She seemed disconcerted by his direct question and lowered her eyes to the floor again.

Elder Logan answered for her. "Sister Gemma is gifted with kindness and patience. She often guides our novitiate sisters in adjusting to their new life. She is working with a new sister now." Elder Logan turned toward the young sister. "How is Sister Charlotte doing? She seemed to have a conflicted spirit when last I saw her."

Adam's hand froze and his head came up at the name. But there were many Charlottes. The Charlotte he longed to see was in Virginia. He looked back down at his sketch and began shading in the girl's face as she answered the elder.

"She works hard to satisfy the duties required of her, but she has not yet left behind her worldly thinking. Sister Martha said she received a letter from the world yesterday, and she seems much subdued today." A fleeting look of concern chased across the young sister's face.

"Has she confessed her worry to you?"

Elder Logan seemed to have no concern that Adam was listening to them talk of the new sister convert.

"Nay. She is to make confession to Sister Altha, not me."

"I see. Where is our new sister now?"

"In the ironing room at the Gathering Family House. I am not gifted with pressing. I always scorch something, but Sister Charlotte is in capable hands with Sister Dulcie helping her to learn the proper methods while I assist Sister Altha this week. Sister Altha has need to write to our sister societies and her arthritis makes such difficult."

Adam couldn't keep from smiling at the thought of the Charlotte he knew, the senator's daughter, trying to press anything other than perhaps a flower between the pages of a book. While she might not have been the usual Southern belle with her peculiar penchant for honesty, she certainly would have never picked up an iron. She had servants for that. He doubted she would even know what an iron looked like. He shook his head a little at the image that came to mind of Charlotte in Shaker dress, wielding an iron. That was too ridiculous to even consider. He would not find Charlotte Vance among the Shakers.

An older woman came in the door behind the young sister called Gemma. Her eyes narrowed and her mouth screwed up in a sour look when she saw Adam. It was the same old sister he'd seen on the path weeks before. The woman whose sketch had made Sam Johnson shudder. But Adam felt as if the spirits were smiling down on him as he began sketching her face in the corner above the young sister's. The contrast was remarkable.

"What goes on here?" she asked, turning her frown on Elder Logan. "I thought this man was to draw our stairways. If so, why does it appear Sister Gemma is the object of his eye?"

Elder Logan didn't seem upset by the old sister's cross tone. "He wanted to draw a young sister, and so when Sister Gemma came, I allowed him to sketch her face. I saw no harm in that."

"There's always harm when one of the world comes among us."

"Please, Sister Altha, we must be considerate of our guest."

"Yea, it is so." The old sister turned toward Adam and almost lost her frown. "I ask your forbearance and forgiveness. I spoke without kindness."

"Don't be concerned on my account. I'm grateful to be allowed to do the drawings. Especially of the stairways. My editor is very anxious to have that illustration for his newspaper." Adam gave her the smile that generally won him whatever he wanted from women, but it only brought a scowl back to her face as she ushered the younger sister down the hall and into one of the rooms out of sight. The door snapped shut behind them.

"I hope you spoke truth when you said you sketched quickly, for I have doubts that Sister Altha will allow Sister Gemma to return." Elder Logan smoothed his hand over his mouth as if to rub away a smile.

"She didn't seem too happy with the idea." Adam turned his sketchbook back to the lines of stairs climbing the wall. "But worry not. I got enough. My mind captures the image of a face as I sketch, much the way those newfangled picture boxes do, and then I can recall that image and finish the details of the sketch even if the subject is no longer actually in front of my eyes. For some reason I have more difficulty with inanimate objects, when it would seem that those would be the easier to draw since they don't move."

"Take all the time you need to properly do your work. One of Mother Ann's basic teachings that all Believers must take to heart is to do our work as if we have a thousand years to live, and as if we might die tomorrow. Such advice would serve even an artist of the world well, I should think."

"I hope it doesn't take me a thousand years to get this right," Adam said as he rubbed away one of his lines. Simply getting the correct curvature of the handrail wasn't enough. He wanted to capture its innate grace.

Later, with three sketches of Sam's stairways safely tucked away, Adam wandered out of the building where those of the world were greeted and lodged. He would sleep in one of the upper rooms come nightfall. When he had followed Elder Logan up one of those beautiful stairways to the room he'd been assigned, Adam had been more than pleased with the light that had flooded the room. If he rose early enough in the morning, he should be able to complete the drawings to leave with Elder Logan, who had promised to post them to Sam come Monday morning. It was an added convenience that the Shakers operated a postal office right there in the village.

"We try to be self-sufficient inasmuch as we are able," Elder Logan had told him. "And then we market our excess to the world along with the many other items we produce with an eye on the needs of those with whom we trade. However, I must confess the current threat of conflict very much concerns us as it threatens to close our trade routes. You say you are recently from Washington. Were any there yet seeking a way to peace?"

"I wasn't privy to the circle of power, but the city is full of men responding to the President's call to arms. Peace did not seem likely."

The elder frowned and shook his head sadly. "I had feared it was such from the reports in the papers. Our traders who have come back from the states that have fallen away from the Union tell us the populace there also talk of nothing but the first battle to come. They are much more interested in buying guns than brooms and seed. As if there will no longer be need to continue sweeping or eating. And alas, that may become too true for many if bullets start flying."

"At least here in Kentucky I've heard the government is voting to stay neutral." Adam tried to offer a cheerful word for the worried man.

The frown on Elder Logan's face grew darker. "I do not see how such a policy will be possible to enforce. Already we hear of enlistment camps being set up on the state's borders both to the north and to the south to gather men into their armies. Thankfully we gather only the fruits of peace here. If only those of the world desired to do the same."

Now with the sun sinking lower in the west, Adam studied the Shaker men and women he passed on Harmony Hill's pathways to see if they carried the same peace as Elder Logan so obviously did. It was hard to tell, for many of the people he met kept their heads bent with their eyes intent on the ground at their feet. Some who did glance up at him seemed to begrudge his presence on their pathways, as if simply being near one from the world might taint the peace they sought. A few turned and followed a different path that kept them from passing close to him.

~ A bell rang, perhaps to signal the end of the working day, because more men and women began filing out of the various buildings and walking toward the larger family houses. Adam moved off the pathway to keep from being an obstruction to their orderly flow. He leaned against a tree and wondered how it would be to live such a cloistered life.

He searched their faces as they passed by for some hint of why they might have withdrawn from the world. Were they simply seeking the perfect life of peace that Elder Logan seemed to have found? But many didn't carry the elder's peaceful expression. Some looked tired from their day's labor. Other faces were as devoid of expression as a smooth river stone. Their blank looks made Adam wonder what feelings they were taking such pains to conceal.

The men's faces were easier to see than the women's, whose features were shaded by their white bonnets. The few female faces he did glimpse brought to mind the old sister's suspicious look rather than young Gemma's easy smile. Perhaps because it was only the older sisters who dared look his way. The younger women kept their eyes so diligently on the path in front of them that Adam would not have been surprised to see one of them stoop down to retrieve a lost coin or some other bit of treasure.

The paths were emptying as the houses swallowed up the Shakers. Only a few stragglers remained, and those walked with quick steps to keep from being late for whatever was to happen next in the village. The evening meal perhaps. The sun had disappeared below the horizon and twilight was gathering. Adam felt the grumble of his own stomach as he pushed away from the tree to head back to his assigned room where Elder Logan had said someone would bring his meal.

It seemed a strange life. Everything so ordered and serene. Elder Logan claimed all strife had been removed for those who dwelt there, but how could one live in a tranquil sea day in and day out? A man needed the water of his life stirred by breezes. Else he stayed in the doldrums and wasted away for lack of challenge. And yet here were all of these men and women seeking those doldrums. It was more than Adam could understand. And certainly nothing he could ever want.

He was so deep in thought that he didn't notice the two sisters coming toward him on the pathway until the older sister put out a hand to stop the other, a young black woman, from passing too closely to him. He moved off the path to give way to them. The older sister stepped faster to move between him and the younger sister. In the fading light it was difficult to see the young sister's black face under the white cap even though she didn't duck her head away from him. Instead her eyes widened in surprise as she peeked around the older sister at him.

He stepped forward to get a better look at her face. "Do I know you?" he asked.

She seemed to want to stop, but the older sister didn't allow it as she put an arm around the girl and hurried her past Adam. "Come, Sister Melana. It is not proper for us to speak with those of the world without first receiving permission from the elders and eldresses."

"But I only wanted to ask if he'd come for her."

"His business here is no concern of ours."

"But . . ." The girl tried to look back at him, but the other sister tugged her along.

Adam watched them until they disappeared into the brick family house. Melana. Not a familiar name, but even so, something about the woman's face tugged at his memory. If he could have gotten a better look at her, then he might place where he'd seen her. Perhaps she'd been a servant from one of the great houses he'd visited in Frankfort, and now she'd found freedom here with the Shakers.

But who in the world would she think he might have come for? He shook his head a little as he started back down the path. She must have mistaken him for someone else. He knew no one among the Shakers.

20

The day after Selena's letter came, Charlotte got up at the sound of the rising bell. She knelt in pretense of prayer. She put on the Shaker dress and cap and went into their biting room where she forced food into her stomach. She listened to Dulcie's chatter in the pressing room as she pushed the iron across the fabric. And she was glad for the toil that brought sweat to her face and made her shoulders ache, because it took some of her mind off the ache in her heart.

She had lost her home. Her life. She had nothing. She who had always planned and arranged and made things happen as she wished. Now there were no wishes left. Grayson would never be hers. She had nothing left but this shell of Charlotte Mayda Vance that the ones around her called Sister Charlotte. Her father had cut her off. In spite of Selena's words to the contrary, Charlotte knew the woman would see that the wound never healed. She had outflanked Charlotte once more.

She couldn't blame it all on Selena. She was the one who had let foolish pride set her feet on this strange path. She should have stayed at Grayson and kept her place. They couldn't have forced her to go to Virginia. Her father wouldn't have pushed her out the door. But no, Charlotte had gone through that door herself. Had run out that door.

The thought tormented her as she pushed the heavy irons over the woven fabric of the sheets. She didn't want to think. She closed her mind to everything but the task at hand. Pick up one iron and move it back and forth until it cooled and then pick up another one to do the same.

Dulcie touched her shoulder when it was time for the evening meal and led her out of the pressing room to where Gemma waited. Gemma was smiling, talking about a man drawing a staircase. Charlotte paid scant attention as she let Gemma's words float on the surface of her mind like leaves on a still pond. If she started listening, really listening, her mind might awaken and she would have to think of losing Grayson again.

She sat at the evening meal and didn't dip any food onto her plate even when Gemma edged the bowls of potatoes and beans closer to her. Sister Altha frowned at her across the table but could say nothing because speaking wasn't allowed in the room where they ate. Each group of four Shakers had their own set of serving bowls in front of them so that no one had to ask for a bowl to be passed. The food was good and plentiful, but Gemma had greatly stressed that Charlotte must Shaker her plate, which meant she must eat every bite of whatever she might take from the bowls. Charlotte had forced down the morning meal and the meal at noon, but now she only stared at her empty plate and was glad no food was there. What was it Selena had written? That at least she would be well fed.

After the meal was over, they once again knelt in silent prayer before filing out of the biting room to retire to their rooms for a time of rest and meditation.

Sister Altha stopped Charlotte in the hallway. "Are you unwell, Sister Charlotte?" There was no hint of sympathy in her voice.

"Nay," Charlotte answered.

"You did not eat."

"I felt no appetite."

"A Believer must take care of her body in order to maintain proper health and strength for her duties."

"Yea, so you have told me. I will eat tomorrow." Charlotte said the words she thought Sister Altha wished to hear. She just wanted the woman to go away so she could return to her dark box and shut away all thought.

But Sister Altha was not satisfied with Charlotte's answer. "Is there some wrong you have need to confess? Sin can fester in one's soul and lead to blackness of the mind. But with proper confession, Mother Ann can bring your spirit back into harmony."

"Yea, so you have told me."

Sister Altha stood unmoving in front of her waiting for Charlotte to say more. When Charlotte didn't speak, Sister Altha's face tightened with disapproval before she said, "I fear, my sister, that you seek the blackness of sin and that your presence here is nothing but a farce."

"Nay, Sister Altha. I want to learn the Shaker way." What other choice did she have now? She had no place to go. She would become Sister Charlotte. She would learn to dance in worship. She would work with her hands. She would never again stand and let a servant dress her in a ball gown she could not button or unbutton. That Charlotte was gone, lost to her own foolishness.

That didn't mean she would never see Grayson again. She would. Somehow. Some way. But until she figured out that new way, she'd bide her time here among these strange people where, as Selena had written, she would be safe and well fed. The war that was threatening the country seemed far removed from this place where peace was sought by all true Believers. And sometimes found. Edwin claimed to have found it. Gemma wore it like a crown of light. Eldress Sadie preached it. Sister Martha knew it. Sister Altha demanded it.

Peace. If it was all around her, then surely some of it would wear off on her no matter what else was happening at Grayson or in the country. She had told Adam Wade she was going to do the unexpected. But she had not expected the road she chose to be so full of crooks and turns that even she had not foreseen.

She remembered Mellie's words as they rode into the village a few weeks earlier. How she'd said they were being swallowed by a whale just as Jonah had been in the Bible story. The village seemed that different and strange. But the three days in the belly of Jonah's whale was long past, and here she remained with no hope of being spit out for a second chance for many more days.

All she could do was bend her spirit, wipe away her thoughts, and search for the right words to pray when she knelt in obedience to the Shaker rules. They did not order her to silently pray any special words. The prayer was to be from her heart. Perhaps she could discover the proper words to convince the Lord to let her be spit out of the belly of the whale the same as Jonah was once he prayed with a reformed heart.

Mellie. At least that was one thing that had gone right with her plan. Mellie was as safe and well fed as she was.

Charlotte was glad when Sister Altha ceased speaking and left her alone in the hallway. She was relieved when Gemma didn't think it necessary to accompany her to the outhouse. She welcomed the cool dark air that made her feel even more invisible. She wanted to walk into the shadows and dwell there for a while. Perhaps forever.

"Miss Lottie." The whisper came from the corner of the building. "Over here, Miss Lottie."

Charlotte moved toward the sound of Mellie's voice, but couldn't see her. A hand reached out and pulled her to the side of the building. Even with Mellie directly in front of her, Charlotte could barely make out her shape in the darkness. Her cap was gone, along with the large white collar and apron from her dress, and her black face melted into the night.

Mellie snatched off Charlotte's cap and turned her toward the building. "Here," she said as she handed the cap to Charlotte. "We won't be as easy to spot with the white hidden."

"What are you doing, Mellie?"

"Same as you. I told them I had to relieve myself, and then I hid out here hopin' and prayin' you'd come along without your guard before they come huntin' for me. I prayed strong as I could, and praises be, he give me the answer I wanted. The one I had to have. Thank the good Lord above." She kept her voice low, just above a whisper. "That's one thing these Shaker folks has got right. All the prayin' time. But they done messed up on a bunch of other things."

Charlotte grabbed Mellie's shoulders. "Slow down and tell me what's going on."

"I guess I better. They liable to show up after us any minute and there is a lot to tell." She rushed out the words. "Has he come for you?"

"Who?" The black sadness filled her heart. "Not Father. He . . ." She hesitated and then pushed the words out around the lump that wanted to form in her throat.

She hadn't cried when she read the letter or since, but now with Mellie there beside her, the tears wanted to break free. "He says I'm no longer his daughter."

"Who says? Massah Charles?" Mellie's voice carried disbelief. "That can't be right."

"I got a letter."

"Well, that woman must've made him write it. She got your daddy under some kind of devil spell."

"I've not only lost Father to her, Mellie. I've lost Grayson." Charlotte choked back a sob.

"You'll figure somethin' out, Miss Lottie. Don't you always." Mellie put her arms around her and pulled her close. "Didn't you figure out a way to keep that woman from sellin' me down the river? And that wasn't no easy thing."

"I'm glad I did that much right." This time Charlotte couldn't hold the sob in.

Mellie leaned back from her and shook her a little. "Now don't you go cryin' on me or I'll never get what needs sayin' said."

Charlotte swallowed hard and peered at Mellie's face, but her expression was hidden in the shadowy darkness. "All right. What needs saying?"

Mellie didn't speak right away, as if now that she had the chance to talk, she didn't know which words to say. Charlotte didn't think her heart could grow any heavier, but she was wrong. Even before Mellie spoke the words, Charlotte knew what they were going to be.

"I don't know if I ought to tell you this or not, but I's always trusted you, Miss Lottie. Nate's runnin' away. Goin' north." Again she hesitated before she pushed out the rest of her words. "I'm goin' with him, Miss Lottie."

"No, you can't do that. It won't be safe. He might get caught, and if he gets caught and you're with him, then no telling what might happen." Charlotte grabbed Mellie's arms and held onto her as though she'd never let go.

Mellie didn't try to pull away. "I has to, Miss Lottie. I love him." Her voice sounded sad, excited, and frightened all at the same time.

Charlotte loosened her hold and pulled in a deep breath. She didn't know what to say.

Mellie put her hands over Charlotte's and pulled them away from her arms. She held her hands softly as she went on. "I loves you too, Miss Lottie. You knows I do. And Mammy. Can't nobody love their mother more than I love Mammy, but we's already apart. Her there cookin' for Massah Charles 'til you figure out a way to get her free. And me here." She squeezed Charlotte's hands a little before she turned them loose. "I don't know as how I can explain, but this way I feel for Nate, it's different love. I has to go with him. Even if I die, I has to 'cause I'll die in my heart if I don't."

"Wait and get the Shakers to take you across the river. They take trips to their other villages in the north. Tell them you want to live at one of them." Charlotte's mind was racing, trying to think of a better way. "Then you can run away from there to meet up with Nate."

"You always has good plans, but I's already decided. The' ain't no turnin' back. I'm goin' tonight. Now. I got my papers." She touched her bosom and Charlotte heard a rustle of paper. "They give them to me to keep. So I'd feel free, they said. I want to feel free, Miss Lottie. Really free and not just stuck here with these folks who has a funny idea of free with all their rules and watchin' eyes. You don't really want to be here either, do you?"

"I don't know. I can't go home. So where else could I go?" Charlotte said.

"What about him? Has he come for you?"

"Has who come for me? What in the world are you talking about?" Charlotte frowned at her.

"That artist gentleman."

"Adam Wade?" Charlotte stared at Mellie with disbelief. She couldn't really be meaning that Adam was there at Harmony Hill.

"Right. The artist man. He was on the path when me and Sister Cora come back from the washhouse after our workin' time."

"Are you sure?" Charlotte asked with doubt in her voice even as she was remembering Gemma's chatter about somebody drawing the spiral staircases in the visitors' house. She hadn't paid attention to the words then. She was too busy shutting everything out, but now they echoed in her brain. She'd said the man from the world had even drawn her likeness.

"Sure as night follows day. We passed right by him. But Sister Cora, she wouldn't let me say nothin' to him. More of them rules."

"Did he know you?"

"He didn't act like it. It was goin' on dark and me with the Shaker garb on. Well, it ain't no wonder he didn't know me. He only talked to me that one time at the party anyhow. It was Mammy he drew the picture of. She liked that."

"He drew my picture too." Charlotte thought of the drawing hidden behind the drawer in the chest. But the face on that paper was the old Charlotte. The lost Charlotte. Not this woebegone Sister Charlotte who followed after the other sisters like a blind sheep and bent her will to theirs.

"He done more than that." Mellie leaned her head over very close to Charlotte's face until Charlotte could see her eyes gleaming in the early darkness. "Remember I saw you in the garden 'fore he left, and I already tol' you a man kisses a woman like that he aims to be back."

"He can't be here for me. How would he even know I'm here?" Charlotte tried to ignore the way hope fluttered awake in her heart just at Mellie's crazy imagining that Adam Wade had come for her.

"Somebody coulda tol' him. Maybe your papa."

"Father wouldn't tell him. He wouldn't tell anybody. Me being here is not only an embarrassment to him, the general knowledge of it might cost him votes. Think how the opposing party could use it against him. The senator's daughter running away from home. Dancing like a heathen in church."

"Not like heathens. Leastways most of the time. Most times they could be right at Grayson dancin' in the big room," Mellie said.

"But not for the same reason."

"For sure. It ain't to catch a man." Mellie blew a snort of air out her nose. Silence stretched between them for a moment before she went on. "You can go home, Miss Lottie. The Massah, he won't stay mad at you once he sees you face-to-face. He'll be like that daddy in the Bible what runs to meet his wayward boy." Mellie's voice was soft, urging.

"There wasn't a stepmother in that story," Charlotte said.

"You's right there," Mellie agreed, but then her voice softened again. "But he's loved you longer than he has her."

Charlotte stared down at the ground as she said, "I can't go home. At least not yet. I'm not starving. There's no need for me to look at the pig food with hungry eyes like the prodigal son in that story. There's plenty of food here. I am safe and well fed." Charlotte's ending words were flat, without feeling.

"Then if you don't want to go home, go find that artist feller. He's got to be still here. It was nigh dark when I saw him."

"No." The word came out sharp and clipped.

"I's hearin' a lot in that no, Miss Lottie. I know you good as I knows myself. Maybe better. You in love with that man."

Charlotte didn't have to be able to see Mellie's face to know how she was staring at her with narrowed eyes, seeing straight through her even in the darkness. She didn't try to argue with Mellie. Not now. Not when her heart was already too bruised to think about love. Instead she grabbed Mellie's wrist. "You can't tell him I'm here."

"You's right there. I can't tell him nothin'. Remember. I'm leavin' with Nate. Soon's we get through huggin' and cryin' our goodbyes." Mellie put her other hand gently over

Charlotte's. "You's the one that needs to tell him. You's the one he's come for."

"He's not here for me. He's here for his work. To draw the Shakers." She said the words as firmly as she could, not for Mellie, but to keep hope from spreading its wings and trying to take flight in her own heart. Adam Wade had no plans that included Charlotte. No one did. Not even Mellie.

"Then ask that sour old Sister Altha to let him draw you." There was a smile in Mellie's voice. "That ought to get things rollin' in the right direction."

"Oh, Mellie, I don't know what I'll do without you." Charlotte pulled her close and breathed in the familiar scent of her hair and skin. "I'm so afraid for you."

"Don't you be scared for me. You done give me a chance. You give me my papers. They say up north a black face don't have to be turned down to the ground all the time. That a person like me can be hired out and collect her own pay. Nate and me, we'll be all right. The Union army ain't signin' Negroes up to fight, but they's usin' them to build bridges and roads. He hears tell that them Yankees ain't all that worried about whether a man has papers. Not so long as he has a strong back."

"I'll pray for you," Charlotte said and she meant it. She'd have a purpose now when she knelt to pray as the Shakers demanded. She reluctantly stepped back from Mellie.

"And me for you." Then in the darkness Charlotte saw Mellie's teeth shine as her smile spread across her face. "That you and that artist gentlemen will meet up in some more gardens. Maybe he'll ask you home to walk in his garden."

"I don't think he even has a home."

"You don't have to have walls and a roof, Miss Lottie. Where the most of your heart is, that's where home can be." Mellie touched Charlotte's cheek. "Mine's with Nate, but I'll be leavin' a chunk of it here with you." She pulled her hand away as she turned to go. She stopped before she went two steps and turned back. With tears in her voice, she said, "When you go home to Grayson and see Mammy agin, you tell her I'm takin' her love ever' bit with me."

And then she was gone. Melting away in the darkness. Charlotte stood very still staring after her. She could just make out

Mellie, and then another figure rose up out of the grass and joined her before the two disappeared into the trees beyond the village houses. Charlotte watched the spot for a long time before she finally looked up at the dark sky and was glad for the clouds that covered the stars and moon. "Keep it dark, dear Lord, and lead her steps safely over the river."

No prayer had ever risen more sincerely from her heart. She stepped back up on the pathway and positioned her cap over her hair. She would not think about her father or Grayson. She would not think about Adam Wade somewhere in the village. He had not come to Harmony Hill seeking her. If he saw her in the Shaker dress, he would laugh at her foolishness. It was all a game with Adam. A game he had won with the kiss he had stolen from her before he left. He would have no interest in playing another round. She could not let him see her here.

She mashed her lips together tightly so that she wouldn't recall the softness of his lips on hers. She would not allow her mind to run after him. She would not allow her heart to yearn for his touch. Mellie was

wrong. She wasn't in love with him. It had
been a game to her too. A silly game she
had no chance of winning any more than
she'd had any chance of pulling Edwin
away from the Shakers. She had gravely
underestimated Edwin's need for spiritual
peace and order in his life.

And now she would continue down the
path she had chosen perhaps without
proper thought, but even so her feet were
upon it. If she was going to forget about
Charlotte Mayda Vance and become simply Sister Charlotte seeking the gifts of
simplicity and peaceful harmony, then she
would do it the best she could. She would
dwell on obedience and prayer the way
Sister Altha told her to. She would learn
to work. She would let more sincere
prayers rise from her soul. And she would
be safe and well fed.

The next morning, she filed out of her
room with all the other sisters when the village bell rang to summon them to meeting. She didn't sing loudly, but she did add
her voice to the gathering song. She went
into the meetinghouse determined to be a
proper novitiate. She had not expected to
see Adam Wade on a bench just inside the

door. He had his sketchbook open, drawing feverishly. She turned her head away before he could look up and see her face.

The Shaker mother must have taken pity on her at that moment and moved Sister Martha up beside her instead of Sister Altha. She took hold of Sister Martha's arm and whispered, "I feel sick, Sister Martha. I fear I might lose my breakfast. Please may I return to my room?"

"My dear sister, you are pale as a sheet." Sister Martha's wrinkled face looked concerned. "Lean on me and I will take you across to the infirmary."

Charlotte peeked out of the corner of her eyes. Adam had raised his head and was looking her way. She couldn't let him recognize her. She couldn't. He would think she had lost her mind. And he wouldn't be too wrong. A tremble chased through her as she tugged her cap down to cover her face.

Sister Martha patted her arm. "There, there, child. Calm yourself. We will find some medicine to ease your stomach."

Charlotte attempted a weak smile toward the old woman as they caused a disruption in the orderly stream of sisters coming in the door and pushed past them out into the open air, but she doubted there was medicine for what ailed her. Her heart was pounding at the thought of the artist in the room behind her. If only he had come for her.

As she let the old sister lead her across to the large stone building, Charlotte looked over her shoulder at the last of the sisters going in the meetinghouse. She tried to tell herself she was glad she'd escaped without Adam seeing her. She was. She couldn't have borne his laughter. Yet each step away from the meetinghouse took more effort as her heart yearned to once more stand in front of him, gaze into his blue gray eyes, and hear his voice in her ears.

With a start, Charlotte realized Mellie was right. Charlotte had allowed herself to fall in love with Adam Wade. Oh dear heavenly Father. She had done nothing right for weeks.

21

By the time the big bell sounded to summon the Shakers to worship, Elder Logan had already ushered Adam inside the meetinghouse and to a bench just inside the doors. Adam would have preferred the opposite side of the large open room to get a better view of the Shakers' faces as they came in, but he didn't complain as he settled on the bench with his sketchpad to wait. There would be plenty of faces and scenes to capture from any direction.

His fingers had been tingling with the anticipation of sketching something new and different ever since the elder had informed Adam after breakfast that he would be allowed to do illustrations of their worship experience.

"As long as you behave respectfully," the old man had added.

Adam didn't plan to be anything but respectful. At least outwardly. His inward thoughts were between him and the good Lord. Not that he expected the Lord to pay much attention to anything he thought. The Lord would be more than occupied with listening to the prayers his faithful worshipers all across the country would be sending up to him on this Sunday morning or maybe watching these Shakers dance their worship to him.

Adam hadn't expected the Shakers to start singing before they were inside the building, but minutes after the bell rang, one voice began and others joined in, the sound growing stronger by the minute. The Shakers' voices lifted into the air, alerting the Lord that they were coming. It was a sound of holiness. A sound of deep commitment. Something he'd never felt except to his art. But as he listened, chills walked up and down his spine.

Then as each Shaker stepped through

the door into the meetinghouse—the men through one door and the women through another—he or she fell silent. Inside there was only the sound of soft-soled shoes moving across the wooden floor to the benches while outside the song went on.

Adam searched through the faces. Not because he expected to know any of the Shakers, but because he wanted to understand these people as he sketched them. Why had they chosen to abstain from the normal impulses of life to dedicate themselves to worship and working in this cloistered community? He supposed he was dedicated to work. He'd given up most of the usual pursuits of a man his age and instead lived in pursuit of his next picture. But that work was for him. It wasn't worship, as Elder Logan claimed the Shakers' work to be.

So many people. Many more than he had expected. He'd seen them on the pathways, but it seemed different when they all filed into the building. He spotted Edwin Gilbey. So the man had done as he said and come to live in the village. He saw the young sister, Gemma, and mentally reviewed his sketch of her to be sure he'd done justice to her beautiful face. He let his eyes dwell extra long on the few black faces under the caps all the sisters wore, but he didn't see the black sister who'd tried to talk to him on the pathway the night before. Or perhaps he simply didn't recognize her in the light of the day.

But there was the older sister who had hurried the two of them past him. Her face, so stern and unyielding the night before, now looked troubled as she glanced to the left and right as though searching for someone. Perhaps the same sister his eyes were seeking. The one who thought he might be at Harmony Hill to carry someone away from the Shakers' paradise. When the woman caught him watching her, she glared at him without welcome before going on across the room to take her place on the benches.

Adam pushed aside the distraction of his curiosity about the missing black sister to start drawing the Shakers spilling into the meetinghouse. A disturbance at the sisters' door pulled his attention away from his sketch as one of the sisters abruptly turned to go the opposite direction. Not a usual oc-currence if the frowns that darkened the other sisters' faces were any indication as she pushed between them back toward the door. An ancient-looking Shaker sister took hold of the younger one's elbow and joined the rebel Shaker sister moving against the flow of women entering the meetinghouse.

He wondered at first if the younger one might be the Negro sister he had been watching for, but then she reached up to pull her cap down and her hand was white as a lily. Not the hand of a working woman, but the hand of a lady. He kept his eyes on the top of her cap as she and the old sister managed to make it past the line of inflowing sisters to the door. Something about her tickled his memory.

He stood up to follow her for a better look, but a Shaker brother stepped in front of him. "You must stay on the visitors' bench until all are inside and, then if you wish to leave our meeting you must do so quietly out the brothers' door, my friend." His voice was firm. He looked to be in his middle years with a barrel chest and muscular arms that stretched tight the sleeves of his dark coat. There was no way Adam could push him aside to go check out the departing sister if the man didn't give ground.

"Sorry." Adam stayed where he was. "I'm not accustomed to the separate doors for the sexes. I was simply concerned for the sister who was leaving. Do you think she was ill?"

"If so, Sister Martha will see to it that she has proper care." The man settled his eyes on Adam for a moment before he asked, "Did you know her in the world before she came here?"

"I'm not sure. I didn't get a good look at her, but something about her seemed familiar. Who is she?"

"She's new to our Society and her name escapes my memory. There are many sisters." The man looked over his shoulder toward the sisters' door now empty as the last of the Shakers had come into the building. "I can ask another if you have need to know, but our meeting is commencing and silence at the proper times is expected."

"Yes, of course. Forgive me. I promised Elder Logan I would abide by the rules and not disrupt your service in any way."

"That would be well."

It wasn't exactly a threat, but Adam noted that the man sat on a bench near him instead of crossing the room to join the other Shaker brethren as they sat ramrod straight on their rows of benches, facing the sisters perched primly on like benches across from them. For a brief moment, Adam considered breaking his promise and doing something outrageous like asking one of the sisters to dance, simply because he hated rules for rules' sake. He glanced over at the Shaker brother who continued to watch him warily. There was little doubt the man would escort Adam out of the building and perhaps the village if he had such a lapse of good sense. So he swallowed his penchant for rebellion, turned to a fresh sheet in his sketchpad, and settled down to work.

The first dances were sedate enough. The Shakers marched back and forth and then made circles within circles as the lines of men and women wove around each other in obviously practiced patterns of movement. Some of the faces were animated as they sang and danced. Others were stiff and without expression. Occasionally on some signal that Adam never caught, the entire body would clap their hands or stomp their feet. There were no musical instruments other than the voices of the singers. The songs were simple and repetitious and the dances almost hypnotic as they shuffled back and forth in time to the voices.

Then just as Adam was wondering if all the reports of the Shakers' wild dancing had been nothing more than stories, the mood in the building changed. He could almost feel the charge in the air when the singers picked up the tempo and many of the dancers also started singing. The sound bounced off the walls and sent some of the dancers into a frenzy as the order of the dance completely broke down. A good number of the men and women began to throw their hands and feet out wildly as they leaped about in no particular fashion while shouts and screams against the devil took the place of the singing. Rules had obviously flown out the window, and those Shakers under the spirit were dancing and shouting in whatever way the spirit led them.

Adam stopped sketching and stared. He spotted Edwin Gilbey with his eyes closed and trembling violently before he collapsed to the floor. A couple of the brethren pulled him off to the side. He saw the stern sister who had worn such a dark frown as she had shooed the young Sister Gemma from his sight the day before now wearing a peaceful, otherworldly look on her face as she spun in place with her hands lifted to heaven. A few of the younger-looking Shaker men were jumping into the air and making whooping noises with their hands clapping against their mouths as if they were children playing Indians.

A Shaker woman stopped her leaping directly in front of Adam to stare at his face as she shouted, "Away from me, Satan." She pushed the palms of her open hands toward him and began stomping, and the intensity of her feeling twisted her plain features into something fierce. Others caught the stomping fever from her until the building vibrated with the banging of feet against the floor. Some added to the noise by slapping their hands on the benches as if they were drums.

The man Adam had thought remained close by to guard the Shakers against his presence now moved in front of Adam to protect him from the fury that had overtaken so many of the Shakers but that seemed not to have affected him in any manner. Adam looked over the man's shoulder and caught sight of Elder Logan. He wasn't stomping or shouting, but was smiling serenely as he stood like an oasis of peace in the midst of the bedlam. Adam picked up his pencil and drew as quickly as he could. He wanted to capture that peace amid the fury.

Then as suddenly as it had started the furor died away, and those who had collapsed on the floor either crawled to the benches or were carried there by others while the remaining dancers began the orderly sedate marching back and forth. The singers' voices controlled the tempo of the meeting once more. Adam listened to the words of the song as his pen flew across the page almost without thought.

> O the simple gifts of God, they're flowing like an ocean,
> And I will strive with all my might to gather in my portion.
> I love, I love the gifts of God. I love to be partaker,
> And I will labor day and night to be an honest Shaker.

The singers repeated the song until all the Shakers had recovered from the fervor of their worship and began filing out of the building. Adam followed the last man out the proper men's door to watch the lines of Shakers walking back to their houses in disciplined columns of two. An odd people. He had thought to come among them, draw their faces, and be able to understand why they lived as they lived, but some things were beyond his understanding.

He didn't stay for the midday meal. Instead he took the food Elder Logan had kindly asked the sisters to pack for Adam's journey and headed his horse toward Frankfort. Before he went back east, he wanted to check out how the state's legislature was doing at maintaining a neutral stance and staying out of the coming conflict. Adam aimed to maintain a neutral stance too, but he had no intention of missing the conflict while his competitors sent their illustrations of the action into the living rooms of the citizens. Most in Washington thought one battle would have the Confederate states begging for mercy, but nobody expected that attack to be launched for weeks, perhaps months, as the army was still gathering.

Plus, Adam no longer had an excuse to go to Virginia since Sam Johnson had telegraphed him not to worry about that illustration of General Lee in his Rebel uniform. It had been easy enough to take a picture already on file of the general in his Federal uniform and have someone redraw him in Confederate gray. Sam knew how to satisfy his readers, but he also knew how to save a dollar.

After a couple of hours, Adam spotted a creek along a deserted stretch of the road where he could let his horse drink. The creek, full from the spring rains, sparkled in the sun as it rushed along its rocky bed in a hurry to join up with a river somewhere downstream. The day was warm, and Adam slid out of the saddle to splash the cool water up on his face. He munched on the Shakers' meat and bread and watched his horse graze. The birds were in full song over his head, and off in the distance a dog barked like it might be trailing a rabbit. Here was real peace, Adam thought. Nature's peace. He'd met few travelers even on the more populated portions of the road.

On the Sabbath, the faithful rested. He imagined his own mother and grandfather sitting in their Boston parlor in their dark Sabbath clothes. His grandfather would be reading the Bible. His little brother Harry would be trying not to doze on the couch. And Jake, well, Jake was gone from the picture now the same as Adam was. Jake was in Washington learning to march and shoot a gun. Hardly a Sabbath day occupation. Maybe Adam should have found a way to make Jake go home the way Phoebe wanted. But the boy was nineteen. A lot of the volunteers were even younger.

Adam's horse raised his head and pricked his ears forward, bringing Adam away from his thoughts. Something was running up the creek. Adam moved over to the horse and caught its reins before he reached into his saddlebag for the gun he carried there. He didn't often have occasion to pull it out, but in some of the places he'd been in the West, it was good to be prepared.

He checked the load and kept it pointed at the ground as the hairs on the back of his neck stood up. Trouble was coming. He didn't know how he knew, but he knew. The baying dog was still some distance away but getting closer. Perhaps it was on the trail of a fox or deer instead of a rabbit. His horse pranced sideways nervously, and Adam clucked his tongue to calm him as he climbed back into the saddle. It was probably just some locals out running their dog. Nothing that had to involve him in any way.

He was turning his horse away from the creek to head back to the road when he caught sight of a flash of blue through the trees that lined the creek. Adam's hands froze on the reins. It wasn't a deer the dog was trailing, but a person. He could hear the panting breaths of the runner along with the water splashing now. A runaway slave and absolutely nothing he could do to help the person as much as he might want to. It was against the law to interfere with those trying to capture a runaway. And in a godforsaken place like this, it wouldn't matter what was legal or what was not. He was liable to be shot for his trouble. Even so, he sat like a stone on his horse and waited for the poor man to come into sight.

It wasn't a man, but a woman grasping up her skirts and running through the knee-deep water. She stopped when she saw him, her eyes wide and frightened. Then she dropped her skirts down in the water and put her hands over her heart.

"Is you really there, Mr. Adam?" she gasped as she tried to catch her breath.

22

He recognized her at once. Not only as the black sister from the Shaker village, but now here with panic alive on her face, he knew why she had tried to speak to him. She was Charlotte's maid he'd met at Grayson. And it didn't matter what the law said anymore.

"How far behind you?" He got straight to the point.

"Don't know." She pushed the breathless words out as she stared back down the creek and shuddered with fear. "They wouldn't believe my papers. Tried to steal them from me."

"Grab that stick there in the water." He shoved his gun in the back of his waistband before he guided his horse down into the creek. When she obediently held up the stick, he said, "Now rip off a piece of your dress to tie to it."

She tried to do as he said, but the skirt's cloth was too tightly woven. "It won't tear."

He grasped the top of her sleeve and jerked the seam loose. She slipped it off her arm and with trembling hands managed to tie it to the stick. "What's this gonna help?"

He didn't take time to answer her as he reached for her to pull her up on his horse.

The creek water swirled around her skirt as she stared at him and didn't take his hand. "You best leave me be and ride on, Mr. Adam. They got guns. They'd a done shot me if I hadn't been worth more to them breathin'. But you, they might think it sport to shoot a Northerner like you."

"Take my hand, Mellie." He remembered the name Charlotte called her. "Hurry or my blood will be on your head."

She let him pull her up in front of him and awkwardly straddled the horse as she stuffed her full skirt under her legs. She grabbed hold of the horse's mane to steady her seat, then held up the stick with her other hand. "What am I supposed to do with this?"

"Hold on to it a minute." He walked his horse down the creek a little way until he found a spot where the bank was rocky. "Now drop it in." He watched the stick to be sure the current caught it and swept it downstream before he turned his horse to the bank. The dog was getting closer and now he heard a man shouting.

At the sound of the man's voice, Mellie began shaking so hard that Adam wrapped an arm around her waist to keep her from tumbling off the horse. She leaned back against him and whispered, "Lord a mercy, help us."

The words carried such raw feeling that even Adam hoped some higher power might be listening, but he wasn't ready to depend on that alone as he guided the horse through the trees. He wanted to kick his heels into the horse's flanks and push him to a full gallop, but it was wiser to go quietly like a fleeting shadow the chasers might not notice. Perhaps because of Mellie's simple prayer, a line of Scripture surfaced in his mind from all the passages his grandfather had forced him to memorize in his school. *Yea, though I walk through the valley of the shadow of death, I will fear no evil.*

As if Mellie had heard his thoughts, she whispered, "Puts your hand over top us, Lord, and bring us on out a this dark place."

Once back out on the road, the sun was too bright, pointing them out as something not right to anybody who might see them. A white stranger with a Negro woman in a bedraggled Shaker blue dress riding in front of him on his horse. That would be something a person would remember if the slave catchers talked to them. So maybe the darkness was more to be desired after all. Adam went off the road again at the next stand of trees. He needed to come up with a plan. He couldn't hear the dog or the men chasing Mellie anymore, so that was good. But they wouldn't give up. She must have looked like easy money to them. They'd keep looking.

When he was sure no one could see them from the road, he dismounted and helped Mellie down. Her legs almost gave way with her, and he had to hold her up until she was able to pull herself together and step away from him.

"You was an answer to prayer, Mr. Adam, but you's can go on and leaves me here now. I can make my way on to the freedom river from here."

"You're a long way from that river, Mellie. And even if you can get there, how do you plan to get across to the other side?" With the horse's reins in his hand, Adam leaned back against a tree and studied the problem in front of him. It wasn't like him to get pulled into this kind of mess. What was it Jake had said about him? That he was an observer. He didn't get involved. And now here he stood with a fugitive slave in the middle of nowhere with no idea of what to do next. "Everybody will know you're a runaway."

She lifted her chin. "I ain't no runaway. Leastwise no runaway slave like as how you're meaning. I did run away from them Shaker people, but they ain't likely to send nobody after me. They knowed I was free and could do what I wanted. Miss Lottie give me my papers." She touched her bosom. "That woman Massah Charles brung home was wantin' to sell me down the river, but Miss Lottie didn't let that happen. She took me to that Shakertown and told me to stay there where I'd be safe."

"But you didn't stay."

"I couldn't. Not after Nate come after me."

"Nate? Who's Nate?"

"He come from Grayson like me." She stared down at the ground, her defiance gone. "Only he don't have no papers. We was goin' north where that might not matter."

"Where is he? Did they catch him?"

"No, sir. Least not that I knows. I tol' him to go on. They hadn't seen him. I tol' him they couldn't take me since I had my papers." Mellie's lip trembled. "They said they didn't care about no papers. That paper burned right easy. And that good, healthy breeding stock brought top money where they was headed. I didn't wait to hear no more. I think they thought I was too scared to run, but I give them the slip and was makin' headway till they set their dog on me."

"So where's Nate now?"

She shook her head. "I ain't got no way of knowin'. I made him promise to go on. He didn't want to, but weren't no need in both of us gettin' caught. And I thought I'd be right behind him soon's as I showed them men my free papers."

"How were you supposed to find him?"

"He told me about this house up 'round the river. Some place called Maysville. Nate knew the way. He drew a map in the dirt. It just looked like chicken scratchin' to me, but I pretended I understood the way so he'd go on." She looked up at Adam. "You know where he was talkin' about?"

He met the woman's dark brown eyes. "I might be able to find out." What other choice did he have? He couldn't just leave her there. Not and ever look Charlotte in the eye again, and no matter how much he tried to deny it, he wanted to see Charlotte again. "If you do something for me first."

Fear flashed in her eyes, but then she squared her shoulders a bit and took a step toward him. "Whatever you want, I'll do."

He held his hand out to stop her when he realized what she was thinking. "Nothing like that, Mellie. I'm not a monster like those men you were running from. I just want to know where Charlotte is."

Her shoulders slumped and she mashed her mouth together. "I can't tell you that.

She asked me not to and I ain't never broke my word to Miss Lottie."

"I know she's been sent to a school in Virginia. I just need to know what town."

Mellie frowned a little and opened her mouth to say something, but then shut it tight.

"It might not be safe for her in Virginia," he added.

Mellie looked almost sad as she said, "I'd help you, Mr. Adam, but I don't know nothin' about Virginia 'cept the Shakers say there's fixin' to be a war there. You needs to go ask Massah Charles about Miss Lottie. He can tell you where she's at."

"Why's it such a secret?"

"Miss Lottie, she sometimes gets over-proud and then shamed if things don't go the way she thinks they should. What with Mr. Edwin turnin' her down and then that woman tearin' apart her home, things has gone bad lately." She looked straight at Adam's face again. "And she don't trust you, Mr. Adam. I'm thinkin' she's lovin' you, but she's not trustin' you. She thinks you's just playin' with her, that that kiss in the garden didn't mean nothin'. But I'm thinkin' she might be wrong from what I can see on your face."

"It won't matter if I can't find her."

"You two is suited. Neither one wants to admit you need any lovin', but I think Miss Lottie's findin' out different and maybe you will too."

When he just looked at her without saying anything, she sighed and went on. "I thank you for helpin' me out back there, Mr. Adam. I wouldn't have got away without you. But guess I'd better be movin' on north now." She looked around and then started off in the wrong direction.

Adam let her walk a ways before he called after her, "That's south."

She turned to look back at him. "You sure?"

"Surer than you are." He couldn't keep from laughing. "Come on back here. We need to come up with a plan."

"That's Miss Lottie too. Always with a plan. I'm hopin' yours has a better chance of workin' than that last one of hers."

"What plan was that?" Adam asked casually as if he didn't care what she answered.

"You ain't trickin' me into breakin' my word to Miss Lottie." She planted her feet on the ground and crossed her arms in front of her chest. "I done tol' you. You gonna have to ask Massah Charles. That's who."

"All right, Mellie. I know when I'm beat." He let out an exaggerated sigh as he beckoned her toward him. "No more questions about Charlotte. But we better put our heads together to figure out a way to this house in Maysville Nate told you about."

The plan was simple. They waited till almost dark and then rode in the gathering twilight to the nearest town. There at daylight, Adam bought train tickets to Maysville for him and the slave he was taking to his sister. Nobody thought a thing out of the way about it. Mellie rode in the baggage car with a few other slaves. One of them had heard about the house on the way to freedom, and he whispered what he knew to Mellie. A rusty roof with an edge of tin curled up on the left dormer, and if it was safe to come to the door, a white wooden flower box between the second and third posts on the porch.

It was late afternoon when they got off the train in Maysville and near dark before they found the house. Out of sight behind a nearby barn, Adam gave Mellie most of the money in his pockets and then smiled a little as he wrote out Phoebe's address again in case she made it all the way to Boston. Phoebe was going to have a houseful of servants before he was through, but it served her right. None of this would be happening if she hadn't insisted he do that wretched portrait of Selena Vance. But then he wouldn't have met Charlotte either, if not for Phoebe. Right now he wasn't sure if he should thank her for that or wish Charlotte from his thoughts forever. Love complicated things. Yet every time he remembered Mellie's words saying Charlotte loved him, his heart practically floated inside his chest.

He didn't go with Mellie to the house. He told her goodbye in the deepening shadows.

"The good Lord will bless you for your goodness, Mr. Adam."

"I didn't do this for the Lord," Adam said.

"I knows who you did it for. Miss Lottie." Mellie stared at him in the dim light. "If I ever sees her again, I'll tell her I ended up safe 'cause of you."

"But is she? Safe?"

"She's safe enough, but what good is it to be safe if a person don't never get the chance to know love?" She didn't expect him to give her an answer as she went on. "Me and Nate, at least we wasn't too scared to try."

"I hope you find him."

"I will. Either here or on the other side."

Adam knew she wasn't talking about the other side of the river. She brushed his hand shyly with her fingertips before she started toward the house. Then she turned back to him to say, "Ain't no need lookin' for her in Virginia."

"Did she go to the Shakers with you?" He frowned, hardly able to believe he gave that idea enough serious consideration to even speak the question aloud, but at the same time the memory of the lady's hand pulling down the Shaker cap to cover her hair popped into his mind.

Mellie stared back at him. "I just told you she wasn't in Virginia. You got to ask Massah Charles the rest of it."

And then she was slipping from shadow to shadow until she was on the porch. The door opened and hands pulled her inside.

No one saw her. He'd done what he could. For Charlotte.

The next morning, he went to the train station with no sure destination in mind. He could go to Frankfort and find Charles Vance. He could find out about Charlotte and about Kentucky's determined neutral stand. But he already knew about Charlotte. As hard as it was to believe, that had been her pushing her way out of the Shaker meetinghouse to escape his notice. He was sure of it. He was also sure if she hadn't wanted to see him two days ago, she wouldn't want to see him now.

And if she'd gone to the Shakers, it would have been to chase after Edwin Gilbey. Some plan she had, according to Mellie. A plan that hadn't worked out. But for certain a plan that included no thought of Adam.

What of his own plans? Was he going to just toss them aside because he'd kissed a pretty redhead? So what if he couldn't get her out of his thoughts. So what if every time he picked up a pen or pencil he wanted to draw her eyes. That didn't mean he had to rush back to the Shaker village to beg to see her and

perhaps suffer the humiliation of being refused. It would be better to give it time, to
see if his infatuation faded. Besides, the
war drums were beating louder. He couldn't
miss the battle chasing after a woman in
Shaker blue.

He stepped up to the ticket window and
said, "Next train to Washington, D.C."

He ignored the way his heart grew suddenly heavier. It was the right decision.
The only decision for him. He couldn't be
tied down. Not by a woman. Even one as
entrancing as Charlotte Vance. There'd be
time for love later on. After the war. After
he had the pictures he wanted.

She was safe at the Shaker village. He
smiled a little at the thought of Charlotte
living the Shaker life. It was almost more
than he could imagine. A Southern belle
in drab Shaker dress. Working with her
hands. Dancing for the Lord instead of to
capture a husband. No husband-capturing
would be going on in the Shaker village.
Not even if she was still trying to convince
Edwin Gilbey to stand by his promise to
her. That wasn't going to happen. Adam
had seen Edwin's face during the Shaker

worship. He would not give up his new-found passion with the Shaker way.

So it wasn't as if Adam had to worry about Charlotte marrying another before he returned. If he decided to return. Not as long as she was with the Shakers. While there was much he still didn't know about the Shakers, everybody knew the normal bonds of marriage were strictly taboo in their society. Charlotte would be safe both from the impending war and a hasty marriage.

Life matters shouldn't be decided in haste. If he truly loved Charlotte, if she truly loved him, a few months wouldn't make that much difference. Better to hesitate and be sure than to jump into a quagmire that might trap him forever. He believed that. He was sure of it, but even so his feet very reluctantly climbed the steps up onto the train. His mind was telling him one thing, but his heart wanted to run back in the other direction.

He found his seat and looked around to see if he could spot a likely subject for his pencil. But when he opened his sketch-book, he began drawing Charlotte's hand pulling the Shaker cap down to cover her red hair, running out the door away from him. What was it Mellie had said? That at least she and her man weren't too scared to try for freedom and love. And as he drew, he imagined a tremble in Charlotte's hand.

When he got to Washington, he sent a telegram to Senator Charles Vance. *Want to see Charlotte. Where is she?*

In spite of the drawing Adam had made on the train where every line he remembered of the Shaker sister running from the meetinghouse matched perfectly his memory of Charlotte, it seemed necessary to have absolute proof that it had really been her in that Shaker dress. Mellie had kept telling him to ask the senator.

He got a return message the next day. *In Virginia. Miss Josephine's School for Young Ladies. Tell her all well at Grayson.*

Adam read the telegram from the senator three times. Then he stared at the sketch he'd drawn on the train. And he wasn't sure which was the lie.

23

As the days passed and became weeks, Charlotte found a certain comfort in being relieved of the need to make decisions. No more plans to go awry. Instead she got up every morning at the sound of the rising bell and followed the path laid out for her. She didn't have to think. Just do.

She discovered her hands were strong and capable, work was not offensive, and a sincere prayer could take wing from her heart up toward heaven. Now when she knelt to silently pray at the appointed times, her mind didn't stay blank. At first her timidly offered prayers were for Mellie's safety and that only, but as the prayers piled up, other thoughts began to come to mind. Even when she stumbled around in her mind searching for proper words, she rose from her knees with a lighter spirit. In her heart the assurance grew that someday, somehow there would be answers. She prayed for Grayson and her father's forgiveness. She prayed for her countrymen both to the north and to the south as soldiers massed in the east for battle.

While the Shakers had withdrawn from worldly living, they did not avoid news of what was happening in the world outside their village. Instead the leaders read newspaper reports at meetings and expressed much concern over what war could mean to their Shaker communities here in the state and all across the northeast. It was feared that even if Kentucky did block the war from between her borders with a neutrality stance, the conflict between the states would greatly hinder their travel into the South where the Harmony Hill traders sold most of their products. The Shakers prayed often and with much conviction for the peaceful preservation of the Union and a just end to the abhorrent institution of slavery.

That was a prayer Charlotte echoed fervently in her heart. She knew her father claimed Grayson could not survive without slavery, but perhaps he was wrong. He was wrong about Selena. He could be wrong about much else.

Sister Martha claimed those of the world were often plagued by wrong thinking and that Charlotte's father demonstrated an obvious lack of understanding when he refused to accept the wisdom of Charlotte's desire to seek spiritual peace among the Believers. When the letter from Grayson and the departure of Mellie had threatened to plunge Charlotte into a dark state of melancholy, the elders had taken pity on her and replaced Sister Altha's stern guidance with Sister Martha's gentle encouragement. Sister Martha, while not straying from the uncompromising Shaker tenets, was gifted with patience as she listened to Charlotte's hesitant confessions of what the Shakers considered wrongs.

And unlike Sister Altha, she voiced no condemnation of Mellie for leaving the village. In those first days after Mellie ran away, Sister Altha had refused to even allow Charlotte to speak Mellie's name as she ranted about the worldly destruction that would surely swallow up their "former sister."

Thankfully Sister Martha had not shown the same indignation and encouraged Charlotte to speak to her of Mellie leaving the village. She had responded with sad kindness. "It is a sorrow to lose our sister, but each who comes among us must choose her own path. Our Sister Melana chose as many do. I regret to say it is not uncommon for those in the Gathering Family to cling to their worldly desires and slip away from our village."

Not long after Mellie left, Gemma began working with a new novitiate and Dulcie became Charlotte's instructor insofar as her work duties. They finished their stretch of ironing duty and then spent a few weeks in the kitchen peeling mounds of potatoes for the giant pots and kneading and shaping dozens of loaves of bread every morning. In spite of the mind-numbing sameness of the chores, Charlotte found the kitchen to be an amazing place where it seemed the Shakers had fashioned a new tool to make nearly every chore easier and quicker. The cupboards were built into recesses in the wall to keep the floor uncluttered. The work area was open and full of light from the tall windows. Huge ovens accommodated the large multiple-loaf pans. The smell of the bread baking and the clang of spoons in the pans made Charlotte wish she could look up from her chores and see Aunt Tish standing in front of the stove instead of Sister Wilma who was in charge of this kitchen.

Dear Aunt Tish. She'd heard nothing from Grayson since Mellie had left the village in the middle of the night. No news at all. Sometimes Charlotte stood on the southwest side of the village and stared overland toward Grayson. She could not see even the first Grayson fence post, but her mind dwelt on the roll of the land and the graceful lift of the Grayson manor house dormers. She imagined standing in her mother's garden and sometimes, if she couldn't block the thought in time, Adam came from the shadows to enfold her in his arms. At those times she regretted running from his eyes. It had been the right thing to do. The only sensible thing to do. And yet, she wished now she had thrown caution to the wind and dared his scorn and laughter. At least then her heart wouldn't wonder.

Sister Martha said it was best to shut away such wondering. Not about Adam. Charlotte saw no need to confess her wayward thoughts about him. But she did sometimes speak of her wish to see Grayson again.

"It's best for our spirits to look forward rather than back," Sister Martha instructed her at those times. "We cannot change what has been done, although we can beg Mother Ann's forgiveness for our sins, but we can change how we live in the days ahead. Our minds must engage in proper thinking. Mother Ann teaches that our thoughts are character molds. They shape language and action. So with proper thoughts you can come to know peace here at Harmony Hill."

Charlotte pretended to believe her. Sometimes she even pretended to herself, and when she and Dulcie were assigned to the duty of gathering rose petals to make the Shakers' rose water to sell to those of the world, the pretense was not so hard. She liked being out in the sun among the roses that brought to mind memories of her mother, who had loved roses above all other flowers. Her mother was every inch a complete lady.

Charlotte smiled when she thought of how distressed her mother would surely be if she could see Charlotte in bonnet and apron, cutting the roses and then stripping the petals from the stem. She didn't know which would upset her mother the most—Charlotte working like a common servant or the destruction of the roses. The rose petals were to be stripped at once to keep the sisters from the temptation of keeping one of the roses intact to sinfully enjoy its beauty by placing it in a vase. To Charlotte it seemed more of a sin to deny themselves the beauty of the roses so freely given by the Lord. So now and again she stole a moment to admire a bloom she had plucked from the bushes before she tore off the soft petals and let them drift down into her basket.

When Dulcie noticed her lifting a pink rose close to her face to catch its sweet fragrance, she warned her. "We are not to smell the roses, Sister Charlotte. It slows the progress of filling our baskets."

"But the fragrance brings peace to my spirit, and aren't we all to seek such peace?"

"Sister Altha would tell you such peace is found through prayer and laboring of our songs in meeting. Not in shirking the proper performance of your duties."

"And what do you say, Sister Dulcie? Do you not want to bury your nose in one of the roses and let the fragrance fill your head?" Charlotte ran her finger across the velvety petals of the perfectly shaped rose she held.

Dulcie looked at the rose in her own hand, then laughed softly as she stripped off its petals before reaching for another bloom. "I have been with the Believers long enough to know that if I stuck my nose in one of the blooms to revel in its scent, an angry bee would be deep among the petals ready to sting me for my waywardness."

"Yea, Sister Dulcie, but would not the bee sting our fingers as well when we pull off the petals?" Charlotte asked with a smile.

"Better a stung finger than a stung nose."

"But we work with our fingers and not our noses."

Dulcie looked up from her work with a hint of exasperation on her face. "You are being purposely contrary this day, Sister Charlotte."

"Yea, you are right." Charlotte pulled the petals from the rose. "I will confess my contrariness to Sister Martha and beg your pardon."

"You know my pardon is always readily given." Dulcie seemed to struggle to keep her face solemn as the Shakers preferred while they were engaged in their work duties before she went on. "But what you have to remember is that I must confess my wrongs to Sister Altha. If you would like to trade confessors, your Sister Martha for mine, then I will sniff the roses and you can worry about the bee stinging your nose."

"I think that is a trade I'd best not make until I become a more dedicated sister."

Dulcie stood up. She glanced around quickly to see if anyone was nearby. Then she looked straight at Charlotte across the rosebush and asked, "And do you plan to become a dedicated sister?"

"I have stopped making plans." Charlotte turned her eyes away from Dulcie back to the roses. She picked off a bud just beginning to unfurl and stripped its petals without hesitation. Then she looked back at Dulcie, who was no longer watching her but staring away down the row of roses to where some of the little girls were gathering the baskets of petals. "And what of your plans, Sister Dulcie?"

She didn't answer Charlotte. Instead she said, "A wise decision, my sister. Many plans are better not made, for they do naught but tear holes in your heart."

"They will call you mother again," Charlotte offered softly.

Dulcie didn't acknowledge her words. Instead she said, "Work time is wasted in idle chatter, Sister Charlotte." She brushed the tears sliding down her cheeks away with an impatient hand as she bent her head back to her task. "There are many rose petals yet to gather."

Later that day, during their rest time after the evening meal, Charlotte did confess her contrariness to Sister Martha, but the old sister barely listened.

"As long as you realize you did wrong, my sister, and vow to do better on the morrow." She waved away Charlotte's words as if she thought her wrong was of such little consequence it was hardly worth notice.

"Yea, Sister. I vow to be kinder to my sisters tomorrow and more diligent in my duties."

"Such an attitude will serve you well," Sister Martha said by rote. Then she pulled a bulky envelope out from under her apron. "You have a letter." Her faded blue eyes sparkled as if she were presenting Charlotte with a prize.

Charlotte kept her hands in her lap. She had no desire to read more words of censure from her father. Nor did she want to allow hope that they might be happier words spring up in her heart only to have such hopes trampled by whatever words were on the paper Sister Martha was holding toward her. "Must I read it?" Charlotte asked.

Sister Martha's eyes softened in understanding. "This is not like the other letter." She reached to take one of Charlotte's hands and turn it over so she could place the envelope on it. Her eyes brightened again. "This is from that artist who put our stairways in *Harper's Weekly* as he promised he would. It was a very fine drawing and the illustration of our dance was done with respect instead of ridicule. So often that is not the case when those of the world report on our worship."

"Yea, I saw the newspaper." Charlotte stared at her name on the envelope.

"He claims he was acquainted with you in the world. Is that true? You didn't speak of it while he was here." Sister Martha was watching her very closely.

"I did not think it important." Charlotte tried to keep the tremble out of her voice. How could just looking at how Adam Wade's hand shaped the letters of her name make her heart want to jump out of her chest? She pulled in a steadying breath. "How did he know I was here?"

"That is an interesting question." Sister Martha's eyes were boring into Charlotte now, seeing more than Charlotte wished her to see. "Perhaps if you choose to look at what he sent you, then you will know the answer."

When Charlotte still made no move to pull the letter out of the envelope, Sister Martha went on in a kind voice. "The Ministry has already looked at it as they do all letters. He sent nothing evil."

"But shouldn't I shut it away as part of the world?" Charlotte said.

"If that is what you wish. I will take the letter away and the Ministry will decide if it should be returned to the one who sent it." Sister Martha reached toward the letter.

Charlotte pulled it back from her fingers. "Nay, it might be best if I read it rather than imagine what it might say."

"That could be wise." Sister Martha sat back and looked pleased. Whatever was in the envelope seemed to be of no mystery to her. "But you may be surprised."

"I am already surprised. Just holding it."

Charlotte pulled in a slow breath as she took the paper from the envelope. It was thick, the same sort of paper as that with the sketch of her face, hidden in the bureau behind Sister Martha. Charlotte unfolded the paper. It was a sketch of her running out of the meetinghouse on the day Adam was in the village.

Sister Martha actually chuckled. "Now I understand your illness that morning, my sister."

"I did not wish him to see me." Charlotte stared at the drawing. Alone it revealed nothing of whether Adam knew whom he was sketching. Adam made many sketches. However, in an envelope bearing her name, it revealed a great deal.

"It appears that he did in spite of your hasty departure." Her smile disappeared. "How well are you and Mr. Wade acquainted?"

"Hardly at all. He was at Grayson for a week or so doing a portrait of my father's wife. He left when word came of the shelling of Fort Sumter. As an illustrator he was needed in Washington to report on the decisions being made there."

Sister Martha sighed as she shook her head. "And such sorrowful decisions for our country, I regret to say." Then she seemed to push aside worries of the impending war as she pointed toward the envelope. "There is more."

Charlotte pulled out a scrap of paper obviously torn from Adam's sketching pad and heard his voice in her ear as she read the words he'd written.

I can't believe this is you, Charlotte, but then when I look at it, I can't believe it is not. If it is and you're

reading this, write to me and tell me the story behind the picture. It has me puzzled. On a side note, M is working for my sister in Boston. N is running errands for a captain in one of the Union regiments. Both are safe. The Potomac Army is equipping to march on Richmond. Some think that will squash the rebellion. I am not so hopeful. Relieved you are not in Virginia. M told me that and nothing more so she did not break her promise to you. It is only the picture that makes me imagine you in Shaker blue. Am I imagining right?

Adam

Charlotte read through the letter again, letting her eyes linger on the welcome news about Mellie. She had no idea how he knew about Mellie or how she had ended up in Boston with his sister, but she had no doubt that was who the M in his letter meant. It was an answer to prayer and worth any laughter she might imagine between the lines of his letter. She folded the drawing and the letter and placed them back in the envelope.

Sister Martha seemed to be waiting for her to speak, but when she did not, the old sister asked, "Will you write to him to relieve his puzzlement?"

"Nay, I think not." He would expect answers from the Charlotte of Grayson, and that Charlotte was lost.

Sister Martha watched her quietly for a long time. At last she said, "I fear your heart runs after him."

"Nay, such is not allowed." Charlotte said the expected words. A Shaker sister denied any such feelings of the heart.

"My dear child," Sister Martha said kindly as she reached over to lay her wrinkled hand on Charlotte's arm. "I have been a Shaker for over fifty years. I was one of the first to come together with this Society here at Harmony Hill, and I have seen many Shaker sisters come and many go. My own dear daughter of the world was one such who went. All because her heart chased after an outsider. I didn't understand it then, but the years have given me more wisdom. The Shaker way is a hard path for some to walk."

"Do you think I should step away from it?" Charlotte looked up to meet her eyes.

"I think that is something only you can decide."

"Sister Altha would warn me about eternal damnation."

"Such is a concern in any life," Sister Martha said so softly Charlotte could barely hear her words. "I worried for many years about such a fate for my daughter in the world, but one day the Lord delivered me from those worries. While Sister Altha often tells me I should be sterner with the young sisters in our Society, I have come to believe that each must find her own path to the Lord. Sometimes that path leads through our village just as yours has, and when that happens, then it is good to tarry here until you are sure of your true way."

"But I see no way." There was despair in Charlotte's voice.

"You will. There is a reason your feet have been set on our path. Perhaps you will decide our way is good. We feel much love one for another here in this place.

The laboring of our songs brings joy down to us. We give our hands to work and our hearts to God. It is a good way. A way of much peace for those whose feet are firmly set upon our path."

"As yours are," Charlotte said.

"Yea, as mine are." Sister Martha smiled and patted Charlotte's arm before she stood up. "The Ministry would like you to correspond with Mr. Wade, for they feel he will send firsthand news of the conflict he warns is about to take place. The elders and eldresses are much interested in knowing the movement of the troops in case there is some way to buttress our villages from disasters that might come upon us due to the war. But if you choose not to, I can write in your stead and not reveal that you are among us."

Charlotte ran her fingers across the writing of her name on the envelope in her lap. "Nay, I will write."

"The Ministry will, of course, read whatever you write before it is posted," Sister Martha warned.

"That will cause no concern." Whatever words she decided to write would reveal nothing of her heart, even though Sister

Martha did speak the truth when she said Charlotte's heart ran after him.

"Very good. You will be supplied with paper and ink." Sister Martha was obviously pleased with Charlotte's decision.

For two days, Charlotte mulled over what she might write to Adam. In the end, she kept her letter short and to the point.

> **Dear Adam,**
>
> **Thank you for your letter. I have lost my place at Grayson, so I am here at Harmony Hill. The Believers have received me among them with great kindness. Mellie was here with me, but she had no desire to stay. I am much relieved to know she is safe although now I am the one puzzled as to how Mellie ended up in Boston with your sister.**
>
> **It seems there are puzzles all around. Some more terrible than others like the prospect of sister states taking up arms against one another. Such a thought saddens me. Saddens all of us here at Harmony Hill and worries us as well. If you have the time or opportunity,**

we would count it a boon if you would share with us the progress of the war or the possibility of peace from your front row seat to the conflict.

My sisters and brothers send their kind regards and wish me to tell you their gratitude for your proper depiction of their village in Harper's Weekly. *They have hopes your pictures might bring converts into the village.*

Charlotte

Three days after the letter was posted, Sister Martha came to find her in the rose garden to tell her she had a visitor. In spite of Charlotte's best efforts, her heart bounded up in her throat at the thought that it might be Adam Wade. Come for her.

24

Of course it wasn't Adam. Her letter answering his would not even have reached him yet, much less given him time to make his way back to Harmony Hill. Besides, she had no reason to imagine him coming back to the Shaker village just because he knew she was there. The words in his letter had been curious. Nothing more. In answer she had been careful to allow no words to spill out of her pen onto the stationery that might encourage him to think she desired his return.

Nor was it her father come in answer to her prayers to mend the rift between them. Instead Perkins, Grayson's overseer, perched uncomfortably on the Shaker chair in the small, bare room in the Trustee's House, twisting his felt hat between his hands until it had little chance of ever regaining its original shape. She could not have been more surprised if President Lincoln had been sitting there waiting to speak to her.

The chair legs scraped against the wooden floor as Perkins jumped up when Sister Altha led Charlotte into the room. Sister Martha trailed behind them. Even though he had obviously come seeking Charlotte, he seemed just as shocked to see her as she was to see him.

He took in her Shaker dress and cap. "They told me that letter you sent came from over here, but I thought they had to be wrong. Charles Vance's daughter a Shaker? I couldn't believe it."

Charlotte had no answer for that as she stared at Perkins and wondered why he was there. Unless it was to deliver a message from her father. She didn't know whether to hope for that or dread the words he might say. The way the man kept staring at her made her uneasy.

She'd rarely spoken to the man at Grayson. If some message needed to be relayed to him in her father's absence, Gibson took care of it. She had no real reason to avoid him. Perkins had never said the first wrong word to her. The corners of his thin lips always lifted in what passed for a smile any time he greeted her, but when she was a child, just the sight of him striding up the steps into the house to speak to her father was enough to send her running to hide her face in Aunt Tish's apron. Aunt Tish would stroke Charlotte's head and murmur that she had no reason to fear Perkins, but Charlotte had felt the tremble in Aunt Tish's hand when she spoke the overseer's name.

That tremble kept Charlotte's fear alive, and then when she grew old enough to know what Perkins did for her father at Grayson, her fear was replaced with uneasy revulsion. Someone had to see that the slaves worked, her father told her. He said slaves were like children who must be disciplined when they didn't do as they were told. Sometimes the punishments had to be harsh, but a young lady like Charlotte had no need to dwell upon those realities of plantation life. Such thinking could damage a young lady's delicate mind the same as too much education. So it was best for her to remember that some things were the bailiwick of men and that she should concentrate on thoughts and occupations more becoming a lady such as reading poetry or doing needlework.

Now Charlotte tried to push aside the familiar distaste of being near Perkins as she waited for him to tell her what he wanted. The man had aged in the months since she'd seen him. Deep lines creased his weather-beaten face, and unruly gray hairs sprang up from heavy eyebrows that almost met over his narrowed eyes as he frowned first at Charlotte and then the two Shaker sisters with her.

"Why are you here, Perkins?" Charlotte asked. She saw no reason for the niceties of a polite greeting.

"I could ask you the same." He kept eyeing her much too boldly.

"That's hardly your concern." She was surprised to hear a little of the old Grayson Charlotte's commanding tone. When Sister Martha touched her arm to remind her to be kind, Charlotte softened her voice before she went on. "But since you are here, I assume there is a reason you came to speak to me. Is something wrong with Father?"

"No, no, not so far as I know. He's still in Frankfort. Trying to legislate the war out of Kentucky."

"That's good to know," Charlotte said, then waited for him to explain why he was there, but he seemed dumbstruck by her Shaker dress.

Sister Altha lost patience. She leveled her severest look on him and spoke briskly. "You asked to see our sister, Mr. Perkins. A request we granted since you claimed it to be a matter of some importance. So come forth with whatever it is you want. We do not wish to be kept from our duties overlong."

Perkins glanced toward Sister Altha, but didn't answer her. Instead he looked back at Charlotte. "It'd be better if they weren't in here."

"Nay, it is necessary for us to be here," Sister Martha said quietly before Sister Altha or Charlotte could speak.

He shifted uneasily on his feet and twisted his hat again. "All right. I'll just be out with it. Though the mistress will fire me without thinking twice if she finds out I came here. But the wife said I had to. That I couldn't sell Tish down the river without trying to stop it."

Charlotte felt like she'd just been punched in the stomach. She could barely get out the words. "Sell Aunt Tish? You can't do that."

"That's what I tried to tell your father's wife, but she's done hired this fancy cook from up north. She let Tish cook for the field hands for a while, but now she says that's a waste of resources since Tish can run a manor kitchen and would bring a fair price on the market. She says Tish has to go." He looked straight at Charlotte. "That's why I'm here. I mean I've sent plenty of slaves down the river, but it don't seem right to do that to Tish."

"Father won't let her."

"That's just it. She don't have to ask him. He wrote out a paper giving her permission to do whatever she wants, and she ordered me not to tell him." Perkins looked down at the floor as though suddenly ashamed to meet Charlotte's eyes.

"I've been at Grayson for thirty years. I'm too old to find a new place."

Charlotte wasn't concerned about his problems. Only Aunt Tish. She couldn't let Selena sell her. She had to stop this insanity. "I'll buy her."

Relief flashed across Perkins's face as he looked up at her. "That's what I was hoping you'd say." He pulled a wad of bills from his pocket and held them out toward Charlotte. "I'm even willing to put in a hundred dollars out of my pocket, long as you don't tell Mrs. Vance."

Charlotte stared at the money between them as the realization of the truth of her actual poverty slammed her in the heart. She had no money. She had nothing. She'd left it all at Grayson.

Sister Altha drove that truth home as she said, "Do you have wealth we know nothing about, Sister Charlotte? If so, you were to have turned such over to the Ministry when you came among us. We have all property in common here."

Charlotte shut her eyes and saw Aunt Tish looking at her with belief when Charlotte had promised to someday free her.

She felt near tears as she said, "Nay. I have no money."

"I thought not," Sister Altha said.

Perkins dropped the hand holding the bills back to his side. He looked beaten, but Charlotte couldn't accept that. She had to find a way to stop Selena. Paper money was not the only thing of value in the world.

She fastened her eyes on Sister Altha to make an appeal. "I brought a necklace and ring with me that I gave over to you. And a horse. They had some value. And I know where I can get another very fine gold necklace."

"You would not steal it from your father of the world, would you?" Sister Altha looked at her with a good bit of suspicion.

"Nay. It is buried beside my mother's tombstone. It was hers, but she would want me to use it to keep Aunt Tish from being sold." Charlotte looked at Sister Altha. "Please, I beg of you. I'll do anything you ask if you will help buy her for me."

"For you?" Sister Altha said.

"To free her," Charlotte amended.

"And will she run away as soon as she gets here to Harmony Hill as Sister Melana did?" Sister Altha narrowed her eyes on

Charlotte as though it was her fault that Mellie had left.

"Sister Altha, we cannot hold Sister Charlotte to blame for our former sister's lack of commitment," Sister Martha said in a soft voice but one that carried a hint of censure.

Sister Altha looked over at Perkins who had not stuffed his money back in his pocket. "We are not heartless, Mr. Perkins, but we are unable to purchase every slave we see being maltreated. Oh, that we could."

"You wouldn't have to repay my money," Perkins said. When Sister Altha didn't say anything, he looked as if he were choosing his next words carefully. "You might want to remember that someday Miss Charlotte here may inherit the Grayson land. If she stays with you, she'd have to give it over to you, wouldn't she?"

"Our charity is not dependent on such concerns. And even if it were, it remains to be seen whether our sister will be able to pick up the cross of sacrifice and become one with us here at Harmony Hill." Sister Altha frowned as she sent a side glance toward Charlotte. "I have many doubts as to that ever happening."

"She's been with you a good many months now when she could have been dancing in parlors and sitting on garden benches twirling her parasol." Perkins kept his eyes on Sister Altha. As a man used to seizing the upper hand in any confrontation, he had recognized the person with power in front of him.

"He speaks true words, Sister Altha," Sister Martha agreed quietly as she motioned with a barely lifted finger for Charlotte's silence. "Sister Charlotte has been working diligently in our Society."

Sister Altha's eyes narrowed on Charlotte. "And what say you, Sister? Are you willing to make such a bargain?"

"I may never own the land now that my father has remarried." Charlotte didn't try to lie to Sister Altha. "So it may not be mine to give, but if I do receive some land as any inheritance, I will deed you one hundred acres. I'll put it in writing and that will be true whether I remain with you or not."

"But you say that may not happen."

"Yea, that is true." Charlotte stared at Sister Altha. "All I truly have is the labor of my hands. I promise it to you for a year if you will buy Aunt Tish." She didn't know if it would be enough, but it was all she had.

Sister Martha spoke up. "Our Society does not deal in human bondage."

"Do not be so quick to find fault with her plan, Sister Martha," Sister Altha said without looking over at the older sister. Instead she was smiling slightly at Charlotte. "We do not talk of bondage here. We speak only of commitment. Do we not each commit to working with our hands for the good of all? It would not be right of us to deny our sister the blessing of giving the gift of self for such an honorable reason. To do so might hinder the growth of her spirit."

"Your thinking is faulty, my sister," Sister Martha warned.

Charlotte put her hand on Sister Martha's arm. "Please, Sister Martha, let Sister Altha approach the Ministry with my request."

"It is not right," Sister Martha insisted.

"Yea, it is. Many years ago I promised Aunt Tish her freedom if ever I had the means to provide it. I beg you not to deny me this means." What was one short year of her life to live in bondage to a promise when Aunt Tish had lived so many years in bondage to chains?

"It is not a decision for me to make," Sister Martha said with a little sigh. "The Ministry will so decide. In the past they have chosen to purchase the freedom of some— not for the guarantee of a return but only out of kindness."

"You speak truth. And because of Sister Charlotte's willingness to bend her spirit, I will speak in favor of the kindness of rescuing this poor woman from the evils of slavery." Sister Altha almost smiled as she looked at Charlotte. "You will need to fetch the necklace," she said as if the decision had already been made by the Ministry. She reached for the money in the overseer's hand. "What price has been set on this woman of whom we speak?"

Perkins surrendered the money willingly. "Eight hundred. She is an excellent cook and knows many domestic skills, but her age has lowered her price."

"Very well. Come with me and if the Ministry allows this purchase as I feel certain they will, we will arrange the funds while our sister fetches the necklace of which she speaks." Sister Altha was all business now.

Brother Willard, who was almost as old as Sister Martha, drove Charlotte and the old sister to Grayson that afternoon. At Charlotte's request, he pulled the Shakers' wagon in among some trees a little way from the house where they would be hidden from easy view. Charlotte had no wish to see Selena or for Selena to see her.

Of course Selena might not even be at Grayson. She might have gone to a summer home somewhere in the north. Or to Frankfort to be with Charlotte's father. That would give her the chance to attend all the fancy events that were held in the capital. Charlotte wondered if Selena was planning entertainments at Grayson. Perhaps not, since so many in the county were pro-Secessionist while Charlotte's father would be maintaining his unyielding support of the Union even as he roundly condemned the President's talk of abolishing slavery.

If she was at Grayson, Charlotte hoped Selena would be taking her afternoon rest on the front veranda, as was the usual custom for ladies in the summer months.

Charlotte could almost see the tray of sweet iced tea and shortbread cookies covered by a white linen cloth on the glass table beside the wicker chair. There might even be a young slave girl stirring the air and keeping the flies away with a palm leaf fan if visitors had come to call.

The thought of whiling away a summer afternoon so lazily seemed almost foreign to Charlotte now as she made the short walk to the graveyard. The July sun was hot. So the moment she was out of sight of Sister Martha, Charlotte stripped off the Shaker cap to let the slight breeze ruffle her hair. It was good to feel Grayson land under her feet and have Grayson air filling her lungs. Every inch of her skin tingled with joy as she lightly ran her hands over the bark of the trees and wished her shoes gone so the grass could tickle her toes. She was home.

But not to stay, she reminded herself sternly. Perhaps never again to stay. That was no reason she couldn't rejoice in this moment as she paused at the edge of the stand of trees and looked toward Grayson's manor house. The rear of the house was plain in comparison to the front. No dormer windows. No veranda spreading out with shady welcome. The porch on the back was a working porch where servants shelled beans and shucked corn. She looked for Aunt Tish, but could see no one moving about.

That was good. Charlotte slipped across the open field to the graveyard where once again she felt concealed by the trees shading the graves. She'd promised Sister Martha she wouldn't linger, but once at her mother's grave, she touched the headstone warm from the day's sun and remembered the last time she'd touched the stone. Adam Wade had backed her into it, expecting her to kiss him. She hadn't. She'd wanted to, but she hadn't.

Would she ever again have the chance to feel his lips on hers? He was following the army into battle. Not to fight, but to draw illustrations of the conflict. That didn't mean he might not be in harm's way. And she, what of her? She had promised her hands to the Shakers. It was better to push all thought of Adam Wade far from her mind. She had told Sister Altha she would pick up the cross of sacrifice and carry it without complaint. She was no longer the

Charlotte who was born to the manor house and a lady's life of ease. She was Sister Charlotte with a duty to do. Retrieve the necklace for the Shakers to sell to help gather the money needed for Aunt Tish's freedom.

She knelt down to feel for the edge of the circle of grass she had lifted up to bury the necklace. "I know you won't mind, Mother," she said aloud as she pushed the trowel she'd brought with her into the ground.

"Are you Mayda?" a timid voice asked behind her.

Startled, Charlotte whirled around. The trowel banged against the tombstone and bounced out of her hand. A boy was watching her with large, frightened eyes.

"Mayda?" she asked when she found her voice.

"Come out of the grave to haunt my mother." The child pointed a finger at the tombstone. He was very slender and too pale either from the fright of staring at a haunt or perhaps a recent illness that had kept him in out of the sun for too many days. "Little Jim says I'd better watch out for Grayson ghosts trying to chase me and

Mother away." He paused a minute as if getting up his nerve to say his next words. "Ghosts like you."

"Do I look like a ghost?" Charlotte asked with a little smile.

"Not the way I imagined, but Miss Pennebaker says I don't always imagine things right. Like being a whaleboat captain. She tells me that really wouldn't be so much fun, that I'd have to start out swabbing decks and eating fishhead stew." He came a couple of steps closer. "Have you ever eaten fishhead stew?"

"I don't think I have, but then ghosts don't have much need to eat."

"You're not a ghost," the little boy said.

"Oh? Then who am I?" Charlotte laughed before she turned away from him to pick up the trowel and shove it into the ground to find the box she'd planted there only a few months before.

"My sister."

Charlotte froze as chills ran up her back. Perhaps instead of her being the ghost, this child was. Her little brother grown older in some sort of spirit world and haunting the graveyard where his little body was buried. Charlotte shook her head at the

foolishness of her thoughts. The child behind her wasn't a ghost any more than
she was. She dug deeper in the hole until
she felt the hard edges of the box. She lifted
it out of the dirt before she turned back to
the boy. "Why do you think I'm your sister?"

"You have red hair. Ghosts don't have
red hair, but my sister does."

He had to be Selena's child, even if he
had little resemblance to her. "All right.
You've caught me. I'm not a ghost. But who
told you I'm your sister?"

"Mother." The boy had lost his nervous
fright at the thought of ghosts and now
merely looked curious. "Is it a long walk
from Virginia?"

"Virginia?"

"From your school there. I would have
thought it would be a very long walk. I had
to ride a train with Miss Pennebaker when
we came here from Boston. I wanted to
come on a ship, but Mother said I couldn't."

"Grayson doesn't sit on the ocean, and
my school is not quite so far as Virginia,"
Charlotte said. "You must be Landon."

"You know me then," the child said as if
it was a common thing for the people he
met to know him without introductions.

"Your mother told me you were coming to Grayson."

"But you were already gone when I got here. Did Mother make you leave?"

"Why do you say that?" Charlotte sat back on her heels and studied the child's sincere face. Not only did he not look like his mother, he seemed to have little of her ways.

"I don't know." He looked down at his shoes as if worried he'd said something that was going to get him in trouble. "It's just that Mother's very good at making things happen as she wants. That's why Miss Pennebaker says I won't get to be a whaleboat captain. Mother would never allow it. She says I have to be a gentleman." The little boy peeked back up at Charlotte. "Do you know what gentlemen do? Besides not going barefoot and always being polite."

Charlotte looked at the child Selena was pushing forward to take Charlotte's rightful place at Grayson, and in spite of that, she laughed and took pity on this pale boy who was doomed to years of attempting to please Selena. "Gentlemen might not harpoon whales, but they ride horses and practice shooting."

"I know. That's so they can go to the army and be captains and generals and not have to march on the ground." Landon looked worried again. "But I don't want to shoot people. I'd rather harpoon whales."

"Then perhaps someday you will," Charlotte said as she stood up and brushed the dirt off her hands on her apron. "Sometimes a gentleman or a lady does the most unexpected things. Now I must go back to my unexpected path."

"Can I tell Mother I saw you?"

"Do you think she'll believe you? As you said, it is a very long walk from Virginia." Charlotte looked at him with raised eyebrows before prizing the top off the powder box. She lifted out the necklace and dropped it down into her pocket. Sister Martha would be getting worried.

"Perhaps I will keep it a secret. Brothers and sisters have secrets, don't they?"

"They do."

"I hope you come back," Landon told her. He looked sad to see her go.

"I might. Someday." Charlotte smiled at the boy. Selena must have stolen him from another mother. "Until then, I'll share a secret with you. Gentlemen can go barefoot as long as their mothers don't see and they don't complain if they happen to step on a bee."

She left him sitting on a stone unlacing his shoes. She forgot to put her cap back on. Sister Martha had to remind her to cover her hair before she climbed up in the wagon. Brother Willard kept his eyes averted until she had done so.

Sister Altha was waiting to take the necklace when they got back to Harmony Hill. She said an elder would see to the details of selling the necklace and dealing with Perkins.

Two weeks later, Sister Latisha was introduced at meeting. Aunt Tish stood at the edge of the dancers and raised her hands to the heavens as tears streamed down her face. For the first time Charlotte's feet weren't reluctant to join in the laboring of the Shaker songs.

25

It took weeks for Charlotte's letter to make its way to Adam where he was camped with the Potomac Army waiting for the generals to give the order to march south. He'd put *Harper's* address on the letter he'd sent to Harmony Hill since he had never been anywhere that Sam Johnson didn't eventually track him down.

Adam could have stayed in a hotel and only come out to the encampments during the day the way many of the reporters and illustrators did, but he wanted more in his pictures than what he saw on the outside as the men passed the time marching drills and playing baseball or mumblety-peg. In order to capture the mixture of eagerness and fear, boredom and excitement, loneliness and comradeship in their faces, Adam had to sit down among the men and become one of them, even if his weapon of choice was a pencil and not one of the Lincoln guns.

He got on well with the men. Few questioned his courage the way Jake had. They didn't need him fighting alongside them to win the day. They much preferred the thought of their coming moments of derring-do being captured by his pen. Most were full of bluster when it came to talk of putting down Johnny Reb. Theirs was the holy cause, the divine duty of preserving the Union.

The preachers who roamed about the camps told them so right before they offered what might be a last chance for salvation. Some of the men of God wore the uniforms of the various state regiments. Others came out of the city to preach to any who would turn his head to listen. None seemed to consider the prayers of the preachers in the Southern pulpits not so many miles away across the Virginia border calling down the Lord's blessings on their cause of freedom from the oppressive North.

So while the army paused on the brink of warfare, Adam filled up book after book of sketches. More than Sam Johnson and all the newspapers and magazines in the country could ever use, but he kept sketching, seeking that perfect scene to show people the gritty face of war.

At night he put his sketching tools aside and gathered with the men around campfires where the talk generally turned to home. Charlotte filled Adam's mind at those times. He started a dozen letters to her in the near darkness, but he always ended up feeding the scraps of papers to the fire.

He assured himself that it wasn't because some of the words he wanted to write frightened him. That wasn't it at all. He didn't have to write those words. He could write of simple things like the sound of a soldier strumming a guitar and singing a song about a girl back home or the way the sparks from the fire rose up toward the stars. No, he burned his words because there was no need writing to her at Harmony Hill if she wasn't there. He hadn't seen her face or one tendril of red hair. He could be mistaken. He wavered between being sure he was mistaken because he couldn't imagine Charlotte with the Shakers and being sure he wasn't mistaken because his fingers had formed with such ease the lines of the Shaker sister running from the meetinghouse.

Of course he drew her into many of his pictures when she was nowhere near. She was the young lady sitting in the shadows deep in her carriage while her servant unloaded baskets of food for the soldiers. She was the lady dipping her full skirts out of a soldier's way as she walked down the street. She was the girl peeking around the curtains in the townhouse on the square to watch the soldiers go through their drills. She was the face in his dreams.

That didn't mean he had to chase after her with letters that might not even find her. Or be welcome if they did. Mellie had claimed Charlotte loved him, but even if that was true, would that be enough to pull her away from her beloved Kentucky? He couldn't settle in one place. No matter how grand the house or how beautiful the woman. The desire to capture the truth in pictures burned too strongly inside him. He had to be where things were happening and not tied to hearth and home. So he told himself it was better if she didn't write. Better for him to burn his own words to her. He had to follow the army. He had no time for love. At least not now. Not until after the war was won.

Then Sam Johnson's messenger came to pick up Adam's sketches and brought his mail. He sifted through the pile. Copies of *Harper's Weekly* and other newspapers. Letters from his mother and Phoebe. He didn't have to open them to know they would be more of the same words they wrote every time, telling him to send Jake home. A waste of ink. There was the usual hastily scrawled and barely legible letter from Sam asking for this or that illustration. Adam flipped through half a dozen envelopes from other editors with checks for illustrations he'd sent them. And there, mixed among those letters, was the small envelope with the handwriting he'd never seen but that his heart recognized at once. His name formed by Charlotte wearing Shaker blue.

He swept his eyes over the words of her letter, swallowing it whole, and then let his eyes go back to the top to read it again slowly, savoring each pen stroke. Her words revealed little. But she had written. She was at the Shaker village. She wanted him to write again. The letter said the Shaker elders wanted him to write of the war, but he wouldn't be addressing the letters to them. He'd be addressing the letters to Charlotte. And even if his words revealed no more than hers, they would still be read by her eyes. Her hand would write the response. And that seemed to be enough. For now. He wondered if she would think the same.

How could he know? He'd only talked to her those few times, and while he'd thought he was seeing the girl she was, he could not imagine that girl wearing Shaker dress by choice. And yet she was. The letter he held proved it. He read the words again. *I have lost my place at Grayson.* No explanation. Just a statement of fact. He saw Selena's hand in that. And Selena's only. The senator thought his daughter in Virginia.

Or did he? Perhaps he had lied because he feared his constituents knowing his daughter had gone to the Shakers. The Shakers' worship was considered at best odd and, at worst, heretical. Not something a politician with his eye on the governorship would want to be tied to in any

way. The senator had enough problems
already with the divided feelings over Union
or Secessionist in his district.

Adam decided not to mention the senator or the school in Virginia in his return
letter. Instead he would do as Charlotte
asked and send news of the war. The answers to their personal puzzles would have
to wait until they were once more face-to-
face. He could get a train and be there in
two days. He could run after her if she ran
from him again.

But the war might not wait for his return.
Rumor had the army moving south within
the week to strike at the new Confederate
capital at Richmond. One swift thrust and
the rebellion would be ended. So he wrote
of the soldiers and sent a sketch of President Lincoln reviewing the troops and another of a soldier polishing his rifle stock.
Not a picture the peace-loving Shakers
might want to see, but they'd asked for news
of the war. War meant weapons. At the end
of his letter, he wrote, *I remember the garden. No puzzles there. With fondest regards,
Adam.*

The next day General McDowell sent
down orders for the army to pack up their

gear, load up the tents and camp stoves, hitch the horses to the artillery pieces, and head south to end the rebellion. Spirits ran high among the men. A few rounds of artillery and Johnny Reb would hightail it for home before the soldiers much more than had time to ram in their second load. Then the Union would be restored, and they could march home to a hero's welcome. Thoughts of maybe falling in battle were pushed aside on that July day as they fell in line to begin the assault on Richmond.

Adam didn't dwell on what the next few days might hold either. At least not unless he was talking to one of the Mexican War veterans. Then with their words of caution in his ears, he worried about Jake and all the eager volunteers who were marching toward the field of battle with only a few months of playing soldier on a practice field.

But he wasn't worried about his own danger. He wouldn't be engaging in battle. He'd be the observer Jake had accused him of being. Rightly enough. He'd be drawing the pictures to make the people who read the news hear the echo of the artillery fire in the safety of their parlors. He and others. Matthew Brady would be there with his photography equipment that captured the images on glass plates. Adam had seen the van that carried the immense amount of equipment the man needed for the magic of those pictures. Adam preferred his sketch-pads. Much lighter traveling.

But Brady's van wasn't the only vehicle horses were pulling down the dusty roads behind the army. Not everybody was content to sit in their parlors and wait for the news to be delivered to their doorsteps. A glut of carriages choked the road. A few like Brady's van carried reporters, but more carried citizens tagging along to witness the spectacle of the Rebels' defeat. Congressmen and their wives. Foreign observers and diplomats. Ladies and gentlemen. Many of them had servants following along with hampers of food, as though marching off to battle was simply a good excuse for a pleasure jaunt and picnic.

Adam found the Massachusetts regiment and rode alongside Jake. The boy had at least relented enough to move from a foot soldier to the cavalry. That was the best Adam had been able to do for Phoebe and his mother. And he'd only been able to do that by convincing Jake he'd have more opportunity to engage the enemy on horseback. An infantryman might be limited to one charge at the enemy, but a man on horseback might charge and wheel about and charge again. Adam had no idea if that was really true, but it was surely safer to be on a horse than marching on foot across an open field in the face of artillery fire. He intended to do all he could to see that Jake survived the battle. Something Jake seemed to give no consideration to at all.

"You will remember not to do anything foolhardy," Adam said as they jogged their horses slowly alongside the marching men.

"You mean charge the ramparts to save the day?" Jake laughed. He was in such high spirits that he was almost floating above his saddle. "It'll be good to finally have some ramparts to charge."

"I've talked to some of the old soldiers who say the troops aren't battle ready," Adam warned.

Jake waved his hand in dismissal. "Those old geezers." He looked around to be sure none of the veteran soldiers were near enough to overhear him. "I mean we're glad they're along and all. They've been a great help getting us in shape. But I want you to tell me how a man can be battle-hardened the way they say we need to be without going into battle."

"I don't guess he can."

"So they were bound to be green at their first battle too. But green or not, we're going to chase those Johnny Rebs all the way back to Richmond and teach them a thing or two. We'll give you plenty of fodder for your pens."

"Just don't you be fodder for the Confederate cannons."

"I wager they won't even stand and fight. We're thirty-five thousand strong. Thirty-five thousand! Nothing can stand against a force that big."

"They've been amassing troops too." Adam looked over at Jake and saw a hint of worry under Jake's bravado. He looked so young, his blond whiskers scarcely thick enough to put a beard on his chin. Maybe Adam shouldn't be pushing reality at the boy. There was no turning back for any of the soldiers now. Not with honor.

"They don't have that many, do they?" Jake took off his hat and wiped the sweat off his forehead. The uniforms were hot in the July sun. "Somebody said only twenty thousand under Beauregard, the scoundrel. We'll pay him back for Fort Sumter. In spades."

"What about Johnstone?" Adam couldn't seem to help himself. "Rumor has it he has upwards to ten thousand men or more."

"Out toward Shenandoah. Not where General McDowell has us heading. The general has it planned out. I've heard he sent some troops out that way to keep Johnstone's bunch occupied. We'll have Beauregard beat before he even knows to holler help. You just watch."

"That's what I do best."

"Every man has his duty," Jake said.

Adam heard the jibe in Jake's words, but he just kept his horse in a steady jog alongside his brother and pretended he didn't. He didn't want angry words between them on the eve of battle.

The next couple of days they heard reports of a few skirmishes, but nothing of importance as the army continued south. They came across places the Confederates or perhaps citizens with rebellious leanings had thrown trees across the roads to impede the movement of the Union artillery and slow the advance of the troops.

The delays hindered General McDowell's battle plan, and discipline among the citizen soldiers was lax. Men wandered away from their ranks at will to fill their canteens or pick handfuls of blackberries. No voice of command rose above the melee of the army's advance to keep the volunteers in line.

Early Sunday, the Union army met their first real resistance at the Bull Run stream near Manassas. Men accustomed to sitting on church pews on Sunday mornings lined up for battle against brothers and friends. Even to Adam, who hadn't regularly attended Sunday services since his school days, it seemed wrong to fire the first volleys to tear apart the country on a Lord's Day.

But when he said as much to one of the reporters taking notes on the formation of the troops, the man snorted a laugh through his nose before he said, "Those boys down there will be doing more praying this day than they ever did in any church building. You can take my word on that. And the people back home are gonna want to read all about it. Unanswered prayers and all."

"What makes you say they'll be unanswered?" Adam asked.

Bud Keeling had been writing for the *New York Times* since before Adam was born. He had the reputation of going anywhere to chase a story. And it was rumored that sometimes he wrote the story and sent it in before the event even happened so the *Times* could beat all the other papers with the headline. He had once told Adam that being first with the news paid off better than accuracy and that things pretty much happened the same, time in and time out. Or at least the part people wanted to read about.

"You been getting religion, Wade?" he asked now as he looked around at Adam with an indulgent half smile. "If so, maybe you should tell me why you think they'll be answered. And how you think the good Lord up above decides which prayer to answer when Billy Yank meets Johnny Reb after they fire their loads and fix their bayonets. Both good boys with mamas back home down on their knees in church praying their sons will come home in one piece."

"I don't know." Adam's eyes went to the Union soldiers firing at a badly outnumbered group of Confederates trying to stop their advance. General McDowell's feint had worked and the Rebels were caught almost totally by surprise except for a few Rebel companies left to guard the bridges over Bull Run. It seemed Jake might be right and they would have a clear road all the way to Richmond. The artillery guns flashed fire and the shells whistled as they passed over top the Confederate force to crash through the trees on the hill before plowing into the ground and throwing up plumes of dirt.

"Don't nobody know the answer to that one. Anybody tells you they do, you can know they're lying." Bud pushed his hat back on his head and spat on the ground. "Me and you, we just have to tell the story. Each in our own way."

Adam drew the lines of the artillery guns belching smoke. The Confederates weren't running. Instead they were lining up to march into the face of the Union guns. He wondered, if he was down there as a part of that line, would he be afraid? "You ever been scared, Bud?"

"What's the matter? You think I'm not human?" Bud didn't wait for Adam to answer. "You get around a man what claims to have never been afraid, you give him a wide berth. He'll get you killed. A good dose of caution can keep a man breathing."

Adam nodded toward the men running forward, loading and firing their guns at one another on the field below them. "No chance for caution on a battlefield."

"I don't know." Bud frowned into the bright sun as he stared down at the battle. "Look how the boys in blue are just flopping down on the ground while the gunners fire over their heads at the Johnny Rebs." Bud scribbled something down in his notebook before he went on. "Don't seem to be hitting much though. Firing high. Whoever's giving the orders better be telling them to mount a charge before the Rebs have time to bring up reinforcements."

Adam drew some quick lines to show the Union soldiers on the ground, waiting the order to charge. The midday sun beat down on them without mercy. Even so, the Union was winning the day in spite of what Bud thought of their methods. Adam felt a terrible sorrow for the Confederate soldiers lining up for a last-ditch effort to slow the Union's advance. Their line was thin. Adam couldn't see their faces, but he could see how they stood shoulder to shoulder ready to march into the jaws of death. Their bravery was almost visible in the air above their heads. All at once they began their charge with a terrible cry that seemed to come from deep within them. Terror and courage exploding in an eerie scream that echoed through the Rebel line. And the battle that should have been won already by the Union soldiers went on.

The smoke of the musket fire and artillery pieces settled around the soldiers until it was hard for Adam to see what was happening. He wanted to go find Jake, but instead, as the sun crawled across the sky, he divided himself from the reality of men screaming and dying below him and became nothing more than a vehicle for his pencils drawing the scenes of battle.

26

The Union took the bridge over the Bull Run stream and charged forward on the cusp of victory. People in the carriages cheered them on, and a few reporters moved closer to better see the action as the army advanced up the rise to finish off the Rebels. But they met surprising resistance. Soon news came winding around to where Adam and Bud Keeling were observing the battle that a new Southern brigade under General Jackson had formed a defensive line on Henry Hill. The Union generals had delayed long enough to allow the Confederates to get some artillery pieces in place, and exploding shells began to rain down on the charging troops.

The stolid resistance knocked the wind out of the Union charge, and the men began to fall back. A couple of regiments quit the field entirely while others regrouped for a second assault, but the officers seemed confused as to the battle plan. Without leadership, many of the troops moved about totally bewildered as to what to do next. To give cover, the artillery company was ordered forward, but no supporting company was assigned to protect the artillery's new exposed position. In short order the gunners were overrun and the Union howitzers silenced. After that, the dying began in earnest.

Up beside Adam, Bud Keeling swore under his breath. "The right hand don't know what the left is doing down there." He shoved his notebook in his pocket and glanced over at Adam. "Tide's turning, Wade. Best pack up your stuff and find your horse. Unless you want to spend some time with the Rebels. Not something I'd recommend. I hear tell they aren't too hospitable to Yanks like us even when we aren't shooting at them."

The retreat began orderly enough as those soldiers still standing began to fall back. But then the Rebels charged down the hill toward them, and the boys in blue threw down their muskets and bayonets and abandoned their wounded to run for their lives. Here and there a captain or other officer called for the men to re-form a line, but their voices were swallowed up in the chaos. Horses reared and fought against their traces as the Confederate shells shrieked overhead and exploded around them. Some of the horses hitched to artillery pieces ran uncontrolled through the fleeing soldiers and added to the carnage of the day.

Other drivers kept their horses under control as they waited to cross the bridge back to the north, but then a shell hit a wagon on the bridge. A horse let out an unearthly scream and fell in its traces. The other three horses scrambled madly to keep pulling in spite of the dead horse, but the shell had also splintered the front wagon wheel. The heavily loaded wagon skewed to the side, totally blocking the bridge and the army's escape route.

Now all semblance of order disappeared

as the retreat became a rout, and men unable to cross the bridge plunged into the Bull Run stream to fight their way to the north side. Soldiers who had escaped the shells and bullets of the battlefield were swept away in the swift current of the stream.

Adam sat on his horse, removed from the action, and watched. He didn't pull out his sketchpad. There was no need. The scene before him would be etched in his memory for life. The acrid smell of the battle smoke assaulted his nose as it gathered in thick clouds over the battlefield to mercifully obscure his view of the bodies of men who had fought their last battle. Dead horses lay among them, and Adam no longer had the sure feeling that a soldier was safer on horseback than afoot.

He guided his own nervous horse down into the smoke-covered field, picking his way through smoldering shell fragments, splintered tree limbs and bodies. The corpses were already black with flies in the summer heat. Adam wanted to turn his eyes away, but he made himself look at the faces even as he dreaded seeing that of his brother.

A soldier struggled to his feet to plead

for help as Adam passed by. He cradled what was left of his hand against his blood-soaked coat. His eyes staring out of a face blackened by gunpowder looked even younger than Jake's. Adam could have turned away from him and continued his search, but he didn't know if Jake was out there among the dead and the dying. He knew this boy in front of him needed a doctor to stop his bleeding. So he lifted the young soldier up on his horse and rode away from the battlefield. Only after he got across the stream and found the house the doctors had commandeered for a field hospital did he realize he'd plucked an Alabama Rebel from the field of battle. It didn't seem to matter.

The Confederates, satisfied with the spoils of victory left on the battlefield, didn't pursue the Northern army across Bull Run. The wounded Potomac Army limped back to the capital where the state regiments began to count up their losses. There were many.

The biggest to Adam's mind was their loss of confidence. They'd marched out of Washington sure they'd overwhelm the Rebels and end the war. Now they knew the Rebels weren't going to cave at the first show of force. Now they knew their leaders had failed to lead them effectively. Now they knew the war was not going to be ended on a picnic-filled day at the battlefield. The worst blow of all was the way many of the city's citizens openly celebrated the Confederate victory, some even being so bold as to fly Rebel flags on their porches.

Adam made a quick sketch of a Union soldier with one arm wrapped in a sling bandage tearing the Confederate colors off a porch post. It was the kind of conflict-laden illustration Sam Johnson liked best.

That night he finally found the Massachusetts 5th Regiment and Jake encamped not far from the White House where President Lincoln was reputed to be gathering with the Secretary of War and his top generals to figure out what had gone so wrong at Bull Run. Jake didn't want to talk about the failings of the army. He didn't seem to want to talk at all as Adam crouched down beside him where he was staring at the remnants of a cooking fire.

Adam's relief to see his brother uninjured was tempered by the boy's morose face. He wasn't the same cocky young soldier who had ridden away from the city, sure he was going to personally chase the Rebels all the way back to Richmond. While he had escaped the battlefield without any flesh-and-blood wounds, he hadn't escaped unscathed. Somewhere on the inside he was bleeding. At Adam's suggestion, they walked away from the other men to be alone in the silky black of the night. To the west the sky rumbled as lightning flickered on and off in a kind of warning signal.

As they moved through the camps without speaking, here and there raucous laughter made it evident some of the men had turned to alcohol in an attempt to wipe away the memory of battle. Jake didn't even turn his head toward the sound, so deep was he in his own gloom. Adam was determined not to speak first for fear he'd say the wrong words that might make whatever was spearing Jake's soul stab deeper. They stopped at the edge of a stand of trees and looked back at the camps spread across the opening. Here and there a campfire flickered, and the officers' white tents pulled light out of the night.

Once they stopped moving, the silence

between them became almost suffocating. Adam finally broke his resolve to not speak first and asked, "You want to talk about it, Jake?"

Jake kept his eyes forward, and for a long minute Adam didn't think he was going to acknowledge his words, but then he muttered, "I ran away."

"The whole army ran away," Adam said.

"No," Jake said. "Not everybody."

The seconds ticked by as Adam waited for him to explain, each one seeming ten times as long as the last. Finally Jake said, "Not Bill Pickworth."

"Who's Bill Pickworth?"

"You met him. Black hair, skinny, not too tall, ears sticking out like some kind of monkey. Nobody paid him much mind. He was just there, you know. Never had much to say."

"Yeah, I remember him now." Adam thought of how the boy had looked as he sat on the fringes of the campfire before they marched to Bull Run. He couldn't have been more than sixteen, with wide brown eyes that seemed to be swallowing every sight whole. "What happened to him?"

"He didn't run. Not even when everybody else did. He stood there and loaded his gun and kept firing the way a soldier is supposed to. He didn't run." Jake looked over at Adam. "But I did."

Lightning flickered across the sky, but it wasn't enough for Adam to see Jake's face in the dark. He didn't really need to. He heard the sorrow in his voice, not as much for Bill as for the loss of who he'd thought he was himself. A soldier ready for battle.

"There are times when it's the better part of valor to quit the field," Adam said. "To live to fight another day."

"Tell that to Bill Pickworth," Jake said as he stared back down at his feet.

"Can I?"

"I don't know. I didn't see him fall, but he's not here. He must be dead or captured."

Adam didn't try to deny the truth of Jake's words. Instead he let the silence gather around them. It would just make Jake feel worse if he tried to coddle him.

After a minute, Jake went on. "He saw the elephant and didn't run."

"The elephant?" Adam frowned into the darkness.

"Yeah, that's what the old guys had been telling us. That a man can't measure his courage until he actually looks into the face of danger. Do you stand and turn the elephant back or do you run like a yellow-bellied coward?" Jake kept his eyes on the ground. "And now I know. I saw the elephant and ran like the coward I am."

"Do you want to go home, Jake?" Adam directed his words out into the night and didn't look at Jake as he waited for his answer.

It was slow in coming. "I can't go home. I enlisted for six months."

"Phoebe would pay someone to take your place."

"Do they let you do that?" There was a touch of hope in Jake's voice as his head jerked up to look toward Adam.

"I don't know. Maybe. Money can buy most anything."

"Not self-respect." Jake let out a long sigh.

"No, not that."

"I don't want to be a coward. I want to be able to look a man like Bill Pickworth in the eye and stand shoulder to shoulder with him in battle."

"The war is far from over, Jake. There will be other battles."

"But what if I see the elephant and run again?"

"You won't." Adam put his hand on Jake's shoulder and squeezed it a little.

"How do you know?" Jake sounded like he used to when he was a little boy in some kind of fix he hoped Adam could make right.

"I know you." He stared straight at Jake's face. In the darkness all he could see was the shine of his eyes. "You mess up, but you don't stay messed up."

Jake let out a huff of breath and moved out from under Adam's hand as though he wasn't sure he could accept Adam's words. The storm had come close enough that the wind had picked up and carried with it the smell of rain, but it looked like it might go around them. Adam hoped so. The men were dispirited enough without thunder crashing down to remind them of the artillery fire they'd escaped but many of their comrades had not.

Jake was quiet a moment before he said, "Were you afraid, Adam?"

"I wasn't fighting."

"I know, but I saw where you were. It wasn't that far removed from the field. You could have been hit by a shell or even the musket fire. A lot of the bullets were going high."

"I didn't think about it, Jake. I only thought about what I was seeing. And you. I worried about you."

"Did you pray for me?" Jake didn't wait for Adam to answer as he looked up at the clouds rolling across the sky and went on. "I prayed. Like I never prayed before."

"To live?"

"No, to be able to look a man in the face and shoot him dead if I had to. I didn't know if I could." Again Jake's little-boy voice came out. "I shouldn't have prayed that, should I? To be able to shoot another man."

"You'd best ask somebody who knows God better than me for that answer."

"Or maybe just ask God."

"Yeah, or maybe that." Adam pushed away from the tree he'd been leaning against. Talking about God was making him uneasy. As they began walking back to Jake's camp, he thought of Charlotte and wondered what kind of answers she was finding among the Shakers. They believed some woman was the daughter of God. But at least they believed something.

As if Jake heard his thoughts, he asked, "Do you believe in God, Adam?"

"Well, sure. Everybody believes there's a God out there somewhere." Adam tried to wave off Jake's question as if it didn't bother him. "Only heathens say there's no God."

"But Mother always said it wasn't enough to believe in a God out there." Jake looked back up at the sky where fingers of lightning sliced through the darkness. "She said you had to believe in God in your heart. Inside you." Jake pounded his fist against his chest. "She said it was like love. That you could believe in love, but until you felt it in your heart, it didn't mean a thing."

Adam wanted to change the subject and talk about the storm, the war, anything but God. Or love. But he didn't. Instead he said, "I used to pray. I prayed for Daddy to come home. He didn't. I prayed when Grandfather said I should. He still beat me."

"So you stopped praying."

"I stopped."

"Completely? You didn't pray any when the shells were screaming over your head?"

Adam could feel Jake staring at him, but he didn't look over at his brother. He could have. It would have been too dark for Jake to see how unsure he felt. "I wanted to pray for you, Jake. I wanted the Lord to hold a hand over you and keep you safe. But I was like you and your prayer about shooting somebody. How could I pray just for you when there were so many dying? If the Lord held his hand over you, over me, over every man on the battlefield, then we'd be in a bowl with no way to wage war."

"But wouldn't that be good?"

"Perhaps." Adam looked at Jake then. "But what of the Union? What of freedom?"

"Some questions don't have answers, do they, Adam?"

"I don't know. Maybe our lot is to seek the answers."

Long after Adam left Jake to return to his hotel room, the questions with no answers whirled in his head. He tried to push them aside so he could concentrate on getting his sketches ready before Sam Johnson's man knocked on his door at first light. He didn't have to have answers, only illustrations. But as he flipped through his sketches, the sounds of exploding shells and men dying echoed in his ears, and he wanted to rip the drawings into a thousand pieces. He shoved aside the scenes of death and pulled a writing tablet toward him.

Dear Charlotte,

You won't mind if I don't call you Sister Charlotte, will you? Thinking of you as a Shaker sister will take some time. It appears that how that came to be will remain a puzzle at least for now. Tell me of your life there. It has to be very different from that of a Southern belle, but as I told you at Grayson, even then you were not like most young ladies I have had the pleasure of meeting in drawing rooms across the South.

I realize you have probably not had time to receive my earlier letter, but this night as I sit in the capital surrounded by a wounded army, I seem to need to put pen to paper again to you. To tell you of the first real battle of the war at a stream called Bull Run near the town of Manassas in Virginia. The Rebels won the day. It appears the Confederates aren't as ready to be beaten as the Union generals had hoped. I have a sketchbook full of the most horrible scenes of war. My pens seemed to be dripping blood on the paper. I will send you a couple of sketches, but you can see more in Harper's *if the Shakers read such. And it sounded as if they do if they saw their stairways on those pages.*

Here in Washington the generals will meet and the soldiers will be given new guns to replace those left behind on the field of battle. The armies will meet again and I must be there to draw more pictures. It is what I do.

It is good you are in a place where peace can bloom undisturbed like roses in a garden. Tell me of your garden and I will let my hand trace the flowers you see and hope that once the battle smoke clears there will still be flowers to pick in our own personal gardens.

Yours, Adam

He folded a picture of the army lining up for battle and then one of the carriages of onlookers, wagons, and soldiers all vying for a place on the road north as they retreated. Last he picked up a small book where he sometimes jotted bits of scenes to keep the sights fresh in his mind. He drew the bench under the dogwood tree beside Grayson's veranda. The one where he was sitting when he first saw Charlotte. She would know.

27

Charlotte settled into the routine at Harmony Hill. Up with the rising bell, work at whatever duty she and Dulcie were assigned, kneel in prayer, partake of the bountiful meals in silence, attend the meetings, and give ear to the teachings Sister Martha pushed at her. And each time Charlotte's eyes fell on Aunt Tish in her Shaker dress with a smile of freedom lighting up her face, she felt glad to turn her hand to whatever task the Shakers asked of her. She felt no trace of resentment in her heart when she looked ahead at the months she'd promised to Sister Altha.

Sister Martha told Charlotte she need give no thought to that promise. "The Ministry had no part in the words of Sister Altha speaking of your service in exchange for our Sister Latisha. That is not the Believers' way. We have ever believed in the freedom of choice. While it is our hope that those who come among us will choose the way of salvation, no one is forced to stay here against her will. Our sister erred in asking such from you and has confessed her wrong thinking."

Sister Altha might have confessed, but Charlotte saw in her eyes that she still considered Charlotte bound by her words. Charlotte didn't tell Sister Martha that. The deal was between Sister Altha and her—no one else. Sister Altha had gotten the Ministry to do what Charlotte asked. Charlotte could do no less than what she had promised in return.

She didn't think about what would happen if Adam Wade did actually come seeking her at Harmony Hill the way she often dreamed he might. At night when sleep was slow to come, she lay in her narrow Shaker bed and remembered Adam seeking her out in her mother's garden.

That didn't mean he would ever really search for her again. Adam Wade was a man of the world who had enjoyed a pleasurable dalliance with a pretty girl. She had no reason to imagine anything more, but she did. And the imaginings were sweet.

The first letters and sketches came in August. Sister Martha carried them to Charlotte. The summer heat sapped Sister Martha's strength, and although climbing the stairs to Charlotte's room made her breath come hard, she brought the letters there to Charlotte during the time of rest after the evening meal.

It was a diversion, she said. "A gift to lighten the burden of my advanced years. You and the letters from the artist."

"But news of the war is distressing." Charlotte looked up from Adam's letter. She tried not to let Sister Martha note her eyes lingering on the sentences mentioning gardens even as her mind did welcome the thoughts he'd intended to spark with his words and the sketch of the garden bench. She thought of how she would write to him of the rose gardens at Harmony Hill. There would be no need to tell of stripping the blooms of their beauty.

"Yea, it is ever so with wars that men of the world seem prone to engage in. But here at Harmony Hill, we will continue to gather peace to our bosoms and pray to keep the war from our village."

But days later, the Kentucky State Guard under the lead of John Hunt Morgan held a muster on the road that ran directly through Harmony Hill. The Guard leaders deemed the Shaker village a good central spot for men from the surrounding towns to join forces on the way south. Only weeks before, both North and South had promised not to recruit inside Kentucky's borders, but the promise was ignored as the cocky young men noisily gathered to march to the aid of the Confederacy. Not so far away across the river bottoms, a man offered his farm as a place for Union recruits to be mustered into service. When word first came of that, a few young Shaker men had slipped away from the village to sign up to save the Union. The elders promptly went after them to fetch them back into the peaceful life at the village.

❧

Charlotte pulled her bonnet forward and kept her face away from the young men in the street. She knew many of them from social gatherings and political functions, but she had no desire for them to recognize her in turn. As was their custom, the Shakers provided the men who asked with food and drink. The Believers never turned any wayfarer away hungry or in need.

"And these men are surely in need. If not of food then of spiritual rectitude," Sister Martha said with a sad shake of her head when she came to get Charlotte from the hat-making shop to help with the extra cooking. "It is as Elder Quinton says. Such a grievous sorrow to see fine young men, though of the world, so ready to learn the best way to let out the heart's blood of the ones they march against. You can see them out there practicing the thrust of their lances." Sister Martha glanced over at Charlotte to be sure she was paying attention. "All the while calling themselves Christians. It cannot be. Mother Ann teaches us that."

"Yea," Charlotte agreed. If she had learned nothing else while with the Shakers, she knew the value they put on peace. And yet at the same time, they seemed to hunger for news of the conflict as evidenced by their desire for her to carry on a correspondence with Adam.

Sister Martha went on with the rest of her little sermon. "Our testimony is for peace, now and always. No Christian can use carnal weapons or fight. Not and be true to the faith. We oppose wars of households, and wars of nations. All wars are the result of lusts for lands and for women. Those who marry will fight." She often repeated this teaching of Mother Ann along with other tenets as if by mere repetition she could plant the words in Charlotte's heart where they might become as deeply rooted there as they were in her own.

And so as the war clouds grew darker and Charlotte obediently walked the Shaker way, the letters back and forth marked the weeks and months that passed.

⚘

August 11, 1861
Dear Adam,
It is not necessary for you to call me sister if the word sits uncomfortably on your tongue or does not flow easily from your pen. It has come to sound familiar to my ear. Aunt Tish, Sister Latisha now,

has joined with us here and rejoices in the freedoms of the Shaker way. If you have the opportunity, please pass that news on to Mellie at your sister's. Tell her she can write to us here if she wants. The Ministry allows letters as you surely already know since your letters have been given to me.

Elder Quinton read portions of your letter at meeting. We had, of course, already heard news of the Battle at Bull Run, and were greatly disheartened by the Union defeat as it seems you were as well. The Believers seek peace in their villages and they can see that the country at war around them will greatly disturb that peace.

Roses of all colors bloom here in the Shaker gardens. My mother's garden bloomed with the same. I will hope the terrible smoke and fire of battle did not destroy every rose in the gardens you see.

As always,
Charlotte

September 15, 1861
Dear Charlotte,

Peace would be desired by many now, but it appears peace is far from reach. A new general has been put in command of the eastern army after the defeat at Bull Run. General McClellan is insisting on discipline among the troops even as more recruits are enrolled in the army every day. Discipline was greatly needed as many in our companies of soldiers were out of hand for some weeks after their return to Washington. It is rumored there won't be another major campaign before spring as the army licks its wounds and the leaders come to understand the need for intense training.

I hear that the peaceful neutrality Kentucky so desired has been shattered and a provisional Confederate government has been established in the southern part of your state. Is there not another Shaker village in that area?

The soldier in the sketch I enclose is my brother. He is nothing like me. I have also drawn your Shaker roses as I imagine them from your words. The gardens here bloom with the last roses of summer. But some roses never fade from a man's memory.

Your friend,
Adam

❦

October 30, 1861
Dear Adam,

The Believers are very busy with harvest and I am going to the fields to help gather the seeds for their seed packets in the spring. The work dries my hands, but they have lotions that keep the skin from cracking. The elders worry their usual market routes to the south will be closed come spring unless the war ends very soon which as you indicate does not seem likely. We saw your sketches of the battle in Harper's Weekly. *The scenes of death caused much distress among us.*

We have heard little news of note

except of course the conquest of the southern part of our state by the Confederates. My father must surely be beside himself. I think of him and Grayson often, but have no news from either since Sister Latisha came among us. They allow her to work in the kitchens almost exclusively since her rheumatism makes field work difficult. The Believers are kind to their elderly and infirm. Sister Latisha received a letter from Mellie, as did I. As you may know, she and Nate are married and she is expecting a child. The Shakers believe both to be sin and so Mellie's news was no reason for rejoicing here, but I am thankful to know she is safe.

An older sister named Martha has been instructing me in the Shaker way with great kindness. She is very patient with me even though I am slow to learn some of their tenets. Edwin, on the other hand, has embraced the peace of the village, and it is plain he is not the same Edwin I grew up with and once unwisely considered marrying. Even as I am not the same Charlotte. The Believers consider the individual family unit as the reason for much of the trouble in the world. That is why they live as brothers and sisters only.

The sisters picked the last of the roses for the rosewater before the frost last week. Thank you for the sketch of the roses and your brother. His eyes are much like yours. Sister Martha kept the sketch of your brother for the journal she keeps of the news of the war. Though I wrongfully desired to do so, I could not keep the one of the roses for it served no purpose other than ornamentation which is not allowed here.

I miss the garden and all that was in it at Grayson.

As always,
Charlotte

November 25, 1861
Dear Charlotte,
I can't imagine you working in the field as a common laborer. What

**would your father say if he knew
you were doing so? Does he
know?**

*Here in the capital the men are
settling into their winter camps. Some
have been given leave to go home for a
few weeks and others haven't waited
for leave, but have simply deserted
their posts. I consider deserting mine.
I am not enlisted in the army as the men
are, but I am obligated to Mr. Johnson
of* Harper's Weekly *who wishes me to
winter with the army and to stay abreast
of the political maneuvering of the
President and his Cabinet. I have gone
to some of the parties and
entertainments, but the gardens here
are cold and without beauty.*

**I send a sketch of the President.
He looks very grave and ages by the
week. I will send you no more
pictures of roses, but we both must
remember the rose sleeps under the
snow of winter and blooms again
with new life in the spring.**

**Your servant,
Adam**

December 29, 1861

Dear Adam,

My father has other problems on his mind with his support of the Union. There are many with Secesh sympathies in his district and I can only imagine the problems he may be having. It would be my mother who would be horrified by my day-to-day activities if she still lived.

She would be surprised, as you may be as well, that I enjoy working with my hands at useful enterprise. While some of the duties are tedious and tiring, there is purpose in the performing of those duties. Unlike the tedious needlework pushed on a young lady as the proper way for her to idle away the time. Here there is no idle time and the needle is plied to make useful things such as dresses or shirts to wear or hats to sell. They let me try to spin silk from the cocoons of their own silkworms, but that is a skill that takes much practice. I am better suited to weaving baskets. Another thing that is hard on the hands, but there is no shortage of their medicinal lotions.

I do miss my books, but Sister Martha says it is best to read the books about Mother Ann's life and study her precepts and teachings. Even so I think of the garden of books in my father's library and cannot always keep from regretting that I can no longer pluck the flower of one of those stories to bring the beauty of its words to my heart. The Ministry might strike out these sentences for they believe the beauty of anything lies in its usefulness and if the words only sing to one's heart and do not instruct in right living then such words are better left on the shelf.

It is good to think of the rose sleeping under the snow and to imagine it blooming again when I am able to return to the garden.

As always,
Charlotte

February 7, 1862

Dear Charlotte,

The New Year has commenced. Your letter was late making its way into my hands due to the heavy snow in the east. The messenger could not come to bring my mail for over two weeks. I felt fortunate to receive it before I left the winter camps around Washington, D.C.

Mr. Johnson asked me to go west to observe and illustrate the troops under the command of General Ulysses S. Grant who has undertaken the task of securing the Mississippi River for the Union and disrupting the Confederates' supply lines to Kentucky and Tennessee. Yesterday with the help of newly equipped ironclad ships, he surrounded Ft. Henry on the Tennessee River and easily defeated the Confederate forces there. When the fort's commanding officer asked for the best terms for capitulation, General Grant gave no ground and called for immediate and unconditional surrender.

With no chance for reinforcements, the Rebels had little choice but to lay down their weapons and be taken prisoners. Fifteen thousand of them. Some of the prisoners are being sent north, but others were paroled with the provision they won't take up arms against the Union again. A condition there is no way to enforce, but there is also no way to handle such a large group of prisoners.

The victory with so few losses is a good beginning for the Union forces in the west and may cheer the worried masses in the north. Bud Keeling, a reporter here, has sent in a report calling the taciturn Grant "Unconditional Surrender" Grant. He claims his story in the NY Times will make Grant an immediate hero. I doubt the General cares as he focuses on moving to his next objective which some say may be Ft. Donelson on the Cumberland River. Keeling and I are on one of the ironclads, but if the river narrows, we will have to find horses or march with the men. I will send a sketch of the ironclad for your Sister Martha's journal whenever I am able to post this missive to you. Not an easy thing in the midst of war.

It is difficult for me to imagine the Southern belle I met at Grayson now stirring soup and spinning thread. Are you gathering eggs and milking cows, too? What an image that brings to mind. One I am tempted to draw. But it's far nicer to imagine you walking the snow-covered paths in the garden as you wait for the return of the rose.

Ever your friend,
Adam

☙❧

April 20, 1862
Dear Adam,

It took your letter some time to reach Harmony Hill. We hope you are still in health although we have heard of the many dead at Shiloh. It seems wrong to have a battle where thousands died or were wounded named after a church on the battlefield. The Lord must shudder at such brazenness. Sister Martha says the Believers' Mother Ann would do worse than shudder at the total disregard of peace and love. The elders and eldresses have us laboring many dances for the swift arrival of peace. The whirling and dancing are the Shakers' way of reaching for the spirit. I have learned many of the dances and songs. It is very different from the church I attended in town, but I never have to worry about dozing off. Meeting is too lively for that, but you know. You were here to witness their meeting one Sunday.

Sister Martha says to thank you for the picture of the ironclad and wonders if you might include a sketch of General Grant in your next letter even though it appears he has lost some of his hero appeal. The papers indicate some in the North are calling for his removal due to the losses the army suffered at Shiloh. Still the Union came away victorious in the way battles are counted. The Believers were glad to hear that news and also of the abolishment of slavery in our great capital. I can only hope that the same will soon be true in Kentucky even though my father would argue against such an idea. But daily I see Sister Latisha's face and I am glad.

Sister Martha also asks me to remind you there is need to watch your words in your letters. She and they, the Ministry, are anxious to hear from the war front, but they will not allow wrong words such as those when you wrote of sketches that have naught to do with the war.

Sister Martha understands that you are not that familiar with the Shaker way, but she wants you to know that she and the Ministry would welcome your questions if you should seek to learn more of the truth of the Second Coming of Christ who was their Mother Ann. That is the actual name of the Shakers, you know. The Believers in the Second Coming of Christ. Shakers is the name attached to the Believers by those of the world, but the Believers often use it themselves now. Shaker seeds and brooms and chairs are much sought by those of the world or were before the war disrupted so many lives. And gardens.

Brother Edwin signed the Covenant a month ago and has given over Hastings Farm to the Believers. His people were freed. Two stayed here at Harmony Hill, but most went north to begin their new lives. It is too perilous for a freed slave here as they are seized for work on the roads or bridges without warning or recompense.

I will pray for your safety and watch for your illustrations in Harper's Weekly.

With prayerful concern,
Charlotte

May 21, 1862
Dear Charlotte,

I am picturing the beauty of the gardens at Harmony Hill. While I am beginning to understand the Shakers don't cultivate their gardens with the beauty an eye might behold in mind, as an artist I can't imagine not noticing nature's handiwork. I have been privy to so much beauty in gardens, but such beauty can seem very remote when the battles are raging around me. At times the battlefield scenes keep playing through my mind long after the guns fall silent. Then it is good to have the memory of a beautiful garden to dwell on in order to shut out the visions of death.

I am back in the capital where a new offensive is being planned. The men look more like soldiers now but it remains to be seen how well they will fare when once more they are ordered to march against the Rebel army. I also hear reports of rumblings to the south, some near your state. Guerilla bands are destroying rail lines and bridges and raiding the countryside for supplies. The Shakers might do well to think of what means they might take to protect their property if those raids should come near Harmony Hill.

Here is Sister Martha's picture of

General Grant. He doesn't look prepossessing but some think he is the best general for winning the day the Union has. At least he does not run from the fray.

Assure Sister Martha and the others that I had no intention of offending them with any of my words. I will consider my words more carefully before I pen them in future letters. As I consider the garden.

In appreciation of your concern,
Your friend, Adam

❧

June 15, 1862
Dear Adam,

Sister Martha thanks you for the picture of General Grant. She has not been well and often is unable to walk. The Shakers have put wheels on a chair for her and I push her to meals and meetings, but she must stay on the lower floors. She has no fear of dying but instead welcomes the thought of stepping across the divide into heaven. She thinks she must be over 90 years old but has forgotten the year of her birth. She and a daughter came into the Shakers in 1806. The daughter left the village, but Sister Martha has faithfully followed the Shaker way in her many years here. She says I have been a gift to her, but even more she is a gift to me as I accustom myself to this new life after losing my place at Grayson.

Sister Latisha has heard that many of our people there are gone, either sold to the south by Selena or they have run away to the north. I hope they all ran away. Father would not like to hear me say that, but he has been blinded by his obsession with Selena. Besides he hears me say nothing. I have not spoken to him since I came to Harmony Hill. I am beginning not to care so much. Although I do long to walk again in the garden as I did before I came here.

Mellie has sent word her baby boy is healthy and even more important, was born free. She says she named him Nathaniel Adam. A proper name for a free child. If I have done nothing else right in my life, I did right by stealing her out of Selena's hand. We heard of the battle at Fair Oaks. Another Union victory or so it seemed in the accounts the elder read to us. Were you there?

We pick the roses again for the Shaker rosewater.

As always,
Charlotte

July 7, 1862
Dear Charlotte,

I was at Fair Oaks as you ask in your last letter. It seems I have been at every battle or so my brother, Jake, tells me. He is at turns envious and grateful to have not been in the midst of the battle more than he has. He was at Fair Oaks and survived to fight again. That is all any soldier can wish for in this war. To gain an honorable victory and leave the field of battle with all limbs intact. The scenes around the hospital tents and houses are more than I can bear to draw and more than the readers could bear to see. Severed arms and legs are thrown out in a pile like so much stove wood and the flies come in clouds. Forgive me for putting that picture in front of your eyes. I should mark out those words, but I will not. It is part of war and I know you are one to face the truth.

It was strange to celebrate Independence Day with our nation so disastrously divided, but I hear the Southern troops celebrated the day with as much enthusiasm as those in the North. It is a strange time when Americans are shooting at Americans. Brothers at brothers, friends at friends. Who is the enemy?

Here is a picture of a little drummer boy with an Indiana regiment. The boy can't be over ten. But he beats the drum in cadence as the regiment marches into battle. He brings to mind Selena's son whom I

met the last time I was at Grayson.
Have you met him? He wants to be a
whale boat captain. At least he is not
marching out to war like this poor
child.

We will both walk in the garden
again. I am sure of it.

Your friend,
Adam

⋞⋟

July 17, 1862
Dear Adam,

We are unsettled here as word has
come to our ears that General John
Hunt Morgan and his cavalry men
are invading the state. They are not
an army such as led by General
McClellan or General Lee in that they
do not line up for battle against an
opposing army, but rather raid the
countryside and take whatever they
want. The Believers are very
concerned about losing their horses
and wagons to such raiders. There is
much talk of hiding the horses
should General Morgan's troops

come this far north and the news
that comes in seems to indicate they
are headed this way leaving a path of
destruction behind them.

Your sketch of the young drummer
boy brought tears to Sister Martha's
eyes and to mine. Sister Martha still
struggles to talk without getting out
of breath, but at least she is no
worse except when she thinks of the
raiders disturbing the peace at
Harmony Hill.

It seems strange to think of our
gardens of peace being disturbed
here, but the elders impress upon us
it is a possibility and we should be
on guard. I wonder at the condition
of the gardens at Grayson. Sister
Martha says it would be better if I
forget Grayson, but there are some
things that are hard to put out of my
mind and the garden is one of them.
So many things flowered in that
garden.

As always,
Charlotte

And so the year passed as the battles grew fiercer and edged nearer to Harmony Hill. There was no peace in Adam's letters or in Charlotte's heart. Except in the memory of the garden.

28

As July thunderstorms gave way to August heat, the news of General Morgan and his band of guerillas storming northward through the state toward Harmony Hill stretched the peace in the Shaker village to the breaking point. Rumors of barns and houses burned to the ground and of confiscated horses swept through the countryside like the wind rushing in before a storm. A man-made storm that struck like lightning and left a path of destruction.

At every meeting an elder from the West Family House stood up and prophesied doom for the village at the hands of the guerilla raiders. The Shakers could not defend their property. They had no weapons or any intent to have weapons. Even so, they had no desire to lose their horses or see their crops ruined before harvest. They sent some of the brethren out for news and appealed to their Mother Ann and the Eternal Father to keep the raiders far from their village. But each report that came in indicated the guerillas coming straight toward them.

Charlotte felt the tension that swept through the village, but her worries were more for Grayson. She saw no reason for the raiders to bother the peaceful Shakers, but her father's house was different. His Union sympathies were no secret.

In spite of her concerns, she didn't try to contact her father to get news of Grayson. She had written him in June when she turned twenty-one, but had no response. Not even through Selena. Her pride kept her from writing again. Her year of self-imposed servitude in exchange for Aunt Tish had come to an end, but she saw little choice except to stay where she was

at Harmony Hill. One day passed into another with little difference except on the
rare days a letter came from Adam.

When her eyes feasted on the words he
wrote to her, she couldn't keep from dreaming of one day seeing Adam again. She
imagined him desiring her hand on his
arm, her lips surrendering to his. The way
he never failed to mention gardens in each
letter seemed to hint at that, but she could
hardly expect him to desert the battlefield
to seek her in the Shaker gardens. And so
she waited as the fearsome shadow of
the war edged closer to Harmony Hill and
Grayson and darkened her mind with
worry. She waited and she prayed.

At Grayson, she'd taken little time for
more than a token childish prayer whispered occasionally at bedtime, sort of the
way one might wish upon a star. Not out of
any real belief, but simply on the off chance
it might help one's fortunes. Then she'd
come to Harmony Hill and become Sister
Charlotte who was required to kneel in silent prayer every morning and night and
before and after every meal. At first she
had merely assumed the posture of prayer
while allowing her mind to meander wher-

ever it willed, but then Charlotte had begged the Lord for Mellie's safety after she left the village.

Something about those prayers had awakened her spirit like spring showers sprouted the seeds in a freshly planted garden. Before she came to the Shakers, she had chased after her own answers as she tried to prove herself worthy. Now she felt the gentle hand of the Lord hovering over her, promising her answers, but even more, promising her love not because she was the senator's daughter or the heiress to Grayson or even Sister Charlotte, but because she was Charlotte. Simply Charlotte.

And she kept praying. For Aunt Tish. For Sister Martha. For peace. For the soldiers on both sides of the conflict. For Adam. Some of those prayers she let rise from her heart without words, for it was surely wrong to pray for love while she wore the Shaker dress and pretended to live a life where such feelings were deemed sin.

She didn't pretend so much as to sign the Shaker Covenant after she turned twenty-one in June, even though Sister Martha encouraged her daily to do so. Charlotte knew she stood outside the circle of full belief in their ways. Grayson called to her. Adam called to her. She did not want to stop dreaming of love.

Sister Martha sensed the reason for Charlotte's divided spirit, but she didn't condemn her nor try to push her out of the village. Sister Altha showed no such kindness. Even though she had asked for the promise of Charlotte's labor, she could not seem to accept Charlotte's service or humble behavior. Instead she kept looking at her with suspicious doubt.

"I don't know why the Ministry allows Sister Martha to waste her time with you," she told Charlotte late one afternoon in August when they crossed paths. "It is plain to see you will never walk the Shaker way with commitment. You are only biding your time here. For what purpose, I cannot discern."

"I perform the duties asked of me." Charlotte kept her voice quiet. There was naught to be gained by testing her will against that of Sister Altha's. Even so, she was unable to keep from reminding her of how she had kept her word. "I have done the year you asked for Sister Latisha."

Sister Altha waved her hand in dismissal.

"That was of little worth. Where is the land you promised?"

"I will keep my promise. When and if it is mine to give." Charlotte kept her eyes on the path as she wondered if she dared edge over on the grass to pass around Sister Altha. She was on her way to her room and rest after pushing Sister Martha in her wheeled chair back to the Centre Family House. The humid heat sapped Sister Martha's energy and she could not walk over a dozen steps without losing her breath.

Charlotte started to step to the side, but Sister Altha shifted over in front of her. The woman glanced around to be sure no one was near enough to hear them before she said, "What of your promise to Mother Ann and the Eternal Father? Do you not want to sign the Covenant as Brother Edwin did? You passed your twenty-first birthday, did you not?"

"Sister Martha says it is best to feel sure in one's heart before such a decision is made." Charlotte answered carefully in the meekest voice she could summon. She had no wish to cross Sister Altha, who could see that she and Dulcie worked nowhere but in the laundry house all through the rest of the summer. That was Charlotte's most dreaded duty. That and ironing in the heat-filled upper room of the Gathering Family House.

"Your heart does not run after the truth of a Believer, but after Brother Edwin."

"Nay, that is not true. I have confessed my wrong motives when I followed Brother Edwin here. I have seen how he has embraced your teachings. At Union meeting last week he explained as much. But I yet have much to learn and it would not be right to sign the Covenant until I have a better understanding."

"Sister Martha fools herself thinking you desire such. Speak the truth. You want to run back to your easy life with servants to fan you and bring your food on silver platters." Sister Altha's voice was filled with scorn.

Rather than anger at Sister Altha's harsh words, Charlotte was surprised to feel a sudden compassion for the woman in front of her. She had rarely seen her with a look of peace or happiness. Instead she always seemed anxious to catch someone doing wrong and had no eye for the good even among these people who professed to seek the good gifts of the spirit each and every day.

For a brief moment, Charlotte thought to reach out and touch Sister Altha's arm, but she stayed her hand as she answered calmly, "Nay. While it is true I miss many things about my home before I came to Harmony Hill, I count it a blessing to learn the simple gift of laboring with my hands. There is satisfaction in doing a task well. However menial that task might be."

"I don't believe you." Sister Altha narrowed her eyes on Charlotte.

"Why not?" Charlotte sincerely wanted to know as she met the woman's sour look.

"You have a wrong spirit. That's easy enough to see."

"And what of your spirit, Sister Altha?" Charlotte still felt no anger as she kept her voice as gentle and kind as possible. "In all the years you have been here at Harmony Hill, haven't you ever wanted to seek a gift of kindness instead of one of fault-finding?"

For a moment Charlotte thought Sister Altha might strike her as the sister's face flushed beet red under her white cap. She seemed at a loss for words at Charlotte's effrontery.

Charlotte spoke again. "I beg your forgiveness if my words were ill spoken. Or untrue." She made the last two words a bit of a question.

"You dare to try to give me spiritual lessons. You who cling to your wrong spirit. My spirit is true." Underneath the fire flashing in the woman's eyes, Charlotte thought she glimpsed a hint of doubt.

"As you say, Sister Altha. I am surely wrong." And just as surely to be doing laundry duty for weeks, she thought with an inward groan. She would have to beg Dulcie's forgiveness for not bridling her tongue.

"Be about your duties and stop wagging your tongue about things of which you know nothing." Sister Altha pushed past Charlotte and hurried up the path as if she were late for her own duties.

Charlotte watched her for a moment before sighing and going on toward her sleeping room. She would have to confess her unrestrained words to Sister Martha on the morrow.

But the next day, unkind words were the least of the Believers' concerns after news came that General Morgan's raiders were in the next county and headed their way. Some of the brethren hurried the best horses into the woods to be hidden out of sight. Others hid away some of their stores while the rest of the Shakers prayed their diligent prayers and went about their assigned duties even as they kept an anxious eye to the south.

Charlotte kept her eye a bit to the southeast as she and Dulcie picked beans in the garden. By the middle of the morning, smoke was rising on the distant southern horizon. Too far for Grayson, Charlotte assured herself. Even so, she wanted to set down her picking bucket and run to Grayson to be sure it and her father were safe, but a year of obedience to the Shaker way kept her pulling the beans from the vines as was her duty. Besides, her father would not want to see her.

By the time the bells called them to their midday meal, new plumes of smoke in the sky showed the advance of the raiders. Charlotte found it almost impossible to sit and silently eat her food in the biting room while the feeling of foreboding grew stronger inside her by the minute. The squeak of the benches as the sisters on one side and the brothers on the far side of the room shifted in their seats indicated she wasn't the only one feeling uneasy. When she knelt for her moment of prayer after the meal, she prayed for Grayson even as she wondered if the others prayed for Harmony Hill or perhaps some other worry of their worldly homes as she did.

A few hours later, General Morgan and his soldiers rode into the village carrying the smell of smoke with them, but they held no lit torches. The Shaker elders were quick to offer food for the soldiers and water and grain for their horses with the unspoken hope that with their bellies full they might ride on without doing damage to the village. Even more the Believers never turned away the hungry. It was their duty to be generous and share the bounty of their labor as Mother Ann's teachings demanded, but they'd never had the hungry show up on their doorsteps in such number.

Charlotte and Dulcie were summoned to the kitchen to help prepare the food for the tables the brethren set up out in the open for the soldiers. Charlotte was slicing bread when Edwin appeared at the kitchen door. She knew as soon as she heard him speak her name that he brought bad news.

"Sister Charlotte. Elder Logan has given me permission to speak to you."

Charlotte looked over at Sister Altha who was overseeing the food preparation in the Gathering Family kitchen. It mattered not whether she received permission. She would still go hear what Edwin had come to tell her, but out of habit, she sought consent. Sister Altha nodded her head once.

Aunt Tish paused in rolling out pie crusts at the work table to reach out to squeeze Charlotte's arm with a flour-covered hand as though to give her courage. Charlotte carefully placed the bread knife on the cutting board before she turned toward the door. She moved across the floor as though pushing her feet through a fast-moving stream.

Once she was face-to-face with Edwin, he hesitated and Charlotte wanted to grab him as she had many times when they were children to shake the words out of him. Instead she moistened her lips and said, "Say what you have come to say."

He pushed the words out all in a rush. "Grayson's burning. Harlan Fulton told me. He says they just came from there. That it is as much as your father deserves for speaking against the Confederate States."

Charlotte remembered Harlan Fulton. He was the hothead nephew of one of her father's fiercest opponents in the county. She'd seen him get into fisticuffs over something no more serious than a spilled glass of lemonade. "Can you believe him?" she asked now.

"Yea," Edwin said. "The smoke rises from the right direction."

Charlotte stepped out of the kitchen but the building blocked her view to the southeast. Even so, smoke hung in the air. It seemed impossible to think that smoke might be from her burning home. Her beloved Grayson. She stared back at Edwin. "And Father? Was he there?"

"He was." Again Edwin looked reluctant to speak. "You might want to go to him. Harlan says he's in a bad way."

"Did they shoot him?" She was surprised at how calmly she asked the words, as if she were doing no more than inquiring after a horse with a broken leg. She wasn't letting herself feel.

"Nay. Harlan claims some among them wanted to, but it turned out there was no need. The senator climbed out a window onto the roof to hide from the raiders but they saw him. He was coming back inside at gunpoint when Harlan says he must have suffered a heart attack."

"Is he dead?" Again the icy calmness in her voice.

"Nay. Not when they rode away. That is why I came to tell you. So you can go to him. To tell him goodbye if you so desire."

"Selena is with him."

"Nay. Harlan says she hardly looked toward him when they carried him out of the house. He said she seemed more worried about what yet remained within the house."

"Perhaps her son," Charlotte said.

"Perhaps." Edwin shrugged as if it was of no matter and of truth it was not. "Elder Logan let me bring you a horse."

"I thought they were all hidden."

Edwin looked quickly over his shoulder to be sure none of the soldiers were near enough to hear her words. "Not all," he whispered.

Charlotte looked up at Sister Altha, who had come to the kitchen door. Her face was set in harsh lines, but it had been so ever since they had begun to prepare the food for the guerilla raiders. It did not change as she said, "It might not be safe for a sister alone among these . . ." She waved her hand as if unable to come up with a proper word of disdain before she finished. "These ruffians who claim to be soldiers but merely loot and burn."

"Please, I beg you not to speak so plainly, Sister Altha." Edwin looked over his shoulder again. "We hope to placate them with food and not anger them with words."

"Yea, you are right, Brother Edwin." Sister Altha lowered her voice.

"Please." The icy calmness deserted Charlotte as her chest began to feel tight. Tight like her father's. "My father may be dying. Please, I must go."

"You need not my permission if Elder Logan has supplied you with a horse."

Charlotte waited for no more words. She was already halfway across the yard to the back fence where she saw the horse tied.

Edwin ran after her. "Wait, Charlotte. Elder Logan requested Harlan's captain get a guard together to ride with you and ensure your safety."

But Charlotte didn't wait. She loosed the reins and, putting one foot in the stirrup, easily swung up into the saddle. She had not been on a horse since she had come to the Shakers, but she hadn't forgotten how to ride. She yanked the full Shaker skirt down to cover her legs with one hand before leaning close to the horse's neck as she urged him forward. She saw no reason to delay her leaving to wait for a guard of the very men who had put a torch to her home and perhaps killed her father. Panic rose in her that she wouldn't be in time, and she dug her heels into the horse's flanks. She hardly noticed when her cap flew off behind her.

29

By the time she cut across the front field to the house, the roof had already surrendered to the flames and caved in. The fire was like a live thing, slamming her in the face with its heat and roaring its victory as it raced up the walls and shot flames out the shattered windows. Her home, everything she treasured, going up in smoke.

Furniture littered the lawn. The hall tree. A rocking chair. The wicker pieces from the veranda. Lamps and other small items were pitched about as though spewed from the windows. Down the way, Perkins was yelling at some men as they pulled the carriages out of the carriage house before its roof caught a stray cinder. The rest of the slaves stood in a tight cluster, staring at the burning house as though spellbound by the flames. Only a few of the faces looked familiar. Twilight was giving way to night, but the fire pushed back the darkness and danced an eerie light on the scene.

Charlotte searched through the other people scattered about the lawn. She recognized some neighbors who must have been attracted by the smoke. Others she didn't know. The child, Landon, leaned against a tall angular woman in a dress not unlike her own without the collar and apron. Perhaps his governess. The boy's face gleamed in the light of the fire, but Charlotte couldn't tell whether he was enjoying the spectacle or mourning his loss.

When he heard the horse, he turned, and there was no doubt that he was glad to see her. He tried to pull away from the woman, but her long fingers dug into his shoulders to hold him there against her as she leaned down to speak fiercely in his right ear. She was so focused on keeping the child under control that she didn't give Charlotte a second glance.

Charlotte didn't see her father. Or Selena. Perhaps her father had been carried somewhere away from the fire. Or hurried off in a carriage to town to find a doctor. Or had a blanket pulled over his body. She shook away that thought. She couldn't be too late.

She tried to guide her horse across the lawn toward Perkins. He would know about her father. But the horse already spooked by the flames neighed in panic as something exploded in the fire with a loud pop. The horse skittered sideways and tried to rear up.

Willis appeared out of the shadows by the horse's head to grab its bridle and throw a bandanna over the horse's eyes. "Your horse won't be wantin' to get any nearer the fire, Miss Lottie. I'd better hold him here for you."

It might have been any day she'd come in from riding. He was that calm. Even with the house burning and her riding up in Shaker garb after being gone more than a year.

"Where's Father? Am I too late?" Charlotte slid off the horse to the ground.

"The Massah's bad, Miss Lottie, but he was still breathin' last I was over there."

"Where?"

"He's out in Miss Mayda's garden or what's left of it. We pulled your momma's faintin' couch out for him to lay on after those sons of the devil set the house on fire." Willis pointed toward the side of the house. "We tried to move him back a ways from the flames before he threatened to shoot us all. Says he has to stay in the garden. You try to talk him back some, Miss Lottie. Where it's not so hot."

"Where's Selena?"

"I ain't knowin' that, Miss." The black man's face went stiff as he turned away from her back to the horse.

It didn't matter. Selena couldn't keep her away from her father now. Nothing could. Nothing but death.

She lifted her skirts and ran across the yard. A few of the neighbors called out to her, but she acted as if she didn't hear them as she hurried on toward the garden and her father. She was almost to the corner of what used to be the veranda when Landon jerked free from the woman holding him and ran to grab Charlotte's skirt. She had to stop.

"I knew you would come, Charlotte. I told Miss Pennebaker you would. She says I don't have a sister. Not really. That you were just part of a game my mother was playing, but she's wrong." Tears glistened on his cheeks in the light of the fire. "Isn't she?"

They were too near the flames. Charlotte gasped to get her breath as she stepped back from the heat, yanking the child with her. He seemed unaware of their danger as his eyes never left her face. He needed her to say yes. So she did. "I am your sister. Come." Wasn't she being sister to a few hundred at Harmony Hill? What difference could one more little brother make? She took his hand. "Let's go find our father."

He wasn't on the couch that stood a little distance from the fire. Instead he sat slumped on a bench much too close to the flames as his longtime valet stood over him stoically fanning air toward his face with a spray of leaves. The heat was overpowering. Selena was nowhere to be seen.

"Father, we have to move back from the fire," Charlotte cried.

He looked up at the sound of her voice, but his eyes showed no recognition.

Ruben spoke up. "Massah Charles won't leave the tree he planted for Miss Mayda."

That tree was the only thing left from the garden Charlotte had known. Her mother's rosebushes and lilacs were gone, replaced by evergreen shrubs and ironwork benches. Selena had wiped away the touch of Charlotte's mother from the garden. Except for the dogwood tree, and now its leaves were scorched and shriveling in the heat of the fire.

"He can't stay here. We can't stay here." Charlotte pulled one of her father's limp arms across her shoulders. Even through her skirt, the bench felt hot against her leg.

Ruben hesitated. "I've always done what the Massah tol' me to do. He tol' me not to let nobody move him."

"I'm not nobody." Charlotte tugged on her father's arm, but there was no way she could move him by herself. "Help me get him back from the fire. Now."

She put authority in the word, but Ruben stared down at the ground and mumbled, "I can't, Miss Lottie. He tol' me."

Charlotte stared at Ruben, nonplussed by his refusal to do as she said. She'd almost forgotten Landon when he slipped around her to push his face right up in front of her father's. "Papa," he said with no hint of panic in his voice. "I'm thirsty. Can we go find a drink?"

Her father put his hand on the boy's head and actually smiled. "Landon, my boy. Where's your mother?"

"I don't know, Papa. But Charlotte's here."

"Charlotte!" And now his smile included her. "When did you get here from Virginia?"

"Virginia?" Charlotte stared at her father, not sure she'd heard him right. But then she remembered Landon asking her the same thing in the graveyard. Could her father have really thought she was in Virginia? "I haven't been in Virginia."

He didn't seem to comprehend her words as he reached a trembling hand toward her. "I've been so worried about you with all the news of battles in the East, but Selena assured me you were safer there than trying to come home." His lips stuck together and made each word a struggle.

"I'm home now," she said as she took his hand. There was so much to say, so much to try to understand, but not here with the fire nearly singeing their hair. "But remember, we've got to get Landon something to drink."

"Yes, yes. Landon." He looked up at Ruben. "Ruben, bring some drinks."

"Yassir. I has them ready down at the end of the garden."

"Please, Papa. It's too hot for me here," Landon said.

Her father looked past them then at the fire before he turned his eyes back to Charlotte. "Grayson's burning, you know," he said as though announcing a rainstorm to her after her head was already soaked. His voice quivered as he went on. "Your mother's crying out to me from the flames. She loved this place. More than she ever did me."

"Nay." Charlotte shook her head a little as if to clear away the Shaker talk before she went on. "That's not true. She loved nothing more than you." She and Ruben pulled him to his feet to begin inching him away from the fire. "A house can be rebuilt."

"Not by me, I fear." He looked down. "I can't feel my feet. Selena won't like that. She does love to dance." His eyes fell on Landon again as they lowered him to the fainting couch. The heat of the flames was not as intense there. "Did you tell me where your mother is?"

"No sir. I don't know where she is."

"She's not in the fire, is she?" He didn't sound worried so much as curious. Then he remembered Landon again. "Of course she's not, lad. I wouldn't want you to think that. I'm sure she's around somewhere."

Ruben had run off toward the slave quarters as soon as they got her father down on the couch, and now he came back with a mason jar of water. Charlotte's father took the jar, but his hand shook so that a good bit of the water spilled out on his pants.

Charlotte eased the jar out of his hand and held it to his lips. "Drink, Father."

He gulped the water greedily before he put his hand over hers on the jar. His hand was still shaking. "I'm so relieved you're safe, Charley. I could have never forgiven myself if something had happened to you in Virginia. Selena shouldn't have let you go after they seceded, but she said you insisted on leaving. That you were angry with me for trying to replace your mother by marrying her. And then when you kept sending my letters back unopened, I knew she must be right." He squeezed her hand. "I'm glad you came home."

Charlotte looked at him and tried to take in what he was saying. Unopened letters? There had been no letters. Her hand started trembling like his as she realized what Selena had done. When water sloshed out of the jar, Ruben lifted it from her hand.

"But, Father," Charlotte said. "I never—"

"Shh, Charley. None of that matters now." He touched her lips with his fingertips to stop her words, then took her hand and squeezed it. "I'm just glad you came home."

"So am I, Father." Charlotte blinked back tears as she tightly held his hand, so familiar, so loved. Selena had lied to them both. She fumbled about in her head for the right words, the gentlest words, to explain how they'd been fooled.

Those words were forgotten when her

father gasped and started jerking on his shirt front. "Why is this shirt so tight? It's binding me."

Charlotte pulled free his buttons, but he still clutched at his chest. He sounded out of breath as he went on. "They thought I was a coward, but it was her. She was the one who made me climb out on the roof. She thought she could sweet-talk them into going away if I wasn't there. But they saw me and accused me of cowardice. I would have rather they shot me clean and true through the heart. It would have been an easier way to pass."

"No, Papa," Landon cried out and laid his head on her father's chest.

"Now, don't take on so, Son." He stroked Landon's head a few times before he looked back up at Charlotte. "You're going to like Landon. He's a fine boy. Wants to be a whale boat captain when he grows up."

"So I've heard," Charlotte said.

Her father looked back toward the fire. "Might be a good place to be right now. Floating on the open sea. The salt air in your face. Searching for that one whale that might take you on the ride of your life."

"You can sail with me, Papa," Landon said.

"You just think about me when you stand in the helm. That will be my ride, Landon." He smiled weakly down at the boy. Sweat beads popped out all over his face. He reached for Charlotte's hand again. "Do you forgive me, Charley? After you left, I wanted to follow you to Virginia to talk to you, but everybody said it was too dangerous, and now look at me. Grayson conquered by the Rebels."

"Not conquered. Never conquered," Charlotte said. "Under us is still Grayson land. Our land." She wanted to take off her shoes and stockings and feel the grass and dirt between her toes.

"Grayson land, yes. But not my land. Your grandfather just endured my presence here. I was the necessary evil to see that the Grayson blood continued even if the name did not." He looked around. "Yours now, Charley. Or what's left of it."

"What of Selena?" Charlotte wanted to sling the woman's deceit in his face, but he looked so sad that she didn't have the heart to add to his sorrow.

"Ah, Selena. I fancied I loved her. You

can forgive me for that, can't you, Charley? I tried to explain in my letters. An old man's last folly." He made a sound that started out a laugh and changed to another gasp of pain as he grabbed his chest. "Too tight."

"Hold on, Father. We'll get a doctor." Charlotte pushed her words at him, willing him to listen and keep breathing, but his eyes glazed over as his head slumped down on his chest. She grabbed him and tried to shake life back into him. "Wait, Father! Wait."

Ruben bent down in front of her with tears streaming down his cheeks. "Ain't no use, Miss Lottie. He's done gone on."

Beside her, Landon let out a pitiful whimper.

Charlotte blinked her eyes and let Ruben gently ease her father away from her hands. "I didn't get to tell him I forgave him. That I never saw his letters," she said softly more to herself than to Ruben or Landon. "I wanted to tell him."

"He knows now," Landon said.

Charlotte looked at the child. "But he died before he heard me."

"The Lord will tell him," Landon assured

her with true faith. "The Lord will want him
to be happy in heaven, so he'll tell him. My
first papa told me that before he died. He
was real sick, but he told me everybody's
happy in heaven. That all the tears stay
down here."

"Listen to the child. He knows what he's
talkin' 'bout. Things is always good up in
paradise even if there is plenty of tears
falling down here," Ruben said as he laid
her father back on the couch with great
care. He pushed her father's eyelids down
over his eyes and folded his arms across
his chest. "I'll get a blanket out of the carriage house."

Charlotte stared at her father's body
and desperately wished he would even yet
gasp and rise up off the couch to talk to
her again. But of course he didn't.

Landon edged closer to Charlotte and
spoke in a small voice. "I wish I could go
hide. It's easier when you can hide."

Charlotte put her arm around him. "Does
it frighten you to look at him?"

"No. It only frightens me that he's gone.
I liked my second papa. I might not like my
third. Or he might not like me."

"Will there be a third?"

"Oh yes. I think Mother already has him picked out. She doesn't like to leave things to chance. She says it's best to always have a plan."

"I used to think that," Charlotte said. She tightened her arm around the boy and felt the trembles shaking him. She turned him toward her. "Here, Landon, hide against me."

He buried his face in her dress. His voice was muffled as he asked, "Can I cry? Mother says young gentlemen don't cry, but I don't think I can keep from it."

"Everybody cries sometimes," Charlotte whispered as tears rolled down her cheek and fell on Landon's messed curls. "Even whale boat captains."

And behind them Grayson burned.

30

August 22, 1862

Dear Adam,

My father was buried last Thursday. Elder Logan, Sister Martha, and Dulcie came to be with me as the preacher from town spoke words over his grave. I'm sure my father's political friends and our neighbors were shocked to see me in Shaker dress with a cap covering my hair. What a change for them to witness, but then the whole nation is in a constant state of flux with the way the current conflict is tearing us apart.

There is much sorrow. Neighbors down the way, the Jacksons, just got word their son was killed at White Oak Swamp. Other neighbors, the Andersons, lost their son at Bull Run a year ago. One fought for the Confederates and the other for the Union, but at my father's funeral, Mr. Jackson and Mr. Anderson stood shoulder to shoulder and grieved with me and with each other. Death is the great equalizer.

Behind us as we stood around my father's grave, smoke still rose from the skeletal remains of my Grayson home. General Morgan's raiders set it afire when they came through here. They did not shoot my father, but the result was the same. His heart could not bear the destruction of his home and his life.

Selena disappeared the night of the fire and was not at the graveside to be a grieving widow. Landon, her young son, is in the charge of his governess and they are at a hotel in town waiting for her to return. The governess says Selena has left him in her charge for extended periods before and that she is confident Selena will return for him. As a mother should. Landon was very sad the day we laid Father to rest. He and Father had established a family bond. So much so that he considers me his rightful sister. I don't mind. He is a charming child. So charming I wonder if Selena can really be his natural mother. I, of course, would not suggest such a thing to him.

The Rebel raiders did no harm to Harmony Hill. The Shakers fed them gladly as they do all who come hungry to their doorsteps and in gratitude the men went on their way without stealing so much as one horse. The elders and eldresses were much relieved. But there is great consternation that General Morgan's raid is only a beginning. A Union cavalry troop camped out in the Shaker pastures not four days after Morgan passed through here. It is unthinkable what would have been the result if they had met in our village.

I remain with the Believers. Sister Martha still instructs me in their ways and says I will surely someday know the peace she carries in her heart if I open my ears to her words. Aunt Tish, Sister Latisha, has embraced the life. In one way she was sorry to hear Grayson was ashes for she knew how it wounded me, but I think she cared not a whit for herself. Grayson wasn't her home. It was her prison.

Every day I recall a new thing to mourn. My mother's portrait. The book of children's poems my grandfather often read to me before he died. The silver bell my mother gave me when I was four so that I could call for help if I was afraid in the night. But they are only things. As Sister Martha says, it is better to give up ownership of all things and to gather only spiritual gifts.

My mother's garden is gone, destroyed by Selena long before the fire completed her work. We will

never again walk among the roses at Grayson.

Sadly,
Charlotte

She was becoming one of the Shakers, Adam thought as he looked up from reading through the letter for a second time. Charlotte a Shaker with no will or spirit of her own. It was almost more than he could imagine, but the proof was there in the words in front of his eyes. He scanned through them again. *Our village. Remain with the Believers. Someday know the peace. Spiritual gifts.*

He shut his eyes and pulled her image into his mind. He longed to look into her green eyes and perhaps take the pins from her beautiful red hair. At times in the last year, Charlotte's letters were all that had kept him sane as he followed first Grant's army in the west before Sam urged him back to the east to be on hand for McClellan's great victory as the general launched his Peninsular Campaign.

The Yankee army marched to within six miles of Richmond, but the Confederates didn't give ground. McClellan was forced to fall into retreat before he was ordered to load his army on boats to join General Pope in northern Virginia where once more the armies were fated to meet at Bull Run Creek. The Union army attacked, this time sent into battle by General Pope in a rash bid to conquer the Southern forces before all of McClellan's men had time to reach the field of battle. But Robert E. Lee, now in command of the Southern army, turned the tables on Pope's forces and launched a surprise counterattack. In a tragic repeat of the first battle at Bull Run, the Union troops once more retreated back to Washington. Yet again there was no great victory to encourage the Northern people.

On the march away from the Bull Run battleground, Adam gave up his horse to a wounded soldier and trudged along the muddy roads with Jake's Massachusetts regiment. Since he often bivouacked with the men, they had become his company. He knew each of them by name and had done sketches of many of the men to send to their wives and mothers. And now those sketches would be all that ever returned

home of some of the men who had fought
their last battle.

Jake no longer worried aloud to Adam
about what he would do when he saw the
elephant. He knew, for he had charged
forward in the face of deadly fire time and
again. He had loaded and fired his gun at
the men in gray and seen them thrown
backward when the bullets found their target. He had heard bullets sing past his
head and watched the men beside him
fall. His horse had died under him, but he
had stood and not run. He had survived to
fight again.

But though he came through the battle
unwounded, he'd been weakened by a
bout with dysentery the week before and
began coughing as they marched away
from Bull Run back toward Washington
in defeat yet again. A defeat made even
more disheartening by the heavy rain beating down on their heads.

The rain made talk impossible, but there
was nothing to say anyway. Nothing to be
done except plod on through the mud. To
move one foot in front of the other and try
not to remember the sight of too many
young soldiers sprawled in death, too many

exploding shells, too many wounds from minié balls that tore muscles asunder and made amputation the only treatment.

Adam wanted to shut from his ears the sounds of horses dying, artillery shells screaming overhead, wounded men crying for help. He wanted to get on a train and ride away from it all. Maybe go west again and be in the wide open spaces where he could sketch the faces of the pioneers pushing the nation westward. In the last year, his pen had drawn too many scenes of battle, sent back too many sketches of Union defeats. Gone were the early dreams of a quick victory and a fast return to peace. At times peace no longer seemed possible. And now it seemed that even the peace he'd always imagined at Harmony Hill was being disturbed by the war.

He looked up from Charlotte's letter as Jake stirred on the narrow bed in front of him. What the enemy hadn't been able to do on the battlefield, the miserable weather and wretched conditions in the camps were doing to his once strong young brother. Jake tried to lift his head up off the pillow, but he was too weak as he was wracked with coughs that tore at his lungs but gave him no relief. Adam stuffed the letter inside his shirt and moved to hold Jake's head. When his coughing was spent, Adam gently wiped the flecks of blood from his brother's lips and held the draught of medicine the doctor had prepared for him to his mouth. He got him to swallow a bit.

Jake's captain had moved him into the makeshift hospital the night before when he'd begun to burn with fever. Adam hadn't been at the camp. He'd gone to the hotel to put the finishing touches on his sketches of the battle. If he'd been there when his brother most needed him, Adam would have never let him be brought to this long, narrow building that had been turned into a hospital for soldiers like Jake who had survived the battle only to be felled by disease. Cots were set up so close together that the men could have reached out and held hands all the way down the line if most of them hadn't been too sick to even realize there was a man in the next bed.

Nurses wearing long white aprons and caps that made him think of Charlotte in her Shaker dress moved among the men to comfort them with a gentle word or, if they were very bad, a dose of laudanum. Most of the women had no training, but simply showed up at the hospital to care for the men. A couple of doctors made the rounds. Twice while Adam watched, the doctors stood up after examining one of the men and let the nurse with him pull the sheet up over the soldier's face. And though he hated himself for it, Adam knew that when he next took out his sketchbook, he would draw that picture.

As the hours dragged by, Adam began to fear the face his pencil might draw under the sheet would be Jake's. Adam had come to sit with Jake as soon as he received word he'd been brought to the hospital, but he should have never left Jake to go to the hotel. He knew his brother was getting sick as they marched back to Washington. He'd heard his cough. He should have stayed in the camp to take care of him.

If he'd been there when Jake first began to burn with fever, he could have loaded him on a train and taken him to their mother and Phoebe. Even now he wanted to pick him up in his arms and carry him home. There Jake might fight off the pneumonia, but the doctor claimed moving him would

surely kill him. That his only chance was
to ride out the fever. To fight off the pneumonia. He was a young man. He had a
chance.

The second morning, Jake seemed improved. The sheen of fever still sat on his
face and the coughing continued to bring
up blood, but at least there was recognition in his eyes when he looked at Adam.

"What are you doing here?" Jake's voice
was little more than a hoarse whisper.

"What do you think?" Adam helped Jake
sit up a little as he put a glass of water to
Jake's lips. The nurse had promised to
bring broth when she saw Jake was awake.

Jake turned his head and looked around.
The water had moistened his mouth and
made his voice stronger. "I don't know. For
sure, there's nothing to draw here that any
of the people back home will want to see."

"You've got that right," Adam agreed in a
voice that he knew at once was too hearty.

Jake eyed him for a moment before he
said, "I must be fearful sick." He made a
sound that might have been an attempt at
a laugh, but it triggered his coughing.

Adam held Jake's shoulders while the
coughs tore at his lungs. In the last few

weeks, Jake had lost so much weight while he battled dysentery and now the pneumonia that his bones almost protruded from his skin.

When at last the coughs eased, Jake wiped his mouth and looked at the blood on the rag. He stared at it a long time before he whispered, "I am fearful sick." He looked up at Adam as if hoping he might deny it.

Adam didn't. Jake needed the truth. "You are. Pneumonia, the doctor says."

"Giles Whited died of pneumonia in May. Homer Martin went down to it in June. Or was it typhoid that got Homer?" He frowned a minute before he shook his head a little. "Doesn't matter. Either way it seemed a wrong way to die in a war." He stared across the room. "Funny, you think about somebody shooting you or maybe getting torn apart by a shell, but you don't think about your body letting you down by getting sick. Not my body anyway. I never got sick back home."

"When you feel a little better, I'll take you home. Once there, Phoebe will see to it that you get well."

Jake smiled. "She would, wouldn't she? This wouldn't be in her plan for me."

"Did she have a plan for you?"

"Oh yeah. Marry well and have hand-some children and become a gentleman with the means to do good. Said it would make Mother happy."

"Not a bad plan," Adam said as he pushed another drink on Jake. "Till the war got in the way."

"That did disrupt her plans. Or at least me joining up did. How about you? Did she have a plan for you too?"

"Probably, but if she did, she gave up on it some time back. For one, she had to accept that I'd never settle for hearth and home over art."

"Couldn't you do both?" Jake asked.

"I never thought so. Maybe because I never met the woman that made me want to try." At least until now, Adam added si-lently as he felt Charlotte's letter touching his skin inside his shirt.

Again Jake looked away from Adam to stare across the room. He turned the rag and spat in it before he muffled a few coughs and wiped his mouth again. His face was very pale as he closed his eyes and sank back on the pillow Adam had propped behind him.

Adam pulled the chair a nurse had found for him up closer to the bed so that he could steady Jake if his head fell to the side in his sleep. But Jake wasn't through talking. He kept his eyes closed as he said, "I was in love once."

"Were you?" Adam said.

"Oona was beautiful. And fun. Her father sold fruits and vegetables to us. He and her mother came over from Ireland. She claimed they had a big farm there. Were richer than we ever thought of being before the potato blight. Her mother hated America, wished for Ireland from the time she got up in the morning until she went to bed at night, but her father refused to speak of Ireland at all. He said there was no purpose to looking back. He had such an accent I could barely understand him when he brought the produce for Mother's kitchen."

"What happened?" Adam asked. Of course, he knew the story. Jake's youth, barely seventeen at the time. The inappropriate girl. Phoebe taking charge and nipping the romance in the bud.

Jake looked at Adam. "You know what

happened." A touch of anger sparked in his eyes.

"Phoebe."

"And you helped her." Jake was hit by another spasm of coughing.

Adam waited until the coughing subsided and Jake was once more lying back on the pillow before he said, "I didn't help her, Jake, but neither did I try to dissuade her. You were too young to think of marriage."

"That didn't mean I couldn't be in love." Jake shut his eyes as if he didn't have the energy to hold his eyelids open. It was a long time before he went on, but Adam knew he wasn't sleeping. At last he said, "Phoebe told me it couldn't be real love, as if she could know. Not married to that old stick she latched on to for his money. If it wasn't your money she used to pay Oona's father to send Oona away, then it must have been his."

"I don't know," Adam answered honestly.

"I should have gone after her, hunted until I found her. I should have, but instead I listened to Phoebe saying what was best for the family. As if that was best for me." Jake blew out a breath that made him cough again. "And now look at me. About to die with nothing to leave behind to ever show I walked this green earth. At least it used to be green before we started blowing up the pastures."

"You're not going to die."

"We all die," Jake said. "Every last one of us." Jake opened his eyes and stared straight at Adam. "Have you ever been in love?"

"I think so," Adam said, shifting in his chair. Why couldn't he just admit to his brother that he loved Charlotte? Perhaps because he hadn't fully admitted it to his own heart yet.

"If you ever are, you won't have to think so. You'll know. I'm glad I at least felt the feeling. You think people will fall in love in heaven?"

"If it makes them happy." But again he was thinking of the Shaker community that was turning Charlotte into one of them. They claimed to be making a paradise on earth, but there was no love between man and woman there.

"Love takes you past mere happiness. At least until you lose it." Jake coughed again and shut his eyes before he went on. "But you never have to wonder with love. If you love somebody, you know. Just like with Jesus. You know."

"What do you know?" Adam leaned forward in his chair to be sure he didn't miss what Jake might say next.

But Jake didn't answer. He had finally fallen to sleep or slipped off into unconsciousness again. Adam stared at his brother's pale face and wished he did know whatever it was Jake knew about the Lord so that he could pray for him. Instead he pulled out Charlotte's letter and read her words again. He wondered if she prayed. It sounded like she might. If only he could rush a letter to her and ask her to pray for Jake. But a letter would take weeks. Jake might not have weeks.

Adam laid his hand gently on his brother's arm. His fingers were trembling and his heart began to pound as he whispered the words, "Please, Lord."

31

September 18, 1862
Dear Charlotte,
   Please forgive me for not writing
sooner to convey my sympathy for
the loss of your father, but it has
been a time of sadness here as well.
My brother, Jake, the one in the
sketch I sent you some months
back, succumbed to pneumonia on
September 10 after the Union army's
retreat from Bull Run once again.
You would have liked Jake. He
embraced life and ran after
adventure. He was only twenty and

had escaped death on the battlefield several times, but what the enemy couldn't do, sickness did. Snuffed out his young life in less than a fortnight.

Phoebe, my sister, holds me directly responsible for Jake's death. I don't disagree with her. He was not much more than a boy and not ready for the army. But he showed staunch courage and acquitted himself well in battle. In spite of what Phoebe believes, I don't think I could have convinced him to quit his company. That said, I could have been with him when he fell so ill. Then I might have been able to see he got better treatment. The army doctors try, but there are so many succumbing to illness in the camps. Pneumonia isn't even the biggest killer. Dysentery is rampant and typhoid and measles have felled many more than bullets thus far. Although too many have died on the battlefield as well.

We are receiving news of the battle at Antietam and are told it is one of the

*most tragic yet with reports of
thousands dead or wounded on both
sides. Some other artist did the
illustrations you will see in* Harper's.
*I had to take Jake's body back to
Boston and have continued here with
my mother for a few days. In truth, I am
glad I wasn't there to draw the scenes.
I am weary of death.*

**How many men can we keep
losing? Why don't sensible heads
find a way to peace? Bud Keeling,
the reporter I may have told you
about, says things have gone too far
to achieve any peace now except
that wrested from the enemy on the
battlefield. He claims that with the
Union finally claiming a victory here
in the east at Antietam, there are
reliable reports Mr. Lincoln will issue
some sort of emancipation
proclamation. Few here harbor the
least doubt any longer that the
President plans to put an end to
slavery. The South will not accept
that and so the fight will continue
until the Union finally overcomes.
I cannot imagine our nation divided**

into two countries if the Union falls. The President must find the generals to win the war.

Forgive me for continuing on and on about the war. I would like to retreat from the conflict. Perhaps go to California far from the sound of cannons. But that is not to be. It is my job to draw the scenes even if they are scenes no one, including myself, wants to see. The people deserve to know what is happening, and at times a picture can tell more than a page of words.

I hear Lexington has been occupied by the Confederates. I hope that has not caused the Shakers at Harmony Hill undue trouble. I don't know where Sam will send me next, but wherever it is, I will take the memory of your mother's roses with me and think upon the beauty in her garden when I am most filled with despair. Keep in mind, as I think I told you once before, that gardens lay dormant every winter and grow afresh each spring.

If you have a moment or your Sister Martha has a moment, your prayers for my mother who mourns her son would be most appreciated.

**Faithfully yours,
Adam**

"Such sorrow in the world," Sister Martha said when Charlotte looked up from Adam's letter with tears in her eyes. "If only all could see the truth of the Believers' way. The truth Mother Ann taught us."

Charlotte wiped away her tears with the corner of her apron as Sister Martha continued her little sermon. "Our testimony is for peace, now and always. Mother Ann taught us to oppose wars of households, and wars of nations, and if we follow her teachings, we will know the peace that is promised the obedient follower."

"But how can we keep wars away? How can we not mourn our loved ones?"

Sister Martha kept her voice gentle even though there was a hint of reproof in her words. "We can love as we should love. As brothers and sisters love. With the proper peace in our hearts, we don't have to worry about wars or the hereafter. We only have to live our lives and do our work as though this could be the last day of our life or as if we might live a thousand years. We seek perfection in all."

"But this mother grieves the loss of her son." Charlotte looked down at the letter she still held. She ran her fingers across Adam's writing. "This brother grieves the loss of his brother."

"Yea, it is so. They know not the peace we have here. They are of the world. I can see that as yet your own mind continues to stray toward worldly thinking. Even after more than a year among us." Sister Martha mashed her lips together and studied Charlotte's face a moment before she heaved a sigh. "It could be I let my desire for news of the war front cloud my judgment and I was wrong to persuade the Ministry to allow you to receive these letters. I fear his words have encouraged you to keep one foot in the world."

"It is true that I have not been able to put my feet solidly on the Shaker pathway," Charlotte admitted. "My spirit seems to seek something more."

"As does our artist friend." Sister Martha

pointed to the letter and then looked straight at Charlotte. "He seeks affection from you and not that of the brotherly sort."

Charlotte looked down quickly to hide the color burning her cheeks as her heart leaped with joy at the thought. If only it could be true. But such a response could not be condoned by the Shakers, even one as kind as Sister Martha.

Again Sister Martha sighed. She leaned nearer Charlotte and laid her dry, wrinkled hand on her arm. "I do not condemn you for allowing the temptations of the world to follow you here. You came into our village unsure of your direction, and since that time, you have stepped forward in your spiritual quest. I see that. But you carry with you the threads of your worldly life. Not only your feelings for this man, but also the attachment to your land and home that you now mourn as this man mourns his brother. You cannot cling forever to both sides. You must decide for the world or for the truth of a Believer."

"What would you have me choose?" Charlotte asked softly without looking up at Sister Martha. She didn't think she would see disapproval on the woman's face, but because of her fondness for the old sister, she feared seeing disappointment there.

"Salvation seems the only choice to me, but many have chosen otherwise."

"Cannot those of the world find salvation without living the Shaker way?" She studied the letter she held in her lap. She did not want to make a choice between salvation and love. She could not believe the Lord required that of her.

"Not true salvation."

"What of your daughter? You told me once that she chose a different way." Charlotte peeked up at Sister Martha to be sure her question wasn't too bold. "Did that condemn her in your eyes?"

"You ask a difficult question. One that I should perhaps not answer, but the two of us, we have naught but truth between us. I know you haven't told me everything that is in your heart, but I also know that what you have told me has been truthful. I can do no less than the same for you."

Sister Martha turned her eyes away from Charlotte's face to stare toward the window. They were alone in the room on the first floor of the Centre Family House that Sister Martha rarely left anymore.

Charlotte carried her meals to her every day. The summer had been especially hot and dry, and the heat had continued into September. Sister Martha could no longer summon the strength to go about the village. Instead she kept busy corresponding with other Shaker villages.

Now as Charlotte waited quietly for Sister Martha to start speaking again, she could faintly hear the bang of pans in the kitchen deep in the building where the sisters were cooking for the hungry soldiers who passed through the village like unending clouds of locusts sucking up water and food. Charlotte thought sometimes it was only the Shakers' prayers that kept the wells from running dry.

Finally Sister Martha looked back at Charlotte. "Often our eyes do not want to behold the truth. Just like with this war. We here at Harmony Hill would like to believe we can keep its conflict from our village, but we cannot. We are in its path and we will suffer some consequences of the worldly struggle. Just as Elder Homer did when the two soldiers held the gun to his head and demanded the horses last week. We would have surrendered a dozen horses to them before we would have chanced harm to Elder Homer, but he refused to give in to their violent demands. In the end his gentle spirit overpowered their evil intents and they went on their way empty-handed."

When Charlotte frowned a little, Sister Martha smiled and held up a hand to keep Charlotte from speaking as she continued. "I see your confusion. You wonder why I speak of the war and Elder Homer when you asked of my daughter of the world. Perhaps because I have no ready answer. I think I once told you of my despair when she first left the village years ago. She was the same as lost to me then. Dead to our Society here."

Sister Martha reached up and absently tucked a strand of gray hair back under her cap before she pulled it down tighter on her head. She patted her feet lightly on the floor as if that might help her come up with the best words to explain. "Of course you have to understand I had already given her up as a daughter. That was required as soon as we joined with the Believers. We were sisters just as you and I are sisters. I embraced the ways of the Society and

I thought she did as well. There were those among the Ministry who thought Gabrielle would become a leader here. She had amazing gifts of the spirit. Many more than I. But then the stranger came into our midst and held out his hand to her and she went with him."

"Did you ever see her again?"

"Once. She came with her firstborn. A girl she called Martha. Named after me. I stood in the visitors' room and told her not to come again. I think I feared losing my own way as I believed she had lost hers." Sister Martha hesitated a moment as if her next words were too hard to speak. "For the little child—she couldn't have been over two—pulled at my heartstrings. I wanted to pick her up and feel her sweet breath against my cheek. But I couldn't deny the way I had chosen any more than my daughter who went to the world could deny her own path. It was how it had to be."

Sister Martha leaned forward until she was looking directly into Charlotte's eyes. "And that is how your path must be, my child. If the seeker comes for you, then perhaps the good Lord will put the right answer in your heart and you will see the proper path before you. You must pray so."

"Yea," Charlotte said. She didn't add that her prayers had seemed empty since the loss of her father. She worried that would make Sister Martha feel the need for more words to buoy Charlotte's spirit when it was obvious her many words had already drained the old sister of strength as she sat back and panted a little to gather her breath.

"We shall pray this nation will find the right answers as well. That the two sides will find a way to cease their hostilities." Again she breathed in and out before she said, "You must get back to your duties. Those in the kitchen at the Gathering House will need your hands."

Charlotte carefully folded Adam's letter and slid it back in the envelope. She wanted to let her eyes dwell on his words again, on his promise of the garden coming back to life after the winter. Perhaps that was what she was feeling, a winter of the soul that had nothing to do with the date on the calendar.

As she hurried back to the Gathering

Family House where there would be a new sack of potatoes or perhaps a basket of apples waiting for her paring knife, she thought the whole country seemed to be deep in a winter of sorrow with so many fields turning to battlegrounds. Sister Martha had been right that no matter how much the Believers desired peace, there was none to be had in Harmony Hill with the Confederate soldiers passing through the village on a daily basis now. Not three nights before, a company had camped in the middle of their village and posted sentries all around. They had been enveloped by the Rebel army. The hungry Rebel army.

Elder Quinton said that the Southern army must have invaded Kentucky simply because there was no food to be had in the South. In truth many of the barefoot Rebel soldiers were ragged and dirty. They were surely out of place at Harmony Hill where, in obedience to Mother Ann's teachings, dirt was chased from every crack and crevice, but there had been little rain for weeks and no way for the men to present a better appearance.

As the dry, hot days of September passed, all attempts to maintain the regular industry of the village had been suspended. Instead the Shakers hurried to pick their corn and fruit to secrete some of it for the winter and keep it from all being devoured by the soldiers passing through the village. There was no time for making brooms or hats and no market for them if they had been made. The war controlled everything now. Even Harmony Hill—where it began to feel as if every soldier in the Confederate army sought food in their village.

They had little choice but to prepare the meals and feed the men who came to their doors famished for food and drink. It was no less than their Christian duty and what Mother Ann would require them do, Sister Altha told Charlotte and Dulcie as they worked side by side in the Gathering Family kitchen.

"She would have us do good in every way we can." Sister Altha frowned, yet it was not crossly but more from sadness. "These poor men need some goodness in their lives."

"Or at least some bread," Dulcie said.

"Yea, at the very least some bread," Sister Altha agreed.

Sister Altha had tempered her attitude

toward Charlotte since Grayson had burned. Charlotte wasn't sure if that was because she felt sympathy for Charlotte or because she thought that now the hundred acres promised might become a thousand if Charlotte inherited the land as it seemed she would. A letter had come to Harmony Hill from her father's lawyer indicating that under the terms of her Grandfather Grayson's will the land was only given over to her father for use in his lifetime. Upon his death Grayson was to pass directly to Charlotte.

Selena would have no claim upon the land if she returned. The letter stated in clear terms that the deceased's widow was entitled to a portion of the personal property of the deceased. But the household goods were now ashes, most of the able-bodied slaves of any worth had slipped away to the North after the fire, and the Confederates had made off with the horses. With Grayson in ruins, Selena had little reason to return except to claim her son. It was rumored she had ridden south with one of the Confederate officers, but that was all it was. Rumors and gossip.

Charlotte didn't care. She'd put Selena

from her mind as soon as she returned to Harmony Hill after the funeral. She had too much to worry about in determining her own path to waste time wondering about Selena's. She did worry about Landon, but there was nothing she could do for him except pray that perhaps father number three would be as kind to him as her own father had obviously been.

Until Charlotte was called from the kitchen to the visitors' room, she had assumed Selena had come for Landon weeks before. But when Sister Altha ushered her into the room, he jumped up off the hard bench and ran to bury his face against her and hide among her skirts as he had at the fire. The smoke no longer circled about them nor did the flames reach for them as they had that night, but even so in some ways the fire would always bind them together.

"Miss Pennebaker says you have to tell them you're my sister the way you said you were." He spoke the first words into her skirt before he peered up at Charlotte with a fierce look that demanded she say the words he wanted to hear, but down under the fierceness in his brown eyes was such a deep well of sadness, it made Charlotte's heart hurt.

He didn't give her time to speak before he said, "Remember?" His voice cracked on the word.

Charlotte tightened her arms around him and pulled him close. She could feel him almost melting against her as the tension drained from him. She forgot about Sister Altha frowning beside her and Miss Pennebaker staring down her long, thin nose at them from where she stood in front of the bench against the wall.

Nobody else in the room mattered as she gently pushed Landon back from her to kneel down and stare straight into his face with eyes every bit as fierce as his own. "I am your sister."

"Thank you," he whispered. His hands gripped the sleeves of her dress so tightly she thought he might never turn her loose. "I've always wanted a sister."

32

"Don't let the child cling to you," Sister Altha said. "Such unrestrained demonstrations of affection are not seemly."

Charlotte squeezed Landon's hands as she pulled free from him to stand up. With her back to Sister Altha, she winked at Landon and smiled even as she kept her voice meek. "Yea, Sister Altha. He has no knowledge of the Shaker way."

"But it is assumed you do, Sister Charlotte."

"Yea." Charlotte smiled at Landon again before she turned toward Sister Altha and bent her head with a show of shame for her improper behavior. "You are right, Sister Altha."

Sister Altha must have seen the dregs of Charlotte's smile, for she blew out a burst of air in exasperation. "Sister Charlotte, explain yourself. Did you not tell us you had no brothers in the world?"

"Landon's mother was married to my father. He is my stepbrother."

"I see. That does not explain why he is here. What of his mother?"

"If you will allow me," Miss Pennebaker spoke up and advanced on them from the bench. Landon dropped his eyes to the floor as the thin, angular woman went on in a stilted voice. "His mother left the boy in my care. We have been at the hotel in town awaiting her return, but it appears that she has been detained. The hotel owner is naturally demanding the money due him and the funds Mrs. Vance left with me are long gone. It is only through the charity of some of Mr. Vance's friends that we have not gone hungry, but charity becomes a burden after a time."

"Yea, so it seems in the world," Sister Altha said with a slight nod toward the governess.

"I would not desert the child, you understand. He has been in my care for well over a year now, and though he is somewhat willful and a reluctant learner, he has a good heart."

She spoke about Landon as if he weren't in the room. He edged a step closer to Charlotte, who let her hand drift over to touch his arm as she said, "A good heart can cover many faults."

"Yes, well." The governess hesitated as if searching for the proper words. "In town it is said that you Shakers practice kindness for the unfortunate."

"We help those who come to our door," Sister Altha said.

"That is what I hoped to hear. Especially since I knew the one he keeps speaking of as his sister resides here with you. Which is the subject of much conjecture in the town, I can assure you." Miss Pennebaker raised her eyebrows at Charlotte before she looked back at Sister Altha.

"Our sister searches for the way to salvation here among us," Sister Altha said mildly.

"Yes, well, I suppose that is a worthy endeavor." Miss Pennebaker looked as if she doubted her own words before she cleared her throat and went on. "Be that as it may, what with the Rebel vagabond army in the area, conditions have become entirely too perilous for me to remain any longer. I have been fortunate enough to obtain a new position with a family in Chicago and have a ticket on a train tomorrow. But quite naturally there is no way I can take the boy with me."

"That is understandable," Sister Altha said. "What is it you ask of us?"

"To see to the boy until his mother returns. It should be the duty of his sister." The woman's eyes settled on Charlotte. "If she really considers herself thus."

"Yea, not only a duty but a desire," Charlotte said. She turned to Sister Altha. "I will do whatever is needed to make a place for him here if that is what he wants." Charlotte leaned over to ask him, "Is that what you want, Landon?"

"I want to stay with you." His brown eyes searched hers.

"It won't be exactly with me. We won't stay in the same houses, but we will be in the same village. We will see one another at times, and you will come to know other boys who can help you learn what is expected of you. They will teach you to work with your hands as do I."

"And you'll always be my sister?" He clutched her apron.

Charlotte touched his cheek and smiled. "I will always be your sister. That will never change. But at Harmony Hill all are sisters and brothers, so you will have many new sisters and brothers."

"I only want you as a sister." He looked worried.

"Here we must follow the rules of the Society," Charlotte said. "But such will be good discipline for a seafaring captain."

"Seafaring?" Sister Altha said behind her. "Of what do you speak, Sister Charlotte?"

The governess answered, "The child goes on and on about going to sea. It is no more than a foolish child's playmaking."

Charlotte didn't look at her, but she had no problem hearing the scorn in the woman's voice.

Landon paid their words no mind as he kept his eyes pinned on Charlotte's face. "You won't leave me like my mother did, will you?"

"She may return yet for you," Charlotte said.

"No. I have ever been a burden to her. Will I be a burden to you? Will you desert me here?"

"Nay." Charlotte leaned close to whisper for his ears only. "I never will."

"Whatever you speak, speak for all to hear, Sister Charlotte."

"Yea, I beg your forgiveness, Sister Altha. I was merely assuring Brother Landon he would not be a burden here." Charlotte stood up and turned toward Sister Altha. She met her eyes. "If I must promise a price, I will."

"Nay," Sister Altha said quickly with a wave of her hand. Charlotte was shocked to see a blush crawl up into her cheeks. "Our charity cannot be bought. You surely have learned that while with us, my sister. We take in many children in need."

"Yea," Charlotte said. There was no need to speak of the promise she'd made and kept for Aunt Tish. It lay in the air between them. But now it seemed to be a matter Sister Altha preferred not to recall.

"Come, we will take the little brother to the Children's House." Sister Altha held out her hand to him with as much of a smile as ever crossed her face before she gave the governess an unsmiling look of dismissal. "Good day, Miss Pennebaker."

Miss Pennebaker fiddled uneasily with the clasp on her receptacle and didn't move toward the door. "There is the small matter of the money due me if Miss Vance would be so generous."

In spite of the woman's stiff manner, Charlotte felt some sympathy for her. She had done her duty by Landon even if she didn't show any fondness for him. "I am sorry, but I have no money to pay you," she said with regret.

The woman's eyes widened in disbelief. "You own Grayson. Over a thousand acres of land and the slaves to work it. You can't stand there and say you have no money. You're rich, Miss Vance. Rich!"

Charlotte stared at Miss Pennebaker, and for the first time since her father's death realized that what the woman said was true. Charlotte was rich in land. She thought of the rolling hills she'd loved to gaze upon from Grayson's veranda. She thought of the stands of trees and the green pastures. She thought of the men working the fields and her fond memories halted. She would not be rich in people. As soon as allowed she would sign papers of manumission for any remaining servants. And land without workers filled no coffers.

"Here at Harmony Hill, we have all things in common," she said after a moment. She still had her hand on Landon's shoulder.

"You have given them Grayson?" Miss Pennebaker sounded shocked.

"Nay. I am yet a novitiate and not a full member of the Society. But even though as you say I may be wealthy in land, I have no cash. Whatever might have been in the house was lost in the fire and all in the bank—if there is any and I do not know for I didn't know my father's business—"

Miss Pennebaker interrupted her. "Mrs. Vance did."

"Yea, but she is not here to reveal what she may have known," Charlotte said with as much patience as she could muster. Her sympathy for the governess was wearing thin. "Be that as it may, any money in my father's name is in his lawyer's hands until the estate is settled. So I do regret that I have naught to give you. Perhaps you can make a claim with the lawyer, Mr. Granville, in the town."

"How much do you want?" Sister Altha asked suddenly.

"Fifty dollars," Miss Pennebaker answered without hesitation.

"The Ministry will give you twenty. And at that you may be overpaid. Come with me." Sister Altha turned on her heel to lead the way out of the room.

In the hall she looked back at Charlotte who was following along behind Miss Pennebaker with Landon. She didn't smile, but Charlotte understood her look. Paying the governess was Sister Altha's way of making amends for the bargain she'd pushed on Charlotte the year before. Charlotte accepted her look with a slight bend of her head. And she knew that when the day came that she left the Shakers—and she suddenly knew without a doubt that day would come—she would deed two hundred acres of her beloved Grayson to them. Not because she owed it, but because here she had found love. From Sister Martha. From Dulcie and Gemma. And now if not love, then acceptance from Sister Altha.

Sister Altha lifted her chin a bit in acknowledgment of Charlotte's nod. "You may take the child to the Children's House, Sister Charlotte. Brother Ballard will help him settle in. He has a joyful way like our Sister Gemma."

Landon hung back and grabbed hold of Charlotte's apron when Brother Ballard reached for his hand. "Why can't I stay with you? You said you are my sister."

"Yea. And I am." She gave Brother Ballard a beseeching look as she pulled Landon a little apart to speak with him. With a kind smile, Brother Ballard stepped back to give her the moment she needed. She turned her full attention on Landon as she tried to explain. "But the Shakers have many rules, and while we are here we must abide by them. It was difficult for me too at first, but bending my will to their ways has taught me much about the strength of my spirit and helped me develop patience. It will do the same for you in the time you're here before your mother comes for you."

"She won't come. Not unless she has need of a son again as she did with my second papa. She knew he wanted a son."

"You're right. He did. As much as I tried, I could not fill that spot in his heart that

desired a son," Charlotte admitted as sadness welled up in her.

"He loved you," Landon said simply. "He
was always telling me about my sister,
Charley, and how good it would be when
you came home."

"But then I didn't." The sadness grew
and sat like a heavy stone inside her chest.

"You came home when he needed you.
To say goodbye." The little boy had his
fierce look on again. "I didn't say goodbye
to my first papa. He loved me like our papa
loved you. He told me he was going to
heaven, but I didn't know he meant that
night. I wish I had hugged him longer. I wish
I had said goodbye. "

A tear slid out of the corner of his eye
and trailed down his cheek. It loosed something inside Charlotte and released the
tears that she had been carrying around in
a tight knot inside her. She knelt down and
pulled the little boy close to let their tears
mix. After a while, when she could find her
voice, she said, "He knew. Just like you
said my father knew." Charlotte rubbed the
tears off his cheeks with her apron and
then dried her own. "The Lord told him."

He watched her and then glanced back

at Brother Ballard, waiting patiently a little ways behind them. "Did the Lord tell you to come here?"

"I don't think so, but sometimes our feet walk strange paths to get where we need to be."

"And where is that?" He frowned as he waited for her answer.

"I don't know, Landon, but wherever it is, I promise to let you walk the path with me if you want. But for a while we need to stay here and do as they ask us. Do you think you can put your seafaring spirit aside for a few weeks and listen to Brother Ballard? It is not a bad thing to learn to work."

"As long as you stay my sister."

"Forever I will be your sister." She did not allow herself to think of Adam and what her promise might mean if he did come back for her. He had told her he could not be tied down. But the promise had been made. Whatever the cost, she would keep it.

In October the news came to Harmony Hill that General Bragg's army was marching up from the south to join with the Confederate troops already deeply entrenched in the central and southern parts of the

state in order to push the Union army out of
Kentucky. With Kentucky in Southern hands,
there would be a clear road to the north
and new supplies of horses and food for
the Rebel army.

Only a day after the news of troop movements reached them, General Kirby-Smith's
army rode into Harmony Hill in search of
food. The soldiers they'd fed prior to this
had been hungry, but they had been respectful as the Shakers brought out meals
for them. These soldiers were too tired, too
hungry, too thirsty to worry about proper
behavior. Brother Quinton said they rushed
the pumps like herds of buffalo at a salt
lick and cared not who they might trample
in the stampede. Then with their thirst
slaked, they flocked around the kitchen
doors and windows like hungry wolves
ready to devour every morsel thrown out
to them. Some even leveled their guns at
their fellow soldiers when it was concluded
the cakes or pies were not divided equally.

The sisters and brethren worked from before daylight until midnight preparing hundreds of meals, and still it was not enough.

33

Adam got off the train in Louisville and headed toward where a man at the station said General Buell's army was mustering in new troops. He could have hired a buggy. Sam wouldn't complain about the expense since he'd sent Adam to Kentucky. Several hansom cabs waited at the station with horses hitched and ready, but Adam wanted a horse, not a cab. Usually at least one buggy horse demonstrated some spirit, and Adam could make a deal with the driver, but today he didn't see a decent-looking animal in the whole row of conveyances for hire.

When he asked one of the drivers about it, the heavily bearded man looked at Adam as though he might have just fallen out of the sky. His answer was a terse two words. "The war."

The war. The war was the reason for everything. Men, who a year before were friends and even brothers, now lined up on opposite sides of the battlefields and fired their muskets at one another. Men not much more than boys died before they even got a good sip of life. Horses were confiscated. Houses burned and gardens left in ruins.

He stopped walking and looked at the sky to get his directions. Then he turned to stare to the southeast. Charlotte was there. Not that far on the train. In her Shaker dress. Or perhaps she had left Harmony Hill to go back to rebuild Grayson. He didn't know. If she had written again, no letter had caught up with him.

After Jake's funeral, he'd gone from Boston to Washington, D.C., to hear the President's speech declaring that unless the rebelling states returned to the Union by January first, he would issue a proclamation freeing their slaves. Then Adam had ridden to where the Potomac Army was once more resting and waiting. It seemed even after the victory at Antietam, the Northern generals had seemed content to sit on their hands and once more do absolutely nothing to achieve an end to the conflict. Rumors were swirling that Mr. Lincoln was ready to replace General Mc-Clellan.

When Adam found the encampment of Jake's Massachusetts Company, many unfamiliar faces occupied the spots around the campfires with new recruits filling the ranks decimated by the last battle at Bull Run. An old sergeant by the name of Hoffman stood up from the camp stool in front of his tent when he saw Adam and came over to offer his sympathies.

"It was a bad one down there and a worse one after we got back. Lost five to typhoid, three to dysentery, and Jake to the lung rot. And that was just out of our company." The sergeant shook his head. "I never thought Jake would go down that way. Strong as an ox when he joined up. A good boy. Brave to a fault."

"Yes." A knot formed in Adam's throat and kept him from saying more.

Sergeant Hoffman turned his eyes away from Adam back toward the men spread out around them to give him time to bring his emotions under control. After a minute or two, the sergeant said, "Plenty more gonna be following him over to the other side. May the good Lord have mercy on us all."

Now as Adam stood staring in the direction of Harmony Hill, he wondered if Charlotte or her Sister Martha was praying for his mother the way he'd asked in his last letter. He had almost written the words to ask them to pray for him too, but he had no right to ask for such prayers. Not after years of pushing the Lord aside as though he were no more important than an old pair of shoes Adam had outgrown.

Yet as he'd sat by Jake through his brother's last hard hours, the need to pray burned within him as he leaned his head over on Jake's bed and wanted to put his own breath inside his brother's lungs to ease his labored breathing. In his anguish he knew no formal words of prayer other than those he'd been taught as a child. *Our Father who art in heaven . . . Now I lay me down to sleep . . . Thank you for the blessing of our food.*

Please don't let my brother die. That should have been easy to pray. The chaplain who came to pray over Jake the morning before he died said things about how the Lord heard and answered even unuttered prayers, but that the answer was not always healing. He said a child of God had to accept the Lord's will.

Adam had wanted to ask him if he thought the war was the Lord's will, but he had bit his lip and stayed silent. It didn't seem wise to challenge a man of God at the same time he was seeking prayers for his brother. Then before night fell, Jake let out one last shuddering breath and did not pull in another. The chaplain's prayers had not protected Jake. But even worse, Adam had not protected his little brother. Adam had stayed on the sidelines and watched while his little brother ran into battle. Always the watcher and not the doer, and now he'd watched his brother die.

The war. The reason for much death. Adam shook away thoughts of Jake. He had to think about drawing the scenes of war. That was his job. He couldn't think about how close he was to Harmony Hill and Charlotte. Not yet. There would come another day in a garden, but first the war.

And it looked as if Sam was right to send him to Kentucky. The man had a nose for where the next battle was going to be. Louisville was overrun with Union troops as General Buell's forces had just made a fast march from Tennessee to Louisville to stop the advance of the Confederate General Bragg and his troops who were trying to drive the Union out of Kentucky. Lexington had fallen to the Confederates and news was coming in that Bragg had left his main army in Bardstown to go to Frankfort for the purpose of installing a Confederate governor.

By the time Adam got to the Union's camp, the soldiers were packing up to move out of Louisville. Reinforced with the twenty-five thousand fresh troops that had been waiting in Louisville, Buell's army of almost sixty thousand marched toward Bardstown to crush the Rebel advance. The Union could ill afford to lose Kentucky.

As they moved swiftly southeast across the state, Adam noted with each mile he was getting closer to Harmony Hill. When the Confederates fell back from Bardstown, it began to look like the armies might meet in Harrodsburg, practically in the Shakers' backyard. That would be sure to disturb the peace they constantly sought.

Adam couldn't keep from wondering if Charlotte was seeking that spiritual peace now. Would she welcome him when his feet finally found his way back to her? This near, he would not leave the area without seeing her. It mattered not that every garden he passed was parched from lack of rain and picked clean of even the smallest corn nubbin by the throngs of soldiers passing through. It mattered not that the gardens at Grayson were shriveled and blackened by the fire. The garden he sought to walk with Charlotte was a garden of the heart. But if she had turned to the Shaker way as her last letter seemed to indicate, her feet would not want to walk in such a garden.

He pushed it from his mind. First the war. First he would draw more illustrations of soldiers and death for Sam to print in his newspaper. Adam had stayed purposely aloof from the soldiers marching in the ranks. He did not want to know their names. He did not want to hear their talk about the sons and daughters waiting for them to save the Union and march home heroes. It was better to just see eyes and noses and mouths with nothing behind them. Not as good for his art, but easier on his heart.

The sun beat down on their heads and dust rose in clouds around them as they marched in the unusual October heat. The countryside hadn't seen rain for weeks, and the creeks where the men might have slaked their thirst were bone dry. The few ponds they came across that still held water were little more than pig wallows, but the men drank anyway, sometimes chasing out the hogs in order to fill their cups or canteens. The sight turned Adam's stomach, and he took tiny sips from his own canteen to make his water last as long as possible.

They didn't make it to Harrodsburg. Instead the Confederates had halted their march by a river that yet held water near a little town called Perryville. With the soldiers and horses so in need of water to drink, the river was more than enough reason for the lines of battle to be formed.

At daylight, Adam found a spot on a knoll with a good view of the rolling countryside.

To one side a big field of drying cornstalks stood in rows waiting to be shocked. Stone fences snaked across the fields giving the possibility of cover to the soldiers. But that would be little help against the artillery the gunners were moving into place.

Adam had seen it all before. The men lining up, advancing into the musket fire. The smoke rising and settling around the artillery guns. The storm of shell, grape, canister, and minié balls. The terrible sounds of the shells screaming overhead. He could have drawn it from memory before the first shell was fired. Even so, it was his job to see it all again and he wondered uneasily if he'd chosen the best viewpoint to watch and record. He wished Bud Keeling was there, because somehow the reporter always knew where and when the action would happen first.

Bud had stayed in the East. Where he said Adam should stay. "I'm not saying Kentucky's not important to the Union," Bud had said when Adam told him he was going west. "But nothing that happens there is gonna compare to what might happen here. Here's where General Lee is. That's who we gotta beat. And if the President ever finds a general who might make that happen, it'll be here in the East. Here's where the big battles are gonna happen. Not out there in Kentucky."

But Adam had come to Kentucky anyway, and now he sat with his sketchpad waiting for another battle. The day had dawned clear, with the rising sun revealing the fall colors in the trees along the little river. On the far side of the river, the Rebels were forming lines, pulling artillery into place, but neither side seemed to be in a hurry to get the battle underway.

The morning hours crept by with only a spatter of gunfire now and again to indicate a few skirmishes. The previous day the information had come down to the reporters that the attack was to commence at dawn before the day's heat drained the men of fighting energy, but then General Buell had been thrown by his horse and injured his back. So instead of riding out to direct the troops, he'd set up headquarters in a house a few miles away from where Adam now sat atop his knoll. Couriers were carrying his orders to the field, so that could be why the troops were slow to move into place.

A young reporter, who had latched on to Adam as a battle-savvy veteran and was dogging his steps, watched the scene below for a few minutes before he yawned and lay back in the dry grass. "Ain't it just like the army. Chase the enemy clear across to tomorrow, and then nobody wants to fire the first salvo." He plopped his hat over his face. "Wake me when they're ready."

For lack of anything better to do Adam drew his picture. The kid was covering his first battle. That was why he could sleep. He had no idea of what was coming the way Adam did. Adam didn't want to think about it as the minutes ticked by. Eventually the artillery would begin firing and the battle would be engaged, but now peace still reigned in the scene spread out below them. Crows cawed as they flew in and out of the cornfield. The soft coo of a mourning dove was almost drowned out by the chirr of grasshoppers in the parched pastures around the cornfield. Adam didn't see the first cow. No doubt the farmers had hidden their stock when they heard the armies were coming to keep the soldiers from having chunks of beef roasting on spits over their fires.

As the sun rose higher in the sky, the reporter continued to snooze while Adam felt the tension growing inside him. He wished he were anywhere other than on that knoll waiting for another battle to begin. He calculated the miles to Harmony Hill and how long it would take him to ride there. He sketched a garden full of roses and then drew Charlotte in the midst of it.

He stared at the sketch a long time and wondered why he hadn't left room for himself beside her. He had never put his image in any of the many sketches he'd done of Charlotte. Was that because he knew in his heart that his dream of holding her in his arms again was just that—a dream that would never come true? Perhaps he was only in love with a woman his imagination had created to be drawn by his pen. Perhaps she was nothing as he remembered and it was only the drums of war that made him wish for love just as Jake had wished for his lost love before he died. To leave something of himself behind even if it was only his memory in the heart of someone who had loved him no matter how briefly.

Maybe the best thing to do instead of

calculating the miles to Harmony Hill would be to forget the kisses in the garden. To leave her in the peace of the Shakers or perhaps rebuilding her Grayson. But then he touched his pocket where he carried the last letter he had received from her, the one he'd read while Jake was in the hospital. It held no words of love. He knew enough about the Shakers to know such would not be allowed by them, but yet she always mentioned the garden. In those words he sought the flowering of love even as his love for her had grown in his heart. He would not forget. He could not forget.

The Rebels fired their first artillery piece when the sun was directly overhead. The young reporter sat up, startled by the noise. But then eagerness lit up his face as he jumped to his feet to get a better view.

"It's started," he said.

"It has," Adam agreed as he turned his sketchbook back to the peaceful pasture scene to begin drawing in the scenes of death.

"How come there aren't any soldiers charging across the field?" the reporter asked.

"They will. The artillery always gets things under way."

Adam tried to recall what the kid had said his name was. Max, maybe. Or Mike. That was it. Mike Putnam. Adam had told him to write his name on a piece of paper and put it in his pocket. A lot of the soldiers had started doing that so their remains could be identified even if they got hit by a shell that blew away their faces. Adam had his name in his pocket on Charlotte's letter. Not that he was worried about his remains. He wasn't one of the green troops about to be ordered to take up positions on the field. He was safe on his knoll.

Mike was on his feet, standing on his tiptoes as if that extra inch would show him even more. "Maybe we should move closer to the action."

"We're close enough." Adam kept his eyes on his sketch.

"But we can't see much from here. How are we going to know who's winning?"

"We'll get the word eventually. Especially if you see the men retreating. Besides, if you think you can't tell much about what's happening up here, believe me, it's ten times worse down there."

"Worse? How could it be worse? That's where it's happening."

"Down there each soldier is standing in one little pocket of what's happening. At least that's what the men I've talked to tell me. Down there in the heat of battle you're as likely to get shot by your own side as the other side if you're in the wrong spot. Better to be up here out of range."

"But . . ." The kid let the word hang in the air between them.

Adam sighed. The last thing he wanted to do was babysit a green newsman. But when he looked up at the kid, Adam saw Jake as he'd been the year before when they marched out to that first battle at Bull Run. Eagerness and fear mixed. At least this kid wouldn't have to run into a barrage of bullets. He could be an observer like Adam.

But the kid couldn't settle down. He kept hopping up at every boom of artillery and then when at last the sound of musket fire signaled the battle had commenced, he couldn't stand it. He looked at Adam and said, "I've got to be down there. I've got to know what it feels like to write about it, don't I?"

"Don't be stupid, Mike. You're not a soldier. You don't even have a gun," Adam said.

"I'm not planning to shoot anybody, just report on what it's like."

Short of tackling him and tying him to a tree, there was no way Adam could keep him up on the knoll out of artillery range. He watched the kid pick his way down the hill toward the cornfield where most of the action seemed to be going on. Cornstalks were flying up in the air as artillery shells dug deep furrows in the ground. Trees on both ends of the cornfield were exploding in splinters from the hits. And the shells kept screaming through the air, killing without partiality.

He saw the kid fall backward when the bullet hit him. Adam wanted to turn his eyes away, wash his hands of the crazy kid, but he couldn't. He saw him turn and begin to crawl. He'd seen dozens of men fall and not ventured into the battle to pull any of them to safety, but he couldn't leave the boy there. It would be like leaving Jake to die again.

Adam closed his sketchpad and looked over his shoulder toward his horse still tied to a tree. The horse had his head up and nostrils flared at the noise of battle, but he was there. If Adam could get the kid back up to the top of the knoll, then he could load him on the horse to take him to a field hospital at the back of the lines.

Adam moved as quickly as he could. There was no need trying to dodge the gunfire because there was no way to know where the next bullet might be. Adam cringed when a bullet whistled past his head, but then he remembered an old soldier telling him once that hearing the bullet was good. That meant the bullet had missed and was seeking out another target. But the one chasing it might be trouble.

The kid had taken a hit to the leg, the minié ball had torn half his calf away, and blood was soaking his britches. Adam put his arm around him to lift him up off the ground as he said, "You're going to have to help."

The kid looked dazed, but he nodded and leaned on Adam as they made their slow progress away from the field of battle. Exploding shells rocked the ground like a volcano about to break through the crust of the earth to add to the destruction.

Adam shut his mind to the bullets. He didn't think about the artillery shells. He just thought about putting one foot in front of the other and getting the young reporter to safety. He hadn't been able to save his brother, but he could save this kid. *Please, Lord.*

The prayer rose unbidden in his thoughts almost at the same instant the shell exploded overhead. Fragments rained down to their left, but missed them. They were making it, moving out of range. A few more steps. Adam could hear the horse whinnying. He didn't know how with the crash of the guns all around, but he did. *Please, Lord.* A few more steps.

He didn't hear the bullet that hit the arm he had wrapped around the kid's waist. He just felt the thud as it knocked both of them forward. The kid cried out, but he didn't stop breathing, so Adam kept moving. He didn't even look at his arm until he was up on the horse with the boy in front of him. Blood was streaming down his hand. His right hand. His drawing hand.

He stared at the wound. The bullet had glanced off the bone of his forearm above the wrist. It was a good ten seconds before he had the nerve to try to move his fingers. The first two moved; the last two didn't. He fished a handkerchief out of his pocket and wrapped it tightly around his arm. A big chunk of his skin was gone, but he could live with that. As long as some of his fingers moved. As long as he could still hold a pen or a brush.

The kid in front of him on the horse groaned and fell forward. Adam caught him and turned the horse away from the battle. He left the boy, still breathing, at a house the surgeons had turned into a field hospital. He didn't let the doctor look at his arm. Waved it off as nothing serious, even though his blood had soaked the handkerchief and his shirt. He couldn't take the chance of losing consciousness and waking up without his hand. The army surgeons were too quick with the knife and saw. He'd chance death before he chanced that.

Please, Lord.

34

On October 8 the day once more dawned hot and clear at Harmony Hill. The pastures and late gardens desperately needed rain, but the air carried so little moisture that the night no longer even licked the grass with dew.

That morning as the sisters left the Gathering Family House to go to their duties, Sister Altha paused to gaze up at the cloudless sky. After a moment she sighed and shook her head. "Not the least sign of rain. It must be the good Lord has turned his face from our village because he can't bear to look down on the misguided soldiers passing along our road on their way to slaughter one another. How sad the sinful hearts of the world."

"Yea." The sisters following her down the steps and out into the village echoed her words with obedient agreement. Charlotte spoke the word without thought.

Sister Altha lowered her eyes from the clear sky to the women behind her. "Never fear, my sisters. In time Mother Ann will convince the Eternal Father to turn his face back to us. When we can shed this odious burden of cooking for the Southern army and can once more go forth in exercising the worship due our Mother and the Lord, laboring songs and attending to proper industry, then the gift of refreshing rain will fall upon our ground again."

Indeed the whole village looked trampled and weary after the onslaught of Confederate soldiers passing through in such desperate need of food and water. But on this Wednesday morning with the road mercifully empty of soldiers, the Shakers set about taking stock of the damages done to their fences and gardens by the pillaging troops.

Charlotte hoped the Confederate soldiers would continue south and leave Kentucky behind forever. Many of the Shakers expressed that same hope as the morning passed quietly. And yet the workers seemed to be continually looking over their shoulders down the road as if fearful the peace of the day wouldn't last.

When Charlotte carried Sister Martha's midday meal to her, the old sister said a messenger had come in with the report of a large army of Union troops chasing after the Confederates.

"I hope the Rebels keep retreating to the south without stopping to engage the Northern army." Concern wrinkled Sister Martha's gentle face. "For if the armies meet, the encounter will surely result in a dreadful battle such as those in the East. Those illustrated in *Harper's* by our artist friend. Another time of death."

Charlotte did pray as she walked back to the Gathering House to partake in her own midday meal. Not just that there would be no battle, although she did fervently pray that. But she also prayed for rain and that Sister Martha would have enough appetite to eat the food she'd taken her. She prayed Adam would be kept from harm wherever he was. She prayed for a clear path, to know where she needed to be.

She wasn't sure why she lingered with the Shakers except that she seemed reluctant to step away from the safe haven of being Sister Charlotte. And didn't she need to stay to see to Sister Martha? And what of Aunt Tish? It was easier to simply be Sister Charlotte, one of many sisters instead of someone who had to make decisions about sifting through the ashes of Grayson and finding a way to keep her promise to Landon.

Then there was Adam. Charlotte dreamed of looking up and seeing him at the Shaker village again as she had last summer. This time she wouldn't run away from him. But even as she was sure of that, she wasn't sure what she would do. Or what he would want her to do. While he had often referred to the garden in his letters, their meetings there had been fleeting. Perhaps she was imagining things to think love could have taken seed in those brief moments together. At least in his heart. She could not deny that it had flowered in her own.

Each of his letters had been like rain

and sunshine to cause her feelings for him to grow. But though she treasured every pen stroke, no one could imagine them love letters. The Shakers would have never allowed any improper words of sinful worldly love to be delivered to her eyes. Yet Sister Martha thought Adam did seek her affections. Affections that were already his if he would only come back to claim them. Then her way would be clear of doubts just as the sky had been clear of clouds for days.

She was hurrying up the steps to keep from being late for the midday meal when a boom that sounded much like thunder rumbled in the distance. Even though she chanced being late and missing her meal, she paused to look up at the sky. The sun was shining as brightly as ever. No storm clouds gathered on the horizon.

Another boom followed the first and then another. Charlotte shut her eyes and shuddered as she suddenly realized that instead of the welcome thunder of nature's rain clouds, these booms were the unnatural thunder of cannon fire. Even as she stood there and listened, men were dying. Men who perhaps only the day before had eaten food she set on a table for them. Men who had smiled and laughed before they marched away to die on this day. She felt so heartsick that she no longer cared about the meal she was missing.

As the afternoon passed, there was nothing to do but shut her ears to the distant booming reports of the cannons and try to close her mind to the image of bleeding and dying men as she worked in the garden alongside Dulcie, gathering the last of the dried bean pods from the vines. But each boom rattled her soul and made her want to put her hands over her ears. Dulcie seemed to feel the same as they picked the beans and filled their baskets without talking, each tensed waiting for the next sound of death in the air.

As the sun began to sink toward the western horizon, the booming continued unabated. When they came out of the garden, Landon broke away from a group of boys trailing after Brother Ballard to run and wrap his arms around Charlotte's waist.

"Is the world coming to an end, Sister Charlotte?" he asked in a voice that trembled.

The child looked so woebegone in his

Shaker clothes and hat that Charlotte wanted to hold him tight against her, but instead she pushed him away before Brother Ballard could reprimand him. She leaned down to look directly in his face as she answered. "Nay. Has not Brother Ballard told you the sounds are from cannons?"

"Like on pirate ships?" he asked.

"Yea, much like that described in storybooks."

"But this isn't in a storybook." Landon looked toward the horizon.

"Nay."

"Brother Landon," Brother Ballard called to him with firm expectation in his voice. "Come back. It is not permissible to run away from the group."

Charlotte gave him a little push toward where Brother Ballard waited for him. "It might be easier if you pay attention to Brother Ballard's rules," she told him.

"I do most of the time. But it's a bad rule if it keeps me from talking to my sister." He turned back to her to ask one last question as he did every time he saw her. "You won't forget your promise?"

"Never, my little brother," she whispered. Only Dulcie was near enough to hear their words, and Dulcie was not a faultfinder. Besides, her mother's heart would understand.

After he hurried back to be the obedient Shaker boy again, Dulcie fell in beside her on the path. "Will you take him with you when you leave?"

Charlotte quickly looked at Dulcie. She didn't say if. She said when. "Leave?" Charlotte said. "What makes you ask that?"

"And what keeps you from answering it?" Dulcie lowered her voice even though there was no one near them on the walkway. "Haven't we ever spoken frankly with each other when we worked as long as we didn't have to worry about spying eyes or listening ears?"

"Yea, forgive me, Sister Dulcie. It is my confusion of spirit that makes the answer difficult. Not your question. But I have promised to be his sister. So either I must stay here or take him if I go."

"I would that I had such a choice." Dulcie sighed.

"Perhaps someday you will." Charlotte's mind raced as she wondered how she could help Dulcie. "If I—"

With the ghost of a smile, Dulcie touched

Charlotte's arm to stop her words. "You can't fix everything for everyone, Sister Charlotte. Even as much as you want to. You must leave some things to the Lord above."

"But I want you to be happy, Sister Dulcie."

"There are many ups and downs to happiness. I think contentedness might be a better blessing."

"Are you content?" Charlotte looked over at Dulcie walking beside her.

Dulcie kept her eyes on the pathway in front of them as they moved on toward the Gathering Family house. "In time I will be. My spirit no longer struggles so actively against the boundaries here. It is not a bad place."

"Nay," Charlotte agreed. "I have learned much about my own spirit here among the Believers."

Dulcie went on as if Charlotte hadn't spoken. "I think seeing the soldiers in the last few weeks has helped me appreciate the peace to be had here at Harmony Hill. I may not be able to hold my children to my bosom, but they are in the bosom of peace. I am thankful for that. If someday the Lord makes a new path for me to walk, then I will step out on it, but now I am not so reluctant to walk the Shaker way as I was." Dulcie turned to look directly at Charlotte's face. "But you don't have to settle for contentment. You can chase happiness. You should chase happiness."

"Yea," Charlotte said as she met Dulcie's honest brown eyes. "My spirit does seek such. If love can bring happiness."

Dulcie lowered her voice even more. "Perhaps not always happiness, but there will be joy." She reached over and squeezed Charlotte's arm. "If your pathway leads there, run along it."

Charlotte's heart leaped at the thought, but she had already spoken too plainly if other ears than Dulcie's happened to hear. Besides, it surely was wrong for her to be contemplating happiness or joy even as the cannonade to the south continued to pound against her ears.

As the evening deepened into night, the thunder of the cannons thankfully ceased. A deep silence fell over the village, but there was little peace in it. It was too easy to imagine the scenes of death and destruction that might lay in the moonlit fields to the south.

Charlotte was awake the next morning before the rising bell. She stared out the open window in the sleeping room to watch the first fingers of dawn creep up into the sky and cringed as she waited for the cannons to start again with the light of day. But no booms came. All was quiet except for the call of a mourning dove and the crickets no night had yet been cold enough to silence. But it appeared the night had silenced the artillery. Perhaps the battle was over.

That proved to be the case as battle-weary soldiers began to straggle back through Harmony Hill. The beginning trickle became a streaming flood by the third day as once again soldiers clustered around the kitchen doors in search of food. As before, the Shaker sisters abandoned all other industry to prepare meals for the hungry troops. The brethren set up a long table on trestles in the yard of the Trustee's Offices next to the road. It not only seemed more efficient to lay the food out in the open in easy reach of the men as they passed through the village, it also kept men with the stain of death on them from too familiar contact with the sisters.

Once again it was the Confederates who came through Harmony Hill, and with them they brought news of the battle. The armies had met near Perryville where the Rebels claimed to outfight the Yankees in spite of being greatly outnumbered. It was only the sheer number of the Union army that had sent the Confederates into retreat back along the main route to the south.

Many had died. Many more had been wounded. When reports came in that churches and houses in the town had been converted into makeshift infirmaries, the Shakers loaded wagons with food and other necessary supplies for the wounded.

"We cannot grow weary of doing good," Sister Altha said as she directed Charlotte and Dulcie in helping gather the supplies to load on the wagons. "Mother Ann instructs us to share of our bounty. In her writings we read of the necessity to do all the good we can, in all the ways we can, as often as we can to all the people we can. That surely includes these hapless and misguided men."

When they had the wagons loaded, Sister Altha looked at Charlotte with a bit of challenge in her eyes. "We have been told there is also need for some to help nurse the wounded. Since you seem to want to keep one foot in the world, Sister Charlotte, and not make a full commitment to our way, I thought you might suit that duty better than a fully committed sister who would surely shudder at the thought of going into the world."

"I will go." Charlotte didn't refute Sister Altha's words. There was nothing to refute, for what she said was true.

35

Some noise pulled Adam back to consciousness. He lay on a narrow cot in a room surrounded by moaning men on other cots. Just like Jake. Except here the heat gathered and pressed down on Adam until it was hard to keep breathing in and out. As he had done every time he regained consciousness since he first awoke in this oven of misery, he shut his eyes and then lifted up his wounded arm where he could see the bandage covering it.

Please, God. The words ran through his mind before he forced open his eyes to see if his hand was still there. A rush of relief swept through him when he saw the bandage had not been shortened while he slept his fevered sleep.

He didn't know how he ended up on the cot in the dim church building surrounded by wounded Confederate soldiers. He knew it was a church because he could see the altar at the front of the room. He remembered going down into the field of battle to help the reckless young reporter. He remembered that the man was still alive when he left him at the house the army surgeons had commandeered. He remembered riding away from there. He remembered how he could think of nothing but Harmony Hill so near. They had a doctor. They had medicine. They had Charlotte.

He remembered turning his horse's head that way, but he remembered nothing else until he woke up on this cot and little since except looking at his arm each time he woke to be sure his hand was still there. He'd seen enough wounded soldiers with empty shirtsleeves and pant legs to know that often as not a raging fever was reason enough for the doctors to get out their knives and saws. But he could not lose his hand. Not his right hand.

His drawing hand. It would be more merciful for the doctors to cut out his heart.

If only he'd made it to Harmony Hill. Then at least if the fever conquered him as it had Jake, perhaps before that happened he would have seen Charlotte. Her touch would have been on his brow, her voice in his ear, and her beauty in his eyes before death took him.

Plus he was confident the Shakers wouldn't amputate his arm. They believed a man should use his hands to work for God. He did not think they would rob him of that ability. But the surgeons who moved between the cots here to check on the wounded were different. They might cut first and ask questions later.

So far they had left him alone except for a few draughts of a vile-tasting medicine that did nothing. But then he was still breathing. He did still have his hand. And the fever came and went. He just needed to get strong enough to get off the cot and walk away from this sick room.

He tried to lift his head up off the pillow, but everything started spinning. He felt so odd that he wondered if he was actually awake. Perhaps he was in a feverish dream.

Perhaps he was already dead and it was his eternal punishment to forever dread the loss of his hand.

Please, God. He couldn't seem to pray further than that, even though the Lord would surely expect more words of pleading from someone who had ignored him for so many years. Was it even right to try to jump back into the Lord's camp simply because he needed help so desperately? All the men around Adam needed help every bit as much. And all those who had died. What made him think the Lord would favor him more than them? He had no right to pray, but yet the words welled up inside his mind again. *Please, God.*

His grandfather would say he was getting no less than he deserved. He'd tell Adam that a man couldn't step away from God and then expect mercy just for the asking. Just by saying "please, God." Surely he would have to earn it with righteous living the way his grandfather had.

The old man had given Adam a curt nod when they'd come face-to-face after Jake's funeral. When Adam asked if he'd seen his illustrations of the war in *Harper's Weekly*, his grandfather's eyebrows had almost met over his eyes in a frown as he fondled the round knob top of his cane. He refused to acknowledge Adam's success as an artist. Instead he said, "But what have you done as a man? All I can see is that you've brought your brother home a corpse."

Adam had brushed off the question then as the sour words of an old man who had never liked him. But now lying there on the cot soaked with his own sweat the question came back to poke at him. What had he done as a man? Why should the Lord listen when he sent up his plea for mercy? The Lord gave him his hand. The Lord gave him his talent. He could take it away.

Please, God. A man somewhere in the room cried out in pain. Adam wondered if he had cried out when he was unconscious with no control of his mouth. The pain was like a live thing devouring him. He thought about how he might draw it. A monster from the deep with pointed teeth and long sharp talons on a dozen arms clawing at Adam. But he could bear the pain. He could overcome the pain. As long as he could stay awake and keep the surgeon's knife from his arm.

The man continued to scream and Adam

raised his head enough to see the doctor and a nurse standing over him. He wondered if the man was screaming because of what they were doing to him. Adam let his head fall back down on the sodden pillow while the man in the bed next to him began to loudly recite the twenty-third Psalm.

"The Lord is my Shepherd," the man said.

Adam could have said the Psalm with him, but he didn't. Instead he tried to remember other Scripture just to shut out the man's screams. He thought about the stories of healings, of the blind man, of the lepers, of the demon-possessed man in the tombs. And then the story of the Prodigal Son popped into his mind. He had not earned his father's forgiveness with righteous living. He had lived riotously instead. And yet the father had welcomed the contrite son home with joy.

"Yea, though I walk through the valley of the shadow of death, I shall fear no evil: for thou art with me." The man beside him repeated that line three times until his voice lost its tremble and grew stronger as he continued. "Thy rod and thy staff they comfort me."

Please, God, forgive me.

"Thou preparest a table before me in the presence of mine enemies: thou anointest my head with oil; my cup runneth over."

As Adam listened to the man, a peaceful feeling came over him. It didn't take away the pain or even the fear of losing his hand, but it was there like bedrock under a flooding stream. It would not be washed away. It did not have to be earned. It was just there. His because the Lord heard his prayer. *Please, God.*

As the man went on with the last of the Psalm, Adam whispered the words with him. "Surely goodness and mercy shall follow me all the days of my life; and I will dwell in the house of the Lord for ever."

When next he woke, he had no idea how much time had passed. He shut his eyes and raised his hand up. This time it didn't take quite as much courage to open his eyes. His hand was there. But so was the pain and the fever. He wanted to beg someone for a drink of water, but his mouth was too dry to form the words. All he could do was grunt.

When she leaned over him, he was sure he was hallucinating. The nurse wore a white Shaker cap and collar. And Charlotte's face. His mind was imagining her face there on the nurse even as he had drawn it in a hundred sketches. Her beautiful green eyes now brimming with tears. The scattering of freckles across her nose. Her soft and inviting lips. He wanted to reach up and touch her, but he feared that would make the image fade and the nurse would turn back into the same older woman with the bulbous nose who had poured the noxious medicine down his throat the last time he awoke.

"Adam."

Even after she spoke his name, he still thought she was only a vision drawn from his desire. It wasn't until her teardrops fell upon his hot cheeks that he realized she was really there looking down at him, bathing his forehead with a damp cloth.

"Adam, can you hear me?"

He reached up with his uninjured hand and touched the tears on her cheeks and then traced his own lips with his dampened fingers. His tongue tasted their salt. "Charlotte," he managed to whisper. "Not much of a garden here."

"A garden needs sunshine and rain." She smiled through her tears, then she lifted his head and held a cup of water to his lips. "And a loving hand to plant the seeds when spring comes again."

"My hand," he whispered as panic at the thought of losing his hand grabbed him once more. He clutched her arm with his left hand and held up his injured arm. He moistened his lips as best he could with his tongue. "Don't let them cut off my hand. Even if they tell you I'll die, don't let them."

Her eyes widened at the fierceness of his words. "But they might not listen to me."

He tightened his hold on her arm. "You are Charlotte Vance, the senator's daughter, the owner of Grayson. You make things happen."

"But I have no right to speak for you."

The darkness was creeping back, making everything disappear but her beautiful face. He clung to the edge of consciousness long enough to push out the words. "You have every right. You own my heart. Promise me."

He could see her eyes on him as he began to slip down into the tunnel of darkness. Her words followed him. "I promise."

⁂

I am Charlotte Mayda Vance, she repeated silently in her head as his fingers relaxed their grip on her arm and he slipped away from her into unconsciousness. *Charlotte Mayda Vance. Daughter of Charles Vance. Granddaughter of Richard Grayson. The owner of Adam Wade's heart.*

But could she keep his heart beating? He was burning with fever. Perhaps the wound was septic. Perhaps the only way to save him was to take his hand. Why had she promised? A binding promise the same as the one she had made young Landon. Dulcie was right. She did think she could fix everything when she couldn't even fix herself.

There was only One who could fix everything. She knelt by Adam's bed and kept her hand over his heart. "Dear Lord, I will do whatever you want if you will help Adam. Whatever I must."

She didn't realize she'd prayed the words aloud until the man in the next bed spoke. "Ain't no use trying to bargain with the good Lord, miss. He done owns it all, you know."

Charlotte turned to look at the man. He had a bandage around his head and his chest. "Are you a preacher?" she asked.

"The men in my company think so, but I never called myself such. But my sainted mother taught me the Scriptures, and believe me, knowing the Word has been a powerful comfort these last few months."

Adam groaned and Charlotte turned her eyes back to his face. She didn't look back at the other man even as she asked, "What should I do?"

"Be not afraid, only believe."

"Is that Scripture?"

"The Lord's very words. Ain't no reason in the world not to trust them. Just say your prayers and get still in your heart and you'll know what to do."

"But what if he dies?" Charlotte whispered the words.

"Been a lot of dying going on and some more in here will be going to meet their Maker afore the day dawns tomorrow. A trip all of us has to make come our time." The man's voice softened. "But you just do your praying. I'm thinking it may not be his time."

Charlotte glanced over at the man with gratitude. "Is there something I can get you?"

"A new ear would be nice." The man attempted a smile as he touched the bandage around his head. "But failing that, a drink of water would be good, and then maybe later between your prayers for your sweetheart there, if you could find me some paper to write to my sainted mother in Alabama, we'd both be much obliged, I'm sure."

Her prayers were ongoing. Even as she walked among the other men, helping them take a drink, turning their pillows, spooning broth into their mouths, her prayers never left Adam. When the doctor came to stand over Adam, she was there by his bedside. She helped unwrap his bandages without quaking. She stared at the wound and felt a turning sickness in the pit of her stomach, but she didn't look away. She couldn't turn her eyes away.

"We may have to amputate," the doctor muttered more to himself than to any ears listening.

"Nay," Charlotte said. She shook away the Shaker word. She couldn't be Sister Charlotte who bent her head and practiced obedience. She was Charlotte Mayda Vance. The owner of Adam Wade's heart and she had made him a promise. She cleared her throat and pushed strength into her voice. "No. You can't cut off his hand."

36

The doctor looked up at her with some surprise and more than a little irritation. "Miss, I suggest you leave the medical decisions up to me. While it is certainly tragic for a man to lose one of his extremities, it is my duty to keep the men here in my care alive." He wore gray Confederate trousers under a surgeon's wrap that showed the evidence of many wounds treated.

"You can't amputate his arm. He instructed me to tell you that." Charlotte looked down at Adam's face in the dim light. What if he couldn't fight off the fever? Nevertheless, she kept her voice firm and sure. She had promised and she had prayed. "I know him. He's Adam Wade, an artist for *Harper's Weekly.*"

That seemed to give the doctor pause. "Hmm," he said as he turned his eyes back to Adam. "Adam Wade. I've seen his illustrations."

"You have to give his arm a chance to heal."

"Or to kill him," the doctor said so grimly that it almost wiped away his Southern drawl.

"There are many ways to die," Charlotte whispered.

"And this way won't be a good one." The doctor's frown grew fiercer as he shifted Adam's arm a bit to better study the wound. He was silent a moment before he gave in. "But I suppose we could wait a few more hours if you're sure he would want to take that chance."

"He would," the man in the bed beside them spoke up. "I heard him telling the girl not to let you get out your saws. Weren't a shred of doubt in his words."

"But did he consider what might happen if we delay proper treatment? You don't think I like amputating arms and legs, do you?" The doctor sounded angry before he let out a long sigh as he wiped his hands on a towel stained with blood. He looked very tired. "Neither do I like pulling sheets up over men's faces."

"You won't." The words were barely audible, but yet it was easy to hear the determination in Adam's voice as his eyes flickered open. He looked first at the doctor and then at Charlotte. He reached for her with his uninjured hand.

Charlotte took his hand and without thought raised it to her lips. With her other hand, she stroked Adam's face as she smiled down at him. The stubble of his unshaven beard was stiff and welcome against her hand.

"So the two of you know each other pretty well," the doctor said as he began to wrap a new bandage around Adam's arm. He didn't wait for her to say anything. "But aren't you one of those Shaker women?"

"Yea," Charlotte said. "In some ways."

"But it appears not in every way." The doctor glanced up at Charlotte with an amused look. "One of your Shaker sisters was telling me earlier that you all don't hold with a man and woman knowing one another in the biblical sense of the word. Is that true?"

"It's true the Shakers believe all should live as brothers and sisters. That the love of a man for a woman causes much distress," Charlotte said softly with her eyes on Adam's. "But I have not been able to forget the garden."

Adam's lips moved, but he seemed too weak to push out any words. He stared at her a moment before his eyelids drooped and then slowly closed. Charlotte's heart jumped up in her throat as she gripped his hand tighter and bit her lip to keep from crying out. Relief washed through her when she saw his chest continue to rise and fall.

"What garden is that?" the doctor was asking. "The one where Eve met the serpent and sin came into the world?"

"For all have sinned and come short of the glory of the Lord," the man in the next bed spoke up again.

"That's God's own truth. Preach it, Sebastian." The doctor glanced over at the man he called Sebastian before he finished fastening the bandage and straightened up. Then he looked directly at Charlotte.

"Keep watch and don't neglect to let me know if his fever worsens. Better alive with one arm than dead with two. Artist or no artist."

When the sun began to go down, the three other sisters returned to Harmony Hill, but Charlotte refused to go with them. She stayed by Adam's bed, bathing his face and neck through the night to keep the fever at bay. Sometime after midnight his breath became more labored and he felt hotter in spite of the cold rags she was laying on his forehead. Torn between her promise to Adam and the doctor's dire warning, she fell on her knees beside Adam's bed and prayed in desperate silence.

Dear Lord, I spoke a promise I shouldn't have spoken even as I have so many times before in my arrogance. Forgive me, Lord, and help me to know what you would have me to do for this man I love. I know Sister Altha would tell me that my sin of loving him has brought on this trouble, but I can't believe it is a sin for me to love him. Is it? His fever burns so hot. Help me to know what to do. Must I keep my promise to him or should I wake the doctor?

She laid her head down on Adam's chest and listened to the fast beating of his heart. In the bed next to Adam's, Sebastian raised up to ask, "Is he worse, Miss?"

"He's very hot. Do you think I should wake the doctor?" She lifted her head to look across at Sebastian. "I prayed for the Lord to help me know what to do, but I still don't know."

"Be still, and know that I am God."

Charlotte knew that was Scripture and even as she heard those words, she remembered the verse Sebastian had offered her earlier. "Be not afraid, only believe," she whispered. "I'm supposed to trust him, aren't I?"

"We all are, miss. We all are. So just get still in your heart and see what he's telling you. Then you gotta believe it. I ain't never knowed him to lead me wrong."

She shut her eyes and sought the peace of spirit that she knew Sister Martha had. The gift to be simple and depend totally on the Lord. She couldn't be a Shaker like Sister Martha, but she could stop trying to fix everything herself and put her hand in the Lord's hand. Bit by bit into the quiet stillness in her mind came the picture of a garden. Not the garden at Grayson. Not any of the gardens at Harmony Hill. But another garden. And there in its center was Adam with his sketchbook. Adam holding a pencil, capturing the beauty of the garden on his paper.

She stood up and dipped the cloth in the basin once more and gently swabbed Adam's face. Across from her, Sebastian breathed out a satisfied sigh as he lay back on his pillow. "But the mercy of the Lord is from everlasting to everlasting."

As the first light of dawn began pushing through the windows, Adam's fever broke.

❧

Adam rose up out of the darkness that had held him captive and slowly opened his eyes. But this time instead of lifting his arm to see if his hand was still there, he sought sight of Charlotte. It mattered more that she be there than his hand. He tried to speak her name, but his voice came out as little more than a croak.

Even so she leaned over him. Tendrils of her beautiful red hair had escaped her Shaker cap to fall around her face. She smiled at him. "The doctor says you are better, Adam. Thanks be to the Lord."

She raised his head and held a glass to his lips. He swallowed the water greedily.

"And my hand?" He still didn't raise his arm up to look at it. He kept his eyes on Charlotte's face. With her there beside him, he could bear whatever she said. "Were you able to keep your promise?"

"It was a promise I should not have made, but one that the Lord honored."

At last he lifted his injured arm off the bed and wiggled his fingers. He welcomed the pain that shot up his arm. His hand was still there. His fingers would hold a pen or a brush again. He moved his fingers again and laughed out loud at the pain.

Charlotte laughed too, understanding his joy without him having to explain. "He must have more pictures for you to draw," she said.

"But not of the war," he said.

"It's not over." All traces of her laughter disappeared.

"Far from it," Adam agreed. "But I have drawn my last scene of death."

"Then what will you draw? As well as I remember, you don't care for doing portraits."

"True." He tried to lift his head up to see

her better. She helped him to a sitting position and doubled up the pillow behind his back against the wall. After the effort of moving, he had to rest before he could find his voice again. She waited without speaking until he was able to go on. "But there are many scenes of life I can draw."

She didn't turn away from him, but her eyes seemed suddenly shielded as she asked, "And where will you seek those scenes?"

"Wherever you are." He lifted his left hand to caress her cheek. He didn't have the strength to hold it there over a couple of seconds, but the soft feel of her skin remained on his fingertips.

"Grayson is no more," she said.

"Is Grayson the only place you dare seek life?"

"Nay." She shook her head a little and changed her word. "No. The Shakers have taught me that love can flower in many places."

"And have they taught you so well that you don't want to leave them?" he asked.

"They taught me to believe, but not as they believe. I am not a Shaker." Her eyes burned into his.

"Then will you come away from Harmony Hill and marry me, Charlotte Vance?"

Joy exploded in her eyes, but then the joy seemed tempered by something else as she turned her face away from him.

His heart constricted and he could not stay silent to wait for her answer. "I love you, Charlotte. I hoped you felt the same."

She looked back at him. "I do love you, Adam. With all my heart, but I have made a promise to another."

Now anger burned through him. "To who? Edwin?"

"Nay." She didn't seem to notice the Shaker word this time as she laughed. Then the laughter faded from her face. "It's Landon who asked for my promise and I gave it to him. I promised that I would always be his sister and never desert him."

"Landon?" Adam frowned. At first he didn't know who she was talking about, but then the name dredged up a memory of a small boy hiding under a table. "You mean Selena's son?"

"Selena's son perhaps, but also now my brother. Selena left the night of the fire and hasn't been heard of since. Landon's governess brought him to Harmony Hill and the Shakers took him in, but I made him a promise. A promise as real and binding as the one I made you about your hand." Tears trickled out of the corners of her eyes and down her cheeks. "So even though I have often dreamed of putting my hand in yours and walking away from the Shakers, I can't leave him behind to do so."

"Are you saying my competition is a boy of six who wants to be a whaleboat captain?" The twitch of a smile played at the corners of his mouth.

Charlotte looked surprised for a second before she said, "That's right. I remember now. You wrote that you had met Landon."

"Once." Adam let his smile spread across his face as he reached for Charlotte's hand again. "And to tell the truth, I don't think he's big enough to keep me away from you."

"But . . . ," she started.

He reached up and lightly touched her lips to silence her. "Your promise is my promise. Your brother is my brother." He gently brushed away one of the tears on her cheek before he let his hand drop back to the bed. "I ask again. Will you marry me, Charlotte Vance?"

"Yea," she said, smiling through fresh tears brimming in her eyes. She sniffed and wiped them away impatiently. "Wait. I can't answer you with a Shaker yes." She jerked off her Shaker cap and threw it up in the air. "Yes, Adam Wade, I will marry you. Today. Tomorrow. Whenever you want."

"And what of Grayson?" He had to know for sure where he stood in her heart.

Her face softened as she leaned closer until he could feel the whisper of her breath on his face as she said, "You are my Grayson. Now and forevermore."

Her love gave him strength to reach his hand up behind her head to pull her closer. She willingly surrendered her lips to his, dried and cracked by the fever though they were. And there in the midst of a roomful of groaning men, he found the love he'd been seeking. Nothing could ever separate him from that feeling again, for he would carry it always in his heart even unto death and beyond. Such was a gift of God.

The man in the next bed let out a whoop of laughter before he said, "I am my beloved's, and my beloved is mine."

Charlotte raised her head to look over

at the man. "That can't be Scripture, Sebastian."

The man laughed again. "Oh, but it is. King Solomon himself. He went down into a garden and found love."

"And so did we." Adam put his finger under Charlotte's chin and turned her face back to him. He thought he might drown in the beauty of her eyes. "So did we."

ACKNOWLEDGMENTS

Writing a book can be a solitary journey, but few journeys are ever completed without the help of others along the way. That's certainly true for me. I thank all those who have encouraged me over the years by cheering me on and then reading my stories.

I especially thank my editor, Lonnie Hull DuPont, for her enthusiasm for my stories and also her wise comments that help make my stories better. Thanks too to Barb Barnes who makes sure I have all my ducks in a row with her careful editing. I appreciate the great work of the whole team at Revell and Baker Publishing Group who take what I write and turn it into a beautiful book with an enticing cover that invites readers into my story.

I will never be able to thank my husband and family enough for their love and understanding over the years and my kids for learning to sleep over the sound of a clattering typewriter when they were babies.

And of course, I am forever thankful to the Lord for this gift of words and for allowing me the blessing of living my dream to write down stories.

Last but not least, I thank you readers. Without readers, a story is nothing but a bunch of words on paper. You bring the words to life as you let the story play out in your imaginations. Thank you.

Ann H. Gabhart and her husband live on a farm just over the hill from where she grew up in central Kentucky. She's active in her country church, and her husband sings bass in a Southern Gospel quartet. Ann is the author of over a dozen novels for adults and young adults. Her first inspirational novel, *The Scent of Lilacs*, was one of Booklist's top ten inspirational novels of 2006. Her novel, *The Outsider*, was a finalist for the 2009 Christian Book Awards in the fiction category.

Visit Ann's website at www.annhgab hart.com.